W9-BSN-026

ENCYCLOPEDIA OF LIBRARY AND INFORMATION SCIENCE

VOLUME 67

ENCYCLOPEDIA OF LIBRARY AND INFORMATION SCIENCE

Executive Editor

ALLEN KENT

SCHOOL OF INFORMATION SCIENCES
UNIVERSITY OF PITTSBURGH
PITTSBURGH, PENNSYLVANIA

Administrative Editor

CAROLYN M. HALL

ARLINGTON, TEXAS

VOLUME 67

SUPPLEMENT 30

MARCEL DEKKER, INC. NEW YORK • BASEL

HEADQUARTERS
Marcel Dekker, Inc.
270 Madison Avenue, New York, New York 10016
tel: 212-696-9000; fax: 212-685-4540

EASTERN HEMISPHERE DISTRIBUTION
Marcel Dekker AG
Hutgasse 4, Postfach 812, CH-4001 Basel Switzerland
tel: 41-61-261-8482; fax: 41-61-261-8896

WORLD WIDE WEB
http://www.dekker.com

LIBRARY OF CONGRESS CATALOG CARD NUMBER 68-31232

ISBN 0-8247-2067-9

Current Printing (last digit):
10 9 8 7 6 5 4 3 2 1

PRINTED IN THE UNITED STATES OF AMERICA

CONTENTS OF VOLUME 67

CONTRIBUTORS TO VOLUME 67

ENEKO AGIRRE, Associate Professor, Faculty of Computer Science, Universidad del Pais Vasco/Euskal Herriko Unibertsitatea, Donostia, Basque Country: *An Intelligent Dictionary Help System*

A. E. A. ALMAINI, Professor of Electronic Engineering, School of Engineering, Napier University, Edinburgh, Scotland: *Logic Design*

XABIER ARREGI, Associate Professor, Faculty of Computer Science, Universidad del Pais Vasco/Euskal Herriko Unibertsitatea, Donostia, Basque Country: *An Intelligent Dictionary Help System*

XABIER ARTOLA, Associate Professor, Faculty of Computer Science, Universidad del Pais Vasco/Euskal Herriko Unibertsitatea, Donostia, Basque Country: *An Intelligent Dictionary Help System*

SUVOJIT CHOTON BASU, Assistant Professor, Cisler College of Business, Northern Michigan University, Marquette, Michigan: *Business Process Reengineering*

SUSANNE BØDKER, Associate Professor, Department of Computer Science, University of Aarhus, Aarhus, Denmark: *Cooperative Design*

JEFFREY D. CAMPBELL, Department of Information Science and Telecommunications, University of Pittsburgh, Pittsburgh, Pennsylvania: *Document Processing*

ARANTZA DIAZ DE ILARRAZA, Associate Professor, Faculty of Computer Science, Universidad del Pais Vasco/Euskal Herriko Unibertsitatea, Donostia, Basque Country: *An Intelligent Dictionary Help System*

MAREK J. DRUZDZEL, Decision Systems Laboratory, School of Information Sciences and Intelligent Systems Program, University of Pittsburgh, Pittsburgh, Pennsylvania: *Decision Support Systems*

CSABA J. EGYHAZY, Associate Professor, Department of Computer Science, The Northern Virginia Graduate Center, Virginia Polytechnic Institute and State University, Falls Church, Virginia: *Intelligent Web Search Agents*

FABRICE EVRARD, Maître de Conferences, ENSEEIHT, Toulouse, France: *An Intelligent Dictionary Help System*

ROGER R. FLYNN, Department of Information Sciences and Intelligent Systems Program, University of Pittsburgh, Pittsburgh, Pennsylvania: *Decision Support Systems*

KAJ GRØNBÆK, Professor, Department of Computer Science, University of Aarhus, Aarhus, Denmark: *Cooperative Design*

CONSTANZA HAGMANN, Associate Professor of Management Information Systems, Management Department, Kansas State University, Manhattan, Kansas: *Computer-Mediated Communication Systems*

MARGARET HEDSTROM, Associate Professor, School of Information, University of Michigan, Ann Arbor, Michigan: *Electronic Recordkeeping*

ROSS HIGHTOWER, Assistant Professor of Management Information Systems, College of Business Administration, University of Central Florida, Orlando, Florida: *Computer-Mediated Communication Systems*

MAGID IGBARIA, Professor, School of Information Sciences, Claremont Graduate University, Claremont, California: *Adoption of Information Technology*

SOUNDAR R. T. KUMARA, Intelligent Design and Diagnostics Research Laboratory, Department of Industrial and Manufacturing Engineering, The Pennsylvania State University, University Park, Pennsylvania: *Software Agents in Logistics Replanning*

ROGER MCHANEY, Assistant Professor of Management Information Systems, Management Department, Kansas State University, Manhattan, Kansas: *Computer-Mediated Communication Systems*

CARL MACHOVER, President, Machover Associates Corporation, White Plains, New York: *CAD/CAM*

DIRK E. MAHLING, Ph.D. Senior Client Partner (Knowledge Management Practice), Primix Solutions, Inc., Watertown, Massachusetts: *Computer-Supported Cooperative Work*

YASHWANT K. MALAIYA, Professor, Computer Science Department, Colorado State University, Fort Collins, Colorado: *Software Reliability*

JERROLD H. MAY, Professor of ODS and AI, Katz Graduate School of Business, University of Pittsburgh, Pittsburgh, Pennsylvania: *Expert and Knowledge-Based Systems*

PREBEN HOLST MOGENSEN, Associate Professor, Department of Computer Science, University of Aarhus, Aarhus, Denmark: *Cooperative Design*

MIRANDA L. MOORE, U.S. Army Logistics Integration Agency, New Cumberland, Pennsylvania: *Software Agents in Logistics Replanning*

M. MEHDI OWRANG O., Professor, Department of Computer Science and Information Systems, American University, Washington, D. C.: *A Framework for Knowledge Discovery in Databases*

PRASHANT C. PALVIA, Professor, Fogelman College of Business and Economics, University of Memphis and Project Director, SCB Computer Technology Global IT Center, Memphis, Tennessee: *Business Process Reengineering*

THOMAS K. PLUNKETT, JR., Ph.D. Candidate, Department of Computer Science, The Northern Virginia Graduate Center, Virginia Polytechnic Institute and State University, Falls Church, Virginia: *Intelligent Web Search Agents*

AIRI SALMINEN, Professor, Department of Computer Science and Information Systems, University of Jyväskylä, Jyväskylä, Finland: *Methodology for Document Analysis*

GOUTAM SATAPATHY, Intelligent Design and Diagnostics Research Laboratory, Department of Industrial and Manufacturing Engineering, The Pennsylvania State University, University Park, Pennsylvania: *Software Agents in Logistics Replanning*

KEPA SARASOLA, Associate Professor, Faculty of Computer Science, Universidad del Pais Vasco/Euskal Herriko Unibertsitatea, Donostia, Basque Country: *An Intelligent Dictionary Help System*

JACQUES SAVOY, Institut Interfacultaire d-Informatique, Universite de Neuchatel, Neuchatel, Switzerland: *Another Statistical View of Infometrics Phenomena*

LUTFUS SAYEED, Associate Professor, Business Analysis and Computer Systems, College of Business, San Francisco State University, San Francisco, California: *Computer-Mediated Communication Systems*

AMANDA J. C. SHARKEY, Ph.D., Department of Computer Science, University of Sheffield, Sheffield, England: *Combining Artificial Neural Networks*

CONRAD SHAYO, College of Business and Public Administration, California State University, San Bernardino, California: *Adoption of Information Technology*

AITOR SOROA, Associate Professor, Faculty of Computer Science, Universidad del Pais Vasco/Euskal Herriko Unibertsitatea, Donostia, Basque Country: *An Intelligent Dictionary Help System*

WILLIAM E. SPANGLER, Assistant Professor, College of Business and Economics, West Virginia University, Morgantown, West Virginia: *Expert and Knowledge-Based Systems*

MICHAEL B. SPRING, Department of Information Science and Telecommunications, University of Pittsburgh, Pittsburgh, Pennsylvania: *Document Processing*

MANFRED STEDE, PH.D., Technische Universitat Berlin, Projektgruppe KIT, Berlin, Germany: *Computer Modeling of Storytelling and Creativity*

DAVID M. THOMPSON, Computer Systems Analyst, U.S. Air Force Pentagon Communications Agency, assigned to the Policy Automation Directorate, Office of the Undersecretary of Defense for Policy, The Pentagon, Washington, D.C.: *Intelligent Web Search Agents*

ADOPTION OF INFORMATION TECHNOLOGY

Introduction

This article provides a general overview of existing literature on new information technology (IT) adoption by individuals and organizations. The rate of successful IT adoption depends on the adopter's perceptions of the ITs' relative advantage, compatibility, and complexity, as well as its triability and observability (*1*). We use the S-curve categories to discuss adoption for each level of analysis—individual and organization. The S curve classifies adopters of new IT into innovators, early adopters, early majority, late majority, and laggards. The citations used are only representative of existing literature, and are not exhaustive. The discussion starts with the premise that IT has the potential of profoundly transforming individual and organizational welfare—that IT offers both an opportunity and a challenge (i.e., an opportunity to increase productivity and effectiveness and a challenge to keep the motivation of perpetually learning newer and sometimes complex ITs), and that, whether the adoption of IT occurs voluntarily, through sanctions, or by the encouragement of outside parties, successful IT adoption is mainly determined by the quality of the technology itself, the quality of the information the technology provides, usage of the IT, user satisfaction from the use of the system, the system's impact on individual behavior, and the system's overall impact on organizational behavior (*2*). The article concludes by suggesting that since proliferation of newer and more powerful ITs is apt to continue unabated well into the twenty-first century, there is a real need for individuals and organizations to devise new ways of identifying, learning, and implementing new technologies. Individual lifelong learning and organizational learning are two recent constructs that capture the essence of survival in an increasingly IT-dependent society.

Background

It is an accepted fact that IT "will change the world more permanently and more profoundly than any technology so far seen in history and will bring about a transformation of civilization to match" (*3*). It is also accepted that IT has the potential of enhancing individual and organizational* performance. Information technology is defined here as any system, product, or process whose underlying technology base is composed of computers (both hardware and software), workstations, and/or computerized communication networks of all types, including Local Area Networks (LANs), Wide Area Networks (WANs), Metropolitan Area Networks (MANs), intranets, Internet, robotics, and smart chips (*4*). Recognition of the potential of IT has led individuals and organizations to invest enormous amounts of time and money in IT. Information technology is so pervasive that more than 50 percent of workers in the developed world rely on it to produce their goods and services. For example, today's world financial markets could not function without IT. Similarly, supermarket checkout counters, travel reservation systems, or just-in-time production systems could not function without IT. It is now fashionable to refer to our generation as the information society.

Despite the evident opportunities offered by IT, however, such as increases in output or decreases in cost, there is no clear evidence, at least in the United States, that IT consumption has raised productivity. For example, "profitability rates have been falling in US industry in the last decade despite the new investments in information technologies" (*5*). As such, much of the investment in new IT may not have led to successful results after all. Some of the cited reasons for nonadoption are inability to learn "how to change organizations faster than humans naturally want to change" (*5*), technically deficient information technologies that are threatening to its users, low user satisfaction from usage of the IT, and a high knowledge burden requirement to master the technology. Others are: users getting information that is not necessary for decision making, low individual or organizational ability to recognize the value of new information and adopt it for productive ends, and the lack of adequate means to realistically measure the costs/benefits of IT. In short, there is skepticism about how quickly one should adopt a new IT.

> At the level of the individual firm, the problem will be to overcome the resistance to change, both by individuals who feel threatened by such changes and by those who doubt the potential returns available from the large investments necessary in the new technologies. At the national level, countries may become laggards if, for example, they fail to provide an IT infrastructure adequate to enable their firms to take advantage of the new ways of doing business, ways that shrink the effects of time and distance (*5*. p. vii).

This article provides a general overview of existing literature on new IT adoption by individuals and organizations. The guiding questions are: Why do individuals or organizations decide to adopt or not to adopt IT? How can individuals and organizations know that IT adoption has been successful? Why do people adopt IT at different rates? The article is divided into two parts. The first identifies the general attributes of adoption of innovations (*1*) and generalizes them to IT adoption. The second part

---

*The terms adoption, use, consumption, and acceptance are used interchangeably. Also, the terms information technology and information technology systems are taken to be synonymous. Organizational adoption looks at adoption by aggregates; namely, departments, agencies, Strategic Business Units (SBUs), or companies.

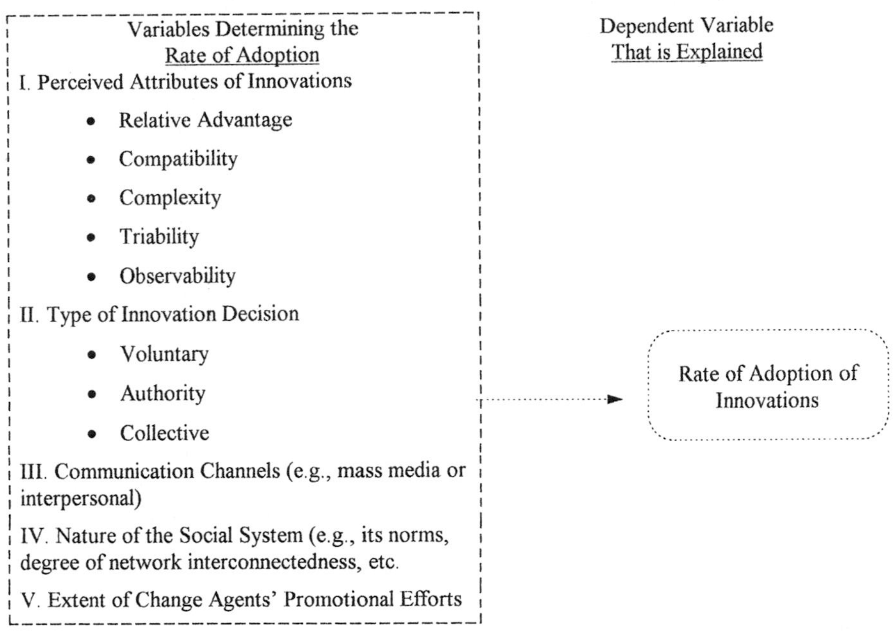

FIGURE 1. *Variables determining the rate of adoption of innovations* (1, *p. 207).*

discusses the rate of IT adoption based on Rogers's S curve (*1*). A conclusion is provided at the end of the two parts.

Part 1: Adoption of IT Innovations

According to Rogers (*1*), the rate of adoption of an innovation* depends on the perceived attributes of the innovation, the type of innovation decision, the communication channels used to advertise the technology, the nature of the social system in which the IT implemented, and the extent of the promotional efforts of change agents. (See Fig. 1.)

PERCEIVED ATTRIBUTES OF INNOVATIONS

The perceived attributes of innovations are relative advantage, compatibility, complexity, observability, and triability. *Relative advantage* is "the degree to which an innovation is perceived as better than the one it replaces" as measured by the monetary gains, convenience, enjoyment, and satisfaction derived from its use. The greater the relative advantage, the higher the rate of adoption of the innovation.

*In this discussion, any new IT is considered an innovation.

Compatibility is "the degree to which an innovation is perceived as being consistent with the existing values, past experiences, and needs of adopters." For example, the implementation of a new IT in a work environment that has had previous experiences with poorly designed systems is much harder than the implementation of a new IT in an environment that has had prior good experiences with a well-designed system.

Complexity is "the degree to which an innovation is perceived as being difficult to use." The level of enjoyment one gets from using a new innovation is inversely proportional to the degree of complexity one encounters. *Observability* is "the degree to which the results of an innovation are observable to others." Individuals may adopt a specific IT in order to gain recognition to make themselves indispensable. *Triability* is the degree to which an innovation may be experimented on by someone before adoption. Ability to pilot enables potential adopters to reduce uncertainty and become acquainted with the new innovation.

A number of research studies have investigated the efficacy of these attributes to the adoption of new IT (*6, 7*). Moore and Benbasat (*6*) used the attributes as a basis of developing an overall validated research instrument to measure the various perceptions of adopting an IT innovation. All attributes had fairly high alpha coefficients: relative advantage, 0.90; compatibility, 0.86; complexity (also called ease of use), 0.84; observability (also called result demonstrability), 0.79; and triability, 0.77.

Relative Advantage

This construct captures both objective and perceived advantages of adopting the new IT. The literature shows that IT researchers have used different measures to assess the relative advantage of a new IT compared to the one it replaces. Six general interrelated and interdependent measures have been identified: IT quality, information quality, use, user satisfaction, individual impact, and organization impact (*2*).* The measure(s) selected by any researcher depended on their research intentions. Figure 2 shows the relationship between the various measures.

At the *IT quality* level, researchers have used "more engineering-oriented performance characteristics of the [IT] in question" (*2*). Specifically, research studies compared the new IT with the old one by focusing on resource and investment utilization (*8*), reliability (*9*), online response time (*10*), perceived usefulness (*7*), and accuracy (*11*). Overall the studies found that any new IT that ranked higher in one or a combination of these factors had a higher chance of getting adopted compared to one that ranked lower. Other researchers have focused on measuring the relative advantage of the quality of the information generated by the new technology.

The perceived relative *quality of information* generated by a new IT in the form of reports is another determinant of successful IT adoption. Bailey and Pearson (*10*) identified thirty-nine IT-related items for measuring individual satisfaction with information quality. Out of the thirty-nine items the most important ones were accuracy, timeliness, reliability, completeness, relevance, precision, and currency.

*McLean and DeLone (*2*) reviewed 180 research studies on measures of information system success and came up with six measures: system quality, information quality, use, user satisfaction, individual impact, and organizational impact. We think these measures apply to IT success as well.

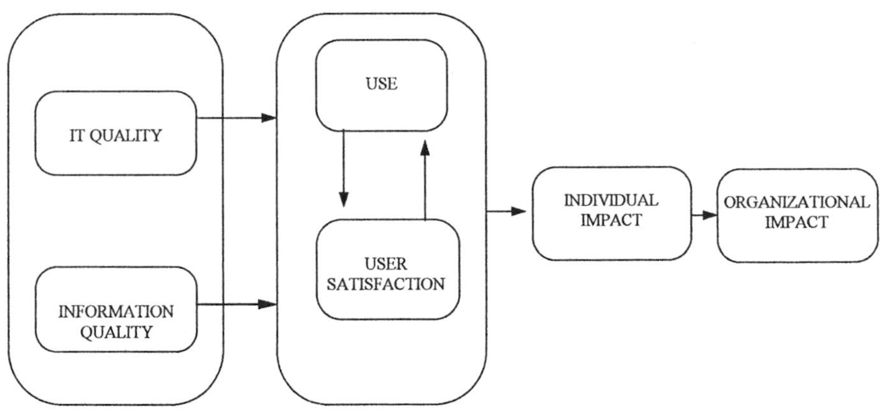

FIGURE 2. *IT Success model (adopted from Ref.* 2*).*

Other researchers have used other attributes of information quality such as uniqueness, conciseness, clarity, and readability (*12*); and sufficiency, understandability, unbiasedness, and quantitativeness (*13*). Ahituv (*14*) summarized the relative value of information into four main multiattribute utility category measures: timeliness, content, format, and cost/benefit. Timeliness includes a class of attributes related to the time factor in information update and retrieval. These factors are: currency/recency, response time, and frequency. If a business transaction occurs in time t_0, the related record may be updated later at time t_1, and the user of this information may get a processed report at time t_2. The *currency* of the data presented to the user is measured by the difference $t_2 - t_0$. The currency of the file is measured by the difference $t_1 - t_0$, and the *response time* is measured by the difference $t_2 - t_1$. The *frequency* of the reports is measured by the number of times the user receives updated information for decision making. For example, if you have a bank account, monthly frequency statements may be sufficient. If you manage your own shares, however, you may need daily or continuous updates of information from the stock exchanges.

Content attributes relate to the meaning of the information provided to the users. The attributes of content include: accuracy, relevance, exhaustiveness, redundancy, and level of detail. *Accuracy* refers to the integrity of the data used to produce reports. *Relevance* refers to the pertinence of the information to the decision at hand. *Exhaustiveness* refers to completeness or comprehensiveness of the information. Often one can have relevant but incomplete information. *Redundancy* is the degree of repetitiveness of the information. *Level of detail* refers to the aggregation level of the data. The optimal level of aggregation is obtained when any extra detailed information does not improve the decision being made and any more aggregation would worsen the decision.

Format attributes relate to the mode of presentation of the information. The attributes of format include: medium (hard copy, visual display, plotters, graphs, microfilm), layout (order of columns and rows, sequencing of detail and totals, etc.), and graphics design (colors, letter sets, fonts, etc.). Research studies on the format attributes have relied on the IT adopter's perceptions with respect to the medium, layout, and graphics design due to the problem of obtaining quantitative measurements.

Cost/benefit refers to the economic value of the new IT relative to the old one. Focus has been on a reduction in fixed and/or variable costs, avoiding certain costs incurred while using the previous IT (e.g., overtime, stationery); profit enhancement through increased sales volume; and customer goodwill. The problem is that some benefits and costs are intangible and cannot easily be assigned monetary values. For example, it may be difficult to justify a new IT that could be used by a police 911 emergency services system to save lives. In this case how does one trade off between the benefits of saving a life and the cost of the IT?

Overall, research studies that compared existing ITs to newer ones found that newer ITs that ranked higher on the timeliness, content, format, and cost/benefit attributes had a higher chance of getting adopted.

Given a relatively higher-quality new IT that provides higher-quality information, the other measure of successful IT adoption is the *actual or reported use* of the information generated by the new IT. (See Fig. 2.) Some studies have measured actual usage by collecting data through hardware monitors; that is, connect time (*15*), number of functions utilized (*16*), and actual charges for IT use (*17*). Other studies have measured IT use by questioning managers about their use of the IT (*18–20*). In either case, the success of an IT innovation will be measured by the degree to which the adopters rely on it, their feelings of ownership of the IT, and the degree to which the IT becomes part and parcel of the standard operating procedures in the workplace (*21*). Moreover, in order to measure the actual use of a newly adopted IT, such use should be voluntary. We propose the discussion of voluntariness to the section on type of innovation decision.

Each interaction with an IT creates a certain level of *user satisfaction*.* Increased satisfaction leads to repeated use of the IT, which in turn increases the user satisfaction level even further (hence the double arrows linking IT use to user satisfaction in Fig. 2). Using this measure to evaluate the success of a new IT adoption has wide appeal (*2, 10*). Also, a number of research studies have found that user satisfaction from using a specific IT is related to their attitudes toward that IT (*22, 23*), so it is recommended that whenever user satisfaction is used as a measure of IT adoption the user's attitudes should also be included in order to control for the biasing effects of the attitudes in the analysis.

As shown in Fig. 2, *IT quality, information quality, use, and user satisfaction* have a joint *impact* on the *individual* behavior of the IT adopter. It is generally accepted that information created by an IT is not valuable until it is meaningful and useful to its user. The IT impact on the individual adopting the technology could include any of the following: a reduction in the average time to make a decision, an increase in the confidence in the decision make, an increase in the number of participants making the decision, increases in productivity, and an increase in the number of reports requested by higher-level managers. Researchers have used both quantitative and qualitative

*Other measures related to user satisfaction are *user enjoyment* and *user appreciation.*

measures to evaluate the impact of IT on individual adopters. Quantitative measures include test scores, amount of performance improvement, time to make a decision, number of members participating in making a decision, and number of reports. Qualitative measures include perceptions of improvement in decision making, perceived confidence in the decision, and the amount of money the adopters are willing to pay for the new IT.

Most managers are eventually concerned about the bottom line. It is therefore of interest to assess the *organizational impact* of new ITs at the unit, department, or overall enterprise level. Figure 2 shows that the aggregate of all individual behaviors resulting from IT adoption leads to organizational impact. Several measures of IT organizational impact are available in the literature: cost reduction (*24, 25*), cost avoidance, increase in sales volumes (*26, 27*), reduction in overall operating expenses (*28*), and return on IT investment (*29, 30*). Current research has focused more on measuring the impact of IT on the organization structure (*31*), determining any increases in customer switching costs, erecting barriers to new firm entry into the industry, differentiating among products and increasing organization bargaining power with suppliers (*32, 25*).

Summary. Relative advantage is "the degree to which an innovation is perceived as better than the one it replaces," as measured by the monetary gains, convenience, enjoyment, and satisfaction derived from its use. The greater the relative advantage, the higher the rate of adoption of the innovation McLean and DeLone (*2*) reviewed the IT literature and identified six categories that can be used to assess the relative advantage of new ITs, namely: IT quality, information quality, use, user satisfaction, individual impact, and organizational impact. Figure 2 shows the relationship between the various measures.

Compatibility

One characteristic of IT is that it requires people to think and work differently. This emanates from the ability of IT to open organizational boundaries, integrate and coordinate work, speed up work, change the way work is done, provide faster feedback systems, and change perceptions of status and power (*33*). Information technology can therefore place a significant amount of cognitive burden on users, who may not only be unsure about their job situation but may also have to invest in education and training in new skills. *Compatibility* is the degree to which the new IT is perceived as being consistent with the existing values, past experiences, and needs of adopters. In Fig. 2, compatibility belongs to the individual impact category. Whenever there is a lack of compatibility, passive or active resistance may occur.

It is therefore recommended that users be involved in decisions leading to the acquisition and implementation of the new IT. As recommended by Osterman (*33*): "Beyond investing in people early, through education, training in new skills and so forth, it turns out to be helpful for the organization to develop flexible human resource policies that enable and encourage the organization to capitalize on the new IT. Employees at all levels are more inclined to experiment with new ways of working if they know their standing in the organization will not be affected by their learning process" (p. 220).

Several studies have identified compatibility as an important factor in IT adoption. One classical study is the one reported by Markus (*34*). In the study by Moore and Benbasat (*6*) a factor analysis grouped compatibility with relative advantage.

Complexity

Complexity is a relative measure of perceived cognitive burden imposed by the new IT. In Fig. 2, complexity belongs to the IT quality category. Measures of complexity include ease of use (*7, 35, 36*), ease of learning (*37*), and enjoyment (*38*). The more user-friendly a particular innovation is, the greater its potential for adoption.

Triability

The ability to try out a new IT before integrating it into the routine activities and standard operating procedures of the workplace is an important measure of IT adoption. Triability affords individuals and organizations and opportunity to investigate the relative advantages, compatibility, complexity, and observability of the new IT. The study by Moore and Benbasat (*6*) found that although triability and significantly less weight than other factors in an organizational context, it should be of great concern for organizations that would adopt IT at their own risk.

Observability

Observability includes the ability to demonstrate the results (benefits and costs) of using the IT to potential users, as well as making the results visible to others within and outside the organization. Users are more likely to use a new IT if they feel that using it will bring higher approval and recognition from management and/or colleagues. In Fig. 2, observability could belong to the user satisfaction category.

Summary. A new IT that is perceived to be relatively useful, compatible, and easy to learn and use, that has observable results, and that can be used on a pilot basis is more likely to be adopted than one that is lacking in any or all of these attributes.

TYPE OF INNOVATION DECISION

There are three types of innovation decisions: voluntary, authoritative, and collective. Innovations requiring the adopter's voluntary decision to adopt are generally more rapidly adopted than innovations that are mandated by an organization or other external pressures (*1*). Voluntariness of use is the degree to which the use of the IT is perceived as being voluntary or of "free will." In Fig. 2, the type of innovation decision belongs to the individual impact or organizational impact category.

At the individual level, management may mandate (authoritatively) the use of a specific IT or may provide incentives for those who use the specific IT. Sometimes management may even enact policies that discourage the use of a specific IT. The decision to adopt may also be made by a few IT champions in the organization and then imposed on the rest of the business unit or department.

At the organizational level, an organization may be forced to adopt specific ITs in order to survive competition in their industry. In this case, IT becomes the cost of

FIGURE 3. *The Kurt Lewin and Edgar Schein change model.*

doing business. For example, a new bank may adopt ATM machine technology as the cost of doing business, irrespective of whether the benefits of implementing ATM technology have been proven in the specific area of operation. These circumstances deny the adopter the freedom to reject the IT.

According to Ajzen and Fishbein (*39*), it is often not actual voluntariness that influences behavior, but rather the perception of voluntariness. This means the rate of adoption will be increased if the people championing the adoption of the IT (change agents) can successfully make the adopters believe that they are the ones who are choosing to adopt. To accomplish this, change agents must understand the dynamics of change. Lewin and Schein (*40*) proposed a three-stage model for managing change. (See Fig. 3.)

Unfreezing is a process of removing old habits and creating a climate receptive to change. Moving is the process of learning new work methods, behaviors, and systems. Refreezing is the process of reinforcing the new changes so that the new work processes and behavior are accepted as part and parcel of the job. When a new IT is introduced, IT professionals become the agents for change. An understanding of the dynamics of change can help change agents understand how to make IT implementation more successful.

The number of people involved in decision making is another factor that may affect successful IT adoption. Rogers (*1*) observed that the more people or institutions involved in making an innovation adoption decision, the slower the rate of adoption. Few studies in the IT adoption literature have focused on this aspect. One notable study is the one by Keen (*41*). He noted that increasing the number of people involved in the IT adoption decision could be a tactic to prevent successful implementation. He called this phenomenon counterimplementation.

COMMUNICATION CHANNELS

The communication channels used to spread information about the relative advantages, compatibility, complexity, triability, and observability of the new IT can also influence the rate of adoption. Mass media are recommended when the new IT is relatively simple to use. Interpersonal contacts with change agents are recommended when the new IT is perceived by potential adopters to be complex.

NATURE OF THE SOCIAL SYSTEM

This includes the norms of the organization in which the new IT is being adopted and the existence of interpersonal network influences on potential but skeptical adopters. In an organization receptive to new IT ideas, opinion leaders play a significant role in providing innovation-evaluation information critical to decreasing uncertainty about the new IT. Opinion leaders are those adopters who act as role models in influencing others' opinions about innovations. As will be discussed later, these people belong to the early adopters category.

EXTENT OF CHANGE AGENTS' PROMOTIONAL EFFORTS

The rate of adoption is also influenced by the extent of the promotional efforts of the change agents. The more opinion leaders the change agent can convert, the greater the rate of adoption. The rate of adoption and the extent of the change agents' efforts may not be direct or linear, however. Rogers (*1*) observed that the rate of adoption is greatest when opinion leaders adopt and continues to grow with little promotion by change agents after a critical mass of adopters have been established. A critical mass is defined as the point at which enough adopters have accepted the new IT to cause the perceived cost-benefit of adoption to shift from negative to positive.

Overall Summary for Part 1

Left to their own volition, not all individuals, organizations, or nations are receptive to IT adoption; there is considerable skepticism about the real benefits of IT adoption. The rate of adoption of an innovation depends on the perceived attributes of the innovation, the type of innovation decision, the communication channels used to advertise the technology, the nature of the social system in which the IT is implemented, and the extent of the promotional efforts of change agents. It is often not the actual voluntariness of the decision to adopt a new IT that influences behavior, but rather the perception of voluntariness. Change agents who understand the dynamics of change can play a role in influencing successful IT adoption.

Part 2: Rate of IT Adoption Categories

In Part 1 we discussed the important elements of successful IT adoption. We noted that despite the overwhelming opportunities offered by IT, however, not all individuals or organizations may implement a new IT at the same rate. Even when the adoption decision is mandated (authoritatively or collectively), users may not implement the full features of the new IT at the same rate.

One way to describe the rate of IT adoption or consumption is to use the S curve of adoption and normality developed by Rogers (*1*).* According to the S curve, the first 2.5 percent (minus 2 standard deviations) of individuals or organizations to adopt IT are called the innovators. The next 13.5 percent (between mean minus 1 standard deviation and mean minus 2 standard deviations) are called the early adopters. The next 34 percent (between mean and mean minus 1 standard deviation) are called the early majority. The next 34 percent (between mean and mean plus 1 standard

*Although some research has found only weak support for the S curve (*42*), many studies have supported its applicability, especially in the early days of the introduction of a new IT (*43, 44, 1*).

deviation) are the late adopters, and the remaining 16 percent (above mean plus 1 standard deviation) are called the laggards.

INDIVIDUALS

Innovators. This first 2.5 percent of IT users include venturesome or cosmopolitan individuals who either have enough resources to acquire and experiment with new IT or can have their organizations buy the technology for them. The value of IT to innovators is the potential returns that may accrue for being the first to try a potentially beneficial technology. People working in beta and alpha test sites for new software applications belong to this category. Innovators command a certain amount of social prestige and peer respect for being at the cutting edge of IT. Observability and triability are the two main attributes at play here.

Early adopters. These are the next 13.5 percent of people to perceive the relative advantage, compatibility, and observability of a new IT and who are willing to pioneer its use. Early adopters are valued as change agents and as such have high subjective norms (*39*). A person's subjective norm refers to the importance the person attaches to opinions of referent others. "The early adopter knows that to continue to earn this self respect of colleagues and to maintain a central position in the communication networks of the IT system, he or she must make judicious innovation decisions." (*1,* p. 264). As such early adopters are motivated by the respect they obtain from their peers.

Early majority. This is a group of individuals who adopt IT because it has been proven to work. Comprising 34 percent of the IT adopter category, the early majority is the first most numerous group to implement the new IT. As such these individuals bring in a "critical mass" of IT users. This group frequently interacts with the early adopters to get guidance on how to use the new IT. Moreover, they provide interpersonal networks to the late majority.

Late majority. These are skeptical individuals who adopt IT either for fear of losing their jobs or due to peer pressure. Like the early majority, they comprise 34 percent of the new IT adopter categories. Also, individuals in this category may not have enough resources to spend on IT and hence have to rationalize each expenditure they consider risky or uncertain.

Laggards. These are the remaining 16 percent of the adopters who may fear computers, have negative attitudes toward computers, or have the fear of using poorly designed systems. Laggards tend to be suspicious of new IT and change agents. They want to be sure about the costs and benefits of adopting the new IT before accepting it. Similar to the late majority, individuals in this category may not have enough resources to spend on IT.

Summary

Individuals can be innovators, early adopters, early majority, late majority, or laggard, depending on the impact of the rate of adoption variables on them. There are both intrinsic and extrinsic factors influencing how adopters perceive the rate of adoption variables. Innovators value IT for the potential returns that may accrue by being the first to try a potentially beneficial technology. They hope that by the time other groups catch on, they will be high up on the learning curve. Early adopters are motivated by the respect they obtain from their peers and their value as change agents. The early majority are risk-averse individuals who join the IT bandwagon only when it has been proven to work. The lake majority are skeptical individuals who adopt IT as the last resort. Finally, the laggards adopt the new IT only when they can ascertain all the benefits and costs.

ORGANIZATIONS

Innovators. This includes the first 2.5 percent of organizations that adopt a specific IT. Such organizations either have enough resources to acquire and experiment with new IT or have an influential MIS department manager who has a secure budget for new IT. The value of IT to innovator organizations is the competitive advantage that may accrue to being the first to try a potentially beneficial technology.

Early adopters. These are the next 13.5 percent of organizations to perceive the relative advantage, compatibility, and observability of a new IT and willing to pioneer its use. Most organizations in volatile industries (e.g., computer hardware, computer software, telecommunications, and entertainment) are forced to become early adopters of new IT. Volatile industries are ones characterized by cutthroat competition and uncertainty. For example, IBM's late move into the PC market cost it significant competitive advantage. Early adopters devise ways to use IT to lock in customers and lock out suppliers early and as such tend to maintain their market share, which in turn increases their chances for long-term survival and profitability. As such early adopters are motivated by the customer loyalty they obtain because of their innovative efforts to provide higher-quality products and service.

Early majority. This is a group of organizations who adopt IT because it has been proven to work. Comprising 34 percent of the IT adopter category, the early majority is the first and most numerous group of organizations to implement the new IT. As such it forms part of a critical mass of IT-using organizations. This group of organizations sometimes assigns specific individuals the role of reading the literature on the experiences of the early adopting organizations in order to get guidance on how to use the new IT. Other organizations employ people from the early adopting organizations so that they can benefit from their experiences. In other instances, organizations may acquire or enter into strategic alliances with early adopting organizations in order to learn from them.

Late majority. These are skeptical organizations who adopt IT for fear of being swept away by the competition. Like the early majority, they comprise 34 percent of the new IT adopter categories. Organizations in this category may not have enough resources to spend on IT and hence have to rationalize each expenditure they consider risky or uncertain.

Laggards. These are the remaining 16 percent of the adopting organizations who may believe "If it ain't broke, why fix it?" Laggard organizations tend to be suspicious of new IT and the hype that surrounds new ITs. They want to be sure about the costs and benefits of adopting the new IT before implementing it. Similar to the late majority, organizations in this category may not have enough resources to spend on IT.

Summary

Organizations can be innovators, early adopters, early majority, late majority, or laggard, depending on their mission, culture, the nature of the industry they are in, their structure, and the impact of the rate of adoption variables on the long-term profitability and survival of the organization. The decision to adopt or not to adopt is mainly driven by demands from the internal and external environment of the organization. For example, organizations with a culture that emphasizes "internal control," "creativity," and "individual autonomy" are more likely to adopt new IT than one that emphasizes "external controls," "conformity," and "hierarchies" (*45*).

Innovators value IT for the potential returns that may accrue by being the first to try a potentially beneficial technology. Early adopters are motivated by the customer loyalty they create by providing better products and superior service. Such organizations hope that by the time other organizations catch on, it would be difficult for them to tap into their market share. The early majority are risk-averse organizations that are in relatively stable operating environments. Most public sector organizations fall into this category. The late majority are skeptical organizations that adopt IT as the last resort. Finally, the laggards adopt a new IT only when they can establish all of its benefits and costs.

Conclusion

We conclude by suggesting that since the proliferation of newer and more powerful ITs is apt to continue unabated well into the twenty-first century, there is a real need for individuals and organizations to devise new ways of identifying, learning, and implementing new technologies. One way to do this is to have a clear understanding of the factors that influence successful adoption of IT. This article used the variables that affect the rate of adoption of IT innovations (*1*), the categories of successful IT adoption (*2*), and the S curve (*1*) to provide a general overview of existing literature on new IT adoption by individuals and organizations. The variables that influence successful adoption and the categories of successful IT adoption are interrelated. For example, one cannot discuss the relative advantage of a specific IT without considering IT quality, information quality, usage of the information provided by the IT, user satisfaction, individual impact, and organizational impact. The use of the S curve will allow individuals and organizations to position themselves with respect to where they fit in their rate of IT adoption. It seems that individual lifelong learning and organizational learning are the indispensable characteristics of the very survival of an increasingly IT-dependent society: One caveat, though: "management can promote the acquisition of skills by creating a climate supporting continuous learning in general and by encouraging experimentation with IT tools in particular" (*46,* p. 275).

REFERENCES

1. E. Rogers, *Diffusion of Innovations,* 4th ed., Free Press, New York, 1995.
2. E. R. McLean and W. H. DeLone, "Information System Success: The Quest for the Dependent Variable." *Info. Syst. Res.,* **3**(1), 60–95 (1992).
3. I. Ajzen and T. J. Madden, "Predication of Goal Directed Behavior: Attitudes Intentions, and Perceived Behavioral Control," *Journal of Experimental Psychology,* 22, 453–474 (1986).
4. M. S. Scott Morton, "Introduction," in *The Corporation of the 1990s: Information Technology and Organizational Transformation,* M. S. Scott Morton, ed. Oxford University Press, New York, 1991.
5. L. C. Thurow, "Foreword," in *The Corporation of the 1990s: Information Technology and Organizational Transformation,* M. S. Scott Morton, ed. Oxford University Press, New York, 1991.
6. G. C. Moore and I. Benbasat, "Development of an Instrument to Measure the Perceptions of Information Technology Innovation." *Info. Syst. Res.,* **2**(3), 192–221 (1991).
7. F. D. Davis, "Perceived Usefulness, Perceived Ease of Use, and User Acceptance of Information Technology." *MIS Q.,* **13**(3), 319–340 (1989).
8. C. A. Kriebel and A. Raviv, "An Economics Approach to Modeling the Productivity of Computer Systems." *Mgt. Sci.,* **26**(3), 297–311 (1980).
9. A. Srinivasan, "Alternative Measures of System Effectiveness: Associations and Implications." *MIS Q.,* **9**(3), 243–253 (1985).
10. J. E. Bailey and S. W. Pearson, "Development of Tools for Measuring and Analyzing Computer User Satisfaction." *Mgt. Sci.,* **29**(5), 530–545 (1983).
11. S. Hamilton and N. L. Chervany, "Evaluating Information System Effectiveness. Part 1: Comparing Evaluation Approaches." *MIS Q.,* **5**(3), 55–69 (1981).

12. E. B. Swanson, "Management Information Systems: Appreciation and Involvement." *Mgt. Sci.,* **21**(20), 178–188 (1984).
13. W. R. King and B. J. Epstein, "Assessing Information System Value." *Decis. Sci.,* **14***(1), 34–45 (1983).*
14. N. Ahituv, "A Systematic Approach Toward Assessing the Value of an Information System." *MIS Q.,* **4**(4), 61–75 (1980).
15. M. J. Ginzberg, "Finding an Adequate Measure of OR/MS Effectiveness." *Interfaces,* **8**(4), 59–62 (1978).
16. G. I. Green and C. T. Hughes, "Effects of Decision Support Training and Cognitive Style on Decision Process Attributes." *J. MIS,* **3**(2), 81–93 (1986).
17. L. L. Gremillion, "Organization Size and Information System Use." *J. MIS,* **1**(2), 4–17 (1984).
18. R. W. Zmud, A. C. Boynton, and G. C. Jacobs, "An Examination of Managerial Strategies for Increasing Information Technology Penetration in Organizations," *Proceedings of the Eighth International Conference on Information Systems,* Pittsburgh, Pennsylvania, Dec. 1987, pp. 24–44.
19. L. Raymond, "Organizational Characteristics and MIS Success in the Context of Small Business." *MIS Q.,* **9**(1), 37–52 (1985).
20. E. Kim and J. Lee, "An Exploratory Contingency Model of User Participation and MIS Use." *Info. Mgt.,* **11**(2), 87–97 (1986).
21. A. W. Trice and E. M. Treacy, "Utilization as a Dependent Variable in MIS Research," *Proceedings of the Seventh International Conference on Information Systems,* Dec. 1987, pp. 227–239.
22. M. Igbaria, "User Acceptance of Microcomputer Technology: An Empirical Test." *Omega,* **21**(1), 73–90 (1993).
23. R. J. Kauffman and P. Weill, "An Evaluative Framework for Research on the Performance Effects of Information Technology Investment," *Proceedings of the Tenth International Conference on Information Systems,* Boston, Dec. 1989.
24. N. L. Chervany, G. W. Dickson, and K. Kozar, "An Experimental Gaming Framework for Investigating the Influence of Management Information Systems on Decision Effectiveness," MISRC Working Paper no. 71-12, MISRC, University of Minnesota, Minneapolis, 1972.
25. H. R. Johnston and M. R. Vitale, "Creating Competitive Advantage with Interorganizational Information Systems." *MIS Q.,* **12**(2), 153–165 (1988).
26. S. Rivard and S. L. Huff, "User Developed Applications: Evaluation of Success from the DP Department Perspective." *MIS Q.,* **8**(1), 39–50 (1984).
27. W. G. Chrismar and C. H. Kriebel, "A Method for Assessing the Economic Impact of Information Systems Technology in Organizations," *Proceedings of the Sixth International Conference on Information Systems,* Indianapolis, Indiana, Dec. 1985, pp. 45–56.
28. J. C. Emery, "Cost/Benefit Analysis of Information Systems," *SMIS Workshop Report Number 1,* Society for Management Information Systems, Chicago, 1971.
29. P. Weill, "The Relationship Between Investment in Information Technology and Firm Performance: A Study of the Valve Manufacturing Sector." *Info. Syst. Res.,* **3**(4), 307–333 (1992).
30. D. F. Perry, "Assimilation Innovative Technology: A More Comprehensive Model," *Proceedings of the Fourth International Conference on Information Systems,* Houston, Texas, Dec. 1983, pp. 281–297.
31. J. Y. Bakos, "Dependent Variables for the Study of Firm and Industry-Level Impacts on Information Technology," *Proceedings of the Eighth International Conference on Information Systems,* Dec. 10–23, 1987.
32. M. Porter, *Competitive Advantage,* Free Press, New York, 1985.
33. P. Osterman, "Impact of IT on Jobs and Skills," in *The Corporation of the 1990s: Information Technology and Organizational Transformation,* M. S. Scott Morton, ed. Oxford University Press, New York, 1991.
34. M. L. Markus, "Power, Politics, and MIS Implementation." *Commun. ACM,* **26**(6), 430–444 (1983).
35. D. A. Adams, R. R. Nelson, and P. A. Todd, "Perceived Usefulness, Ease of Use, and Usage of Information Technology: A Replication." *MIS Q.,* **16**(2), 227–247 (1992).
36. K. Mathieson, "Predicting User Intentions: Comparing the Technology Acceptance Model with the Theory of Planned Behavior." *Info. Syst. Res.,* **2**(3), 173–191 (1991).
37. S. Belardo, R. K. Kirk, and W. A. Wallace, 'DSS Component Design Through Field Experimentation: An Application to Emergency Management," *Proceedings of the Third International Conference on Information Systems,* Ann Arbor, Michigan, Dec. 1982, pp. 93–108.

38. M. Igbaria, J. Iivari, and H. Maragahh, "Why Do Individuals Use Computer Technology?: A Finnish Case Study." *Info. Mgt.,* **29**, 227–238 (1995).
39. I. Ajzen and M. Fishbein, *Understanding Attitudes and Predicting Behavior,* Prentice Hall, Englewood Cliffs, NJ, 1980.
40. E. Schein, *Process Consultation: Its Role in Organizational Development,* Addison-Wesley, Reading, MA, 1969.
41. P. G. W. Keen, "Information Systems and Organizational Change." *Commun. ACM,* **24**(1), 24–33 (Jan. 1981).
42. R. B. Cooper and R. W. Zmud, "Information Technology Implementation Research: A Technological Diffusion Approach." *Mgt. Sci.,* **36**(2), 123–139 (1990).
43. V. Gurbaxani, "Diffusion in computing Networks: The Case of BITNET." *Commun. ACM,* **33**(12), 65–75 (1990).
44. V. Gurbaxani and H. Mendelson, "The Use of Secondary Analysis in MIS Research," in *The Information Systems Research Challenge: Survey Research Methods,* vol. 3, K. L. Kraemer, ed. Harvard Business School, Boston, 1991.
45. P. S. DeLisi, "Lessons from the Steel Axe: Culture, Technology, and Organizational Change." *Sloan Mgt. Rev.,* **83** (fall 1990).
46. R. B. McKersie and R. E. Walton, "Organizational Change," in *The Corporation of the 1990s: Information Technology and Organizational Transformation,* M. S. Scott Morton, ed. Oxford University Press, New York, 1991.

MAGID IGBARIA
CONRAD SHAYO

ANOTHER STATISTICAL VIEW OF INFOMETRICS PHENOMENA

Introduction

Given that library and information research techniques traditionally employ empirical methods for analyzing various library phenomena (*1–3*) and that computers are widely employed to accelerate the collection, storage, and diffusion of electronic information, there is now an even greater need to use numbers and statistics in order to explain and justify decisions made by librarians. Moreover, available technologies such as CD-ROMs, and both local and wide-area networks (Internet), allow us to manage and distribute larger volumes of information. We thus may now propose various experiments that extend across several countries and that also facilitate the collection of various observations, from which summary descriptions can be drawn. In view of all these current success stories, it only seems natural to assume we have all the available and pertinent data required to analyze the various librarian processes required in making more rational decisions. Moreover, we might also hope to learn something from these large seas of numbers, from which interesting patterns may emerge or can be discovered more or less automatically [e.g., based on various data-mining strategies (*4, 5*)].

The pragmatics of experimentation reveal other realities. Often, in fact, the stored information is not accurate. It may contain errors, and values may be missing (*6*), as depicted in the criminal history records described in Ref. *7*. For example, typing errors may occur when entering numbers, decimal points may not be placed at the right position, OCR (optical character recognition software) may not perfectly recognize a given text, and even numerical computer errors may occur (*8, 9*). From this we might conclude that the precision represented by stored or displayed numbers is often an illusion.

Since our data world contains errors and missing values, we should thus question whether the calculation of a sample mean is always the most appropriate method of depicting the central tendency of a sample. We should perhaps consider using other and more robust statistical methods (*10, 11*; e.g., the median or the trimmed mean). More precisely, the first section will explain some of the reasons justifying the choice of robust statistics when working with data containing errors and will reveal the advantages and disadvantages of the sample median and sample mean as central tendency measures.

Using these statistics, however, may lead us into a situation in which the associated standard error may be quite hard to compute. In other investigations, we may be in a situation in which assessing the accuracy of a more complex statistic such as the ratio of two random variates, and for which a neat formula may be quite hard to derive (or may not exist). To resolve these difficulties, the second section will present the bootstrap methodology (*12, 13*), which is useful in deriving a good approximation for the numerical value of the standard error associated with various statistics. To achieve this goal, we will introduce an example for which we already know the exact standard error formula. We have chosen this instance in order to allow the reader to compare values obtained by the bootstrap method with those derived from textbook formula.

Choice of a Summary Statistic

To obtain a general tendency expressed by a single number for a given set of observations (*14*), we must first consider whether the underlying variable is nominal (e.g., a book written in English, Spanish, or French), ordinal (e.g., the user's knowledge valued as novice, intermediary, good, or expert), or quantitative (e.g., the price, the time spent to . . .). In the first case, only the mode or the case having the maximal frequency may be a valid source of information. For ordinal variables, we may consider the mode or the sample median. Finally, for quantitative variables, we may consider the sample mean or the sample median. The sample median is represented by the value in the middle of the sorted sample (or by the average between the two values in the middle of the sample when the sample size is even). For example, the median and the mean of the sample {14, 15, 16, 17, 18, 19, 20} are both equal to 17. What then are the differences between these two statistics?

When we introduce a zero value in our sample, leading to {0, 14, 15, 16, 17, 18, 19, 20}, the sample median is evaluated as (16 + 17) / 2 = 16.5. The introduction of this value zero represents a very different value compared to the rest of the sample, leading to a sample mean value of 14.9. Such a number does not seem typical; after all, six of the eight values are greater than 14.9. Since the sample mean is sensitive to the presence of extreme scores, we know that it is not a particularly good location measure when the distribution is skewed and/or truncated. Moreover, when the sample contains errors often represented by values very different from the general tendency, the sample mean may not be a representative indicator. By contrast, the median is not dramatically changed by the new value, and therefore represents a more robust summary statistic (*10, 11*) that can also be used in the presence of noisy information or errors in the data. If for this latter case, we suspect that it can represent a significant percentage of error (e.g., between 2% and 4%), and we suggest using the trimmed mean as a method of summarizing the general tendency of the underlying phenomenon. The α% trimmed mean is obtained by computing the sample mean after removing the α% of the more extreme values in the sample. For example, the 25% trimmed mean of our last example is 16.5. (The average of the sample {14, 15, 16, 17, 18, 19} is obtained by removing the smallest and the largest values.)

As another example, when collecting information about the delivery time from a given bookseller measured in days, we obtain the following sample: {27, 18, 12, 36, 9, 7, 4, 6, 0}. The sample mean is 13.22 and the sample median is 9. Of course we may wonder what the value 0 means. For example, the book was in stock at the bookseller or it may indicate an input error (e.g., the clerk forgot to put a 1 before the digit 0). In another case, the presence of extreme values is also questionable as, for example, in information retrieval (*15*), in which an average precision of 0 for a request reflects the fact that the retrieval scheme is unable to find any relevant record (because the user wrote a query that was too restrictive or introduced a spelling error).

On the basis of these considerations, we really need a robust summary statistic such as an estimator of less sensitive to extreme values. For example, in evaluating the retrieval effectiveness, the median seems to be a better measure than does the sample mean (*15*). The trimmed mean can also be considered as an estimator of location, for which the behavior is not affected by extreme (and often suspicious) values in the sample.

Instead of limiting the summarization of a phenomenon to a single number (e.g., the time needed by a user to consult an online catalogue system and retrieve a given set of books), it is often a good idea to represent the main characteristics graphically. For example, a histogram or a distribution curve (polygon) is usually applied for a quantitative variable, while a pie chart or a bar chart is usually used to depict a nominal or an ordinal variable. Moreover, we may also consider the box-and-whisker plot. (See Fig. 1.) Within this graphical representation, a solid rectangle is formed by the position of the three quartiles. The first quartile (or the 25th percentile), denoted by Q_1, is the value such that 25 percent of the observations are smaller (and the rest larger). The second quartile Q_2 is the median (50% of the values are smaller and 50% are larger), and the third quartile Q_3 corresponds to the value such that 75 percent of the sample values are smaller. Moreover, the two extreme values (the minimum and the maximum) are indicated with a vertical dashed line. From this picture we may see that the range depicted by the solid rectangle indicates 50 percent of the observations (corresponding to the difference between Q_3 and Q_1). Also, both the position of the solid rectangle along the dashed line and the position of the median inside this rectangle indicate whether the underlying distribution is fairly symmetric (rectangle

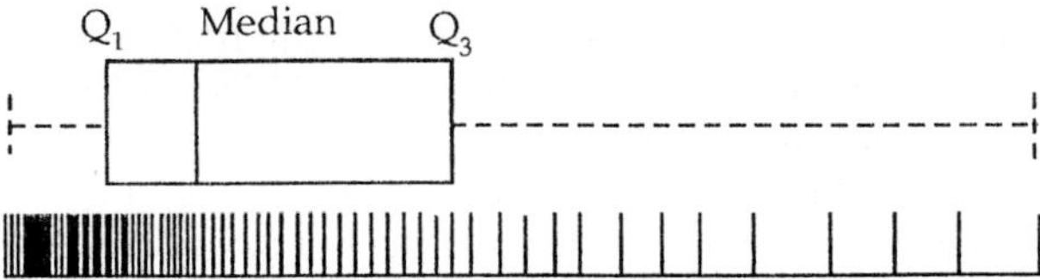

FIGURE 1. *Box-and-whisker plot (upper) and the corresponding sample values (below).*

depicted near or around the center of the figure; median depicted in the center of the rectangle) or asymmetric (e.g., right-skewed as shown in Fig. 1). In the latter case and as indicated before, the median is a more appropriate measure of the central tendency.

Such overall statistics as average precision, however, may hide performance irregularities that occur among observation samples (e.g., a drunk driver may walk along a white line, and in mean, this driver will be on the line, but only in mean!). Limited to a point estimate, a given statistic is thus not especially interesting, and we need some indication about the standard error associated with such a statistic. To achieve this objective, the bootstrap method can be a useful tool.

The Accuracy of Our Measure

In analyzing a phenomenon, we usually prefer the sample mean (denoted by $\bar{x}$), because this measure displays interesting properties. We know both its expectation and variance, which provide a general idea of the accuracy of this point estimator. Moreover, based on the central limit theorem, the distribution of $\bar{x}$ will be approximately normal as the sample size n gets larger, thus we may write the following well-known formulae:

$$\bar{x} = \frac{1}{n} \cdot \sum_{i=1}^{n} x_i \tag{1}$$

$$\hat{\sigma}_{\bar{x}} = \sqrt{\frac{S^2}{n}} \qquad \text{with } S^2 = \frac{1}{n-1} \cdot \sum_{i=1}^{n} (x_i - \bar{x})^2 \tag{2}$$

$$\bar{x} \doteq N\left(\mu; \frac{\sigma}{\sqrt{n}}\right) \tag{3}$$

in which the symbol $\doteq$ means that the random variable approximately follows a Gaussian distribution. This formulation leads us to construct confidence intervals around the observed sample mean and hypothesis testing. While such an approximation can be good if n is large, it can be quite inaccurate for the small sample size actually available or if the sample of observations contains some errors. Moreover, other location statistics are not necessarily represented by such a neat formula as Eq. 3, and the assessment of the accuracy of such an estimator can be quite hard compared to the expression depicted in Eq. 2. Some authors (e.g., Ref. *14*) therefore suggest that the median must be considered only as a descriptive measure. As another example, Stigler (*16*) shows that the trimmed mean does not always follow a normal distribution and that the estimation of the standard error associated with this estimator can be quite hard to assess.

To assign measures of accuracy to virtually any statistical estimators, we suggest using the bootstrap methodology (*12, 13, 17, 18*). Within this paradigm, we do not have to rely entirely on the central limit theorem to obtain a numerical value of estimator accuracy. Such an approach is very attractive, and in this case we should use the median instead of the mean to measure the central tendency of a sample. Moreover, the same methodology can be used to derive the accuracy of other statistics, such as the linear correlation coefficient or the trimmed mean.

The basic idea of the bootstrap approach is simple and can be explained as follows. From a given population, we have to obtain a sample of observations denoted by $X = \{x_1, x_2, \ldots, x_k, \ldots, x_n\}$ of size n. If we know the real population distribution, we may compute the underlying parameter of interest (e.g., the median or the mean). Since this population distribution is usually unknown, we want to estimate the parameter θ (e.g., the median, the mean) by a point estimate noted $\hat{\theta}$ based on the sample of observations. The aim of bootstrap methodology, however, is not to provide another formula to calculate such an estimator, but to achieve a measure of accuracy (or to indicate a "degree of uncertainty") for any statistical estimate.

For example, we have a sample of $n = 9$ values measuring the time in minutes needed to find a given document in our library. To summarize this sample, we suggest using the median, which in this case in 9.

Sample	x_1	x_2	x_3	x_4	x_5	x_6	x_7	x_8	x_9	median
value	27	18	12	36	9	7	4	6	0	9

Is this simple value able to provide a good indication of the general tendency of the underlying population? Clearly not. We also need an estimate or an idea of the variability of this measure. The general bootstrap algorithm is depicted in Fig. 2, and the underlying ideas will be described using our previous example.

To obtain a measure of the standard error associated with practically all estimators, the computer generates a set of bootstrap samples $X^{*i} = \{x_1^*, x_2^*, \ldots, x_k^*, \ldots, x_n^*\}$, for $i = 1, 2, \ldots B$, by random sampling with replacement from X. Each bootstrap sample X^{*i} contains members of the sample X, some appearing zero times, some once, some twice, and so on.

From our sample we have drawn ten bootstrap samples, and from each of them we have computed the corresponding median. From these samples, as shown in Table 1, we can see that some observations may appear more than once in a given bootstrap sample (e.g., the number 12 appears three times in the first bootstrap sample, and the observation 4 never). It can thus be deduced that the probability that a given value x_k (e.g., 4 in our case) does not appear in a bootstrap sample is approximately 0.368.

This process guarantees that each value x_k^* is mutually independent of each other and identically distributed (i.i.d.) from an empirical distribution function attributing probability of $1/n$ to each value x_k (nonparametric bootstrap). A note of caution must

TABLE 1

Example of our Data Set Together with Ten Bootstrap Samples

Sample value	x_1 27	x_2 18	x_3 12	x_4 36	x_5 9	x_6 7	x_7 4	x_8 6	x_9 0	median 9
X^{*i}										$\hat{\theta}^{*i}$
1	0	12	0	12	9	12	0	7	7	7
2	6	27	36	27	12	18	6	7	27	18
3	4	9	27	18	6	0	6	0	0	6
4	0	0	0	27	18	18	4	0	18	4
5	36	7	9	6	6	0	36	4	18	7
6	7	12	27	7	7	4	18	0	0	7
7	12	9	18	0	12	0	36	0	0	9
8	7	6	4	0	4	27	7	4	6	6
9	4	12	4	4	4	9	12	9	9	9
10	6	9	6	27	4	27	0	0	27	6

Estimator accuracy measurement for $\hat{\theta}$
Given $X = \{x_1, x_2, ..., x_k, ..., x_n\}$, a sample of size n;
for i = 1, 2, ..., B (e.g., B = 50 to 1000)
    Generate $X^{*i} = \{x_1^*, x_2^*, ..., x_k^*, ..., x_n^*\}$, a bootstrap sample drawn
        with replacement from X, and with x_k^* ~ i.i.d.;
    Compute the statistic $\hat{\theta}^{*i}$ corresponding to each bootstrap
        sample X^{*i};
next i

Compute $\hat{\sigma}(\hat{\theta}^*) = \sqrt{\frac{1}{B-1} \cdot \sum_{i=1}^{B} (\hat{\theta}^{*i} - \bar{\theta}^*)^2}$ with $\bar{\theta}^* = \frac{1}{B} \cdot \sum_{i=1}^{B} \hat{\theta}^{*i}$

FIGURE 2. *General bootstrap algorithm.*

be stated here. The bootstrap approach is not an "assumption-free" method due to the requirement that the observations be independent and identically distributed (i.i.d.).

From each sample X^{*i}, we may compute $\hat{\theta}^{*i}$, the bootstrap replication of $\hat{\theta}$ computed according to the same function that was applied to compute $\hat{\theta}$ from X as shown in our example (the last column in Table 1). As an example, the median of the first bootstrap sample {0, 12, 0, 12, 9, 12, 0, 7, 7} is 7, and the median of the second bootstrap sample is 18.

Finally, the value of $\hat{\sigma}(\hat{\theta}^*)$, the standard error estimator associated with $\hat{\theta}^*$, can be considered as a good approximation for the numerical value of the standard error associated with $\hat{\theta}$. (See formula at the bottom of Fig. 2.) From our example, we may compute with the average of our ten $\hat{\theta}^{*i}$ values, leading to $\bar{\theta}^* = 7.9$. Based on this average, we may compute $\hat{\sigma}(\hat{\theta}^*)$ according to the expression shown in Fig. 2, which

TABLE 2

Standard Errors for the Sample Mean and the Sample Median

Statistics \ B =	50	200	500	2000	5000	∞
θ = mean standard error $\hat{\sigma}(\hat{\theta}^*)$	2.901	3.324	3.593	3.603	3.677	3.688
θ = median standard error $\hat{\sigma}(\hat{\theta}^*)$	4.095	4.434	4.612	4.770	4.761	4.767

gives 3.84 as the numerical value of the standard error associated with the median 9 in our case. Of course, ten bootstrap samples are clearly not enough to obtain an accurate estimate of the standard error, and the computer will repeat this procedure B times. If we are interested in a main tendency estimator, a value for B greater than 500 can be viewed as sufficient for achieving acceptable accuracy. If the estimator θ is the 95th percentile, however, B must be greater, because estimating the standard error associated with such an estimator depends on the tail of the distribution, in which fewer bootstrap samples occur.

The main computational difficulty in such approaches resides in generating uniform random numbers, a well-known problem in computer science (*19*). There are some fairly good solutions described in (*20, 21*), however. Also, by using Excel, we may simulate such a simple process in order to obtain an estimate of the standard error associated with the simple statistic, such as the mean or the median.

As an example illustrating the reliability achieved by this nonparametric bootstrap method, we will evaluate the accuracy of both the sample mean and the sample median of our example shown in Table 1. From this sample we can easily compute the sample mean and the sample median, together with the standard error of the sample mean (computed according to formula 2). Obtaining the exact value of the standard error for the median is slightly more complex, but for a small sample size, the required computation is not very hard. (See Ref. *13,* p. 61.) These exact values are reported in the last column of Table 2. From the data depicted in Table 2, it can be seen that as the constant B gets larger, the accuracy of the standard error gets closer to the limit value (shown in the last column). We thus have an informal proof supporting the validity of the bootstrap methodology.

The bootstrap method may, however, sometimes fail to give an appropriate numerical value of the standard error for an estimator θ, as mentioned in Ref. *12* (p. 81). For example, it could be misleading to apply bootstrap methodology, at least as described in this article, to estimate the standard error associated with the maximum of a distribution (*22,* section 5) or other estimators very close to the tails of the underlying distribution.

As a final word, please note that the sample size used in our example is clearly not large enough to obtain a reasonable estimation. The set of possible values is very small and the resulting distribution is highly discrete. Moreover, for the median and with this limited sample size, the exact computation of the standard error does not represent a real difficulty. The aim of this example, however, was to give to the reader an idea of the bootstrap method's accuracy. For a larger sample size, the estimation of the standard error for the median can be done using the bootstrap approach (*15*).

Conclusion

The aim of this article was to take another look at the statistical and computational aspects underlying each experimental procedure. In order to deal with real sampling situations, which tend to contain errors and missing values, it would be more appropriate to apply more robust statistical methods (*10*) than the sample mean to adequately analyze and summarize the central tendency of a sample. As an example, this article suggested using the sample median or the trimmed mean instead of the sample mean as a location measure. It is usually not wise to summarize a sample only by one value, however, and we must also know, or at least have a rough idea, about its variability or standard error.

To answer to this question, the second chapter introduced the bootstrap methodology, a new computer-intensive approach. As an example, we demonstrated how one can apply this approach in a nonparametric fashion. In this case, the new statistical method required that the observations were independent and identically distributed, thus retaining the advantage of relieving the investigator from having to make unrealistic or unverifiable assumptions imposed by statistical models.

Based on a computer simulation, we have demonstrated that the numerical values of the standard error obtained by the bootstrap approach were closely related to those derived from textbook formulae. Moreover, using the bootstrap approach, the investigator avoided having to derive formulae that would be hard to come by.

The bootstrap approach is not an "assumption-free" method, however, and naturally a larger sample size is preferable to a rather limited sample size. Moreover, if we suspect that the sampling is subject to various erroneous manipulations or that the resulting sample contains many errors, even robust statistics and the bootstrap methodology cannot compensate for these errors in order to achieve a good estimate of the underlying population.

More advanced topics about using linear regression, establishing confidence intervals, or conducting statistical inference using the bootstrap method can be found in Refs. *12* or *13,* and some real examples in evaluating the comparing the retrieval effectiveness for various search systems are described in Ref. *15.*

ACKNOWLEDGMENTS

I would like to thank V. Rousson for reading and commenting on an earlier version of this article. This research was supported by the SNSF (Swiss National Science Foundation) under grants 20-43′217.95 and 20-50′578.97.

REFERENCES

1. L. Egghe and R. Rousseau, *Introduction to Informetrics: Quantitative Methods in Library, Documentation and Information Science,* Elsevier, Amsterdam, 1990.

2. D. H. Kraft and B. R. Boyce, *Operations Research for Libraries and Information Agencies,* Academic, San Diego, CA, 1991.
3. B. R. Boyce, C. T. Meadow, and D. H. Kraft, *Measurement in Information Science,* Academic, San Diego, CA, 1994.
4. S. M. Weiss and N. Indurkhya, *Predictive Data Mining: A Practical Guide,* Morgan Kaufmann, San Francisco, 1998.
5. D. Fisher and H. J. Lenz, eds., *Learning from Data,* Lecture Notes in Statistics, vol. 112, Springer-Verlag, New York, 1996.
6. T. Redman, "The Impact of Poor Data Quality on the Typical Enterprise." *Commun. ACM,* **41**(2), 79–82 (1998).
7. D. M. Strong, Y. W. Lee, and R. Y. Wang, "Data Quality in Context." *Commun. ACM,* **40**(5), 103–110 (1997).
8. G. Sawitzki, "Testing Numerical Reliability of Data Analysis Systems." *Computa. Stat. Data Anal.,* **18**(2), 269–286 (1994).
9. G. Sawitzki, "Report on the Numerical Reliability of Data Analysis Systems." *Computa. Stat. Data Anal.,* **18**(2), 289–301 (1994).
10. P. J. Huber, *Robust Statistics,* Wiley, New York, 1981.
11. H. Rieder, ed., *Robust Statistics, Data Analysis, and Computer Intensive Methods,* Lecture Notes in Statistics, vol. 109, Springer-Verlag, New York, 1996.
12. B. Efron and R. J. Tibshirani, *An Introduction to the Bootstrap,* Chapman & Hall, New York, 1993.
13. A. C. Davison and D. V. Hinkley, *Bootstrap Methods and Their Application,* Cambridge University Press, Cambridge, U.K., 1997.
14. L. G. Grimm, *Statistical Applications for the Behavioral Sciences,* Wiley, New York, 1993.
15. J. Savoy, "Statistical Inference in Retrieval Effectiveness Evaluation." *Info. Proc. Mgt.,* **33**(4), 495–512 (1997).
16. S. M. Stigler, "The Asymptotic Distribution of the Trimmed Mean." *Annals Stat.,* **1**(3), 472–477 (1973).
17. B. Efron, and R. J. Tibshirani, "Bootstrap Measures for Standard Errors, Confidence Intervals, and Other Measures of Statistical Accuracy." *Stat. Sci.,* **1**, 54–77 (1986).
18. C. Léger, D. N. Politis, and J. P. Romano, "Bootstrap Technology and Applications." *Technometrics,* **34**(4), 378–398 (1992).
19. D. Knuth, *The Art of Computer Programming: Seminumerical Algorithms,* 2nd ed., Addison-Wesley, Reading, MA, 1981.
20. S. Tezuka and P. L'Écuyer, "Efficient and Portable Combined Tausworthe Random Number Generators." *ACM Transac. Modeling Computer Sim.,* **1**(2), 99–112 (1991).
21. P. L'Écuyer and S. Côté, "Implementing a Random Number Package with Splitting Facilities." *ACM Transac. Math. Software,* **17**(1), 98–111 (1991).
22. P. J. Bickel and D. A. Freedman, "Some Asymptotic Theory for the Bootstrap." *Annals Stat.,* **9***(6), 1196–1217 (1981).*

JACQUES SAVOY

BUSINESS PROCESS REENGINEERING

The concept of business process reengineering (BPR) was first introduced in articles by Davenport and Short (*1*) and Hammer (*2*) in 1990. In their earlier experiences conducting research for consulting firms, both Davenport and Hammer had encountered consultants who talked about "redesigning business processes with the aid of information technology (IT)" (*3*). In 1989, an article by Rockart and Short (*4*) proposed the application of IT to enable change in cross-functional processes. Around the same time both Davenport and Hammer began to separately write articles on reengineering. The seeds for BPR were sown thus. These articles were followed by highly successful books by both Davenport (*5*) and Hammer and Champy (*6*). Both these books still drive the interest on the subject, although there has been considerable research and work in this area by both academics and practitioners.

Why was BPR so well accepted? On the one hand, there were numerous examples of the tremendous benefits of BPR, such as at IBM, CIGNA, and Xerox, but on the other hand, there were also reports that four out of five BPR projects were unsuccessful (*7*). In fact, Hammer and Champy, coauthors of *Reengineering the Corporation,* admitted that reengineering—as they preach it and practice it—works about 30 percent of the time (*8*). That implies a 70 percent failure rate!

As Davenport (*5*) explains, success and failure in reengineering is a complex phenomenon, and might be equated with success and failure of strategic planning. Further, critics of reengineering tend to display an extremely narrow focus. This type of attitude tends to equate reengineering with cost reduction, and therefore deflation of reengineering is bound to happen (*5*). The main reason for BPR can be attributed to business needs. The "bottom line" was that businesses were losing their competitive edge and they needed to respond to changing demands. The new set of demands required businesses to move from size and scale to flexibility, from low price or high quality to low price and high quality, from sustainable competitive advantage to extremely temporary competitive advantage, and from control to empowerment and teamwork.

These changing conditions required some drastic measures to revolutionize the way companies conducted business. It is at this time that BPR emerged and promised to provide the solution that would discard traditional business methods and provide a fresh approach. As Michael Hammer so eloquently said, "at the heart of reengineering is the notion of discontinuous thinking—of recognizing and breaking away from the outdated rules and fundamental assumptions that underlie operations" (*2*). In fact, over the last six years BPR has become so popular that it was ranked as the number one issue in the 1995 key issues study conducted by the CSC/Index consulting group (*9*).

Definition of BPR

There are various competing definitions of BPR, some of which are compiled in the recent book by Grover and Kettinger (*10*). These include such definitions as "the fundamental rethinking and radical redesign of business processes to achieve dramatic improvements in critical, contemporary measures of performance," "the reconfiguration of the business using IT as a central lever," and "the design of a company's core processes and organization structures that limit the competitiveness effectiveness and efficiency of the organization" (*10*).

Whatever the definition of BPR, there are some underlying essential elements that have clearly emerged over the last few years. It is well accepted that BPR deals with cross-functional core processes, promises a radical process change, allows breakthrough performance gains, is enabled by IT, is customer-driven, and is facilitated through empowerment and teamwork. Though most experts on BPR seem to agree on the above elements, the report from the field clearly indicates that there are exceptions to each of these elements (*10*). For example, there have been exceptions to the assumed role of IT, the clean-slate approach and the radical process change especially evident during the implementation stage. Even the breakthrough performance gain has eluded many companies, and they have settled for moderate gains. This has opened the door for new definitions, some of which capture the current status of BPR. Kettinger, Guha, and Teng (*11*) define it as follows: "Business Process Reengineering is an organizational initiative to accomplish strategy-driven (re)design of business processes to achieve competitive breakthroughs in quality, responsiveness, cost, flexibility, and satisfaction. These initiatives may differ in scope from process improvement to radical new processes design" (*11*).

This definition is based on a process management perspective and combines aspects from many fields, including management theory, operations research, and communication analysis.

Regardless of the definition of BPR it is important to note that the focus here is the business process. The importance of this element hinges on the fact that processes are strongly entrenched in and interact with organization strategy, structure, level of technology, and people, therefore it is not possible to view BPR in isolation and ignore this important interaction with other dimensions of the organization.

Dimensions of Business Process Reengineering

The business process concept is a collection of activities that take one or more kinds of inputs and create an output that is of value to the customer. The business process is the focal point of reengineering efforts rather than traditional tasks or functional activities. Figure 1 shows the shift from the traditional functional-oriented organization outlook to a process-oriented outlook. It must be noted, however, that a matrix type of organization did attempt to address the cross-functional aspect, but it was a fairly weak effort. The process view clearly attempts to cut across every required functional unit in the organization to achieve its goal—take the inputs and create the output that adds value.

This goal is far more elusive than most people realize, however. Any change, especially one that radically shifts from traditional beliefs and experiences of the organization and adopts a horizontal, process view is bound to face numerous hurdles. This entails upsetting the employees of the company, redefining the roles of the

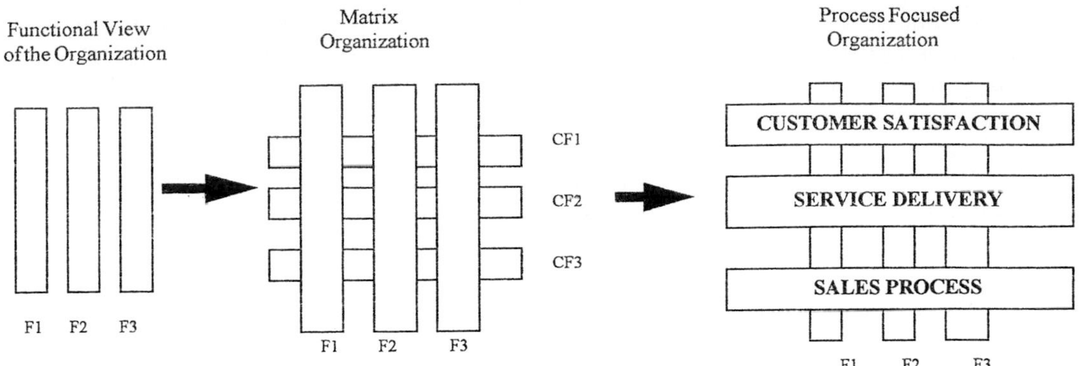

FIGURE 1. *Shift from traditional functional to process-oriented organization. (F1 = marketing function, F2 = finance function, F3 = manufacturing, CF1 = cross-functional activity/project 1, CF2 = cross-functional activity/project 2, CF3 = cross-functional activity/project 3.)*

information systems (IS) professionals, assessing the cultural impacts of the effort, and many other issues. In fact, one can expect at least some repercussions to all the major dimensions of the organization—**the people, the organization structure and strategy, the technology,** and the way the organization conducts its operation. This has led to many companies losing their commitment to the BPR effort after a period of time and settling for partial gains.

Researchers and professionals have been wrestling with the issue of how to ensure a successful BPR project. In fact ProSci, a BPR consulting group, has started a BPR best practices study in which it invites professionals involved in BPR projects to share their experiences on the many dimensions of BPR. The group plans to pool all the responses and provide useful insights into the BPR enigma. Various research studies have also been conducted on the many dimensions of BPR, but with contradictory results. What follows is a brief discussion of some of the major dimensions of BPR and the various views on each dimension.

Goals and Objectives

J. Emery, the editor of *MIS Quarterly* in 1991, expressed the following view on the need for reengineering:

> Reengineering should be an important goal of any effort to develop an IS plan for an organization . . . symptoms of obsolete design concepts are manifested throughout almost any large application developed a decade or more ago—in its failure to satisfy cross-functional needs, its limited functional capabilities, its inability to provide selected and tailored information drawn from widespread parts of the organization, its flexibility in meeting changing needs, and its unfriendly interfaces (*12*).

Though this view clearly calls for the need for reengineering and the development of organization IS plans, it does not mention "specific" goals or needs of the organization that may lead it to reengineer certain business processes. These specific objectives vary for each company, but some of the common ones include improving customer satisfaction, reducing costs, becoming more efficient, and being more competitive and flexible in the marketplace (*13*). For example Federal Express's method of addressing the customer satisfaction goal is to create IS that provide accurate and timely information on the packages. This, coupled with on-time delivery and the ability to provide complete information on the rarely lost or misplaced packages, has allowed the company to keep its customers extremely satisfied.

There are other reasons that lead companies to reengineer, but one of the most popular ones is competition. Hallmark, the Kansas City-based greeting card company committed itself to reengineering to gain competitive advantage and to solve certain aspects of the competitive facet of the company. Because of changes in its business environment the company had to assess the processes involving its stock proliferation its channels of distribution. The company reengineered fairly successfully and in doing so was able to take a leap into the future to stay competitive and conduct business in a new way. In their 1993 book, *Reengineering the Corporation,* Hammer and Champy (*6*) provide a detailed narrative of this BPR effort by Hallmark.

Methodologies and Tools

The last few years have led to a remarkable development in creating new methods and tools for reengineering: "The majority of methodologies for conducting reengineering are the intellectual property of the leading reengineering consulting firms such as Anderson Consulting, CSC/Index Group, Ernst and Young, Mckinsey Co., Nolan and Norton and Price-Waterhouse" (*11*). Most of these methodologies incorporate the assumptions unique to these consulting firms. These consultants promote their methodologies as represented by Barrett (*14*) and Klein (*7*). These methodologies have evolved from many business disciplines, including operations research, industrial engineering, and software development (*15, 1, 16–19*).

In their February 1995 article in *Business Technology,* Goldsmith and Maniace (*20*) profiled the Coopers and Lybrand methodology BreakPoint BPR. Based on their evaluation criteria, BreakPoint was touted to be a highly desirable methodology. Some of the highlights included the fewest phases of all popular methodologies, an integrative approach to BPR, and an easy-to-understand modular approach. The three phases of this methodology were discover, redesign, and realize. Another unique aspect of the Coopers and Lybrand's BreakPoint Workbench is the belief that people, cultures, and structures vary enormously across companies, and thus this methodology incorporates the ability to allow a fairly high degree of customization. There are other methodologies, such as Process Reengineering Life Cycle (PRLC; *11*) and Turbo BPR (Department of Defense). The Department of Defense also provides a choice of four basic methods for BPR, and even allow users to download and tutor themselves on how to use Turbo BPR.

There exists a common thread in most of these BPR methods and tools, however. Usually the common aspects of most BPR methods can be summarized as follows:

- All methods define the project before beginning, although some controversy has emerged with this point recently (*10*).
- All methods have a redesign step.
- All methods include some form of assessment or cost/benefit analysis.
- All methods plan and implement a solution in some manner.
- All methods measure the resulting performance changes.

Jeff Haitt, president of the ProSci Group, writes (*21*) that while deciding on any BPR method or tool it is important to ask certain questions, such as Should you create a vision prior to beginning process and systems redesign? Is it necessary for you to document the as-is processes prior to the redesign work? Should a learning process precede the visioning or redesign activities? The answers to these questions and others will have a major bearing on the final choice of the BPR methodology or tool, but one thing companies need to keep in mind is to ask themselves these questions before they decide on any consultants. This simply stems from the fact that consultants are most familiar with their own methodologies and any choice of consultant will lead to the default selection of the BPR methodology.

The Role of Information Technology

Any review of the literature clearly displays the extreme positions on the role of IT in BPR. Hammer and Champy (*6*) viewed "state of the art information technology as a part of any reengineering effort." They labeled IT as an "essential enabler," since it allowed companies to reengineer business processes. Information technology therefore has a crucial role to play in the reengineering effort. This view has been more or less sustained over the last few years. Venkatraman (*22*) writes that IT has become a fundamental enabler in creating and maintaining a flexible business network. In his 1994 article int he *Sloan Management Review* (*22*) he provides an excellent framework that captures the range of IT's potential benefit on one dimension and the degree of organizational transformation on the other. Clearly the role of IT as an enabler and a major ingredient for reengineering is recognized.

Some researchers raise the possibilities of conflict between the organization culture and the implementation of IT, however. This may result in implementation failure, which may directly undermine the effort to bring about organizational change (*23*). In the last few years researchers and professionals have realized that firms that believe IT is the dominant answer to their process redesign efforts are destined to run against barriers that prevent the integration of technology into the company (*24*). Changing processes by imposing IT through brute force does not lead to solutions. There is indeed a delicate balance involved in which all the ingredients for reengineering need to be judiciously applied to reap the benefits.

It is therefore imperative that managers focus on the appropriate use of IT. It is meaningless to embrace new technology to stay ahead of the competition since this will definitely upset the reengineering effort. It often mistakenly leads to companies deciding on the IT and then gearing the reengineering effort around this technology with dire consequences.

Role of IS Professionals

Unless management gives IS a prominent role in the reengineering project, the effort will be doomed to failure (*25*). Systems development and operation is very often an integrative activity. This emanates from the simple fact that processes that affect more than one part of any organization require the need for cross-functional teams, but in this integrative effort to develop systems most organizations delegate the leadership role to the IS people. Most line managers and external BPR consultants take exception to this view (*26*), however.

Like any other new idea, BPR too has its points of disagreements. Various authors (e.g., *26–29*) have all addressed the issue of appropriate role of IS professionals in the BPR process. The general view is that IS professionals definitely have a major role to play in the BPR process, although this role is not clearly defined. Most experts suggest that managers should strive to make the IS professionals work with the line managers. This may negate the feeling of animosity between the two diametrically opposite groups of people.

In a preliminary report of a research study reported by Markus and Robey (*26*), it was apparent that "internal IS specialists were occasionally left out of BPR projects altogether." This role of IS can be summed up in a statement by Robert Zeibig of Nolan, Norton and Co., where he observes, "the role of IS: leading from behind" (*30*).

Measurement of BPR Outcome

Most BPR methodologies include some form of technique for measuring performance. Usually this is done in the evaluation stage of the BPR process, although the label for this stage may differ, based on the methodology used.

In the process reengineering life cycle approach (PRLC), performance is measured during the evaluation stage. This measurement of performance of the redesigned process should include a wide variety of process measures, such as "process performance (cycle time, cost, customer satisfaction), IT performance (downtime, system use) and productivity indices (orders processed per hour)" (*11*).

Measures can vary from "soft" measures such as morale to "hard" measures such as cycle time. *CFO* magazine reports that more than half of executives (54%) agreed that there was no consistent, reliable measures available. Dave Trimble of ProSci (*21*) concurs that measuring the success of a BPR project is extremely difficult and elusive. Not only do you have to develop the right measure, but you have to measure the right thing. Trimble further recommends developing "metrics," which he defines as "nothing more than a standard measure to assess your performance in a particular area. Metrics are at the heart of good, customer-focused process management system and any program directed at continuous improvement" (*21*).

The secret to developing useful metrics or performance measures hinges on the ability of the metric to measure the right thing, the ability to collect accurate and complete data, and keeping the metrics focused to capture specific, relevant information. Some examples of performance measures reported in the literature include cycle time reduction by 27 percent reduced defects by 38 percent, and diminished labor costs by 18 percent (*11*).

Success Factors

This is perhaps the most intriguing part of the BPR phenomenon. How can a company ensure the proper execution of a BPR effort? Success factors are nothing more than a collection of lessons learned from reengineering projects over the years. Based on reports included in many studies it is possible to develop a general list of factors that contribute to a successful reengineering project.

- Top management sponsorship (strong and consistent)
- Strategic alignment (with company strategic direction)
- Compelling business case for change (with measureable objectives)
- Proven methodology (that includes a vision process)
- Effective change management (address cultural transformation)
- Line ownership (pair ownership with accountability)
- Composition of the reengineering team (in both breadth and knowledge)
- Employee involvement (through communicating and empowering)
- Availability of resources (establishing resource base on front end)
- Establish time limit on the project (decide on time frame to avoid overruns)
- Establish relationship between internal IS professionals and line manager (*5–7, 27, 31, 32*)

This list at best can be termed a "laundry list" since it encompasses a host of factors that have often proved to be essential to the success of any major project, but labeling these factors in this way does not diminish their importance in any manner. The truth is that there is no perfect way to ensure a successful outcome of a BPR project. Methodology has clearly emerged as a major concern for most companies, although each of the above factors cannot be neglected. It has to be appreciated, however, that any BPR effort undertaken by an organization requires a major effort on every possible dimension—structure, strategy, people, and the technology dimension. This can be shown in the form of a framework.

A Framework for Business Process Reengineering

The central premise for BPR is that it requires a holistic view of strategy, structure, process, people, and technology (*19*); that is, BPR is not solely based on how the organization can wield its IT or on some top management prerogative imposed on the rest of the organization. It is in fact a major effort that will require participation from various corners of the organization and will impact and change all of the five dimensions shown in the framework. (Refer to Fig. 2.)

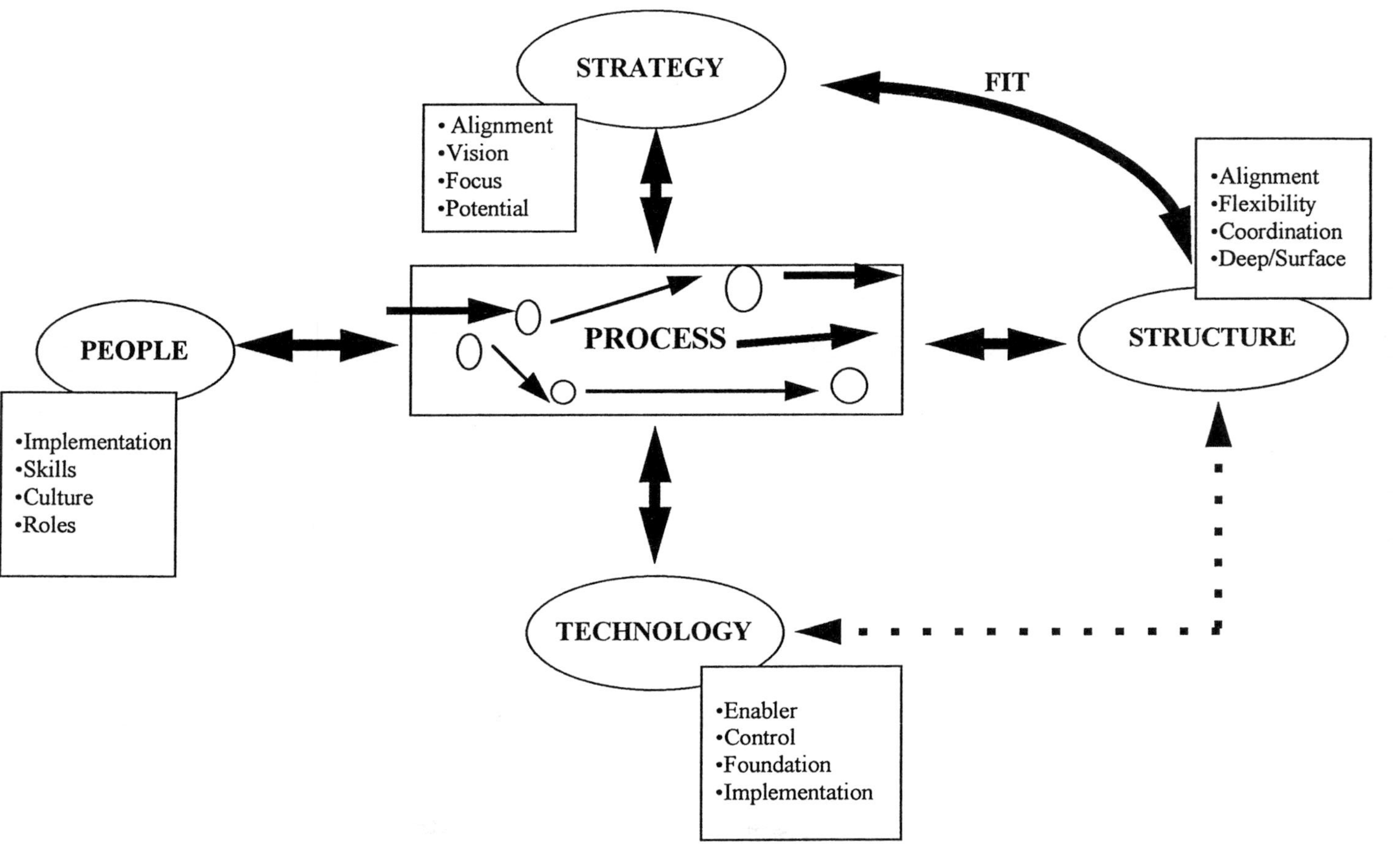

FIGURE 2. *A framework for business process reengineering.*

Future Trends and Research Directions

Davenport and Stoddard (*33*) predicted that like all popular management notions, reengineering would have a life cycle (*34*), which they observed peaked in the United States in early 1994. According to Kutschker (*35*), in 1993 the world market for consultancy for BPR was close to $1 billion, which is predicted to double by 1997. Most authors predict some type of synthesis whereby reengineering will be absorbed into the existing change management methods (*33, 35*). Though this is a perfectly sound explanation for the future of BPR, it is impossible to disregard the host of unanswered questions regarding the success of BPR, its proper measurement, and its effect on the long-term goal of the business and the role of IS/IT.

Davenport (*3*) outlined some possible directions for BPR in the future. The first possibility is integrated process management, whereby reengineering becomes better integrated with other approaches to process management. The second is the application of reengineering toward processes that deal with knowledge work as opposed to administrative processes, where it has traditionally had its major impact. The third possibility entails reducing the cycle time for executing a BPR project. He calls this rapid reengineering, in which the goal would be to speed up the cycle time for reengineering (*3*).

Another area that presents an excellent future for reengineering is in global business processes. These global processes can be distinguished from "local" business processes since they cut across national boundaries. In other words, research needs to be conducted to assess how the framework for BPR changes when the process is global in nature (i.e., it not only cuts across organizational boundaries but also national and cultural boundaries). This is definitely an area in which it is possible to harness the lessons learned from reengineering.

Changing markets, shifting demographies, rapidly changing environments, faster adoption of IT, and the most important factor, customers' demands, are forcing businesses to think globally. The process-oriented view of the organization will prove useful to many companies that rely on global processes.

In his 1994 paper on reengineering in multinational corporations, Michael Kutschker (*35*) conducted case studies of fifty German and Swiss companies and arrived at the following conclusion: "the re-engineering of international business processes needs special attention because the multi-faceted deeper structure of multinational corporations increases in complexity of business processes, thus influencing the options for redesign."

This multifaceted deeper structure in multinationals exists because of the global issues that an organization has to confront to operate globally. In their 1991 paper, Deans et al. (*36*) identified the global issues in the international environment. These issues have been summarized in Table 1.

Nakatani and Yadav (*37*) identified seventeen types of information that should be captured in any model for BPR. Given the complexity of the issues in the international environment it is extremely important to use global IT wisely to facilitate coordination. The management of global IT and handling the cultural differences across national borders is going to present a major challenge to the organizations.

TABLE 1

List of Issues in an International Environment

Environment	Issues
Political/legal	Transborder data flow restrictions, legal restrictions, on hardware and software, telecommunications deregulation, etc.
Technological	Regulatory Strategies, vendor support in foreign countries, price and quality of telecommunications, level of IT sophistication, etc.
Social/Cultural	Local cultural constraints, language barriers, work habits, etc.
Economic	National infrastructure, export restrictions, etc.

Source: Compiled from Ref. *36*.

Ives and Jarvenpaa (*38*) state that "carefully crafted investments in global information technology offer firms an opportunity to increase control and enhance coordination." It is without a doubt that challenges such as geographic transfer of work, global networking, and global service levels require firms to have a high developed and well-managed global IT, therefore one view is that before any BPR effort can begin it is imperative that this global IT strategy be formulated. It is this IT that will provide the initial data to identify the organization's business processes.

Conclusions

Recently there has been a shift in the reengineering community to address the "people" issues associated with reengineering (*39, 40*). This human reengineering approach focuses first on changing people's attitudes toward change and encouraging them to be creative (*41*). Clearly this realization has evolved from bitter lessons learned during failed reengineering projects. Although IT continues to be the enabler it is has become necessary to understand and appreciate the people side of reengineering.

Further, it is important for researchers to bring together their experiences with reengineering and begin to develop the best practices for implementing it.

In conclusion, organizations are cautioned from blindly launching into BPR projects, especially when dealing with global processes. It is important to heed Peter Drucker's (*42*) statement that "concepts and tools, history teaches again and again, are mutually interdependent and interactive. One changes the other" (*42*).

REFERENCES

1. T. H. Davenport and J. E. Short, "The New Industrial Engineering: Information Technology and Business Process Redesign." *Sloan Mgt. Rev.,* 11–27 (summer 1990).

2. M. Hammer, "Reengineering Work: Don't Automate, Obliterate." *Harvard Bus. Rev.,* 104–112 (summer 1990).

3. T. H. Davenport, "Business Process Reengineering: Where It's Been, Where It's Going," in *Business Process Change—Reengineering Concepts, Methods, and Technologies,* V. Grover and W. J. Kettinger, eds. Idea Publishing Group, Harrisburg, PA, 1995, pp. 1–13.

4. J. F. Rockart and J. E. Short, "IT in the 1990's: Managing Organizational Interdependence." *Sloan Mgt. Rev.,* 7–16 (winter 1989).
5. T. H. Davenport, *Process Innovation,* Harbard Business School Press, Boston, 1993.
6. M. Hammer and J. A. Champy, *Reengineering the Corporation,* Harper Business, New York, 1993.
7. M. M. Klein, "The Most Fatal Reengineering Mistakes." *Info. Strat. Exec. J.,* **10**:4, 21–28 (summer 1994).
8. D. Appleton, "Business Reengineering with Business Rules, in *Business Process Change—Reengineering Concepts, Methods, and Technologies,* V. Grover and W. J. Kettinger, eds. Idea Pbulishing Group, Harrisburg, PA, 1995, pp. 291–329.
9. CSC/Index Report for 1995.
10. V. Grover and W. J. Kettinger, eds. *Business Process Change—Reengineering Concepts, Methods, and Technologies,* Idea Publishing Group, Harrisburg, PA, 1995.
11. W. J. Kettinger, S. Guha, and J. T. C. Teng, "The Process Reengineering Life Cycle Methodology: A Case Study," in *Business Process Change—Reengineering Concepts, Methods, and Technologies,* V. Grover and W. J. Kettinger, eds. Idea Publishing Group, Harrisburg, PA, 1995, pp. 211–244.
12. J. Emery, "Editor's Comments: Reengineering the Organization." *MIS Q.,* iii-iv (March 1991).
13. J. A. Ponce de Leon, A. Rai, and A. Melcher, "Alternative IT Strategies: Organizational Scope and Application Delivery," in *Business Process Change—Reengineering Concepts, Methods, and Technologies,* V. Gover and W. J. Kettinger, eds. Idea Publishing Group, Harrisburg, PA, 1995, pp. 187–207.
14. J. L. Barrett, "Process Visualization: Getting the Vision Right Is the Key." *Info. Syst. Mgt.,* **11**(2), 14–23 (spring 1994).
15. J. A. Watts, "Practical Approach to Redesigning and Implementing Business Processes," in *Software Assistance for Business Process Reengineering,* K. Spurr, P. Layzell, L. Jennison, and N. Richards, eds. Wiley, Chichester, U.K., 1993.
16. F. Farhoodi, "CADDIE: An Advanced Tool for Organizational Design and Process Modelling," in *Software Assistance for Business Process Reengineering,* K. Spurr, P. Layzell, L. Jennison, and N. Richards, eds. Wiley, Chichester, U.K., 1993.
17. E. Morris and J. Brandon, *Reengineering Your Business,* McGraw Hill, London, 1994.
18. S. Wang, "OO Modeling of Business Processes: Object-Oriented Systems Analysis." *Info. Syst. Mgt.,* 36–43 (spring 1994).
19. G. Smith and L. Willcocks, "Business Process Reengineering, Politics and Management: From Methodologies to Processes," in *Business Process Change—Reengineering Concepts, Methods, and Technologies,* V. Grover and W. J. Kettinger, eds. Idea Publishing Group, Harrisburg, PA, 1995, pp. 493–525.
20. N. M. Goldsmith and M. A. Maniace, "Coopers & Lybrand Consulting's BreakPoint BPR." *Bus. Tech. (Feb. 1995).*
21. J. Haitt and D. Trimble, Comments and letters, ProSci On-line Tutorials, ProSci Web Site, 1996.
22. N. Venkatraman, "IT-enabled Business Transformation: From Automation to Business Scope Redefintion." *Sloan Mgt. Rev.,* **35**(2) 73–87 (winter 1994).
23. R. B. Cooper, "The Inertial Impact of Culture on IT Implementation." *Info. Mgt.,* **27**(1), 17–31 (July 1994).
24. D. A. Marchand and M. J. Stanford, "Business Process Redesign: A Framework for Harmonizing People, Information and Technology," in *Business Process Change—Reengineering Concepts, Methods, and Technologies,* V. Grover and W. J. Kettinger, eds. Idea Publishing Group, Harrisburg, PA, 1995, pp. 34–56.
25. E. V. Martinez, "Successful Reengineering Demands IS/Business Partnerships." *Sloan Mgt. Rev.,* **36**(4), 51–60 (summer 1995).
26. M. L. Markus and D. Robey, "Business Process Reengineering and the Role of the Information Systems Professional," in *Business Process Change—Reengineering Concepts, Methods, and Technologies,* V. Grover and W. J. Kettinger, eds. Idea Publishing Group, Harrisburg, PA, 1995, pp. 591–611.
27. B. J. Bashien, M. L. Markus, and P. Riley, "Preconditions to BPR Success and How to Prevent Failure." *Info. Syst. Mgt.,* **11**(2), 7–13 (spring 1994).
28. P. Krass, "Building a Better Mouse Trap." *Info. Week,* 24–28 (1991).

29. P. Krass, "The Role of the CIO: A Delicate Balance." *Info. Week* (May 1992).
30. R. Zeibig, "Surviving Business Process Redesign: The Impact on IS," in *Business Process Change—Reengineering Concepts, Methods, and Technologies,* V. Grover and W. J. Kettinger, eds. Idea Publishing Group, Harrisburg, PA, 1995, pp. 650–668.
31. R. D. Galliers, "Strategic Information Systems Planning: Myths, Reality, and Guidelines for Successful Implementation." *Eur. J. Info. Syst.,* **1**(1), 55–64 (1991).
32. ProSci Tutorial Web Site, ProSci Web Site, Module 3—Reengineering Success Factors: Why Do Some Projects Fail and others Succeed?
33. T. H. Davenport and D. B. Stoddard, "Reengineering: Business Change of Mythic Proportions?" *MIS Q.,* **18**(2) 121–128 (June 1994).
34. R. Pascale, *Managing on the Edge,* Simon and Schuster, New York, 1990.
35. M. Kutschker, "Reengineering of Businesses in Multinational Corporations," *Carnegie Bosch Institute International Research Conference,* Nov. 1994.
36. P. C. Deans, K. R. Karawan, M. D. Goslar, D. A. Ricks, and B. Toyne, "Identification of Key International Information Systems Issues in U.S.-Based Multinational Corporations." *J. MIS,* **27**(4), 27–50 (spring 1991).
37. K. Nakatani and S. B. Yadav, "An Extended Object-Oriented Modeling Method for Business Process Reengineering," *Proceedings of Association of Information Systems,* Phoenix, 1996, pp. 167–169.
38. B. Ives and S. L. Jarvenpaa, "Applications of Global Information Technology: Key Issues for Management." *MIS Q.,* 33–49 (March 1991).
39. J. Champy, *Reengineering Management: The Mandate for a New Leadership,* Harper Business, New York, 1995.
40. C. A. Bartlett and S. Ghoshal, "Rebuilding Behavioral Context: Turn Process Reengineering into People Rejuvenation," *Sloan Mgt. Rev.,* **37**(1), 11–23 (fall 1995).
41. R. Cooper and M. L. Markus, "Human Reengineering." *Sloan Mgt. Rev.,* **36**(1), 39–50 (summer 1995).
42. P. F. Drucker, "The Information Executives Truly Need." *Harvard Bus. Rev.,* 54–62 (Jan.–Feb. 1995).

SUVOJIT CHOTON BASU
PRASHANT C. PALVIA

CAD/CAM

Introduction

The use of Computer Aided Design/Drafting (CAD)/Computer Aided Manufacturing (CAM) has become a fundamental part of the business strategies of most industries, particularly with the availability of increasingly low-cost PC-based systems that are adequate for many applications and are available for under $5,000 per seat. CAD/CAM continues to expand from being simply a design, drafting, and manufacturing aid into the kernel around which the company's business revolves. The concept of concurrent or simultaneous engineering in which various disciplines are repre-

The material in this section is adapted from *The CAD/CAM Handbook,* edited by Carl Machover and published by McGraw Hill (1996).

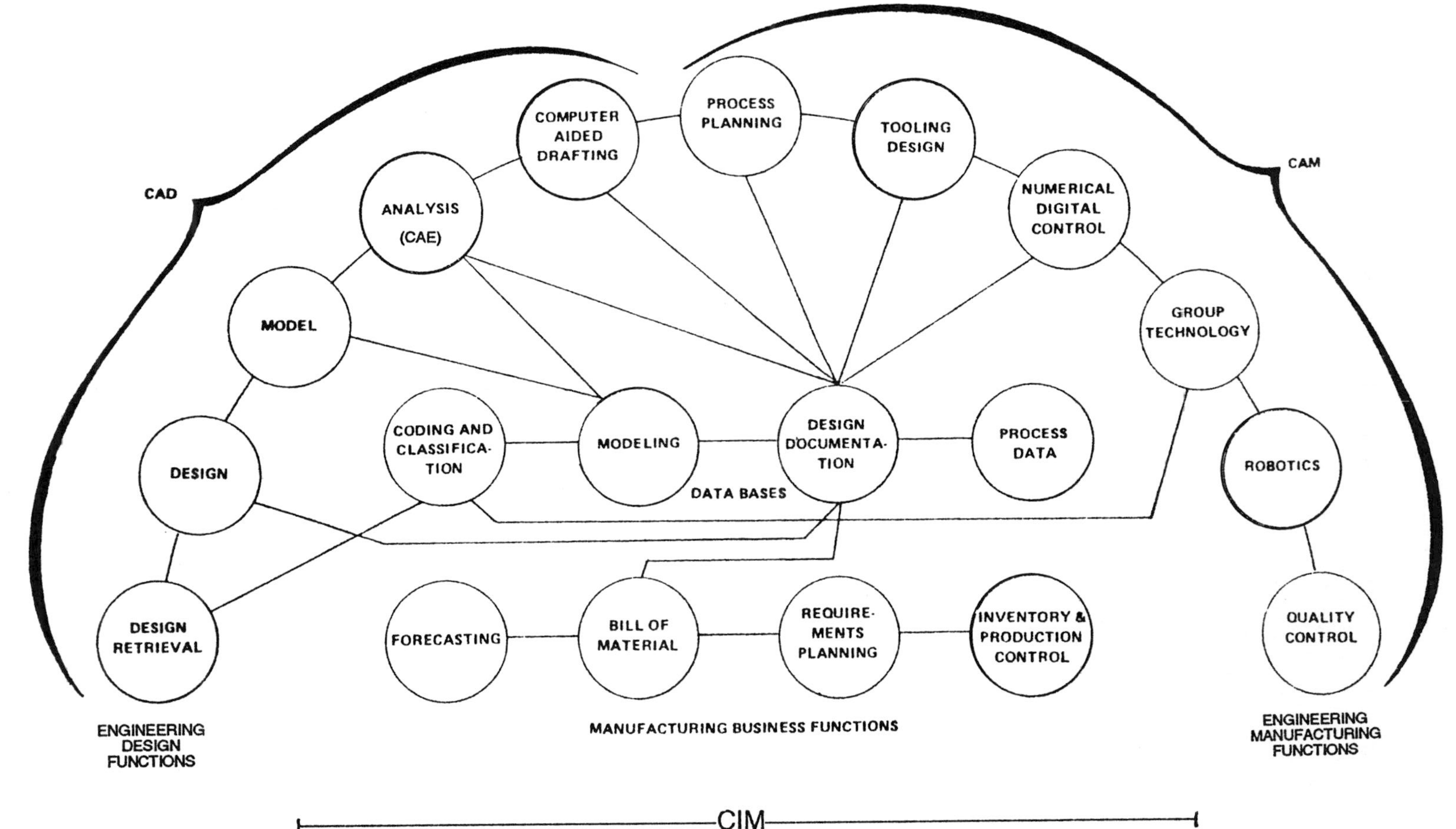

FIGURE 1. *C4 (CAD/CAM/CAE/CIM)*

sented on design and manufacturing teams continues to grow. We are beginning to move closer to the concept of the engineering and manufacturing cycle being tied more closely to the business practices of the company. With the growth of lower-cost teleconferencing techniques, the establishment of worldwide engineering teams is literally becoming practical. Justification is increasingly based on downstream benefits and not on how quickly a drawing can be made or revised.

The design stage has a profound effect on manufacturing costs. Somewhere on the order of 75 percent of the final manufacturing cost is determined during the initial expenditure of 5 to 10 percent involving design.

Figure 1 shows the traditional relationships among the various CAD/CAM/Computer Aided Engineering (CAE)/Computer Integrated Manufacturing (CIM) functions.

What Is CAD/CAM?

Computer-aided drafting or computer-aided design is used to define the geometry for a mechanical part, architectural structure, electronic circuit, building layout, or other item. This information is stored in a computer database, which is the basis for further work and for the production of engineering drawings.

Computer-aided-manufacturing systems provide the data and instructions to automated machines for making parts, assemblies, and circuits, often using the geometric data from CAD as a starting point. Computer aided engineering is used to analyze CAD geometry, allowing the operator to simulate and study how the product will behave so the design can be refined and optimized.

Often associated with CAD and CAM are CAE and CIM. Computer-aided engineering can be considered to be the analysis component of design. The Society of Manufacturing Engineers (SME) has continued to refine its concept of CIM. In 1993, it published *The New Manufacturing Enterprise Wheel*. Figure 2 is a graphical representation of those elements that are the foundation of manufacturing success. Recognizing that CIM had developed a negative connotation in some circles, SME chose not to use it in the title. The new version is said to preserve the "understanding gained from the previous CIM Enterprise Wheel," however.

Applications

CAD/CAM IN PRIMARY MANUFACTURING PROCESSES

Computer-aided manufacturing has played an important role in industry since 1952, when the first numerically controlled machine tool was successfully demonstrated at the Massachusetts Institute of Technology (MIT).

Developed by MIT, Automatically Programmed Tool (APT) is the most widely used numerical control (NC) language in the world.

While the solid model is important for representing part definition, other key factors to a successful manufacturing operation include the following:

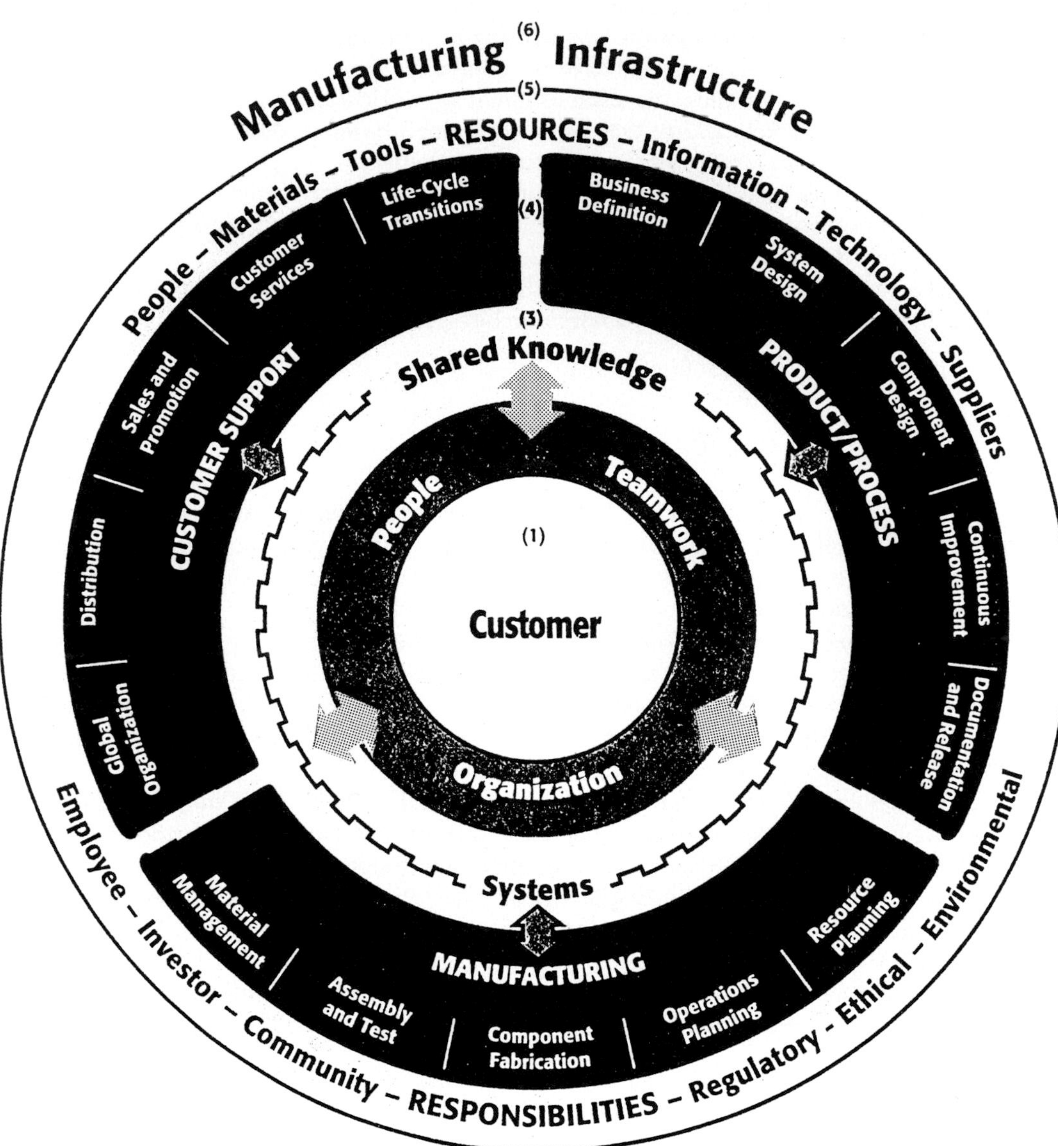

FIGURE 2. *The new manufacturing enterprise wheel.*

- Graphics
- Data Management
- Associativity
- Applications

Applications

The preeminent application of CAD/CAM in manufacturing today is NC programming. Twenty years ago NC only meant the programming of machine tools. Now NC encompasses many facets of the manufacturing environment, from machine tools to coordinate-measuring machines, to fully automated, high-speed machining cells.

Generative numerical control (GNC) is a technology that can be applied to several key components of the manufacturing process. Generative numerical control's technology is based on its ability to take a CAD feature-based solid model, evaluate and recognize the features, and apply rules to each feature to automatically create NC tool paths (machine control data), cutter selection, and work instructions. The strength of the system lies in the "knowledge" embedded in its rules for recognizing features and then selecting methods to machine that feature. Features such as holes, slots, pockets, and faces are recognized by analyzing the solid-model CAD geometry entitles.

Machining Applications

Turning operations
2–2 1/2 application milling
Milling operations
NC verification

Fabrication Applications

Wire electrodischarge machining (EDM)
Flame, waterjet, and laser operations
Sheet metal development
Automated nesting
NC punching operations
Automated tube-pipe bending
Coordinate measuring machines

COMPUTER-AIDED PLANT DESIGN

Plant design involves a wide range of tasks, and activities related to the design and construction of process-oriented facilities, and falls within the broader category of architecture, engineering, and construction (AEC). Plant design usually refers to the design and construction of facilities such as petrochemical plants, power plants, offshore oil platforms, chemical processing plants, and pharmaceutical plants. These facilities are typified by their size and complexity, particularly as it relates to process piping systems.

Today computer-aided plant design is in a state of transition. The advent of personal computer (PC)-based CAD in the mid-1980s changed the face of the plant design systems in use today. The per-seat cost today is in the $10,000 to $15,000 range, with no loss in functionality or performance when compared to the older minicomputer-based systems.

Detailed Design

The focus of nearly every computer-aided plant-design system today is the detailed design of process facilities. This includes the physical design of the facility as well as the schematic design of the major systems, in particular piping systems.

Schematic Design of Piping and Equipment

Piping and mechanical equipment make up the large part of any process facility. It is not surprising, then, that within the context of detailed plant design, much of the focus of software development for computer-aided plant design has been on the design of piping systems.

Physical Design of Piping and Equipment

The layout of piping systems in 3D space lies at the heart of any computer-aided plant design. In fact, this is what distinguishes plant design from other application areas with the AEC realm.

Interactive Design

Structural Steel. The process for using computer-aided plant design for the design of structural steel is necessarily somewhat different from the processes used for piping. In the case of piping, the 3D design data are used to create the drawings and often the input to stress-analysis programs as well. For structural steel, it is usually more productive for the drawings and analysis to precede the 3D structural-steel model.

Other Disciplines. From a 3D modeling perspective, the amount of data required from other disciplines in a plant-design project, such as the Heating, Ventilation, Air Conditioning (HVAC) duct and electrical cable tray, is usually much less than that typical for piping, mechanical equipment, and structural steel. Also, the 3D complexity of the components and component layout is often much less than that for piping.

Downstream Applications

There are several downstream uses of computer-aided plant design. Two of the most important are in piping fabrication and plant construction.

AUTOMATED MAPPING AND GEOGRAPHIC INFORMATION SYSTEMS (GIS)

Electronic imaging and digital map data have now become commonplace.

GIS Versus AM/FM (Automated Mapping and Facilities Mapping)

Mapping using computer technology has been constantly expanding over the last decade. In many areas the digital map by itself is no longer considered sufficient; a database is now required, to be linked to the various graphic elements to produce an intelligent map. For example, a city tax assessor might query his mapping system to show all the parcels of land in a particular zone that had over two acres of land valued between $150,000 and $325,000. A water superintendent who just had a main break might query her computer to determine what valves must be closed to isolate the pipe, where they are located, and what hydrants and customers will be put of service.

Geographic information systems are based on a closed-polygon system, in which each parcel boundary is closed to allow for area calculation. An attached database describes all the attribute data within that boundary. Automated mapping and facilities mapping, on the other hand, is based on a linked-node system. For example, pipes are attached to nodes, then valves, hydrants, and services are attached to pipes. These attachments allow for tracing through the system. The associated database describes the various facility attribute data.

AUTOMOTIVE STYLING APPLICATIONS

Computer-aided styling is a relatively new segment of the CAD process. If well designed, it can serve as a front end to computer design and manufacturing.

The initial goals for these systems were to achieve the following:

- Facilitate concurrent or simultaneous engineering by the generation of a computer database earlier in the design process
- Use computer graphics to visualize new designs prior to the development of physical models
- Reduce the time necessary to develop 3D models by using Computer Numerical Control (CNC) milling machines and the same database used for visualization and analysis to mill out these 3D models
- Use computer graphics to monitor the quality of the production surfaces

The next-generation industrial design will incorporate knowledge-based engineering rules and enhancements to the surface development software. These, along with 3D holographic display systems and the refinement of virtual reality systems, have the potential to further reduce the development cycle. The ultimate goal of these systems is to allow the product designer, who originates the design, to produce data suitable for release to the tooling manufacturer.

CAD/CAM IN THE AEROSPACE INDUSTRY

Aerospace products aren't like automobiles, where one designs and builds a new model every year. Aircraft companies might introduce a new model only every ten or fifteen years. It is therefore essential that companies take every advantage to apply the latest design-build technologies because they will be stuck with them for the life of the program, which can exceed forty years.

Vision

At the heart of the preferred process vision is a CAD/CAM system capable of simulating all of the product parts and assemblies before building any hardware. It can virtually eliminate the hard copy.

Digital product definition (DPD) combined with the latest communications technology makes it possible for designers separated by continents and oceans to work together almost as if their desks were side by side. Indeed, one of the major coordination problems that will need to be overcome is the difference in time zones between various parties.

One Hundred Percent Digital Product Definition

Digital product definition using a CAD/CAM system offers some significant advantages over conventional, 2D manual drawings. For instance, airplane parts can be modeled as 3D elements and easily assembled on the computer to check for part interference and interface mismatches. Weights, balance, and stress analysis can be accurately performed. Cross-sectional views can be easily extracted from solids. Numerical control machine processes can use the digital data to drive manufacturing machines. Production illustrations can be easily and more accurately created. The customer services function can use CAD data as required to generate technical publications.

PRINTED CIRCUIT BOARD DESIGN: CAE AND CAD

Today's Printed Circuit Board (PCB) layout tools are capable of working with submil databases and producing data to manufacture one-mil (0.001 of an inch) traces. Today's high-tech board shop is beginning to move to three-mil traces with two- or three-mil spaces. Mainstream boards include features typically in the range of six to eight mils.

Today the single most significant roadblock to the promise of integrated CAD/CAM/CAE/CIM (C4) is that with few exceptions the various computer-aided tools do not talk to each other very well.

Interactive Design

Despite the maturity of today's CAE and CAD tools and EDA (electronic design automation) marketing hype, most PCB design layout is still performed interactively.

According to *Printed Circuit Design* magazine, the classes of design layout include the following:

- Interactive. The tool requires a significant amount of direction by the user. For example, a user interactively routes a connection by selecting the trace, the function (route), and each vertex of the connection.

- Autointeractive. The user selects functions and is aided by the tool to make connections. For example, to select a group of signals, the user routes one and the route editor routes the group according to the first route.
- Auto. The tools requires a minimum of input by the user. For example, the tool selects the connections to be made (e.g., by net class, by net, or by window).

Typical Uses

Interactive component placement
Auto placement
Routing

High-Speed Design

Multichip modules
Design synthesis

MATCHING THE IMPLANT TO THE PATIENT: A MEDICAL APPLICATION

The human skeleton is both a physically and biologically dynamic system that occasionally breaks down—literally at the connections. Great success has been enjoyed in replacing these painful connections or joints, and CAD/CAM has played a significant role in the speciality of tailor-fitting implants to individual patients.

The leading manufacturers have adopted CAD/CAM strategies so they can meet demanding design requirements and tight delivery schedules for these one-of-a-kind, or custom, implants. These strategies range from the simple deployment of CAD as a traditional design tool to entirely integrated expert systems responsible for both design decisions and NC programming.

The task of creating custom devices is quite different from the traditional approach of "design once and produce many." While engineers can design mass-produced, standard devices by studying cadaver specimens, they must use noninvasive techniques to see into the live patient when designing custom devices. While manufacturers can produce standard devices using techniques that benefit from economies of scale, they must be innovative and efficient in producing the one-of-a-kind parts for custom devices.

The challenge of creating custom devices can be summarized as a three step process.

1. Visualizing the anatomy inside the patient
2. Developing a mechanical design matched to him or her
3. Manufacturing the parts in an expeditious manner

Computer technology assists manufacturers in each of these key areas.

OTHER CAD/CAM APPLICATIONS

In addition to the specific applications discussed in this section, CAD/CAM is used in a wide variety of other applications, including basic design/drafting, Integrated Circuit (IC) design, kitchen design, general industrial design, and location-based entertainment layouts.

What Are the Tools?

SYSTEM CONFIGURATIONS

Although early CAD/CAM systems used a mainframe driving dumb or smart terminals, the "client-server" model has gained acceptance in the last few years. Here supercomputers and various distributed computing systems, including workstations and PCs, are connected and share information. The computer in the *server* role responds to *client* computers' requests for services, such as holding the database, storing applications programs, printing, and filing; theoretically, the server can be located down the hall or around the world.

SOFTWARE

A CAD/CAM system includes a variety of software. In a closed (turnkey) system, most of the software is supplied by a single vendor. In an open (constructive) system, the software may come from a wide variety of sources, including that which is purchased as well as software developed by the user. Some software is the same as one would have in any other computer facility. There is an operating system (traffic cop) which contains utilities, system diagnostics, and high-level programming languages. Typical CAD/CAM software might include software to perform graphic manipulation functions (such as scale, zoom, and rotate) and to perform graphic drawing functions such as character, line, and circle generation. In addition, there may be programs for drawing and manipulating three-dimensional objects and surfaces.

In addition to the pure drawing functions, either the server or the micro used in the workstations has a variety of C4 application software for sophisticated design, engineering analysis, and manufacturing purposes. For example, initial design may be done in 3D using solid modeling techniques. Also, data generated in the production of a schematic to describe a circuit may be transferred back to the server for analysis, or at some of the newer high-performance workstations it could be analyzed locally.

The system may also include design functions and will operate under an operating system such as UNIX, MS/DOS, Windows, and NT. In addition, there are programming languages, typically such high-level languages as C and C++, which support graphics-oriented functions for programming use.

Another issue is the interchange among different systems. In the last decade, the most commonly used application-level interchange specification is IGES (initial graphics exchange specification). That data exchange specification is being replaced

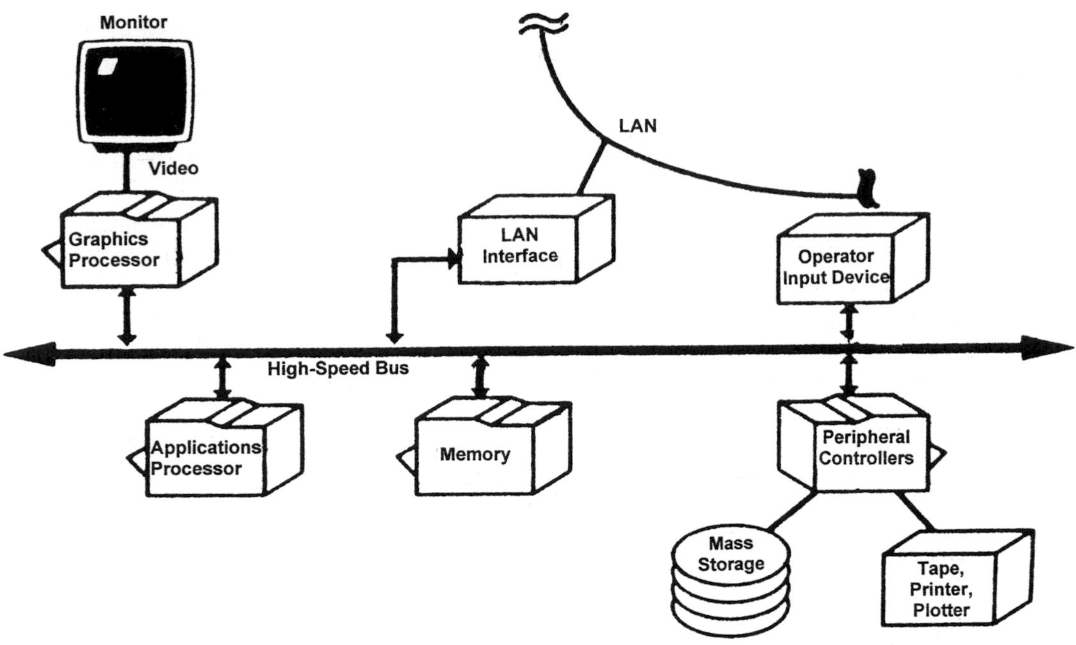

FIGURE 3. *Intelligent workstation architecture.*

by STEP (international standard for exchange of model data), PDES (product data exchange) and direct custom translators.

The software environment also includes various graphic standards, both for the transmission of graphic information and to make the application programs independent of the graphic devices.

WORKSTATIONS AND PCs

Increasingly workstations are the focal point for the user in the C4 environment. Fundamentally, the workstation combines graphic and computational capability within a single unit that includes adequate power, memory, networking capability, and operator control to be used in essentially a stand-alone mode. A typical block diagram for such a workstation is shown in Fig. 3.

Such products as the Tektronix 4051 of the early 1970s provided the impetus for the development of stand-alone low-cost systems. These 8-bit machines have migrated to the point where multi-millions of instructions per second operation is available up to a 32-bit Central Processing Unit (CPU). Products sell in the $5,000 to $100,000 range. Companies such as DEC, Hewlett Packard, IBM, Silicon Graphics, and Sun offer a wide variety of products that have become an increasing part of the CAD/CAM environment. Where the early products were essentially computers with graphics as an afterthought, later generations of products represent very sophisticated computers coupled with very sophisticated graphic systems. It is possible to do elaborate ray tracing, for example, on some of the stand-alone systems and produce results that are breathtaking. While today computation time is often measured in many hours as special purpose hardware and supergraphics workstations are becoming available, such ray tracing and generation of "photorealistic images" begin to approach real time.

Originally the workstation was quite different from a PC. Products that originally started in the home environment, such as the Apple II, were perceived as useful in the CAD/CAM environment only for training and low-performance applications. In the past few years, however, the introduction of very powerful PCs has essentially blurred the line between what a PC is and what a workstation is. At the same time, many of the workstation vendors have begun to reduce the price of their products so that we have low-end products priced in the PC area.

Further, it is possible to buy plug-in cards that significantly improve the graphic performance, response time, and computational capability of many of the PCs.

The performance of workstations today meets or exceeds the performance of yesterday's mini- and mainframe computers.

Most C4 systems use color raster/refresh displays. The ability to create realistic images on a raster display, the ability to use full color, the increasing dynamic capability of the raster systems, and improving price and performance virtually ensures raster domination for the next few years.

Higher dynamic performance is coupled with higher picture quality. The present 760 × 1024, 1024 × 1280, and 1200 × 1600, 60 frame per second are migrating into the 1500 × 2000 range. High frame rates to support stereo are more generally available.

It is common to have 256 colors as standard, with some systems that are designed for very realistic presentations offering as many as 16 million colors.

With the use of the raster as a standard, it becomes quite feasible to use large-screen TV projectors. In the past, one had a choice between $50,000 to $100,000 light valve systems, or several thousand dollar home entertainment systems. A few years ago, however, we began to get midrange-cost products (in the $10,000 to 15,000 range) that provide high-resolution bright images that are quite suitable for engineering applications. For about one-tenth to one-third that price we can get flat-panel color liquid crystal displays (LCD), which can be used for engineering conferencing and training. These products, large, transparent LCD, sit on a conventional overhead transparency and are driven from one of the standard outputs of the PC. Most recently, projectors using a Texas Instruments deflectable picture element chip are becoming available.

Whenever we talk about mechanical design the issue is raised about true 3D. A number of systems have been tried, including various kinds of vibrating mirrors and polarized images. In the last decade, technology based on switchable LCD, used with passive polarized glasses or switched LCD glasses have become available. In the last few years, interest has grown in virtual reality as a CAD/CAM environment.

The prospect of flat panel displays (plasma, light emitting diode, electroluminescent, LCD, etc.) replacing the Cathode Ray Tube (CRT) "tomorrow" is always being raised. These flat panel displays have become the dominant technology in portable units. Today, 10-in. to 14-in. diagonal, full-color, flat panel displays are becoming cost-effective and may at last challenge the conventional CRT in desktop workstations.

HARD COPY

In spite of all the forecasts that hard copy is dying and that we are going to have a paperless engineering office, the amount of hard copy produced still grows at 15 percent per year. While the basic data reference (sometimes called data sets in a C4 environment) will in fact be paperless, this does not mean that paper will be eliminated, because we may still want to distribute that data and make them "portable." For at least the next five years, it looks as though the culturally accepted method of distribution will be paper.

Pen Plotters

The role of electromechanical pen plotters in the C4 application seems to be secure for the next few years, although other technologies such as ink jet are threatening the pen plotter's dominance. It is possible today to buy engineering quality D/E size pen plotters in the $1,500 to $5,000 range.

Drum plotters and flatbed plotters are the two basic configurations, but in the past few years flatbed plotters have been relegated primarily to very large high-accuracy applications, and most of the C4 plotters today are an adaptation of the drum type. Today's plotters will often handle four to eight pens, and the pens can be used either for different colors, or to make black and white plots of varying line widths. Many of today's pen plotters are roll-fed, which makes them low-cost production devices, and accounts for their continued popularity.

For special applications the flatbed becomes very important, particularly in making the equivalent of a photographic negative for IC and PC applications.

Electrostatic Plotters/Electrophotographic Plotters

While it takes fractions of a second to display an image on the cathode ray tube, the time required to plot that same drawing on a precision pen plotter may take tens of minutes.

Electrostatic plotters were introduced to reduce plotting time at the expense of some drawing quality. Essentially these plotters consist of a combination of wire nibs (styli) or Light Emitting Diodes (LEDs) spaced from 100 to 400 styli per inch. As in the drum plotter, the paper's motion provides one axis of deflection, but instead of a pen moving along the other axis, the information is progressively "scanned" across the styli, and these styli place a dot on the paper as needed. The dot is really achieved by having the stylus place a charge on the paper, and then a toning process transfers toner to the charged point.

Unless the plotter data are in raster format, some form of software or hardware scan conversion (raster image processor—R.I.P.) is required between the digital picture file and the plotter. Most plotter manufacturers now supply that software (or its equivalent hardware).

Electrostatic plotters are now available with up to six-foot widths. They are significantly faster than electromechanical plotters, typically producing a drawing ten to 100 times faster. Black and white electrostatic plotters are today available in the \$700 to \$1,000 range per inch width of paper.

Color electrostatic plotters have become available in about the \$1,500 per inch range.

Ink Jet

Perhaps the fastest-growing segment of the C4 hard copy market is the ink jet segment. Increasingly, ink jets (wide format, both monochromatic and color) are competing effectively with both pen plotters and electrostatic plotters. Ink jet units cost about the same as pen plotters, but are faster. While still slower than electrostatic and electrophotographic plotters, ink jet plotter speeds will probably increase over the next few years, tending to offer electrostatic performance at pen plotter prices.

While consumer-oriented ink jet plotters are available for several hundred dollars, units suitable for graphic arts cost in the \$5,000 to \$100,000 range.

Computer-Output-to-Microfilm (COM) Units

Drawing storage is a continual problem for large engineering facilities. Such companies may have 100,000 drawings or more that need to be stored and retrieved. Historically, one solution was the use of microfilm, using computer-output-to-microfilm (COM) units. Although relatively expensive—about \$300,000—COM units are fast and provide adequate accuracy and resolution for drawings that ultimately are blown up to as large as 34-in. ×44-in. (E size). By mounting the microfilm on aperture cards, drawings can be stored and retrieved by data-processing techniques.

While microfilm still continues to be part of the C4 environment, the use of COM for aperture card creation technology has slowed tremendously of late. New techniques for electronic drawing storage using scanners and high-capacity optical disks may in the long term replace microfilm as the mechanism for archival storage.

Other Output Devices

Because color is becoming an increasingly important part of the C4 environment and the images being produced are closer to realistic images requiring large area fills, several other techniques are finding use in the C4 environment. Both jet ink techniques and thermal dye transfer techniques are becoming increasingly price-competitive. Size A jet ink printers are available under \$200, and more typical jet ink and thermal dye transfer systems for A-size products are in the \$5,000 to \$6,000 range, with B-size products in the \$10,000 range.

Laser printer/plotters are capturing an increasingly large part of the graphic output market and also have an application in C4. The black and white versions are used heavily in the office automation and technical documentation areas. A large document laser printer that is designed to compete directly against the large format electrostatic printers is now available. Combination plotters, copiers, and scanners have begun to appear.

In the last decade, 3D hard copy devices for rapid prototyping have also become available to C4 users. Using a variety of techniques, the most common being stereo lithography and sintering, these units operate directly from CAD data to produce 3D parts assemblies and tools. There are a number of other methods currently under development, such as ballistic particle deposition (at BPM Corp. and Incre, Inc.), shape melting (Babcock & Wilcox Co.), MD selective spray metal deposition (Carnegie Mellon), and three-dimensional printing (MIT/Soligen).

Currently priced in the $30,000 to $500,000 range, these units have found broad application in the design and manufacturing environment. Because of the purchase price, a brisk service bureau business has developed around the concept of rapid prototyping.

INPUT DEVICES

The classic joystick, trackball, and graphic tablet continue to be part of the graphics environment. The "popular" input device is the mouse in its many ramifications. The keyboard continues to be the input preferred by the professional and production user, while the mouse and the other techniques will be more comfortable for the less frequent user of these systems.

As more systems deal with 3D data, the user needs a 3D "pointing" and "manipulating" device. These input devices allow the operator to pick a function from the many presented to enter text and/or numerical data into the system, to modify the picture shown on the screen (by moving, deleting, expanding, rotating, etc.), and finally to construct the desired picture.

Most C4 systems have at least one operator input device. Many systems have several devices, each for a different function, depending on the user's needs and preferences.

Keyboards

Several kinds of keyboards are commonly used with C4 terminals. The conventional typewriterlike alphanumeric (QWERTY) keyboard allows the operator to enter commands, symbols, and text, and to request information. The keyboard is often used to enter precise nongraphic data such as dimensions or measurements into a program so that the display will accurately represent all important data relating to a current design.

These keyboards may also include special graphics-oriented buttons—for example, to move the cursor up or down, left or right, or to transmit memory file content back to the host computer.

Ergonomic considerations have promoted the development of new keyboards, which attempt to reduce operator strains.

In some cases the C4 terminal is also equipped with a separate box containing program-controlled pushbuttons (such as a function keyboard or a button box).

Cursor Controls

There is a variety of cursor control devices. These devices let the operator simultaneously develop changing X and Y signals to direct a cursor (a tracking symbol) on the screen.

Including in these devices are the following:

- Thumb wheels/keys. The simplest way to generate cursor movement is by separate X and Y cursor control keys or knobs.
- Trackball. The trackball uses a rolling ball to drive the transducers.
- Mouse. This device is functionally equivalent to a trackball turned upside down. Mechanical, optical, and acoustical mouses are available. Generally, one, two, or three control buttons are packaged with the mouse to control what the mouse function is.
- Joystick. The joystick is similar to the trackball except that it provides a small, batlike handle that the operator moves.
- Data tablet (graphic tablet). Another popular operator input device is the data tablet. Generators within the tablet pulse the lines, producing discrete signals in response to a pencillike stylus moved by the operator. The location of the information is used like the output of other cursor control devices.

Pressure-sensitive styluses have become available for data tablets. Software can translate the user's pen pressure as desired line width or other parameters.

Automatic Digitizers

A decade ago the industry looked for the OZALID approach of putting a paper drawing into a slot, and moments later getting a vector-based CAD representation of that image. While we don't quite have the magic box yet, we can put the paper in the slot and get a pixel representation of the image, have the operator manipulate that pixel representation with various computer aids, and in a short time or perhaps several hours (depending on the requirements) get a good edit of the drawing or a good CAD (vector) representation. This can represent a major improvement in productivity over conventional manual techniques for digitizing a drawing. While originally conceived as a means of putting paper drawings in a CAD system, increasingly they are being viewed as a technique for putting drawings in a form for later electronic distribution, as in product data management (PDM) applications.

Other Input Devices

There continue to be applications for touch input devices, and certainly for data selection. It is unlikely that touch input will be used as the fundamental C4 control, but as graphic terminals move onto the factory floor, the use of touch input as means of calling up data appears to be natural and reasonable.

Techniques of voice input are getting better each year, and occasionally one of the CAD companies offers a voice input option. These are not yet a major factor in the CAD environment, however.

The C4 environment is also beginning to make more use of video, multimedia, and virtual reality. Video serves both as a powerful training tool and as a teleconferencing vehicle.

CAE

While CAE applies equally to both electrical and mechanical product development, this section deals primarily with mechanical. Three major elements represent the core of its components and philosophy, its first principles.

1. The geometry foundation of mechanical design and manufacturing
2. The analysis component of engineering practice
3. The abstract economics of cost justification

MULTIMEDIA

What is multimedia? Whatever you want it to be. It usually involves an intelligent way of combining computer graphics, animation, sound, scanned images, and video so that the user can get needed information most effectively.

Multimedia affects our workstation purchasing strategies. Over the past few years almost no one would purchase a graphic workstation without a color monitor. Today users are reluctant to purchase a workstation that does not have multimedia capability. At a minimum today's workstations include sound capability and provisions to play CD-ROMs. Live video capability is also often provided.

Much of our current experience with multimedia comes from business, education, and consumer applications—video games, product kiosks in stores, information kiosks in museums, reference works on CD-ROM, and in a variety of training situations. Often overlooked, however, are the significant applications for multimedia in C4. These applications are growing and include the following:

Analysis
Design modifications
Documentation
Human factors analysis
Maintenance simulation
Manufacturing assembly instructions
Research
Teleconferencing
Training/simulation

VIRTUAL REALITY

Virtual reality is a new interactive technology that creates a completely (hopefully) convincing illusion that one is immersed in a world that exists only inside a computer. There are essentially three virtual reality configurations—fully immersive, partially immersive, and others.

Virtual reality is used in architecture, art and CAD, computational fluid dynamics, chemistry, entertainment and games, financial analysis, geoscience, geographic information systems, graphic arts, medical, telepresence, training and simulation, visualization, and weather/meteorology.

The technology includes hardware such as head-mounted displays, conventional and stereo displays, input devices (gloves, 3 and 6D cursor controls, etc.) position trackers, video, audio, workstations, PCs and other computer resources, and body suits.

Software includes Virtual Reality (VR) operating systems, VR tool kits, standards and others, as well as application software. Systems include turnkey and constructive, and services include VR laboratories, consultancies and other design services, and publications.

SOLID MODELERS

Solid models are used for the following:

Drafting and product documentation
Structural analysis
Mechanisms analysis
Numerical control programming
Product visualization

The first commercially available solid modelers appeared in the late 1970s. (Euclid from Mantra Datavision was the first general CAD system to include solid modeling.) By the mid-1980s, virtually all major CAD products had solid modeling capabilities.

Most early solids-based systems relied on Boolean combinations of simple primitive solids (blocks, cylinders, spheres, cones, tori, etc.) to build up complex part designs. While Boolean combinations can be used to create very complex designs, they don't match well with the traditional sketching methods that designers have used for most of recent history. The terminology used for these Boolean operations (union, difference, and intersection) is also nontraditional, and it confused designers and other users.

Boolean operations are rather difficult to use in many situations, and many designers found them to be unintuitive and difficult to control. Three types of solid modelers have been in general use.

- Constructive solid geometry (CSG)
- Boundary representation (B-rep)
- Hybrid (B-rep combined with CSG-tree)

A CSG modeler uses a tree structure (often called a CSG tree) to define solid objects as Boolean combinations of solid primitives.

B-rep modelers also use Boolean combinations of primitive solids. The primitives themselves, as well as complex solids resulting from their combination, are defined as a collection of faces, edges, and vertices.

Hybrid modelers use a CSG-like tree structure combined with an evaluated boundary representation, providing many of the advantages of these two types of solid modeling. Most CAD/CAM systems use some form of hybrid approach today.

It wasn't until 1988 when PTC introduced its Pro/ENGINEER product with a fundamentally different approach to design modeling that solids became easily accessible and generally productive. PTC's approach has three basic components that had been known previously, but had not been developed into a coherent commercial product. These components are parametric design, the use of design features, and data associativity. Most other CAD vendors now offer similar capabilities.

Parametric modeling is a type of constraint modeling, as is variational modeling. Designs modeled in a constraint modeler capture many pieces of information about a design's shape and size in the form of dimensional and geometric values. These are related to each other by a set of equations known as relationships or parametric equations. When any dimensional value is changed, the set of equations can be solved to find the effect on all other related dimensions. The geometric description of the design is then updated automatically. Simply stated, constraint-based design allows users to easily make changes to their designs that follow their "design intent" without having to recreate or move primitive solids.

Current state-of-the-art CAD/CAM systems used constraint-based features along with surface and solid models to create design geometry much more efficiently than was possible with earlier CAD technologies.

Constraint- and Feature-Based Design

Constraints are used to create a set of rules that control how changes can be made to a group of geometric elements (such as lines, arcs, and form features). These rules are typically embodied in a set of equations. Three types of constraints can be used.

- *Numeric constraints* provide positions (XYZ locations), lengths, diameters, spline parameters, angular values, and other measurable values.
- *Geometric constraints* include parallelism, perpendicularity, colinearity, tangency, and other nonnumeric parameters that control the positional relationships of one piece of geometry with respect to another.
- *Algebraic constraints* combine numeric and geometric constraints in very simple equations, such as "The diameter of C is one-half the length of A," or extremely complex sets of equations that include IF-THEN-ELSE branches, inequalities, and calls to external subroutines.

Parametric and variational are the two types of constraint modelers in general use. These types have to do with how the set of constraining equations are defined and solved. In parametric systems, all of the constraint equations are captured and solved in the order in which they are created; the design is controlled by a directed graph of operations.

Comparison of Other Approaches

Parametric Modeling Approach. Parametric modeling is based on the geometry construction process in drafting, in which each geometric entity (a point or line) is constructed one at a time in a specific sequence. By remembering the construction sequence, the geometry is reconstructed after a change in a dimension.

Variational Geometry Approach. Variational geometry is based on the realization that all geometric constraints (such as parallelism, tangency, and dimensions) can be converted to algebraic equations. These geometric constraint equations can be combined with user-defined engineering relations to form a single set of equations.

Over time, several additional approaches have been developed that blur the distinction between variational and parametric design by providing some but not all of the capabilities of the two basic approaches. Several hybrid approaches have been developed that make part of the design process behave as if it is parametric and other aspects as if they are variational. One of the most important advantages of using constraint modelers is that they allow the CAD system to capture some of the designer's intentions.

ENGINEERING DOCUMENT MANAGEMENT

An EDMS (engineering document management system) offers the capability to store, retrieve, edit, view, and distribute information digitally. Users manage and digitally manipulate hard copy documents, such as paper or aperture cards, CAD data, and other computer system files. Multifunction systems (plotting, scanning, copying) can also facilitate these functions. Furthermore, an EDMS can store designs and design information in one integrated file. Product data management systems are often a subset of EDMS. Engineering document management and PDM systems are similar applications that organize files using hidden databases and metadata. Both EDM and PDM systems organize files stored in different locations throughout a network into a centralized virtual library. This library is referred to as a document vault.

Engineering document management systems are made to be used across an entire company, while PDM systems are made specifically for the engineering departments of manufacturing and design corporations.

Essential Technologies

Two technologies essential to the document-management process are scanning and printing. The capability to scan existing drawings into a digital archive allows CAD-generated designs and manually created drawings to be merged. The availability of large-format and microfilm scanners now enables drawings to be scanned with the accuracy required to form a proper record of the image at a realistic price.

Equally important is the ability to produce hard copy output, since electronic distribution and viewing is not always possible or even desirable. Reprographics systems therefore must form an integral part of these systems. Further technological enablers include low-cost, high-performance PCs and workstations for viewing and editing and open systems architectures to facilitate communication between heterogeneous hardware and application software. Optical disk technology is also important because of its ability to store large quantities of data. WORM (write-one, ready-many) technology creates a permanent record that cannot be erased.

NETWORKING AND THE INTERNET

The major pioneering efforts in networking were performed in the 1970s by the large computer companies IBM and Digital Equipment Corporation (DEC). These efforts and others at that time were focused on rather closely coupled computers and terminals, and are referred to as local area networks (LANs). Since the needs of the end user to share computer resources over relatively short distances haven't changed much until recently, with minor changes, these early LANs (e.g., Ethernet) are the ones most people use today.

While these network hardware standards were under development during the 1970s, one of the most important networking software protocols was developed by the Defense Advanced Research Projects Agency (DARPA). This transmission control protocol/Internet protocol is better known as TCP/IP.

Where Ethernet, Token-Ring, and a third early standard, ARCnet, described how things should work and set minimal performance levels, TCP/IP was the early protocol that set out the rules and agreements for LAN components to follow. Many of today's most popular networking systems support TCP/IP.

The trends in networking are migrating away from the proprietary, single-vendor standards of the 1980s to more flexible and expandable open protocol standards promising true heterogeneous interoperability.

The three needs driving new networking technology are the need to support more users, the need for much higher bandwidth, and the need to cover longer distances. Most of today's LANs cover relatively short distances, such as within a building, but LANs are now being connected between campuses across the country over WANs. In addition, metropolitan area networks (MANs), which cover more distance than LANs and less than WANs, are being set up around corporations and cities. WANs' growth demands are being fed by rapid increases in remote terminal and laptop usage and will be addressed by economical circuit-switched digital services such as Integrated Services Digital Network (ISDN) and protocols such as TCP/IP over 56 Kbps X 25 lines.

Even more significant are the bandwidth demands of such new applications as multimedia. Simple audio, voice, and video contain significantly more data bits than screens of text, and require higher bandwidths. Beyond the issue of higher bandwidth, new technologies are required to maintain the time integrity of data formats to accurately preserve voice and video files.

Higher bandwidth is promised by very costly fiberoptic cable Fiber Distributed Data Interface (FDDI) (100 Mbps), and its equally fast, shorter-distance copper derivative, Copper Distributed Data Interface (CDDI), both of which require significant hardware and software changes. In contrast, Fast Ethernet, in any of its proposed variants, promises 100 Mbps bandwidth while using most of today's Ethernet cabling and network protocols.

High bandwidth and time-oriented multimedia environments would be served by Asynchronous Transfer Mode (ATM), a promising new technology with 1.5 Mbps to 1.2 Gbps speeds and the capacity to deliver "real-time data" through predictable data rates.

ISDN is a Consultative Committee for International Telephone and Telegraphy model for combining voice and data services. When fully implemented, it will handle full multimedia networking requirements. Of the three major types of ISDNs, the basic rate interface (BRI) is the most popular and is targeted at connecting terminals with computers.

SIMULTANEOUS OR CONCURRENT ENGINEERING

Concurrent engineering helps bring higher-quality products to market faster and at less cost by involving all the players, including customers and suppliers, at the earliest stage possible. Multiple design alternatives can be evaluated earlier, when they cost less and are easier to implement because people are working with "soft" concepts, not handcrafted prototypes.

Such terms as simultaneous engineering, team design, design/build teams, platform engineering, integrated product development, and design for manufacturability are often used interchangeably with concurrent engineering to describe an approach to engineering.

With this approach, all the factors influencing a design, especially manufacturing issues, are considered at the beginning of the production cycle. Normally this is done by a multidisciplinary team that guides a product through its entire life cycle. This is in sharp contrast to the more common scenario in which design engineers create a design and then send it on its way "over the wall" to analysts, who in turn send it to the procurement specialists, manufacturing engineers, shop-floor people, service technicians, and so on. As the design reaches each department, the time and money invested in mushrooms so that minor enhancements might be ignored and major revisions become extremely expensive.

KNOWLEDGE-BASED SYSTEMS

Expert systems, also called knowledge-based systems (KBS), form a branch of AI (artificial intelligence) that makes extensive use of specialized knowledge (i.e., rules-based or inference) to solve problems at the level of a human expert. Artificial intelligence is a subfield of computer science aimed at pursuing the possibility that a computer can be made to act in ways humans recognize as intelligent behavior in each other.

Intelligence is exhibited by the appearance of parametric and feature-based CAD systems (e.g., Pro/Engineer of Parametric Technology, I-DEAS of SDRC, CV CADDS of Computervision, and CDC of Control Data Corporation), CAD tools with associative geometry, the new CAD packages with intelligent user interface (e.g., Master Series IDEAS of SDRC and Vellum of Ashlar, Inc.), and the special rule-based packages for the representation of complex, more-than-just-geometry models, called knowledge engineering systems (KES; e.g., ICAD of ICAD Inc. and the Concept Modeler of Wisdom Systems, Inc.). Knowledge engineering systems bring together the advances of the geometry capability of CAD/CAM software and rule-based and inference aspects, making systems able to capture knowledge beyond 3D geometry (e.g., about materials, finishes, machine tools, billing, and fabrication processes).

THE ROLE OF STANDARDS

Standards, Standards, and More Standards

Standards today address a multitude of arenas, including quality, performance, conformance, safety, and documentation. Industries cannot exist or grow without the thousands of standards that direct their operations. In general, a standard must specify a nominal set of requirements, a minimal level of performance, and a mandatory area of compliance and conformance to specifications.

Standards can be developed in many ways, over long and short periods of time, through voluntary and mandatory processes, and as formal, industry, or de facto standards.

Integration of computer technology into a total system creates a labyrinth of interconnection. At every level of interconnection, there are requirements for standardization. Standards can no longer address only the physical aspects of computer hardware; they must also address software.

De facto refers to a method or product that has become so predominant with a given arena that it is accepted as the standard way something is done or produced. Usually, de facto standards are proprietary technology (developed and owned by a specific company) that is copied or imitated by others, probably for a fee. PostScript by Adobe Systems is a prime example.

Industry standards, on the other hand, are developed with a specific market or industrial application in mind. They are usually produced by industry associations such as the Institute of Electrical and Electronic Engineers (IEEE) or the American Society of Mechanical Engineers (ASME) and pertain to practices that affect that specific industry. They might be offered for formal standardization if they are of general interest to the computer industry as a whole. For example, IEEE 802.3 (Ethernet) was an electronic industry communications standard prior to its adoption as a formal standard.

Formal standardization is conducted by the American National Standards Institute (ANSI) in the United States, and the International Organization for Standardization (ISO) and the International Electro-technical Commission (IEC) in the world community. These voluntary organizations support the formal development and use standards by industry and government. They have no specific authority to enforce the use of these standards other than the commitment by the same industry and government entities to require their use. The requirement for the use of national and international standards is at an all-time high.

In addition to general computer graphics standards such as CGM (computer graphics metafile), several standards are particularly related to CAD/CAM.

Data Exchange Standards. Data exchange standards include those technologies for the sharing, exchange, storage, and retrieval of product information.

One of the first associated CAD/CAM was IGES (initial graphics exchange specification) now being superseded by the international standard for the exchange of product model data (STEP) and its U.S. counterpart, product data exchange using STEP (PDES), both of which have been approved at the initial release level. There is still much development and implementation work to be completed, however, before STEP or PDES can achieve universality.

Continuous Acquisition and Life Cycle Support (CALS). Continuous acquisition and life cycle support is a strategy to accelerate the transition from paper-intensive, nonintegrated product development, design, manufacturing, and support to a highly automated, integrated mode of operation.

Continuous acquisition and life cycle support incorporates three types of standards.

- Functional standards, which define processes, data requirements, data creation, and the content and format of data products
- Technical interchange standards, which control the medium and process of exchanging data between sending and receiving systems
- Data standards, which govern information sharing and data exchange in an open systems environment

VIDEOCONFERENCING PRODUCTS FOR C4

Videoconferencing has been referred to as an "emerging technology" and a "strategic application area" for so long that it's easy to dismiss it as just another great idea that won't be going mainstream any time soon—like a picture phone or practical electric car. The reality, however, is that videoconferencing has suddenly and quietly become a multibillion-dollar business. Engineering companies, particularly those with C4 projects, are among the leaders in adopting videoconferencing products and technologies.

Conference Room Solutions

Videoconferencing allows groups of people to see each other and share ideas without traveling, enabling them to meet without having a meeting. Companies can save considerable money, and engineers can spend much less time on the road and much more time doing what they do best—designing products an processes.

In recent years vendors of conference-room solutions have gone to great lengths to solve the reliability and cost problems that beset early products. Today conference-room products offer much higher quality. Flickering and video drops are rare occurrences, and a host of new features has been added to make the products easy to use. Costs have also dropped considerably; high-quality conference-room solutions are now available from $12,000.

A New Alternative Desktop Videoconferencing

The shortcomings of conference-room products did not escape the attention of a number of computer vendors and software developers, who produced a second technological alternative: desktop videoconferencing.

The first desktop videoconferencing solutions were called shared whiteboards. These products allow users in remote locations to connect their computers via phone lines, view documents, graphics, spreadsheets, and other images concurrently, and annotate the documents using visual "markers."

The next step in the evolution of videoconferencing solutions was bringing face-to-face interaction to the desktop. Several vendors in both the PC and Unix environments now make it possible to transmit a live, full-color, full-motion image of an individual from his or her office to the desktop computers of each participant in the videoconferencing session. Audio can be played on the desktop computer's speakers, so it is not necessary for each participant to hold a telephone while he or she talks.

Management Issues

THE BENEFITS OF C4

Early CAD/CAM systems were expensive and needed full-time operators. It was not at all unusual for some companies to run their systems for two or three shifts.

Buyers saw benefits most often in terms of labor savings: "If we have 10 drafters today and the system's productivity ratio is 2 : 1, then we only need to have five drafters once the system is up and running."

The New Business Environment

The overall business environment has changed significantly in recent years. Perhaps the most important element of the changing scene is that business enterprises no longer have the luxury of time.

The benefits associated with C4 technology fall into two categories: direct benefits, whereby it is relatively easy to assign economic value, and indirect benefits, whereby the value is somewhat more subtle. Let's look at the direct benefits first.

There has been a major shift in justifying these systems from looking at individual drafting/design department savings to recognizing "downstream" benefits that cut across traditional organizational boundaries.

Personnel

Comparing the use of today's drawing production systems to manual drafting is not difficult. Productivity ratios range from 2 : 1 to 10 : 1.

Better Information Management

At many organizations, the traditional drawing vault has been replaced by automated, online document storage. The cost of data storage has dropped significantly in recent years. Large-volume disk storage units cost \$1 to \$2 per million bytes of data, the amount of data it takes to store a typical E-size engineering drawing.

Improved Product Quality

Today's computer systems permit designers to quickly create product alternatives until the one that meets customer requirements becomes apparent. In the past, the cost of making substantial changes once an initial design was completed were sufficiently high that engineering management would frequently put the first workable design into production. By being able to easily make many incremental changes to a design it is possible to create something that will be better accepted in the marketplace as well as more reliable.

Reduced Lead Time

The use of computer design systems combined with effective data management and communication can dramatically reduce the time it takes from product concept to availability. One aerospace firm reported it is now able to deliver commercial communications satellites in 12 months, compared to 36 months just a few years ago.

Reduced Product Costs

As with product quality, manufacturing costs are often affected by actions taken during the design process. One of the ways C4 can affect manufacturing costs is in design optimization, which refers to the process by which the shape of a part can be modified to produce a version with a minimum weight while still meeting critical dimensions and stress criteria. For example, an automobile seat manufacturer was able to reduce the weight of the seats it manufacturers by 20 percent using design optimization software.

Many organizations have found they can reduce production costs significantly by reducing the total number of purchased and manufactured components. They do this by making data on these standardized parts readily available to designers using online data-management techniques.

Increased Manufacturing Yields

The direct transfer of design data to manufacturing eliminates a source of potential errors.

Reduced Duplication of Effort

When the data transfer between the different groups involved in a product's development is handled manually, there tends to be a substantial duplication of effort.

Reduced Inventory

Most companies strive to reduce both work in process (WIP) and finished-goods inventory.

Indirect Economic Benefits

One of the problems associated with using this new technology is that historical accounting procedures may no longer reflect the true value of business enterprise. New approaches are needed to measure the value enterprise's information infrastructure.

Ability to react
Employee morale
Business flexibility
Product liability

MIGRATING FROM 2D TO 3D

The Power of 3D Photorealistic Visualization

For many disciplines, a natural route for 3D data is photorealistic visualization. Today this exciting technology is being used by engineers, industrial designers, architects, videographers, trainers, corporate media specialists, and many other multimedia professionals. From a small, intricate piece of jewelry to a new automobile, the designer can use graphic tools to create extraordinary, realistic products.

Photorealistic rendering products offer extensive libraries of textures, fonts, backgrounds, and prebuilt objects. With a robust materials editor, a user has full control of variables such as transparency, reflectivity, opacity, and luminosity. Designers can experiment and simulate their own unique textures. Scanning is a popular method for capturing swatches of textiles and natural materials such as leather. Effective texture-mapping features allow the user to precisely apply bit maps to 3D components of the design.

Animation

3D animation is not only for the movies! Recently a new wave of inexpensive and feature-packed animation solutions has hit the market. With the emergence of high-performance PCs, animation is now an attractive alternative for contemporary CAD professionals. Here are a few examples of the creative possibilities.

- There are many practical applications for the world of product design. Sales presentations can be very captivating with dynamic animations of rendered 3D models. Early in the design cycle, clients can scrutinize every detail of potential new products.
- Architects are creating fly-throughs of future homes, buildings, stores, and renovations. Months before construction begins, a client can realistically "visit" a new investment. Interior designers can showcase their ideas and proposals as well.
- With real-time dynamic animation of 3D models, engineers are able to observe the interaction of moving parts within a total assembly.
- In simulating an actual production process, mechanical components can be strategically placed in the order of their assembly and animated for the training of a technician or a consumer.

Once considered to be a nonessential extravagance, animation is fast becoming an effective alternative for leveraging new business, promoting product lines, and communicating ideas.

What's New, What's to Come

WHAT'S NEXT?

The C4 industry continues to respond aggressively to the user's demand for interactive graphic systems that can do more faster, for smaller capital investment, and for lower per-seat cost. Today some per-seat costs for production systems are about one-tenth of what they were in 1980.

Memory and computing performance in these C4 systems continues to double (at the same price) about every eighteen months.

The systems of the future will use these increased capabilities to perform more of the C4 functions in real time at the engineer's desk. Continually lower entry-level prices for production systems have accelerated the penetration of C4 into new industries and into the smaller companies.

Growing client-server networks coupled with videoconferencing and the Internet will accelerate the adoption of faster networks.

DISPLAY TECHNOLOGY

While the CRT is predicted to be replaced by various flat panel technologies (plasma, LDC, electroluminescent, etc.), the overwhelming percentage of C4 workstations today and probably well into the next decade will continue to use the CRT. Laptops, which do use flat panel displays (predominantly LCD) are beginning to be used in some C4 applications. Also, larger (12-in. diagonal and 14-in. diagonal) LCD panels are becoming more price/performance competitive, so we may start to see more flat panel display workstations by the end of the decade.

Color is being increasingly demanded for C4 display applications. Large-format color hard copy devices are available and it appears that ink jet technology will become dominant. This will further accelerate the demand for color monitors. As the use of solid modeling grows, the need for wide-spectrum color will increase.

WORKSTATIONS

Workstations and PCs will add more special-purpose hardware processors to enhance picture rendering and manipulation. Distinctions between vector-based and pixel-based images will no longer be important, and C4 workstations will include more image-processing capability, merging real and computer-generated images.

Improvements in user interface ("user-friendly") will continue with the growth of user- and application-oriented menus and other Graphics User Interface technology. The keyboard, graphic tablet, and mouse will continue to dominate the operator input device environment for the next few years, although as the demand for 3D capability continues to grow, 3D to 6D input devices will be demanded.

Stereoviewing will continue to grow as a desirable workstation option, and virtual reality, discussed later, will become quite common by the end of the decade.

Scanners will play an increasingly important role in the C4 environment as a means of entering existing drawings into a C4 system for editing, and for electronic distribution. This trend will be accelerated by the growing use of PDM systems.

SOFTWARE

Major software trends today and tomorrow include the following:

- Increasing importance of graphic and application de facto and legislated standards are accelerating the trend to "open" systems
- Increasing use of expert systems for design, analysis, and manufacturing
- Increasing use of solid modeling, especially incorporating feature-based user interfaces
- Increasing use of parametric and automatic design capability
- Increasing coupling between conventional C4 software and software for creating photo-realistic images
- Increasing use of application-specific software
- Increasing coupling between C4 and technical documentation
- Increasing use of image databases
- Increasing use of object-oriented databases
- Increasing movement to the client-server environment

MULTIMEDIA

We are now entering an era in which users are reluctant to purchase a workstation that does not have multimedia capability. All major (and many minor) workstation vendors (including laptop suppliers) have incorporated various levels of multimedia capability into their products. At a minimum, today's workstations include sound capability and provisions to play CD-ROMs. Live video capability is also often provided.

We expect to see growing use of multimedia in design, production, testing, and training applications.

VIRTUAL REALITY

Several areas of VR are mature enough for off-the-shelf applications (computer graphics, e.g.), while others are not. In some cases, the technology is available but very expensive!

CARL MACHOVER

COMPUTER-MEDIATED COMMUNICATION SYSTEMS

Introduction

The term *computer-mediated communication* (CMC) was developed to represent the use of computers as a means of facilitating human communication. Computer-based systems have gained momentum as a communication and collaboration medium. As the cost of technology drops and user access to networks increases, the number of business, education, and government applications of CMC continues to expand. The current trend toward increased computer-assisted task collaboration has been fueled by the growth of networks as well as economic and organizational pressures. Increased competition and globalization have forced business to become more efficient by taking advantage of new technologies. Scholarly research in the area of CMC has mirrored this growth. The study of a computer's impact on human communication and the resulting complexities have culminated in a relatively broad collection of literature and theoretical papers.

Computer-mediated communication has been described in various ways by researchers and scholars. In liberal definitions, CMC can encompass virtually all computer uses that employ a user interface or involve the manipulation of data. Diverse applications such as statistical analysis programs, remote-sensing systems, and financial modeling programs all fit within this concept (*1*). A narrower view holds that CMC only encompasses those applications that directly involve human communication. From this perspective, CMC is the process by which people create, exchange, and perceive information using networked telecommunications systems that facilitate encoding, transmitting, and decoding messages. In other words, CMC is a means to establish an electronic environment that is accessible to participants who might otherwise be separated by time zones and physical distance (*2*).

Computer-mediated communication scholarship covers a wide range of applications. This is due in part to the number of potential applications for this technology and in part to the number of fields it spans. The term CMC has been used to describe research in such diverse areas as electronic messaging (*3*), office automation (*4*), distributed decision making (*5*), electronic boardrooms (*6*), teleconferencing, informatics (*1*), computer-supported cooperative work (CSCW), decision support systems and group decision support systems (GDSS; *7*), and computer-assisted instruction (CAI; *1, 8*).

In general, CMC systems can be broken into three distinct areas, which are based on applications. These areas are conferencing, informatics, and CAI. While each area has unique characteristics, elements common to all CMC include communication, computers, and information exchange. Rather than attempt to describe each individual area fitting within CMC, this article concentrates on the commonalities shared by CMC applications. The first section develops a general understanding of the primary divisions within CMC by discussing conferencing and communication, informatics, and CAI (*9*). The remainder of this article explores academic research in the area of CMC.

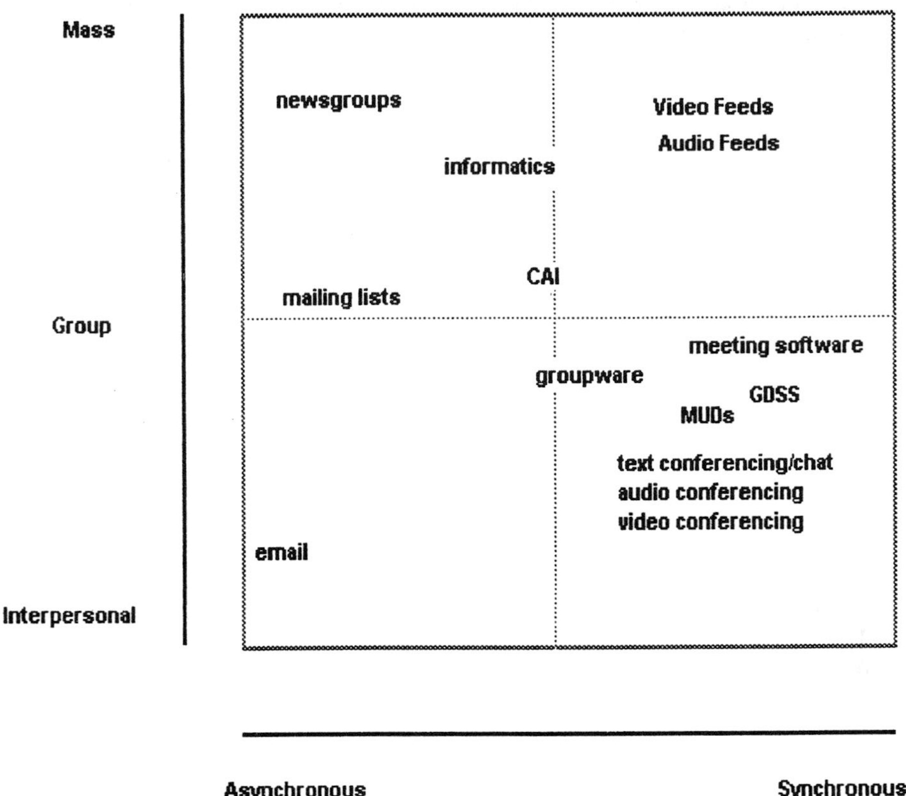

FIGURE 1. *Applications of CMC.*

Primary Divisions Within CMC

CONFERENCING AND COMMUNICATION

A primary use of CMC has been to facilitate direct human communication through conferencing applications. Conferencing has used computer technology in a variety of ways. To understand the types of applications, it is important to view communication systems in two ways: task-related and nontask-related. Task-related communication systems imply applications that concentrate on specific goal completion, with human communication as a necessary link in the process. Group decision support system and CSCW literature supports this view. Conference systems may also have the goal of enabling or enhancing communication. In these instances, systems are not developed with the objective of meeting specific goals or solving problems. Improved communication is the goal instead.

In most conferencing applications communication is either synchronous or asynchronous. Asynchronous communication is not time-dependent. Examples include e-mail and electronic bulletin boards. Synchronous communication, on the other hand, is real-time. An example is an IRC chat system. Figure 1 illustrates the difference.

This article discusses both synchronous and asynchronous applications of CMC conferencing and communication technology, breaking applications down between task-specific and nontask-specific areas of application. Interpersonal, group, and mass nontask-related communication systems will be examined together with task-related areas such as GDSS, CSCW, and CAI.

Interpersonal

Computer-mediated communication systems that are developed specifically for communication support between two individuals or within a very small group can be classified as interpersonal. Interpersonal communication systems can be synchronous or asynchronous, with text-, audio-, and video-based communication being passed between system users. Synchronous communications operate in a real-time or near real-time atmosphere. Text-based chat, video, and low-bandwidth voice communication have all been implemented using computer technologies to facilitate synchronous interpersonal communication. Asynchronous systems can also be based on stored text or audio or video files. While the most common asynchronous interpersonal communication system is e-mail, asynchronous video and audio implementations are becoming more popular. These applications involve digitally storing a video or audio clip and then transmitting it to the receiver, who can listen to or view the message at his or her leisure.

Text-Based Chat. Chat systems provide a synchronous way to communicate with people from all over the world. Any real-time IRC chat systems rely on the Internet as a transmission medium. In general terms, chat systems consist of various separate networks of chat servers or machines that allow users to connect. Once connected to a server, text-based communication can begin. Besides providing a means for interpersonal communication, chat systems are often used to enable communication between larger groups of people. The largest chat networks at this time are EFnet, Undernet, IRCnet, DALnet, and NewNet. In most applications the user will run a program called the client and connect to a server on one of the nets. The server relays information to and from other servers on the same net. Some of the best-known client programs include mIRC, which runs in a windows environment, ircii, which runs under UNIX, and Homer, which runs on the Macintosh. A client connected to a chat network has the option of joining one or more channels. These channels are used to categorize and separate conversations by topics. Chat networks may have several thousand channels available at any time, and the user can generally initiate a new channel. Conversations may be public (everyone in the channel will see the typed messages) or they may be private (communication is between only invited people), depending on the way in which the channel was created.

Video Conferencing. Interpersonal video conferencing facilitates synchronous communication using video and audio. Like many CMC tools, this communication method can save time and reduce travel costs. Video conferencing software currently offers everything from compressed low-bandwidth images on desktop personal computers (PCs) to full-motion, broadcast-quality video. Frequent users may utilize private line video conferencing, and less frequent users may either opt for dial-up access or access other users across the Internet. Video conferencing can be either one-way or two-way interactive and provide a multimedia mix of voice and graphics in addition to video. Personal video conferencing is focused on one-on-one, person-to-person interaction. Other applications of video conferencing might be directed toward larger groups of people. One of the best-known video conferencing software packages is CUSeeMe.

Low-Bandwidth Voice Communication. Audio conferencing programs digitize speech as the user speaks and sends the digital data over the Internet or other transmission media. In order to match sound quality comparable to regular telephone service, most audio communication applications compress sound information before transmitting. In full duplex conversations, sender and receiver can speak and hear the other person simultaneously. In half duplex applications, only one person can speak at a time.

Various commercial products have been developed to support audio CMC applications. Among these are MAVEN and NETPHONE for the Macintosh. In the windows environment, the most popular application has been the INTERNET PHONE, which runs on top of Internet relay chat. It provides many advanced features, such as lists of online users and topics of conversation. Other applications include CoolTalk by Netscape/Insoft, which includes a whiteboard, text chatting, and voice mail; Microsoft's NetMeeting, which is designed to support personal conversation, larger meetings, and application sharing; Webphone, produced by Netspeak; and Quarterdeck's WEBTALK.

The main disadvantage with these low-bandwidth voice communication applications is that most offer proprietary compression schemes, which makes compatibility across applications difficult.

E-mail. Electronic mail or e-mail provides a means of sending text-based messages over a communications channel. E-mail is similar to regular mail, but with an added advantage—speed. E-mail allows both the sender and receiver to asynchronously communicate at convenient times.

Asynchronous Voice and Video. Developed as an extension to e-mail software, asynchronous voice and video applications have become more popular. Digitized voice and video files are transmitted as attachments to e-mail and viewed or heard at a time convenient to the receiver.

Groups

Computer-mediated communication systems have also been developed specifically to support communication within groups. Like interpersonal systems, group CMC has been developed to support both synchronous and asynchronous modes of communication. Text, audio, and video formats can be used to facilitate the exchange of information between system users. In terms of synchronous communication, chat systems, real-time video systems, networked meeting systems, multiple user dialog systems, and group collaboration systems have all been implemented. Asynchronous applications such as the USENET, LISTSERV, and electronic mailing list software have also been developed.

Chat Systems. Most text-based chat systems were designed to support synchronous communication within groups. The same applications used to support interpersonal communication are also used to support groups over the Internet or other computer networks.

Real-Time Video. Several real-time video conferencing software packages are currently available. Of these, CUSeeMe, a software product developed at Cornell University, is one of the best known and most widely used. CUSeeMe allows users to hold desktop video conferences using the Internet as a transmission channel. It is currently available in beta version from Cornell University or as a commercial package from White Pine Software. In order to use CUSeeMe over the Internet with any synchronicity, an ISDN connection is practically required. Users connect to a site called a reflector. Their signal is then sent to other connected users. In addition to video, CUSeeMe also transmits audio and text.

Networked Meeting Software. Networked meeting software generally refers to a package that supports such synchronous collaboration tools as group chats, shared whiteboards, multiusers editors, Web slide shows, and shared applications running simultaneously on the Internet or other network. Several platforms are under development to support these applications. Among these are Yarn and GroCo. Other mainstream vendors such as Netscape and Microsoft are preparing to offer integrated applications supporting this area.

Multiple User Dialog. A variety of multiuser environments have become available to support real-time group communication and collaboration over computer networks. Multiple user dialogs (MUDs) and related systems such as object-oriented MUDs (MOOs) were derived from systems developed by the gaming community in the 1970s and 1980s. Many of the original MUDs have been extended to provide real-time conferencing and collaborative environments. Sometime called text-based virtual realities, these multiuser environments can be used to facilitate group interaction. Multiple user dialogs are generally text-based sites that allow people to connect to the same place at the same time. Unlike conventional chat rooms, they allow program manipulation and interaction through supporting software. In other words, the decision of one user can impact the perceived environment of another user. Synchronous communication is usually a component of the system.

When logged onto a MUD individuals type rather than talk, read rather than listen, and manipulate programs to describe themselves and the current state of the virtual environment. Resulting descriptions are generally text-based and in real time.

Groupware and Collaboration. Groupware encompasses a wide set of technologies used to support interpersonal and group collaboration. Groupware ranges from e-mail to electronic meeting systems (EMS) to workflow collaboration tools. Generally speaking, groupware provides tools to solve *collaboration-oriented* business problems. The general concept driving groupware is the intent to foster collaboration and interpersonal productivity. This is accomplished through the technical automation and enhancement of a variety of tasks. Some groupware applications seek to integrate the functionality of e-mail with other technologies, such as calendar/scheduling software. Others integrate group work processes, workflows, and meetings (*10*).

Newsgroups. Unlike the related asynchronous interpersonal CMC technology, e-mail, newsgroups facilitate group asynchronous communication. Rather than receiving messages directly, newsgroup messages are posted to groups. These groups are organized into topic headings. The user can decide which topics are of interest and choose which messages to view or download. One of the best-known newsgroup systems is called the Usenet, which is an international forum in which asynchronous discussions on a myriad of topics are constantly taking place. Usenet discussion has been described as liberating because of its anonymous nature. As in many applications of CMC, participants are judged on their words rather than on outward appearance, age, or gender. Many different types of newsgroups exist within Usenet, and these groups are organized into the following eight major topic groups:

comp: Computer and computer science-orientated newsgroups
news: Internet news-orientated newsgroups
sci: Technical or scientific-orientated newsgroups
rec: Recreational-orientated newsgroups
soc: Cultural and social-orientated newsgroups
talk: Discussions and debate about what's making news
misc: Miscellaneous
alt: Alternative

The Usenet abbreviations are placed at the start of the newsgroup address and the contents of the group are usually represented in the remainder of the address. Newsreader programs have been developed to allow the viewing of the messages. Some systems download the file for future viewing, while other systems allow viewing without actually downloading the messages.

Electronic Mailing Lists. Like newsgroups, electronic mailing lists are an asynchronous group communication technology. Mailing lists use e-mail technology to disseminate information and facilitate discussion. In many mailing list systems a user subscribes to a list. After acceptance, copies of every message sent to the group will be routed to each member on the list. If the list is moderated each message will be reviewed by a moderator prior to being disseminated to each member. Most mailing lists will have three e-mail addresses. These are as follows:

The subscription e-mail: To subscribe to the list
The list e-mail: To send messages to the list
The administrator/moderator e-mail: To contact the administrator or moderator of the list

Mailing lists fall into two categories, manual and automatic. Manual lists are generally moderated or controlled by a particular person. This person accepts, rejects, or edits message contents. Automatic lists aren't generally moderated; computer programs called robots are used for administration instead. Two common robots are LISTSERV and Majordomo. Other types of mailing lists allow readers to read messages but not send new ones.

Mass

Computer-mediated communication systems have also been developed specifically for mass communication. This means computer systems facilitate one-to-many communication in either a synchronous or an asynchronous mode. While mass communication over networked computer systems is still in its infancy, this technology has been implemented with some measure of success in text, audio, and video formats.

Text. Technologies such as mailing lists, newsgroups, and Web sites have been implemented to effectively allow one-to-many communication. This is particularly true of mediated newsgroups and mailing lists, in which a single individual is able to communicate to an audience that cannot be limited.

Audio. Systems have been developed to present real-time audio over the Internet and other networks. Users with conventional multimedia personal computers, a network connection, and the appropriate software are able to listen to real-time sound "broadcasts." A product released by Progressive Networks called RealAudio Server enables media providers to distribute audio or audio-based multimedia streams over the Internet in much the same way broadcast media operate.

Video. One-to-many video applications are being developed to operate over the Internet and other networks. One of the best-known applications, the Multicast Backbone or MBONE, is a virtual network that originated from an effort to multicast audio and video. MBONE is primary used by researchers developing protocols and applications for enhanced group communication. Multicast provides one-to-many and many-to-many network delivery services. Besides basic networking technology, MBONE researchers are developing new applications in the areas of video conferencing, audio transmissions, and shared drawing whiteboards.

Group Decision Support Systems (GDSS)

The term group decision support systems has been used to describe a particular area within CMC specifically developed from the need to support organizational decision-making processes that are being implemented by more than an individual. Unlike the nontask-specific CMC applications, GDSS are generally used to facilitate a particular task. As such, GDSS can be described as an interactive computer-based system used to support collective decision making. The term *group support systems* is often associated with GDSS, but focuses specifically on the within-group processes. Group decision support systems may also include technologies for outside-group and information-managing communication.

Generally decision makers utilize data and models within a GDSS to communicate and solve problems. Researchers have classified a variety of applications as GDSS, however, ranging from systems to facilitate electronic meetings to systems to support complex decision processes (*11*).

The simplistic GDSS may consist of no more than a personal computer and voting pads combination. In this arrangement questions are answered with a simple yes and no. The results are tabulated real-time and the results are displayed graphically. In more complex GDSS implementations, anonymously entered data can be displayed, and options such as data consolidation, statistical analysis, voting tabulation, ranking, and agenda planning exist.

Other GDSS systems have been developed to support an organizational paradigm of computing. In this view, the GDSS integrates data from corporate transaction processing systems and decision support systems and uses this information to demonstrate various outcomes.

Group decision support systems have been developed for use in several different environments. Among these are decision rooms, local networks, and remote networks. In the decision room scenario, a traditional conference center is equipped with computerized aids. This allows both the advantages of face-to-face communication and electronic interaction to be enjoyed. A local network GDSS is designed to allow participants to interact from their offices. Using their own computers, communication and access to data and decision support is enabled. Remote network systems operate in the same way as the local networks, except the decision makers are not in close proximity.

Group decision support systems applications have been found to enjoy several benefits. Among these are anonymity, extension of group memory, parallel task completion, and the democratization of decision making.

Researchers report anonymity enhances group member participation by reducing inhibition (*11*). Groups working anonymously produce greater numbers of solution clarifications, critical comments, questions about solutions, and total comments. In addition, members were more likely to be critical of ideas, to ask questions about new ideas, and to clarify or add to ideas. Anonymity acts as a buffer between people, disassociating them from their comments. This reduces behavioral constraints on group members and allows them to contribute more freely to the group discussion (*12*).

The efficiency of group work is also improved by a GDSS through the structuring of team member interactions. Resulting time savings allows a greater focus on its task performance and problem-solving activities (*13*). Parallel entry also provides an increase in group efficiency. Members don't need to wait for someone to finish "speaking" before beginning the entry of additional information (*14*).

Group decision support system tools can also enhance group memory. Retaining group memory has been a traditional barrier in face-to-face interaction and often results in information loss. Features of GDSSs such as electronic information capturing and display have been specifically designed to reduce information loss.

A single garrulous person cannot raise his or her voice to dominate a meeting in which GDSS is used. Group decision support systems tend to democratize the process, giving members the same opportunity to express their ideas through their terminal.

Group decision support systems applications are not without shortcomings. The use of GDSS tends to reduce face-to-face interpersonal communication and increase social distances between members. In addition, the technology used to implement a GDSS can make meetings more complicated, particularly to the facilitator.

A variety of commercial products have been developed in the area of GDSS. Among these are VisionQuest, an electronic meeting support software supporting anonymous brainstorming, voting, allocation, and meeting documentation. Like most

GDSS products, it runs in a variety of environments and requires that network software already be in place. Other tools include Autotel Information Systems' Clarity, which provides a permanent record of the group's interactions; CM/1 by Corporate Memory Systems, a graphical meeting map combining a hypertext interface with an object-oriented database to allow groups to collaborate and organize ideas during brainstorming sessions; Group Systems V by Ventana, electronic meeting software that captures anonymous text-based ideas and displays the results in a shared screen environment; and OptionFinder from Option Technologies, an interactive GDSS that allows each meeting participant to vote using a numeric keypad attached to a PC, and then collects, calculates, and graphically displays results in real time.

Computer-Supported Cooperative Work

The study of people working together using computerized technology is the focus of computer-supported cooperative (or collaborative) work (CSCW). While this area can be classified under the umbrella of CMC, the goal of researchers is to develop better ways to use computer technology to further enhance the group work process. Key concerns include trying to better understand the role time and location play in the process. The focus of CSCW is the social interaction of people, not technology. Typical topics in CSCW research include e-mail, shared applications, databases, hypertext, and other technical developments that improve a participant's awareness of other users and their activities. Like CMC in general, CSCW can be divided into synchronous and asynchronous domains. The term groupware is used to refer to the technology used by individuals wishing to collaborate on a project. Computer-supported cooperative work, on the other hand, refers to the field that studies human use of that technology.

INFORMATICS

Informatics is the term used to describe the study and application of information technology to information systems. The computer and related technologies are central to this area of research. Although information is stored, retrieved, and changed by people, the technical system has an active role as the repository and maintainer of organized information (*1*). Study of social impacts of this technology has been termed social informatics. Some common applications of informatics include the World Wide Web, library resources, online CD-ROM databases, gopher sites, and wide-area information server (WAIS) databases. A related area of study is called social informatics, which attempts to understand the social implications involved with using this technology.

World Wide Web

In the latter part of the 1960s, military computer networks across the country were interconnected in a way to ensure sensitive planning and communication were uninterrupted during times of emergency. A key aspect of this development was the lack of a central hub. Since communication was not required to pass through a single point, the network was less vulnerable during times of war. During the following decades, universities and businesses adopted similar technology to link new and existing networks. This growth became exponential, with new sites being added until it became what is now called the Internet—a worldwide network of computer networks. Today no single entity is responsible for the entire Internet. Each connection of a computer or network is maintained by different organizations or individuals. This makes regulation of the vast amount of information transmitted over the Internet virtually impossible.

The World Wide Web (WWW) has evolved as a graphical way of viewing information over the Internet. Documents called Web pages are collected in Web sites stored in various computers connected to the Internet. Web pages contain text as well as multimedia elements such as pictures, sound, video, and animation. These items are integrated using *hypertext markup language* (HTML) in a way to facilitate communication over the network. Web pages are viewed with software programs called browsers. Several better known browsers are Netscape's Navigator and Microsoft Explorer.

Gopher

Gopher is a distributed document delivery service which began as a campus information service at the University of Minnesota. Users are able to access information from Gopher servers running on Internet hosts in a seamless fashion. The information stored on Gopher appears as a series of nested menus and resembles the organization of a directory with subdirectories and files. From the user's perspective, all information appears to originate from a single location. In actuality, this information may be on the local site or on a remote site using Gopher software. These links to other sites create a virtual network often called Gopherspace. The University of Minnesota maintains a list of all Gopher servers currently in use. Information on Gopher servers can be text, binary images, directory information, sound, or video. In addition, Gopher provides gateways to other information systems.

WAIS Databases

WAIS (pronounced "ways") is a database system that gives users the ability to search databases of articles, books, references, and abstracts. It was also designed as a means to publish information over the Internet at a minimal cost. The wide area information server was developed by Thinking Machines Corporation of Cambridge, Massachusetts, in collaboration with Dow Jones & Co., Apple Computer, and Peat Marwick.

COMPUTER-ASSISTED INSTRUCTION (CAI)

Computer-assisted instruction has been defined as a curriculum-based instruction that is individualized, interactive, and guided: individualized and guided since the computer serves as a tutor providing instruction for one individual; interactive because it involves two-way communication between a student and the computer (*15*).

Computer-assisted instruction systems may also help students in ways that are not covered in the basic definition. Four common CAI situations are: (1) allowing simulation of laboratory experiments that might be too dangerous or expensive for real experiments, (2) creating three-dimensional objects following user specifications (thus freeing time for the exploration of hypotheses and relationships), (3) making large databases available for consultation and research, and (4) using networks and the Internet for either cooperative experiments conducted by users in different locations or participation in remote dialogues that increase the development of critical thinking skills.

CAI History

The central premises behind CAI are not new. Ideas and research derived from the cognitive and behavioral sciences have influenced developments in this field. For example, the theories of B. F. Skinner (*16*) regarding operant conditioning and the importance of providing rewards for goal achievement, the progressivism of education in the 1920s, which represented a radical change in approach toward individual learning and formative education, the emphasis on visual education in the 1930s (which included failed experiments aimed at replacing books with films and radios in the classroom), the TV instruction effort of the 1950s, B. Bloom's taxonomy of educational objectives (*17*), and the instructional systems design (ISD) models of the 1970s have all had an impact on the present status of CAI (*18*).

Implementation of CAI really started when IBM introduced the 360 series of mainframe computers. Better hardware allowed faster computation and presentation of results, which in turn facilitated interaction between user and computer. IBM initially developed CAI systems for corporate training. Computer-assisted instruction received additional impetus during the Vietnam War, when the military establishment felt the need for innovations in training. The support from the military for CAI through grants for research facilitated its adaptation for civilian education uses (*19*).

Four early successes in CAI during the 1960s stimulated the growth of CAI research and implementation: the PLATO project together with its language TUTOR at the University of Illinois; the work by Patrick Suppes at Stanford University, who developed CAI for mathematics and language; the development of the LOGO language by Seymour Papert; and the creation of the BASIC (beginner's all-purpose symbolic instructional code) language. The PLATO project implemented educational computer programs that were highly interactive and of a tutorial nature. The quality of these programs allowed their conversion into microcomputer-oriented implementations (*20*). The Suppes project led to the establishment of the Computer Curriculum Corporation, which provides instructional computer systems with a large body of courseware (*21*). With the Logo language computer is a tutee (a "turtle" on the screen is instructed by the user). Its aim is to make the computer an object to think with and to stimulate the user's higher-order thinking skills.

Types of CAI Systems

During the last thirty years a multitude of CAI systems have been produced by universities, software companies, and individuals. The great majority of systems have been written for microcomputer platforms, especially the IBM-compatible computers. These microcomputer-oriented CAI systems can be classified as tutor applications, tool applications, and tutee applications. In tutor applications the computer can provide drill and practice, tutorials, simulations, problem solving, and educational games. In tool applications the computer is used as a tool helpful in learning (just as a pencil, typewriter, or microscope). In tutee applications the computer acts as the student and the user acts as the teacher (*21*).

The CAI systems of the 1990s tend to use hypermedia and interactivity enhanced by sophisticated computer graphics (and in some cases virtual reality). There is heavy emphasis on learner-centered systems that adapt to the learner as he or she advances in the area of study (*22, 23*). Two other areas of growth are the utilization of computer networking and the Internet to provide learning opportunities for individuals and groups. Computer-aided instruction users can participate in projects, experimentation, and idea exploration by using group-oriented software that has been designed to facilitate these types of activities. Communication through the Internet (i.e., using MOOs and chat programs) is being used by schools to enhance communications and learning (*24–26*).

CAI Implementation Examples

Many examples of CAI put into practice can be identified. Several specific applications and several areas of application are described in more detail.

Computer-Assisted Law Instruction (CALI) is a series of resource materials available to students at different law schools throughout the country. Development was sponsored by the Center for Computer-Assisted Law Instruction, which was established in June 1982 by the University of Minnesota Law School and Harvard Law School. Its objectives were to coordinate distribution and use of computerized instructional materials, support authors in the development of new instructional programs, sponsor research for advancing quality and effectiveness of exercises, establish standards for hardware, software, and courseware, and support and coordinate the sharing of information relating to computer applications in legal education and law. Members contribute the material and receive payment in the form of royalties based on the use of material by students. The database contains exercises on all aspects of the law and is heavily used by students in law schools around the country. (CALI has a total of 165 members, including international universities, corporate members, and most of the major law schools in the United States; *27*.)

Human Anatomy is an interactive program designed to aid in the study of gross anatomy in medical schools. The program comprises over 9,000 images of the human body in various stages of dissection, which students can view as they read through a description of the procedure on a computer monitor. The program is available on computer and video disks or CD-ROM. This courseware simulates traditional dissection by providing video images similar to the perspective seen when performing a cadaveric dissection in the laboratory. By enabling students to study dissection outside the lab the program gives them the flexibility and the opportunity to study at their own pace. Human Anatomy is published by Gold Standard Multimedia, Inc., which offers a complete series of medical programs, including a course in medical ethics (*28*).

A.D.A.M.: The Inside Story is a multimedia introduction to the secrets of the human body. Designed for middle grades 5 through 8, the school edition of this award-winning CD-ROM features the Family Scrapbook, in which animated, modern-day Adam and Eve lead a lighthearted educational tour through each of the body's twelve anatomical systems. The body's "inner workings" are revealed in the context of Adam and Eve's daily activities, making each system's role clear and easy to understand. Over four hours of detailed animations, video, and sound show and explain everything from the basics of swallowing and digesting food to more serious issues, such as coronary artery disease, to the role of less-familiar systems, such as the lymphatic system. *A.D.A.M.: The Inside Story* also features precision-rendered anatomical images for interactive "point-and-click" exploration of the human body, plus a basic dictionary of anatomical terms and challenging interactive puzzles (*29*).

Distance learning systems are another area of CAI. Here, computer networks are used for distance education. The increased availability of broadband transmission channels makes it possible to exchange multiple types of data simultaneously (image, voice, graphics, and software applications). Several high schools and universities are establishing distance education programs; among them the John D. Bracco School in Edmonton, Canada (*25*), Boise State University, Kansas State University, and Harvard Law School. Harvard has established a partnership with Lexis Nexis to implement the Harvard Bridge Project, which will offer the first year of law school in digital form (*30*).

Reference Sites for Other Types of Software. A search of the Internet produces a multiplicity of sources for CAI programs. A partial list of sites in which references to different types of CAI software may be found follows.

1. The University of Capetown's page on computer-based education. An excellent source for links related to computer-based education at all educational levels (*31*).
2. SuperKids Educational Software Review. Excellent unbiased reviews of children's software. Gives ratings from the parents' and children's points of view, as well as an educational value rating (*29*).
3. EENet. A virtual-market online information and communication system serving the needs of the electronics industry. Provides a good list of educational software providers (*32*).
4. Internet Reference Library of Educational Software. Sponsored by California State University at Fullerton, offers good links for computer science, engineering, and mathematics educational software (*33*).
5. PEP Registry of Educational Software Publishers. Provides a comprehensive listing of educational software companies with direct links to their sites (*34*).

CMC Research Summary

CONFERENCING AND COMMUNICATION: INTERPERSONAL, GROUP, AND MASS

Most research on CMC has focused on the differences between CMC communication and face-to-face communication. Face-to-face communication includes a variety of secondary communication channels, including paraverbal (tone of voice, inflection) and nonverbal (body language). These cues help to regulate the flow of conversation, facilitate turn taking, provide feedback, and convey subtle meaning. As a result, face-to-face conversation is a remarkably orderly process. In normal face-to-face conversation there are few interruptions or long pauses and the distribution of participation is consistent though skewed toward higher-status members (*35*). Research has demonstrated that CMC filters many of these secondary communication channels, which has specific identifiable affects on CMC communication. The degree to which these channels are filtered depends on the type of CMC system. For example, video-based media permit more communication channels than text-based media. Recently, two paradigms have emerged in the CMC literature (*36*).

The first paradigm asserts that the affects of CMC on communication are an invariant attribute of the communication medium. This implicit assumption underlies theories of communication "richness" and social presence. Rich media are characterized by multiple communication channels and feedback. It takes more effort to achieve the same level of mutual understanding in "lean" media such as text-based conferencing as in a rich one, such as face-to-face communication. Communication via lean media has been found to be less efficient in terms of information exchanged, less inhibited, more equal in participation, and more task-focused than face-to-face communication. Two recent summaries of this research can be found in McGrath and Hollinshead (*35*) and Scrivener (*37*).

The second paradigm asserts that the effects of the communication medium are transitory and that people overcome media limitations over time. Through repeated interactions, group members adapt to the communication medium and may also adapt the technology and find innovative ways to overcome and compensate for the inherent limitations of the medium. According to researchers in this area, the previously identified effects of CMCS are limited to the initial interactions among group members with a new medium. Recent studies have suggested that CMC groups can communicate as effectively as face-to-face groups if the interactions last for an extended period of time. Three recent articles that summarize this paradigm are Burke and Chidambaram (*38*), Chidambaram (*36*), and Chidambaram and Bostrom (*39*).

Computer-mediated mass communication is a new phenomenon. Besides the literature on the technical aspects of the medium researchers have not established an independent body of literature.

GDSS

Most of the research on GDSS has been led by two groups. The first group is the Management of Information Systems Department at the University of Arizona, which describes GDSS in terms of three facets it calls group process and outcomes, methods, and the environment. Group process and outcomes include a variety of characteristics of the group, the task, and the organizational context in which the system is used. Methods include the tools and procedures built into the system. Environment refers the total system, including hardware and software. Although this research has identified a large number of variables to consider in the development and study of GDSS, the results of much of the research is equivocal and has not clearly established the benefits of GDSS except for a few specific tasks. Good reviews of the research in this area can be found in McGrath and Hollingshead (*35*) and Jessup and Valacich (*7*).

The second group includes researchers at the University of Minnesota. Unlike the first group, which has focused on the systems, the second paradigm developed from behavioral research on groups interacting without computer support and has focused on group process and interaction. The primary theoretical foundation for this paradigm is adaptive structuration theory (AST). According to AST, group members continually adapt the rules and resources available to them to achieve their goals. Reviews of this body of literature can be found in McGrath and Hollingshead (*35*) and Jessup and Valacich (*7*).

COMPUTER-SUPPORTED COOPERATIVE WORK

Computer-supported cooperative work as a separate field of study has only been in existence since the mid-1980s. Its roots are in the area of human-computer interaction, but it encompasses aspects of almost every area of computers and information systems from systems and interface design to the social and behavioral aspects of group interaction. While the research in computer conferencing, GDSS, and other areas is relevant to CSCW, CSCW is broader and more difficult to define. Two recent reviews of this area are Schrivener (*37*) and Mankin, Cohen, and Bikson (*40*).

CAI: ANALYSIS AND CRITICISM

Computer-assisted instruction is an area that fosters heated discussion. Proponents of CAI (*41*) are as adamant as its detractors. The development of CAI systems has suffered from the same malady as most computer-oriented technology; the proliferation of design principles, the lack of standards and quality control, and the explosion in the number of CAI systems available leave the consumers in a bind when trying to choose effective systems (*35, 42*). School systems in the United States tend to introduce CAI and technology without adequate preparation of teachers and students. The lack of training and equipment for instructors causes the CAI systems to be used inappropriately (*43*). The entrance into the CAI market by big entertainment corporations that want to profit from the CAI emphasis is school curricula, could make learning take a role secondary to entertainment. As with most other computer-based systems, we will have to wait and see how technology, market forces, and consumer needs determine which systems will be the ones helping people learn in the future (*44*).

REFERENCES

1. G. M. Santoro, "What Is Computer-Mediated Communication?" in *Computer Mediated Communication and the Online Classroom: Overview and Perspectives,* vol. 1, Z. L. Berge and M. P. Collins, eds. Hampton, Cresskill, NJ, 1995.

2. P. Fisser, J. O. Weghuis, and K. Slotman, *Computer Mediated Communication (CMC),* University of Twente, Enschede, Netherlands. Online distance learning publication. http://www.to.utwent.nl/ism/online95/campus/library/online95/chap4/chap4.htm (1995).

3. R. Johansen, J. Vallee, and K. Spangler, *Electronic Meetings: Technical Alternatives and Socail Choices,* Addison-Wesley, Reading, MA, 1979.
4. R. E. Rice and D. Case, "Electronic Message Systems in the University: A Description of Use and Utility." *J. Commun.,* 131–152 (1983).
5. A. R. Wellens, "Group Situation Awareness and Distributed Decision Making," in *Individual and Group Decision Making,* N. J. Castellan, Jr., ed. Lawrence Erlbaum, Hillsdale, NJ, 1993, pp. 267–293.
6. A. Pinsonneault and K. L. Kraemer, "The Effects of Electronic Meetings on Group Processes and Outcomes: An Assessment of the Empirical Research." *Eur. J. Op. Res.,* **46**(2), 143–161 (1989).
7. L. M. Jessup and J. S. Valacich, "On the Study of Group Support Systems: An Introduction to Group Support System Research and Development," in *Group Support Systems,* L. M. Jessup and J. S. Valacich, eds. Macmillan, New York, 1993, pp. 3–7.
8. P. Ferris, "What Is CMC? An Overview of Scholarly Definitions," http://www.december.com/cmc/mag/1997/jan/ferapp.html (Feb. 22, 1997).
9. Z. L. Berge and M. Collins, "Computer-Mediated Scholarly Discussion Groups." *Computers Ed.,* **24**(3), 183–189 (1995).
10. D. Coleman, *Groupware: Technology and Applications,* Prentice Hall, Englewood Cliffs, NJ, 1995.
11. G. DeSanctis and R. B. Gallupe, "A Foundation for the Study of Group Decision Support Systems." *Mgt. Sci.,* **33**(5), 589–609 (1987).
12. L. M. Jessup, T. Connoly, and J. Galegher, "The Effects of Anonymity on GDSS Group Process with an Idea-Generating Task." *MIS. Q.,* 312–321 (Sept. 1990).
13. M. Alavi, "Group Decision Support Systems." *J. Info. Syst. Mgt.,* 36–41 (summer 1991).
14. C. Thornton and E. Lockhart, "Groupware of Electronic Brainstorming." *J. Mgt. Syst.,* 10–12 (Oct. 1994).
15. L. A. Miller, "Computer Assisted Instruction" [HTML title], available: http://www.nova.edu:80/gtep/SCI/SCI651/CRS124/leemill.html (Feb. 20, 1997).
16. B. F. Skinner, *Cumulative Record,* Appleton-Century-Crofts, New York, 1959.
17. B. Bloom, *Taxonomy of Educational Objectives: The Classification of Educational Goals,* McKay, New York, 1956.
18. P. Saettler, *A History of Instructional Technology,* McGraw-Hill, New York, 1968.
19. T. M. Shlechter, *Problems and Promises of Computer Based Training,* T. M. Shlechter, ed. Ablex Publishing Corp., Norwood, NJ, 1991, pp. 1–20.
20. R. V. Bullough and F. B. LaMond, *Classroom Applications of Microcomputers,* MacMillan, New York, NY, 1991.
21. P. F. Merrill, K. Hammons, M. N. Tolman, L. Christenson, B. R. Vincent, and P. L. Reynolds, *Computers in Education,* Allyn and Bacon, Boston, 1992.
22. E. Soloway and A. Pryor, "The Next Generation in Human-Computer Interaction," *Commun. ACM,* **39**(8), 83 (1996).
23. D. A. Norman and J. C. Spohrer, "Learner-Centered Education," *Commun. ACM,* **39**(4), 24 (1996).
24. R. Cosmann, "The Evolution of Educational Computer Software," *Education,* **116**(4), 619 (1996).
25. V. Dwyer and S. Steele, "High-tech or Glorified Play," *Afterimage,* **23**(5), 13.
26. L. Guernsey, "Student Across Many Time Zones Spend the Summer in the BioM00: On-line Discussion, Virtual Smiles, and Virtual Applause Characterize Biocomputing Class," *Chronicle Higher Ed.,* **49**, A21 (1996).
27. CALI homepage, "CALI: The Center for Computer-Assisted Legal Instruction" [HTML title], available: http://www.cali.org:80/, Area Maintainer: <webmaster@cali.org> (Feb. 20, 1997).
28. Gold Standard Multimedia, Inc., "Gold Standard Multimedia Inc." [HTML title], available: http://www.gsm.com/products/ha/index.html; E-mail: <info@gsm.com>; Area Maintainer: <webmaster@gsm.com> (Feb. 20, 1997).
29. SuperKids, "SuperKids Educational Software Review" [HTML title], available: http://www.superkids.com:80/; E-mail: <editor@superkids.com>; Area Maintainer: <Knowledge Share LLC> (Feb. 20, 1997).
30. C. Klein, "1Ls in Cyberspace: Harvard Joins Race to Create Virtual Classroom," *Nat. Law J.,* **19**(5), A18 (1996).

31. University of Cape Town Computer-Based Education, "Welcome to UCT's Computer-Based Education" [HTML title], available: http://www.uct.ac.za/projects/cbe/; E-mail: <webmaster@uct.ac.za>; Area Maintainer: <Media Services, Department of Development and Public Affairs> (Feb. 20, 1997).
32. EENet, "EENet: Educational Software" [HTML title], available: <http://www.eenet.com/soft/dir/educate.html>; E-mail: <campbell@eenet.com>; Area Maintainer: EENet SYSOP (Feb. 20, 1997).
33. IRL, "IRL: Main Menu of Educational Software" [HTML title], available: http://titan.ecs.fullerton.edu:0080/cgi-irl/mainmenu.pl; E-mail: <http://titan.ecs.fullerton.edu:0080/cgi-irl/mailmenu.pl>; Area Maintainer: <http://titan.ecs.fullerton.edu:0080/cgi-irl/mailmenu.pl> (Feb. 20, 1997).
34. PEP, "PEP Registry, Educational Software Publishers" [HTML title], available: <http://www.microweb.com/pepsite/Software/publishers.html>; E-mail: OCKidTalk@aol.com>; Area Maintainer: Anne Bubnic (Feb. 20, 1997).
35. J. McGrath and A. B. Hollingshead, *Groups Interaction with Technology: Ideas, Evidence, Issues and an Agenda,* Sage, London, 1994.
36. L. Chidambaram, "Relational Development in Computer-Supported Groups." *MIS Q.,* **20**(2), 143–165 (1996).
37. S. Scrivener, ed., *Computer-Supported Cooperative Work,* Ashgate, Brookfield, VT, 1994.
38. K. Burke and L. Chidambaram, "Developmental Difference Between Distributed and Face-to-Face Groups in Electronically Supported Meeting Environments: An Exploratory Investigation." *Group Decis. Nego.,* **4**(3), (1995).
39. L. Chidambaram and R. P. Bostrom, "Group Development (I): A Review and Synthesis of Developmental Models." *Group Decis. Negot.,* (forthcoming).
40. D. Mankin, S. G. Cohen, and T. K. Bikson, *Teams Technology: Fulfilling the Promise of the New Organization,* Harvard Business School Press, Cambridge, 1996.
41. C. Kulik and J. A. Julik, "Effectiveness of Computer-Based Instruction: An Updated Analysis." *Computers Human Behav.,* **7**, 1–2, 75 (1991).
42. R. L. Measelle, "Reinventing Education: New Classrooms for the Information Age," *Vit. Sp.,* **62**(16), 492 (1996).
43. D. Noble, "Mad Rushes into the Future: The Overselling of Educational Technology," *Educ. Lead.,* **54**(3), 18 (1996).
44. R. Furger, "Where's the On Button," *PC World,* **14**(10), 256 (1996).

ROGER MCHANEY
CONSTANZA HAGMANN
ROSS HIGHTOWER
LUTFUS SAYEED

COMPUTER MODELING OF STORYTELLING AND CREATIVITY

Introduction

Soon after the advent of computers in the 1940s, the idea was born to have them process not merely numbers but also human language. The research field of *machine translation* was the first to attract interest, later followed by other kinds of applications, among them the idea to model the processes of storytelling and the underlying creativity. Computer applications presuppose formal theories, and stories indeed seemed to be amenable to formalization, as they were often seen as instances of a small set of schematic templates. In the early 1900s, for instance, George Polti analyzed a wide range of classic plot lines in literature and proposed an inventory of thirty-six basic "dramatic situations," which included such concepts as conflict with a god, mistaken jealousy, faulty judgment, or loss of loved ones (*1*).

In the spirit of such schematic approaches, the concept of "story grammar" originated in the 1970s. Even though story grammars were first developed from the perspective of understanding rather than generation, the idea had influence on the efforts in story production as well. Basically, a story grammar claims that a formal structure can be assigned to a story in analogy to the syntactic structure ascribed to sentences in linguistics. Accordingly, story grammars are represented in the form of rewrite rules; the grammar given by Rumelhart (*2*) starts with the following:

$$\text{story} \rightarrow \text{setting} + \text{episode}$$

$$\text{setting} \rightarrow (\text{state})^*$$

$$\text{episode} \rightarrow \text{event} + \text{reaction}$$

In brief, this means that a story consists of a "setting" element followed by an "episode," in which the setting is a series of "states," and the episode is in turn composed of an "event" and a "reaction" (which are further defined by other rules). In parallel to these rules describing form, a set of semantic rules is supposed to capture the relations of meaning holding between the elements of a story.

Obviously the notion of a story grammar is attractive from the perspective of computer modeling, as it offers a clear account of "storyness" that allows for formally parsing stories in ways very similar to automatic sentence parsing. It was noted however, (see, e.g., Ref. *3*) that a grammatical approach to stories imposed very strict limitations and is not flexible enough to describe the mechanisms that make a story "work." Other theories were proposed, and in artificial intelligence (AI), the work on story generation focused on modeling the *reasoning processes* of the characters acting in a story as well as those involved in story production itself.

Story Generation Systems in "Classic" Artificial Intelligence

An early storytelling program, often regarded as the pioneer of the field, was written by James Meehan for his Ph.D. thesis at Yale University in 1976 (*4*). Under the title "The Meta-Novel: Writing Stories by Computer," Meehan presented a program called Tale-Spin that allowed the user to define a basic setting and a cast of characters together with a particular "problem" that one of the characters sets out to solve. The program has a problem-solving module that holds some knowledge on breaking goals into simpler subgoals that can be solved individually; this aspect of the work is rooted in the tradition of the work by Roger Schank's group at Yale, *Scripts, Plans, Goals and Understanding* (*5*). In the 1970s, this framework of research was very prominent in the research field that nowadays is often referred to as "classic" AI. In a nutshell, the underlying idea was that problem solving in terms of goal decomposition can be seen as the central ability in human cognition, and it can be simulated with computers using symbolic representations of the knowledge in conjunction with procedures manipulating these representations.

The level of problem solving employed in Tale-Spin and thus manifested in the stories is one of straightforward cause-effect links, such as "X is thirsty—X wants water—X does Y to get water—X drinks water—X is not thirsty anymore." To compute these sequences, a set of fairly general rules is instantiated with the specific problem and applied to find the solution. The type of tale might be said to resemble narrations produced by small children, a claim that was indeed explicitly made for a similar program some twenty years later, to which we will turn below. When reading the stories produced by Tale-Spin, one immediately notices the relatively poor "surface quality" of the text: it lacks pronouns and variation in expressions; the sentences are short and have only very few cohesive elements to glue them together. Basically, a text is a sequence of individual short statements, and thus the language sounds quite unnatural—even though one might argue that deficits of this kind are also a "feature" of children's language. On this point, the author acknowledges that "the addition of personal pronouns to the output would have enhanced the quality of the output but were not central to the problem of generating the events of a story" (*6*, p. 197). This issue, too, will be taken up below in the discussion of a later program. At this point, we briefly explain the inner workings of Tale-Spin in producing its stories.

The "knowledge base" coded within the program holds descriptions of eight different kinds of characters and about fifty kinds of physical locations. Problem-solving procedures have been defined for the acts of acquiring objects and information, transfering information, and persuading, bargaining, and asking information. To start story production, the program user defines a list of characters and assigns a goal to one of them. Suppose the user states that "John wants to visit Mary." Then the corresponding problem-solving procedure is triggered, which sets up a transportation goal, which might in turn expand to other subgoals, and so forth. When these procedures are executed to build an abstract "plan" describing the way to the problem's solution, the story is produced as a side effect. On the linguistic side, the program has a vocabulary of fifty verbs and a small number of nouns and adjectives.

In the 1970s, the stories automatically produced by Tale-Spin were quite innovative examples of computer "reasoning." The program treated problem solving as the driving force of story production, thereby advancing the view that coherence of a story arises simply from the fact that one or several characters exhibit rational, goal-driven behavior. This was in line with the contemporary research in AI, and to a good extent in cognitive psychology, in which the capacity of solving problems by applying symbolic rules was seen as a central feature of human intelligence.

Almost twenty years after Tale-Spin, another story generator was written along the lines of the "scripts, plans, goals" research framework. Minstrel by Scott Turner (*7*) also sees problem solving as the central ingredient of stories. To implement it, he uses top-down goal expansion as sketched above, and in addition the more recent AI technique of "case-based reasoning," in which one problem is solved by recalling another similar one from memory and adopting the old solution to the new problem.

Importantly, Turner places problem solving not only inside the story plots, but views the entire process of storytelling as the "purposeful achievement of author goals." Minstrel's stories are in the domain of King Arthur and his noble knights; they are little fables illustrating a moral, such as "deception is a weapon difficult to aim."

As for "surface quality," the same comment made above on Tale-Spin applies here as well. Sentences are short statements and often repeat the same words, as in the schema "A loves B. Because A loves B, A wants B to love A." By employing results from research in "natural language generation," sketched below in the final section, the cohesion of such stories could easily be improved, but again this was not the author's main goal. Instead, the "deeper" process of solving problems on the basis of experience is treated as the central task. The program gets started when the user provides clues to the theme of the story to be developed. Then the system's memory is explored to find similar schemes that have been employed in the past. This process of adapting old solutions to new problems is put forward as a theory of creativity, which will be dealt with below in the section "Creativity and Humor Generation."

In Minstrel, the story production task itself is seen as an instance of problem solving. The story originates by successively applying procedures that refine goals. These fall into four groups: "thematic goals" ensure that the story indeed illustrates the theme given by creating an appropriate sequence of events. "Consistency goals" supervise the resulting story to ensure its consistency. (For example, they can invoke adding material covering the preconditions of some action.) "Presentation goals" are in charge of selecting and ordering the material, and expressing it in English. "Drama goals" serve to create simple forms of tragedy, suspense, irony, characterization, and foreshadowing.

The developer of Minstrel had the artificial stories evaluated by test subjects, and from this inquiry he concluded that the stories are comparable to those written by a younger high school student.

In summary, storytelling in the AI tradition involves relatively deep analyses and formalizations of relatively isolated phenomena; the events of the story are actually simulated by the computer program as a model of human reasoning. A more recent example of work in this category is the Brutus.1 system (*8*), which aims at an algorithmic formalization of betrayal and produces stories around this notion. In all these AI approaches, as a result of focusing on a few specific aspects, the range of things a program can talk about is rather limited, and the stories—being produced "from scratch" by simulating the events within the program—typically sound somewhat unnatural. The storytelling systems discussed in the next section approach the topic roughly from the opposite direction.

Interactive Fiction

In the 1980s the so-called computer adventure games became increasingly popular forms of entertainment. Based either solely on text or on mixed text and graphics, these games would present an artificial world to the player, who could interact with the program by issuing simple commands as to where to go next in this world and what to do; the program (i.e., the representation of the artificial world) would react appropriately. In effect, the player was the protagonist of a story to unfold, and how it unfolded was to a good extent determined by the player. These programs have meanwhile improved considerably, and the field of activities is now labeled *interactive fiction* (IF). Interactivity means that in effect every player/reader encounters a different story, depending on the choices made at the various points of interaction—it can be seen as an advanced version of a hypertext system. In contrast to classical AI storytelling, IF emphasizes breadth over depth; a program has an entire "world" to talk about, but mainly the talk is not produced by deep reasoning but by prestored data and chunks of text. Interestingly, though, some more recent work in IF makes contact with AI, as will be outlined at the end of the section.

The enduring popularity of text adventure games has led to the development of special programming languages for creating IF. Gradually these were enriched with pieces of "world knowledge." An advanced language of this kind is TADS (the Text-Adventure Development System), freely available on the Internet. It supplies a range of readily defined object types equiped with some minimal knowledge about their own behavior. For example, container and vehicle objects "know" that objects placed within them will move with them, and that they will be invisible unless the container or vehicle is transparent. TADS offers a hierarchy of object definitions along these lines, which an author developing IF can employ to efficiently build a system without worrying about programming details.

The same motivation led to the development of the "Erasmatron story engine," which is now a product on the market. Moving even further away from programming languages, it provides an authoring environment enabling users to write IF without knowing how to program. Using this system, the author creates a cast of actors and specifies their personality traits, then sets the stage on which the story will take place. Most important, the author has to define a web of actions defining the behaviors encountered in the story. Finally, the system takes over and the "storytelling engine" builds up a story based on the author's presettings. Choice points are calculated, where the reader can influence how the story proceeds, as in any IF system.

A much more ambitious IF-developing system is built in the long-term research project Oz at Carnegie-Mellon University (*9*). The work in this project centers on the two issues of "believable agents" and "interactive drama," and both have been explored in great detail over more than 10 years. The basis of Oz is again a simulated physical world with characters and an interactor. Several complex modules are then in charge of producing "good" fiction. The "drama manager" of Oz is an attempt to overcome the fundamental theoretical problem of IF: the incompatibility between interactivity and drama. A "conventional" story can be dramatic due to the temporal structure imposed by the author, whereas the reader's free choices in IF might very well take the dramatic coherence away from the enterprise (and the notion of "author" becomes increasingly difficult to define).

Oz responds to this problem with a theory of "plot points," the important moments in a story that critically determine the overall course of actions. By isolating the set of possible plot points, the various permutations of the elements of this set is the theoretically possible set of all stories. Most of these will make little sense, though. The drama manager module of Oz (*10*) uses an evaluation function that judges the quality of a particular series of plot points and thus can tell a "good" story from a "bad" one. Story unfolding in Oz then is a process that is on the one hand driven by the user, who can in typical IF manner exercise choices on how to proceed. On the other hand, the drama manager supervises the activities and notices the important plot point transitions that occur. Using the evaluation function, the module determines a good continuation of the story as developed so far, and twists the virtual world in such a way that the events move in a direction toward a targeted subsequent plot point. This may happen by, for example, changing the physical world model, inducing characters to pursue a certain course of action, or adding new characters. Program and user thus effectively collaborate to produce a good story; even though the user is choosing what to do or say, there is a type of "destiny" created by the author of the interactive drama. This destiny is not an exact sequence of actions and events, but is subtly shaped by the supervising drama manager system.

Besides the drama manager, the second major research area pursued in Oz concerns the creation of "believable characters." The idea is that the quality of a story depends to a great extent on the characters acting "natural" or "lifelike." If the deeds or utterances of a character are unmotivated or senseless, the reader of the story will be disappointed, and rightly so. The Oz group has defined the following six requirements for characters to be believable:

- Personality: Characters should have unique and specific features that distinguish them from other characters.
- Emotion: Characters should exhibit emotions and respond to those of others.
- Self-motivation: Besides reacting to changes in the environment, characters ought to pursue their own goals and desires.
- Change: Depending on their personality, characters should change and grow with time.
- Social relationships: Characters should interact with others in accordance with the status of their mutual relationship. Furthermore, this relationship should change over time and in turn prompt differences in interaction.
- Illusion of life: Various basic requirements, such as the capabilities of movement, perception, memory, or language.

The Oz project is a case in point to demonstrate the convergence between IF and AI. More precisely, it is not the classic AI of symbolic reasoning that receives the most attention here, but the more recent branch of "behavioral AI," which emphasizes the importance of interaction between an agent and its environment. According to this research paradigm, the embedding of agents in concrete situations and the need to continuously react and act is a critical aspect of intelligent behavior. This hypothesis is at the heart of research in believable agents. When the system user engages in an interactive story, the characters encountered need to "respond" instantly and sensibly for the whole environment to be convincing. Classic AI, on the other hand, has always focused on trying to mirror rational problem solving by means of developing reasoning capabilities aiming at "correct" results, thus the reliance on formal logic for implementing such systems. Clearly the Oz interest in believable characters is of a different kind; a character behaving "naturally" needs more (or other) capabilities than that of achieving correctness in rational problem solving.

Classic AI is clearly not irrelevant for the IF endeavor, though. The efforts in constructing descriptions of worlds that allow for simulating the actions of characters and their effects on the world have much in common with traditional AI approaches to knowledge representation. For instance, the CYC project (*11*) is a long-term and large-scale research program aimed at modeling human "common sense" as well as the basic laws governing what happens in a world. To this end, the domain of human understanding is broken into very many individual "microtheories" in charge of modeling such everyday notions as ailments, food preparation, communication, and corporate behavior. These theories are represented in formal logic so that programs can make use of the knowledge in order to reason about events.

The relevance of this research to IF is quite obvious; the more open-ended the process of storytelling becomes and the more options there are for the reader to interact with the virtual world, the more world simulation is necessary on the side of the IF system, as it cannot rely on prestored chains of events any more. When the reader triggers an event in the world, the story must take all the effects of this event into account; the world model must be updated appropriately. This requires the kind of "deep" knowledge that the CYC team tries to formalize.

Natural Language Generation

We pointed out above that computer-produced stories such as those by Tale-Spin or Minstrel lack certain "surface linguistic features"—appropriate anaphoric expressions, for example—that would render the texts more readable and natural. These questions are attended to in the research field of natural language generation (NLG); given some abstract, nonlinguistic representation of text content, how can it be mapped to well-formed and moreover good text in natural language? This includes investigating text structure and thematic development from sentence to sentence, making appropriate lexical choices, and selecting suitable referring expressions in the specific context (indefinite versus definite noun phrase, pronoun, ellipsis).

Surprisingly, there is only little contact between NLG and the discipline of computer storytelling. (An exception is the Oz project. See Ref. *12.*) Applications developed by NLG researchers are, for example, the production of reports from input "raw" data (such as weather reports or stock market reports) and the generation of instructional text such as user manuals. Natural language generation systems, if they are designed in a modular fashion, can to a good extent be reused in different applications. To this end, typical text generators consist of the following two independent modules:

- The *text planning* module, which accepts data structures created by some underlying application program and converts these to an abstract linguistic specification
- The *realization* module, which transforms the linguistic specification into a text in a natural language

If the text planner is versatile enough, it can be configured to accept different kinds of input structures from different applications, and if the interface between text planner and realizer is thoroughly defined, different realizers for different natural languages can be used with the same text planner.

It is therefore feasible to employ existing NLG technology for the purposes of storytelling by designing solely the application supplying the input for a text planner, or at least it is possible to employ existing realization modules and build only a story-specific text planner on top. One system demonstrating this versatility is the SPOKESMAN generator (*13*), which has among several other purposes been used for generating narrations about characters trying to accomplish certain goals, quite similar to the scenarios in Tale-Spin or Minstrel. This particular SPOKESMAN environment was called SAGE (*14*), for "simulation and generation environment." Based on a represented model of a house, the program simulates the actions of a cat and a mouse following their particular goals, and simultaneously produces a verbalization of the events. For this purpose, the standard SPOKESMAN modules are employed. The resulting stories, however, are clearly recognizable as being a side effect of a running simulation, as in the following example (*14*): "Fluffy wants to catch a mouse. He is looking for her. The mouse wants to get cheese. She is leaving a mouse-house. She is going toward it. Fluffy is chasing the mouse. He is going toward her. He caught her. The mouse didn't get the cheese."

If some more *text planning* were performed prior to realizing the individual event descriptions, sentences could be conjoined to form a more cohesive text. To this end, NLG builds upon research in *discourse structure* to devise appropriate formal representations of text content. One approach that was quite influential in NLG is "rhetorical structure theory" (*15*), which posits that the structure of a coherent text can be characterized by the facts that adjacent portions of text are always linked by a certain coherence relation (such as condition, purpose, sequence, elaboration), and that assigning these relations applies recursively to yield a tree structure that defines the rhetorical structure of the entire text. Mann and Thompson proposed about twenty relations, defined in terms of the effects their presence has on the reader's cognitive state. Natural language generation researchers in turn formalized these definitions in order to perform text planning—to achieve a higher-level goal (e.g., to persuade the reader to believe something) it is broken up in a series of subgoals that correspond to establishing rhetorical relations.

Following approaches of this kind, it is possible to generate coherent and cohesive text that tries to achieve particular purposes and can be tailored to various kinds of readers to have a maximum effect. For example, the NLG program Pauline (*16*) reports on the result of a fictitious primary election, and it can be parameterized to take a particular perspective toward the results, which include positive or negative evaluations. The parameters are a set of "rhetorical goals" whose values are set by the user of the program. In response, Pauline decides on which information is included in the text and which is left out, how the information is arranged, which words are used, and so on, so that the text is as brief or verbose as desired or conveys evaluative overtones. Given the same underlying "content" (the election result), the program can thus produce appropriate text variants for different purposes, as represented by the parameter settings.

In conclusion, NLG research can be characterized as looking into the fine-grained details of the theoretical groundwork for automatic language production, of which computer storytelling is but one application.

Creativity and Humor Generation

Work in automatic story generation, being generally in its early stages, usually does not make much reference to attempts of actually explaining *creativity*; that is, the human capacity that is generally assumed to be a driving force behind activities such as storytelling. A notable exception is the aforementioned program Minstrel, which was introduced by its creator as embodying a theory of creativity. As explained above, when Minstrel attempts to solve a problem, it searches its memory for an episode representing a solution to a similar problem, and then tries to adapt the earlier solution to the present problem. In effect, it tries to abstract from the specific details of individual problems and to form generalizations over classes of problems exhibiting the same structure. In the view of Turner (*7*), the set of rules characterizing how old problem-solution pairs can be mapped to new problems explains the nature of human creative behavior.

Under the umbrella of AI, there is some other research on the nature of creativity, but this is usually not immediately related to linguistic production. One relatively small research area, however, builds bridges between storytelling and creativity: the study of *humor* and its production, possibly with computational models. Here it is often proposed to see *metaphor* as the link between creativity and humor. Metaphor, in the view of cognitive linguists, is at the very heart of human cognitive ability; it allows us to view one concept through the lens of another, thereby possibly uncovering analogies that were not perceived before. Two diverse situations are related and reconciled—quite similar to what Turner (*7*) had described, even though he didn't explicitly refer to this process as metaphorical. Humor, then, can be explained as a "perversion of an underlying metaphoric mapping." (*17,* p. 121). Both good metaphor and good humor rely on their ability to surprise the reader; metaphor shows that surface dissimilarities might very well conceal deeper conceptual similarities, while humor deliberately misleads the hearer along a path of convention, which then unexpectedly goes astray. The punch line of a joke very often points to an ambiguity that had so far remained in the dark.

Can the processes underlying humor be explained by computational theories and implementations? There are no very convincing joke-telling programs yet, but some initial steps are being taken. The root of some work on "computational humor" is the "script-based semantic theory of humor" developed by Raskin (*18*). It builds upon the notion of script as referenced above (*5*); a representation of a prototypical flow of event, such as the series of steps involved in going to a restaurant, dining, paying, and leaving. According to Raskin, humor originates when a text is compatible with two different scripts, which—importantly—are in some way opposed to one another: normal versus abnormal, real versus unreal, and so on. When being presented with the text, the hearer or reader first activates in the mind only one of these scripts, the more conventionalized one. Only the punch line of the joke triggers recognition of the other script underlying the narration; this late recognition is based on ambiguity or contradiction.

Extensions to this theory were later proposed by Attardo and Raskin (*19*), who proposed six levels of "knowledge resources" needed to characterize a humorous text, which successively move from the linguistic surface to more abstract representations.

1. The text itself
2. The narrative strategy or expository genre underlying the text
3. The target domain of the joke
4. The situation described
5. The logical mechanism underlying the joke (such as figure/ground reversal)
6. The relation of script opposition

Such steps toward uncovering the "mechanics" underlying humorous text suggest the attempt to build computational models, but these have not been elaborated yet. Some initial thoughts on building joke-recognizing and joke-telling computer programs are given in Ref. *20.*

The work of Raskin and Attardo can be seen as an attempt to find a global, all-encompassing theory of humor. What are the general principles responsible for rendering a certain piece of text humorous? This is an ambitious goal, and—not surprisingly—there have so far been no more than preliminary proposals on what a computational system implementing such a theory ought to look like. A different line of research approaches the problem from the opposite end and examines specific *kinds* of humorous texts in great detail so that a computational model can be developed for this limited domain; the hope, then, is that some general model can later be induced from various models of individual humorous genres.

In this way, Binsted and Ritchie (*21*) investigated *riddles*: simple question/answer jokes usually based on some form of pun. The authors give the example: *What do you use to flatten a ghost?—A spirit level.* The regular structure of these jokes prompted Binsted and Ritchie to develop a schema-based approach to producing them automatically. On the basis of a (humor-independent) lexicon and a set of schemas and templates characterizing the structure of (a subclass of) riddles, their program produces word-substitution puns that rely on the phonological identity (homonymy) of distinct words. The schemata encode knowledge about some semantic relationships and about homophones, and the program employs these schemata to construct such riddles as *What do you get when you cross a sheep and a kangaroo?—A woolly jumper.*

In later work Binsted and Ritchie turned to a similar class of jokes, where the punch line is a distorted form of some popular saying (e.g., a proverb; *22*). They developed a model of producing story puns, which is not implemented yet, but it can be quickly summarized as follows. After choosing a maxim as the basis for the joke, the maxim is distorted by a set of rules, and then a representation of the meaning is built up. For actually producing the story, the authors propose developing an evaluation function that can rate how well a story achieves the desired effect (recall the role of evaluation functions in the drama manager of the Oz system), and for creating the candidate stories they hint at the utility of "genetic algorithms," a class of algorithms drawing a loose analogy between computer programming and the Darwinian notion of genetic variation plus natural selection. The idea is that a system would produce stories by starting with a raw version and successively improving it in small steps guided by the evaluation function.

From small-scope studies of the kind just described, Binsted and Ritchie hope to derive ideas about the ingredients of humor in general, and ultimately to build computer models capable of producing a broader range of humorous texts—an endeavor that can be expected to shed some more light on the nature of human creativity.

REFERENCES

1. G. Polti, *The Thirty-Six Dramatic Situations,* J. K. Reeve, Franklin, OH, 1921.
2. D. E. Rumelhart, "Notes on a Schema for Stories," in *Representation and Understanding,* D. G. Bobrow and A. Collins, eds. Academic, New York, 1975, pp. 211–236.
3. R. Wilensky, "Story Grammars versus Story Points," in *Behavioral and Brain Sciences,* vol. 6, 1983, pp. 579–623.
4. J. Meehan, "The Meta-Novel: Writing Stories by Computer," Ph.D. thesis, research report no. 74, Computer Science Department, Yale University, New Haven, CT, 1976.
5. R. C. Schank and R. P. Abelson, *Scripts, Plans, Goals, and Understanding,* Lawrence Erlbaum, Hillsdale, NJ, 1977.
6. J. Meehan, "TALE-SPIN," in *Inside Computer Understanding,* R. C. Schank and C. K. Riesbeck, eds. Lawrence Erlbaum, Hillsdale, NJ, 1981, pp. 197–226.
7. S. R. Turner, *The Creative Process—A Computer Model of Storytelling and Creativity,* Lawrence Erlbaum, Hillsdale, NJ, 1994.
8. S. Bringsjord and D. Ferrucci, *Artificial Intelligence and Literary Creativity,* Lawrence Erlbaum, Hillsdale, NJ.
9. J. Bates, "Virtual Reality, Art, and Entertainment." *Presence J. Teleop. Virt. Env.,* **1**(1), 133–138 (1992).
10. P. Weyhrauch, "Guiding Interactive Drama," Ph.D. thesis, Department of Computer Science, Carnegie Mellon University, technical report CMU-CS-97-109, 1997.
11. D. B. Lenat, "CYC: A Large-Scale Investment in Knowledge Infrastructure." *Commun. ACM,* **38**(11), (1995).
12. M. Kantrowitz and J. Bates, "Natural Language Text Generation in the Oz Interactive Fiction Project," in *Aspects of Automated Natural Language Generation,* R. Dale, E. Hovy, D. Rösner, and O. Stock, eds. Springer-Verlag, Berlin, 1992, pp. 13–28.
13. M. Meteer, "Portable Natural Language Generation using SPOKESMAN," *Proceedings of the 3rd Conference on Applied Natural Language Processing,* Trento, Italy, 1992.
14. M. Meteer, "Generating Event Descriptions with SAGE: A Simulation and Generation Environment," *Proceedings of the 7th International Workshop on Natural Language Generation,* Kennebunkport, ME, 1994, pp. 99–107.
15. W. Mann and S. Thompson, "Rhetorical Structure Theory: Towards a Functional Theory of Text Organization." *TEXT,* **8**, 243–281 (1988).
16. E. H. Hovy, *Generating Natural Language under Pragmatic Constraints,* Lawrence Erlbaum, Hillsdale, NJ, 1988.
17. T. Veale, "No Laughing Matter: The Cognitive Structure of Humor, Metaphor, and Creativity," *Automatic Interpretation and Generation of Verbal Humor* (Proceedings of TWLT 12/IWCH 96, The International Workshop on Computational Humor), J. Hulstin and A. Nijholt, eds. University of Twente, Enschede, Netherlands, 1996.
18. V. Raskin, *Semantic Mechanisms of Humor,* Reidel, Dordrecht, The Netherlands, 1985.
19. S. Attardo and V. Raskin, "Script Theory Revis(it)ed: Joke Similarity and Joke Representation Model." *HUMOR Internat. J. Humor Res.,* **4**(3–4), 293–347 (1991).
20. V. Raskin, "Computer Implementation of the General Theory of Verbal Humor," *Automatic Interpretation and Generation of Verbal Humor* (Proceedings of TWLT 12/IWCH 96, The International Workshop on Computational Humor), J. Hulstin and A. Nijholt, eds. University of Twente, Enschede, Netherlands, 1996.
21. K. Binsted, and G. Ritchie, "An Implemented Model of Punning Riddles," *Proceedings of the Twelfth National Conference on Artificial Intelligence (AAAI-94),* Seattle, 1994.
22. K. Binsted and G. Ritchie, "Speculations on Story Puns," *Automatic Interpretation and Generation of Verbal Humor* (Proceedings of TWLT 12/IWCH 96, The International Workshop on Computational Humor), J. Hulstin and A. Nijholt, eds. University of Twente, Enschede, Netherlands, 1996.

Manfred Stede

COMPUTER-SUPPORTED COOPERATIVE WORK

Introduction

Computer-supported cooperative work (CSCW) represents a change of perspective in the way we view computers, networks, and the opportunities they represent for people and their work. While the dominating technology-centered view has slowly been challenged by the view of *human-machine interaction,* CSCW introduces *human-human* interaction as the primary focus. In this view the computer is viewed as a tool or a medium that facilitates communication and collaboration among humans rather than acting as a technological computation device.

A number of factors contributed to this change of focus. A first prerequisite factor is the ready availability of computing devices and the extension of these computers as a personal tool to the group. A second prerequisite is the growth of pervasive networking that enables widespread computer-based communication between people and their information appliances. Another factor that spurred the emergence of CSCW is the merging of telecommunications and computing, as network providers seek new applications to exploit bandwidth and widen their service spectrum. Telecommuting, telepresence, mobile offices, and working at a distance further motivated the emergence of CSCW and the concepts connected to it.

Before defining *computer-supported cooperative work* we need to clarify a number of terms and issues in the name that may be misleading. As Greenberg (*1*) notes, CSCW often includes technologies other than computers. Video, cameras, displays, telecommunications devices, and other devices form the hardware components of CSCW systems in addition to computers. Further, CSCW need not be supportive. Often technology and applications can be disruptive to the individual's work or the organizational context. Computer-supported cooperative work technologies are not limited to the concept of "work" in the strict economic sense; they can assist casual and social interactions for learning, discovery, or pleasure as well.

Cooperation in this context is a particularly sensitive keyword. Computer-supported cooperative work systems may at times foster competition rather than cooperation. Systems that support negotiation between groups are examples of CSCW systems that are employed in such competitive situations.

Another source of confusion is the meaning of the word cooperation or cooperative work as contrasted with the terms *collaboration, collective work,* and *coordination.* All these "cowords" apply to group situations and the work context. The distinction between them is not very well established in the CSCW community. According to Sørgaard (*2*), a specific set of criteria (nonhierarchical, autonomous, etc.) must apply for work to be called cooperative. At the core of this view of work is the notion of interdependence between individuals in their work. For many researchers there is a connotation to the term cooperative that assumes compliance, shared sentiments, and so forth. Collective work, on the other hand, is seen by many as a more general term for a group's working in a social context that is not as narrow as the above definition of cooperation calls for.

Coordination often refers to the arrangements of individual tasks according to a number of constraints, such as time or resources, while collaboration often connotes the close interaction of two individuals. Over the last few years the term collaborative work in the context of CSCW has come to mean any type of work that involves more than one individual.

Definitions and Taxonomies

The term computer-supported cooperative work was first used by Greiff and Cashman in 1984 (*3*). It was the title of an interdisciplinary workshop on how to support groups of people in their work arrangements with computers. Since then CSCW has come to mean the large field that is concerned with computer-assisted activity that is carried out by a number of collaborating individuals. While the term CSCW was felt by many to be unwieldy and ill-defined, it has not disappeared but stuck to a field whose boundaries are still unclear. It has become an umbrella term under which people from many disciplines can discuss aspects of system design and use by more than one user.

Bannon and Schmidt (*4*) define CSCW as *"an endeavor to understand the nature and characteristics of cooperative work with the objective of designing adequate computer-based technologies,"* while Suchman (*5*) defines it as *"the design of computer-based technologies with explicit concern for the socially organized practices of their intended users."* From this discussion it should have become clear that CSCW is still an evolving field that covers a wide spectrum, ranging from social and organizational research to the development and deployment of computer-based technologies. Recently the special interest group for organizational information systems (ACM SIGOIS) focused on CSCW, reflected in its mission statement.

Computer-supported cooperative work is often used synonymously with the term *groupware.* That term was originally coined by Peter and Trudy Johnson-Lenz (*6*) to mean *"intentional group processes and procedures to achieve specific purposes plus software tools designed to support and facilitate the group's work."* Generally the CSCW community has adopted a slightly different view. Computer-supported cooperative work is viewed as the overall scope of research, development, implementation, deployment, evaluation, and so on, while groupware is viewed as the technology that supports group work. Dyson (*7*) notes that *"groupware is about as useful a term as singleware."* She goes on to state: *"More than a way of coding or building applications, groupware is a way to define, structure, and link applications, data and the people who use them."* Ellis, Gibbs, and Rein (*8*) emphasize the task and goal aspect of groupware: *"computer-based systems that support groups of people engaged in a common task (goal) and that provide an interface to a shared environment."* This goal-focused view of task interaction is augmented by Lynch, Snyder, and Vogel (*9*): *"Groupware is distinguished from normal software by the basic assumption it makes: groupware makes the user aware that he is part of a group, while most other software seeks to hide and protect users from each other... Groupware... is software that accentuates the multiple user environment, coordinating and orchestrating things so that users can 'see' each other, yet do not conflict with each other."* Finally, Malone (cited in *10*) defines groupware as *"information technology used to help people work together more effectively."* Groupware is thus the combination of multiuser software and hardware that supports the activities of more than one person in order to accomplish a task.

In addition to the terms CSCW and groupware a number of related concepts are often used. We frequently find the terms *workgroup computing* or *team computing.* This term arose to particularly denote the extension of personal computers to small groups. The focus here is the size of the group. Workgroup computing is directed at a closely knit set of individuals working together. This small group (four to twelve people) is frequently referred to as a *team,* thus the term team computing. This distinction makes sense when it is contrasted with applications that are written to be used enterprisewide (many hundreds of users) or even for the Internet (thousands of users).

Extending the size of the group turns workgroup computing into *organizational computing,* which spans a wide variety of settings from domains as diverse as business, hospital administration, professional organizations, or the military. Organizational computing is often used by researchers who are concerned with the impacts of computer and communication technology on organizational design, operations, and performance.

Collaborative Computing is a term used to cover research in CSCW and computer-mediated communications. People in this field particularly emphasize the development of computer and communication technologies to support group work. In this sense it is rather close to groupware, since the design of cooperative systems and group support technology is a central theme in collaborative computing. Topics in collaborative computing cover groupware architectures and environments, the theoretical basis of collaborative systems, models of collaboration, evaluations of and experiences with collaborative systems, the relationship between collaborative systems, user interface tools and techniques for collaboration, and the use of multimedia technologies for collaboration.

Computer-supported cooperative work as a multidisciplinary field had input from many different sources. Among the major origins are computer and information science, sociology, organizational design, and human-computer interaction. Each one of these fields maintains a special interest or flavor in CSCW. Organizational design is often associated with organizational computing, while computer and information science is close to collaborative computing. Arising from the tradition of human-computer interaction and user-interface design we find a niche in CSCW that is concerned with multiuser interfaces. This work approaches CSCW from the system's component that connects the user to the application. The multiuser interface explicitly acknowledges that the interface and the application(s) behind it are shared by a number of users. This requirement imposes a number of design constraints and demands on the interface. The accommodation of multiple pointing devices and the questions of what to show to all the users and how often to update their displays are issues that arise from this perspective.

To organize and systematize the various views and systems that have arisen in CSCW, Johansen (*11*) developed a widely used 2-by-2 matrix (Fig. 1). This matrix uses *time* and *space* as the two major dimensions to differentiate between systems and applications. Each dimension has two values, which are *"same"* and *"different."*

		Space	
		Colocated	Distributed
Time	Synchronous	Electronic classroom Interact. liveboards Whiteboarding Workstations	Video Desktop Large screen Whiteboarding Content sharing Telepresence
	Asynchronous		Discussion Boards Case annotation Email Struct. Discussion

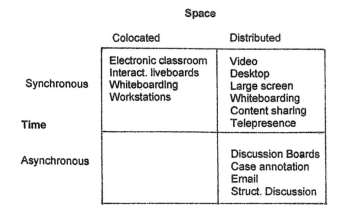

FIGURE 1. *Time/space matrix for CSCW.*

According to this simple classification, activities can happen in the same space or in different spaces, or activities could happen at the same time or at different times. Group members can collaborate at the same time or work whenever they please. The team can meet in a conference room, or the team could be located in offices on different floors, or even in different buildings spread over the country or the face of the earth. Usually the terms synchronous and asynchronous are used to denote same-time versus different-time activities. On the space dimension the terms colocated and distributed are used to indicate same space versus different space. The cell representing colocated and asynchronous settings is frequently left blank since it is easily subsumed by the more powerful asynchronous and distributed cell. Once the time constraint is relaxed, it is no longer necessary to return to the same space. Even though examples for this type of work exist (shift work, war rooms), none of them features prominently in CSCW.

This basic taxonomy is easily extended. First, the space dimension can be seen as *group proximity.* The values on this dimension then become *multiple individual sites, one group site,* and *multiple group sites.* This classification was developed in particular for electronic meeting rooms by Nunamaker et al. (*12*).

A further extension can be created by adding group size as a third dimension. Usually small groups or project teams of three to seven members are distinguished from larger task forces (greater than seven). In the business world it makes sense to distinguish between groups or teams, departments, divisions, units, and the whole enterprise or organization. Outside the business context different ways have been developed to categorize groups based on the number of members and the basis for the groups foundation. Research by McGrath (*13*) has led to the following enumeration of social aggregations:

- Artificial aggregations: statistical group or social category
- Unorganized aggregates: audience, crowd, public
- Units with patterned relationships: culture, subculture, kinship group

- Structured social units: society, community, family
- Deliberately designed social unit: organization, suborganization, crew, project group, team
- Less deliberately designed social unit: association, peer group, circle of friends

Another important dimension along which CSCW and groupware can be categorized are the varying application domains. A meeting system used in education will differ from a meeting system used in a business context. Engineering tasks usually require different tools from administrative tasks. The following list of task and application domains can only serve as a first attempt and needs to be augmented as new systems are built and applied to an ever-growing set of domains:

- Engineering
- Administration
- Manufacturing
- Research and development
- Banking and insurance
- Logistics and warehousing
- Decision making
- Teaching and learning
- Authoring
- Drafting
- Entertainment
- Software engineering
- Project management
- Military planning and operations

Social, Behavioral, and Organizational Foundations

Computer-supported cooperative work often starts by studying groups at work. Sociologists, social psychologists, and anthropologists (in particular ethnographers), have contributed a large amount of CSCW studies that lead to a number of surprising results regarding the reasons for success and failure of systems. This work has also led to a refinement of tools and methods that were borrowed from the originating disciplines.

Among the technologists in CSCW a development could be observed that had happened earlier in the human-computer interaction community. Technologists as tool builders looked to the social sciences, expecting a set of prescriptive rules or guidelines. Social sciences for the most part are not design sciences. Social sciences do not intend to create; their focus is descriptive, analyzing and describing social, organizational, and behavioral phenomena. The CSCW community, just like the HCI community, has spent and is still spending some energy at reconciling this difference in approach. As new teams of product developers or researchers form, this question is often confronted in the form of *interdisciplinary* versus *multidisciplinary* research.

McGrath (*13*) offers a framework for the study of groups that focuses on the relations between group dynamics and the elements that influence it.

- The properties of individuals
- The relationships among individuals as members of the group (i.e., the group's structure)

- The properties of the environment in which the group functions
- The task or situation to be carried out by the group
- The "behavior setting," which he defines as the fit between the group's structure and task

In addition, McGrath has included time, interaction, and performance into his theory of groups. Criticizing most of the existing work on groups because of the ad hoc or artificial laboratory conditions under which the data had been collected, he proposes three functional classes of group behavior: (1) production of instrumental results, (2) member support within the group, and (3) group well-being. These functional classes can be matched with four operational modes of the group: (1) inception, (2) problem solving, (3) conflict resolution, and (4) execution.

From the organizational side, Mintzberg (*14*) makes a major contribution to CSCW. He first distinguished five major parts of an organization: (1) the operating core, (2) the strategic apex, (3) the middle line, (4) the technostructure, and (5) the support staff. The operating core comprises the workers or professionals who are mainly concerned with creating the product or service the organization sells. The strategic apex is usually equated with the CEO and the board of directors or other such positions, while the middle line consists of middle management. The technostructure includes the specialists who design and redesign the process in the organization and the way the company does business. The support staff comprises all those specialists who provide support to the organization outside its operating workflow. Certain coordination and cooperation strategies come about as one of these five organizational elements dominates. These strategies are as follows:

- Direct supervision. A supervisor gives direct orders to work, thus coordinating the work of many workers.
- Standardization of work processes. The general work procedure is designed in such a way that the execution of an activity is always done in the same way.
- Standardization of outputs. Coordination is accomplished not by specifying how to do the work but by what needs to be produced. One person's output becomes another person's input.
- Standardization of skills. The workers are trained in a standardized way so that they coordinate automatically with others.
- Mutual adjustment. People communicate informally among themselves to coordinate the ongoing work processes and results.

Mintzberg summarizes the relationship between organizational units, coordination strategies, and types of organization in the following table.

Organizational type	Coordination strategy	Dominating unit
Simple structure	Direct supervision	Strategic apex
Machine bureaucracy	Standardization of work	Technostructure
Professional bureaucracy	Standardization of skills	Operating core
Divisionalized form	Standardization of outputs	Middle line
Ad-hocracy	Mutual adjustment	Staff and core

Another framework for analyzing CSCW settings from organizational science is Leavitt's diamond (*15*).

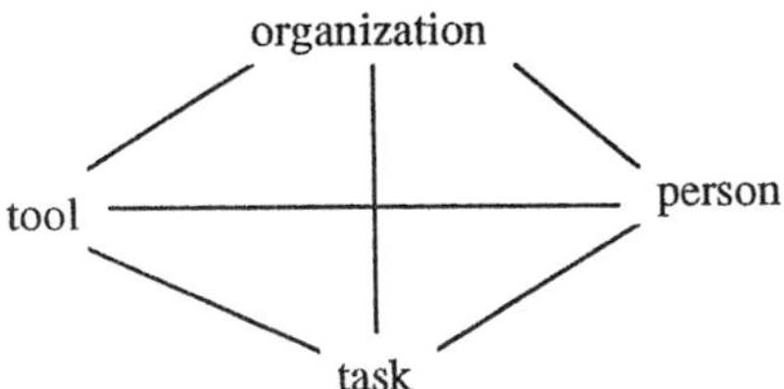

Each dyadic relationship can be analyzed and interpreted. The relationship between person and organization will deal with issues or organizational design and human resources. The triangle between person, tool, and tasks provides a framework to analyze the processes and the quality of systems a person uses in order to do his or her work. Other dyads and triads can be constructed in the same way.

Prerequisite Enabling Technologies

In order to build, deploy, and use groupware, a number of enabling technologies must be in place. Most of these technologies are covered in more detail elsewhere. This section provides a short overview of the prerequisite technologies for groupware and the major concepts that effect the design and implementation of CSCW systems.

Among the most important technologies for CSCW systems are the following:

- Networks
- Connectivity
- Naming and name spaces
- Mail and other communication protocols
- Multimedia technologies
- Hypertext and hypermedia
- Video technologies
- Cross-platform development tools
- Large bit-mapped displays

This list is by no means complete; it merely covers some of the more important enabling technologies that contribute to groupware and CSCW systems in the mid-1990s.

Usually groupware systems require on the basic technological level a reliable and responsive high-bandwidth communications network, the management of sessions over time and distance, a persistent user interface for the user group, and a replicated, interlinked repository of multimedia information.

From the groupware perspective, networks are concerned with the circuit-switching and packet-switching aspects of electronic data transfer. Integrated services digital network (ISDN) in particular, has seen a renaissance, because of its potential for groupware. Integrated services digital network's ability to provide a unified transmission for digital, voice, and video data has made it a prime candidate for the commercial expansion of groupware. Another important cornerstone in the networks area of

CSCW is the open systems interconnection (OSI) reference model, which builds the foundation for many modern networks. This model also addresses the increasingly important issue of network security.

Among the earliest and most basic (groupware) services provided by networks are electronic mail and file sharing. Making data available to other users in this way is a fundamental prerequisite for collaborative work. A networked file system needs to provide the illusion of a uniform central file system. It needs to contain a programming library independent of any particular windowing system, and it needs to support a very large scale, multimedia mail and bulletin board system. A good example for research in this direction is the Andrew file system (*16*). Andrew addresses such complex issues as the need for a distributed file system to cope with scalability and security, database operations as background tasks, unanticipated group work patterns, and caching to reduce contention on centralized resources to make data available as well as transparent.

In supporting group communication, common problems are the growing number of message-handling systems and the need to distribute the message directory system. When focusing on asynchronous communication a number of issues must be resolved, including: (1) the storage and management of message objects, (2) the structuring of information to match the structure of the organization, (3) the management of a distributed message repository, and (4) a database to provide information on the organization itself. Such issues go beyond the X.400 Mail standard. Among other things, roles, message objects, functions, and rules must be defined to accomplish groupware-specific E-mail support.

Multimedia technologies are another cornerstone for groupware systems. The incorporation of images, movies, sounds, and animation allows groups to work with a variety of objects that best represent the entities encountered in their daily work. Multimedia also allows communication in a variety of modes, ranging from asynchronous typed messages, over typed synchronous dialogs (UNIX talk), to videomail and videoconferencing.

Hypermedia are an extension to hypertext. Hypertext allows the linking of words and text blocks in and between documents. Hypermedia extends this idea of linking text blocks to multimedia. Text can be linked to images, videos point to animation, and sound recordings point to explanatory text paragraphs. The joint construction of such hypermedia spaces is an active research and development topic in the groupware community.

User Interface Foundations for Groupware

End users are rarely interested in the underlying technologies or theories of a system. End users need to accomplish work tasks. The aspect of the system that users come in contact with is the user interface. For an end user, the user interface *is* the system. If information can not be accessed through the interface, it does not exist for the end user, even though it may be stored in the system. If a certain action is not represented on the interface, users will not be able to let the system perform it, even though the system may be perfectly capable of doing so.

Conceptually, the user interface maps a set of motor behavior of the users to instrumental functions of the system. This is accomplished through keyboards, mice, moles, data gloves, voice recognition, gesture recognition, whiteboards, and so on. The interface also maps system outputs to a variety of displays. To make interfaces for groups of users in CSCW settings effective, the cognitive models and metaphors that guide interface construction must be carefully chosen.

For "singleware," task-oriented metaphors and models were often sufficient. Examples are the typewriter metaphor for word processing or the spreadsheet metaphor for financial calculations. For groupware, more powerful mataphors and models must be found to express the interaction and task relationships that exist between group members. To accomplish this, groupware employs a combination of techniques and technologies.

- Shared resources (file servers, mail servers, print servers)
- Networked workstations and personal computers
- High-bandwidth networks (FDDI, ISDN)
- Projection devices (LiveBoard, SmartBoard)
- Advanced input devices (microphones, cameras, digitizers)

One of the most powerful metaphors developed during the last decade for user interfaces is the desktop metaphor (*17*). Here the computer screen represents an office desk. On this desk the user finds familiar objects, such as folders, documents, in boxes, out boxes, and writing tools. The resulting interface supports direct manipulation of these objects in small, incremental steps. These steps lead to the final user task goal. All steps are easily reversible to allow for correction. Pioneering research on this metaphor was done by the Xerox Star system. This system is most often known for its user interface in single-user environments, but the Star system also pioneered concepts for electronic communication within workgroups.

Since the desktop metaphor worked well for single users, many researchers tried to expand upon it for groupware. The first step in that direction was the *rooms metaphor.* Objects that are related to a common task can be organized into a specific "room." These objects include information sources, such as documents or databases and tools the users need to operate upon them. This virtual room is shared by all the people working on that task. Certain areas of the room can be made accessible to all group members, while other areas can be restricted to subsets of people. In this fashion users can collaborate on a variety of tasks, such as authoring a paper together, drafting the blueprints for an airplane, or learning about anatomy.

With the advent of videoconferencing on LANs, the rooms metaphor evolved into the *office-building* metaphor. This metaphor can be used in two ways. Either virtual rooms can be grouped to form a virtual office, in which users are able to tailor and modify their system environment at all levels, from global parameters such as colors and spacing to minute details concerning individual applications. Here users may be in a room in the office building by themselves and a minute later they may be joined by a colleague. Small groups can readily form, reform, and disband themselves.

The other way this metaphor is used is to represent the actual layout of the office building and show photos (thumbnail views) of coworkers in their spaces. Video contact can now be initiated by cruising the virtual hallways and knocking on colleague's virtual doors.

Different applications call for different metaphors. Specializations of the above can be easily accomplished. The interface must always suit the group, the task, and the technology available.

Application Classes

Reviewing the current CSCW and groupware landscape a number of application classes can be discerned. The section will review these application classes according to the taxonomy given in Fig. 1.

SYNCHRONOUS/COLOCATED APPLICATIONS

To support teams in negotiating, making decisions, brainstorming, learning, and other activities, a number of systems have been built that can support a group in a meeting room. Examples of such *electronic meeting rooms* are the *Capture Lab* at Electronic Data Systems, the *Electronic Meeting Systems* (*EMS*) at the University of Arizona, a commercial system by IBM, and the CoLab at Xerox PARC. These systems usually consist of a room with special furniture that can be rearranged. The furniture is also designed in such a way that the monitor recedes under the surface of the desk. Users view the monitor through a glass surface on the desk, thus having an unobstructed view of other participants. The tables either form a circle or a semicircle. Sometimes a large bit-mapped device is used instead of the whiteboard or chalkboard. All devices are connected by a LAN. Special software can be written to take advantage of this configuration. Figure 2 shows a sample setup.

The motivation to create such meeting rooms is rather obvious. People experience media such as overheads and flip carts as influencing a meeting in terms of the way

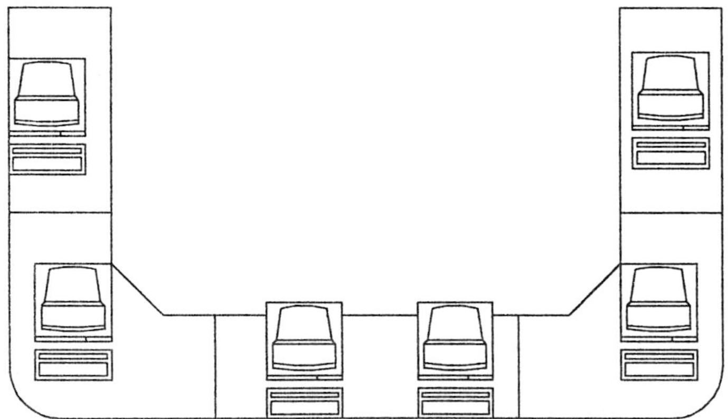

FIGURE 2. *Generic electronic meeting room setup.*

FIGURE 3. *Two videoconferencing rooms.*

people communicate and how well they remember what was said. This influence is to a large degree subconscious, however.

We can classify meetings along their functional dimension: exploration, information sharing, brainstorming, problem solving, decision making, morale building, negotiating, planning, or social structuring. This diversity creates a wide range of design issues concerning the layout of the room, the capability of the software, the performance of the hardware, the selection of user interfaces, and many others.

SYNCHRONOUS/DISTRIBUTED APPLICATIONS

Some meetings cannot be held in the same room. The first step toward distributed support of meetings is the linking of two or more electronic meeting rooms. The ISU H.320 standard for videoconferencing permits building systems that broadcast the image from one meeting room to another. Such systems have cameras that take in views of all participants or focus in on individuals. The camera can be locally or remotely controlled. Figure 3 shows such a setup.

Usually the two rooms also have a document camera that permits sharing documents in addition to viewing participants in the other room.

Removing the constraint of having to go to a special room makes videoconferencing even more comfortable. This type of groupware is referred to as desktop videoconferencing. This arrangement places the camera and the monitor on the person's desk. A number of commercial systems are readily available (Intel ProShare, NT Visit, etc.). Research systems include MMConf (*18*) and Bill Buxton's Hydra units (*19*). Desktop videoconferencing is often augmented by whiteboarding, which allows conference participants to share one or more windows. Users can use different colored pointers or markers to create sketches or notes in electronic ink on a shared space.

This type of whiteboarding is different from document conferencing where the users do not use electronic ink but actually share the same application at the same time. A group of users may share a spreadsheet, for instance. As the users type into the cells of the spreadsheet, other cells that depend on this cell change their values. This is not possible with mere whiteboarding. The final document needs to be saved on one of the user's machines and can then be shared via the file system.

An important issue in designing synchronous software is the question of who sees what and when they see it. One of the most common strategies is called *WYSIWIS (what you see is what I see),* coined after the well-known WYSIWYG strategy developed in human-computer interaction.

Buxton's (*19*) idea of telepresence as established in the HYDRA units carries the idea of videoconferencing an important step forward. Telepresence builds on the idea of media spaces to link participants in a meeting, overcoming the barriers of physical separation. A media space that facilitates telepresence is a computer-controlled teleconferencing or videoconferencing system in which audio, video, and document conferencing form an integrated gestalt. Telepresence in particular is the use of technology to establish a sense of shared presence or a shared space among geographically distributed members of a group.

ASYNCHRONOUS APPLICATIONS

Asynchronous applications subsume those that happen in the same and at different places. Once the time constraint has been lifted, location is no longer an issue. Among the most successful systems in this category are E-mail and the IBM product Lotus Notes, which will be described in more detail later. Asynchronous groupware as a category is by far the one in which most systems—research and commercial—do cluster. Because of the diversity of applications in this group, the following subcategorization will be used: E-mail and bulletin board systems, structured messaging and workflow systems, and knowledge management and collaborative hypertext. E-mail usually starts as a substitute for letter mail. Messages go from one person to another or to a small distribution list. Messages that go to a large distribution list that shares common interests are usually handled by an electronic bulletin board system (also known as conferencing systems). Many of these have sprung up on privately owned machines that are accessible via modem dial-in.

Structured messaging systems were introduced to cope with the flood of E-mail messages, which can easily be generated. These systems represent an attempt to provide users with better methods for filtering, organizing, and managing their incoming E-mail. Adding rules and techniques from artificial intelligence to such structured E-mail systems allows the delegation of this task to so-called E-mail agents. When structured messaging is taken further, it starts to represent the movement of electronic forms. Forms are central to many organizations concerned with administrative tasks. Prescribing and defining the path of an electronic form (e-form) through an organization is the basis for the simplest form of workflow automation system. More advanced workflow systems also employ agents and sophisticated knowledge bases to handle many different processes—to the extent of being able to cope with a number of exceptions to the process.

Some applications focus on the content of documents rather than on the communication aspects. Such systems are shared document bases or collaborative hypermedia systems, and often provide the basis for collecting the design and decision history for products and services in an organization. They become the organizational policy handbook or the organizational memory. In this capacity, such systems form an integral part of knowledge management efforts, which deal with the intellectual capital of organizations at all levels.

ELECTRONIC MAIL AND BULLETIN BOARDS/CONFERENCING

E-mail is one of the most successful and pervasive groupware applications to data. As a basic service it quickly follows the introduction of LANs or WANs. When the technical issues of access, naming, transport, and interface have been resolved, a number of key characteristics of E-mail can be observed, including the following:

- E-mail is asynchronous.
- E-mail is fast.
- E-mail is text-based (but multimedia mail is on the way).
- E-mail can be addressed to multiple receivers.
- E-mail has built-in external memory.
- This eternal memory can be processed by the computer.

E-mail has created a number of studies that try to identify the effects of the medium on the content and quality of the message (*20*). Among the findings are the following:

- The perceived threat to middle management because the user's ability to cross-communicate easily in organizations transcends departmental boundaries
- The loss of form and politeness, which shows in a disrespect for other users (flaming), seeing the message as an impersonal entity
- The development of netiquette and other measures to counter the tendency for flaming and inappropriate behavior on the Internet
- Increasing personal connections in close work groups because of ready availability of other users.

Since E-mail can as easily be addressed to multiple recipients as well as a single recipient, the same technology provides the basis for bulletin boards. Bulletin board systems allow users to post messages to the system and develop threads of discussions that focus on varying topics. Depending on the system, users can view the discussion by thread, user name, date, status of the message, and so on. IBM's Lotus Notes system in its simplest form can be used as a conferencing system.

The introduction of E-mail and conferencing systems very often has profound effects on the structure of the organization and the work performed. While *first-level effects* of technology, such as planned increases in efficiency or productivity gains, are desired by management and foreseeable, *second-level effects* often are not. Second-level effects enable people to do things that go beyond the old technology that is being replaced, but these effects also include unplanned side effects. An example is the automobile, which was invented to make transportation faster and more comfortable (first-level effects), yet also led to the sprawl of suburbs around many cities (second-level effect), which could not have sprung up with a less convenient transportation system. Suburbs, though, were not a planned goal of introducing the automobile to society, and became a *second-level system* effect.

STRUCTURED MESSAGING AND WORKFLOW

Communication is central to CSCW. The growth of electronic messaging and conferencing quickly led to the realization that tools are needed to manage the avalanche of information descending on users. The features of such tools include the abilities to *filter, structure,* and *route* messages. In order to take this burden of the user and handle it (semi-) automatically, systems need to be able to discern from and/or content of the communication. The simplest way to accomplish this is by allowing only the exchange of predefined set of message types. Usually these message types are represented as *forms* or *structured messages* in the system. Incoming messages can thus easily be recognized and analyzed according to their fields.

Malone et al. (*21*) presented Information Lens as an environment for the intelligent management of a large volume of E-mail messages. Information Lens uses the concept of semistructured messages to combine the benefits of rigid, form-based communication with the flexibility of unconstrained E-mail. Users could define new message types if desired or needed. This raised the question of a best or minimal set of message types and how to avoid forms that overlap largely in meaning or that are overspecialized. Information Lens also allowed users to create rules (if-then) that would act as semiintelligent agents on incoming messages, depending on the values in certain fields of the message. Information Lens was applied to a number of domains, including conferencing, calendar management, project management, and engineering change notices.

A number of commercial systems exist that allow the filtering, storing, and structuring of E-mail messages. IBM's *Lotus Notes* system incorporates E-mail, conferencing, document sharing, and many other functions that form a complete groupware environment. *Notes* gives users folders and allows for the creation of rules. Novell's *GroupWise* integrates E-mail, multimedia mail, and calendaring, allowing users to connect E-mail messages into their personal calendars. Microsoft's collaboration environment, *Exchange,* is the third major commercial offering in this category.

This concept was first explored in Coordinator (*22*). Coordinator was based on speech act theory, which postulates that all acts of human speech fit a small finite set of *speech acts.* Examples for such speech acts are: *propose, reject, accept, counterpropose,* and *inform.* Coordinator adhered strictly to this theory, allowing only a limited set of speech acts in response to an incoming one (e.g., only *accept, reject,* and *counterpropose* are choices to respond to *propose*). Coordinator had been deployed in a number of organizations with varying success. Those organizations that kept using it were reported to have succumbed to the system and using speech act terminology even in the cafeteria.

Moving the concept of structured messages even further leads us to the field of workflow. Workflow facilitated by electronic forms traveling along predetermined paths is the simplest form of workflow. Workflow systems try to move work from one person to the next in an organization. Most workflow systems are LAN-based, using a central server to keep track of the state of the workflow. Such systems require process engineers to define all the processes in the organization and create workflow maps for these processes. Such maps resemble flowcharts in that they are mostly sequential steps of operations and decision points as to which branch to follow. More advanced workflow systems (*23*) employ agent technologies.

COLLABORATIVE HYPERTEXT AND KNOWLEDGE MANAGEMENT

Hypertext and hypermedia technology provide the basis for a large number of asynchronous CSCW applications. Being able to link pieces of text or media together in a very flexible fashion provides multiple contributors to create document bases (commercial products: Lotus Notes, Fulcrum, DocsOpen, etc.) that need not adhere to a single structure but present themselves in many different structures at the same time. This flexibility makes hypertext systems ideal for *collaborative authoring* and *collaborative learning.* It allows the creation of collective memories, which in turn are the first step toward the capture of intellectual capital for the management of an organization's knowledge.

An *organizational memory* needs to capture documents and artifacts that represent the expertise of an organization, as well as the processes and decisions that represent the life of that organization. Conklin (*24*) argues that organizational memory systems must be ready to easily capture, recall, and learn organizational expertise. In addition to hypertext as a technological foundation and groupware as a sociological enabler, Conklin argues that organizational memory systems require a rhetorical method. He suggests *IBIS* (*issue-based information system*) for this purpose, which allows structured discussion based on issues and the pro and con arguments participants submit. In addition, a shift in organizational culture is required. The organization needs to appreciate processes as well as artifacts. Organizational memories must be constantly updated to not fall into disrepair or become less useful. The best way to do this is to create an *evergreen process* that continually adds and renews the organizational memory. To keep this evergreen process alive, tending to the organizational memory should not be an additional duty of the workers, but should preferably happen as a side effect of the core work that knowledge workers perform anyhow.

Deployment and Development Issues

Evaluating groupware has always been a challenge, since the software changes its own playing field. A number of studies have been cited in the section on social and behavioral foundations. Jonathan Grudin (*25*) summarizes the lessons learned during development and deployment as follows:

- Disparity in work and benefit. Groupware applications often require additional work from individuals who do not perceive a direct benefit from the use of the application.
- Critical mass dilemma. Groupware may not enlist the "critical mass" of users required to be useful, or can fail because it is never to any one individual's advantage to use it.
- Disruption of social processes. Groupware can lead to activity that violates social taboos, threatens existing political structures, or otherwise demotivates users crucial to its success.
- Exception handling. Groupware may not accommodate the wide range of exception handling and improvisation that characterizes much group activity.
- Unobtrusive accessibility. Features that support group processes are used relatively infrequently, requiring unobtrusive accessibility and integration with more heavily used features.
- Difficulty of evaluation. The almost insurmountable obstacles to meaningful, generalizable analysis and evaluation of groupware prevent us from learning from experience.
- Failure of intuition. Intuitions in product development environments are especially poor

for multiuser applications, resulting in bad management decisions and an error-prone design process.

- The adoption process. Groupware requires more careful implementation (introduction, deployment) in the workplace than the product developers have confronted.

Selected Research Topics

The design of user interfaces to groupware remains a challenge. New designs need to mirror the expanding bandwidth of human-computer dialogs. The high innovation rate in hardware and network services will continue to provide stimulation for innovation in this area. Thin LCDs, color displays, and 3D display devices sketch a possible direction on the output end of the user interface. Data gloves, gesture recognition, and voice recognition do the same for the input end. The further development of agent-based technologies allows a whole new dimension of interfaces, possibly based on an *assistant* metaphor.

The growth of the Internet has also prompted CSCW researchers to consider this powerful medium for the use of groupware. Some people may actually argue that the World Wide Web is a large shared document system and therefore one of the largest groupware applications in existence. A challenge in bringing groupware and CSCW to the Internet and related intranets is the missing ability to collaborate synchronously. CU-SeeMe is a first step in bringing video to the Internet. InternetPhone does the same for telephony. Still, chat rooms and whiteboarding are beyond the capabilities of the Internet.

The integration of video and voice with text during a synchronous conference is another research challenge. While conferencing and editing systems are available that can be used at the same time via the same interface (e.g., POLIKOM), the integration of the spoken word with text documents is not readily accomplished. Scribes must be designated during videoconferences to take notes and capture the content flow of the meeting.

With radio LANs spreading and "road warriors" being equipped with "mobile offices," new challenges will arise for CSCW. One of the most successful products in this category, Lotus Notes, clearly solves one of the most pressing problems in mobile computing: version control between different users. Lotus Notes accomplishes that via an elaborate replication mechanism. As the mobile office grows, users will ask for more services and more convenience, which will have to be translated into advanced groupware functionality.

Further Reading

Computer-supported cooperative work and groupware are extensively covered by a number of conferences and journals. These serve both the research and academic community as well as the business and end-user communities. The largest academic conference on CSCW is the ACM conference by the same name, which is usually held in even years. A sister conference exists in Europe, called European CSCW or

ECSCW, in odd years. The technical and groupware aspects of CSCW are largely covered by the ACM's Conference on Organizational Computing Systems (COOCS), which is also held in odd years. A commercial conference, *Groupware,* is held yearly on the East Coast and the West Coast of the United States, and in at least one European city. The ACM conferences are sponsored by the Special Interest Group on Organizational Information Systems (SIGOIS, soon to be the Special Interest Group on Groupware, SIGGroup) and the Special Interest Group on Computer Human Interaction (SIGCHI). The IEEE Task Group on Office Automation also sponsors COOCS.

The trade press frequently covers topics that are relevant to CSCW and groupware. *BYTE* magazine and *PC-World* frequently publish hardware and software reviews concerning such issues as desktop videoconferencing, E-mail, calendaring systems, or collaborative learning. Special trade magazines exist for multimedia, presentation technology, and other special aspects of groupware. *Virtual Workgroups,* a magazine for electronic collaboration published by BCR Enterprises in New York, has emerged with a wider scope on commercial applications of groupware.

Scholarly journals exist that are dedicated to certain aspects of CSCW. *CSCW-International Journal* is a European publication by Kluwer Academic Publishers and provides an interdisciplinary forum for the debate and exchange of ideas concerning theoretical, practical, and social issues in CSCW. Most of the articles published in CSCW-IJ deal with social, anthropological, or behavioral studies of groupwork and groupware. The now defunct journal *Collaborative Computing* offered a voice to the technical aspects of groupware, publishing articles on the design and architecture of systems. The *Journal of Organizational Computing* focuses on the business and organizational aspects of CSCW.

REFERENCES

1. S. Greenberg, "Computer Supported Cooperative Work and Groupware." *Internat. J. Man-Machine Stud.,* **34**(2), (1991).

2. P. Sørgaard, "A Cooperative Work Perspective on Use and Development of Computer Artifacts," *10th Information System Research Seminar in Scandinavia (IRIS) Conference,* Vaskivesi, Finland, 1987.

3. Greiff and Cashman, ed., *CSCW '84*: Proceedings of the Conference on Computer Supported Cooperative Work, Microelectronics Computer Corporation, 1984.

4. L. Bannon and K. Schmidt, "CSCW: Four Letters in Search of a Context," in *Studies in Computer Supported Cooperative Work: Theory, Practice, and Design,* Proceedings of the First European Conference on Computer Supported Cooperative Work, J. Bowers and D. Bendford, eds. North Holland, 1991, pp. 3–16.

5. L. Suchman, ed., *CSCW '88: Proceedings Computer Supported Collaborative Work,* Portland, 1988, pp. 26–29.

6. P. Johnson-Lenz and T. Johnson-Lenz, "Groupware: The Process and Impacts of Design Choices," in *Computer Mediated Communication System: Status and Evaluation,* Kerr and Hiltz, eds. Academic, 1982.

7. E. Dyson, "A Framework for Groupware," in *Proceedings of Groupware '92,* D. Coleman, ed. 1992, pp. 148–154.

8. C. Ellis, S. Gibbs, and G. Rein, "Groupware: Some Issues and Experiences." *Commun. ACM,* **34**(1), 38–58 (1991).

9. K. J. Lynch, J. M. Snyder, and D. R. Vogel, "The Arizona Analyst Information System: Supporting Collaboration Research on International Technology Trends," in Gibbs and Verrijn-Stuart, eds. 1990, pp. 159–174.

10. D. Coleman, *Proceedings of Groupware '92,* Morgan Kaufmann, 1992.
11. R. Johansen, "Groupware: Future Directions and Wild Cards." *J. of Organiz. Comp.* **1**(2), 219–227 (1991).
12. J. Nunamaker, A. Dennis, Valacich, D. Vogel, and J. George, "Electronic Meeting Systems to Support Group Work." *Commun. ACM,* **34**(7), 40–61 (1991).
13. J. McGrath, *Groups and Human Behavior,* Prentice Hall, Englewood Cliffs, NJ, 1984.
14. H. Mintzberg, "A Typology of Organizational Structure," in *ORGANIZATIONS: A Quantum View,* Miller Friesen, eds. Prentice Hall, Englewood Cliffs, NJ, 1984, pp. 68–86.
15. H. J. Leavitt, "Some Effects of Certain Communications Patterns on Group Performance." *J. of Abnorm. and Soc. Psyc.*, **46**, 38–50 (1951).
16. N. Borenstein and C. Thyberg, "Power, Ease of Use and Cooperative Work in a Practical Multimedia Message System." *Internat. J. Man–Machine Stud.,* **34**(2), 229–259 (1991).
17. J. Johnson, T. Roberts, W. Verplank, D. Smith, C. Irby, M. Beard, and K. Mackey, "The Xerox Star: A Retrospective." *Computer,* **22**(9), 11–26 (1989).
18. T. Crowley, P. Milazzo, E. Baker, H. Forsdick, and R. Tomlinson, "MMConf: An Infrastructure for Building Shared Multimedia Applications," *CSCW 90: Proceedings of the Conference on Computer-Supported Cooperative Work,* Los Angeles, Oct. 7–10, 1990, F. Halasz, ed., pp. 329–342.
19. B. Buxton, "Telepresence: Integrated Shared Task and Person Spaces," *Proceedings of Graphic Interface 92,* Morgan Kaufman, 1992, pp. 123–129.
20. L. Sproull and S. Kiesler, *Connections: New Ways of Working in the Networked Organization,* MIT Press, 1991.
21. T. Malone, K. Grant, K. Lai, R. Rao, and D. Rosenblitt, "The Information Lens: An Intelligent System for Information Sharing and Coordination," in *Technological Support Work Group Collaboration,* M. Olson, ed. Lawrence Erlbaum, Hillsdale, NJ, 1989, pp. 65–88.
22. F. Flores, Graves, Harfield, and T. Winograd, "Computer Systems and the Design of Organizational Interaction." *ACM Transac. Off. Info. Syst.,* **6**(2), 153–172 (1988).
23. D. Mahling, N. Craven, and B. Croft, "From Office Automation to Intelligent Workflow Systems." *IEEE Exp.,* 41–47 (June 1995).
24. E. Conklin, "Capturing Organization Memory," in *Groupware '92,* D. Coleman, ed. Morgan Kaufman, 1992, pp. 133–137.
25. J. Grudin, "Why CSCW Applications Fail: Problems in the Design and Evaluation of Organizational Interfaces," *Proceedings of Computer Supported Cooperative Work '88,* 1988.

DIRK E. MAHLING

COOPERATIVE DESIGN

Cooperative design is an approach to computer system development that emphasizes *active user participation* through exploratory, *experience-driven* design techniques. The roots of cooperative design in Scandinavian system development research will be presented, together with the relations of the approach to software engineering, human–computer interaction, and computer-supported cooperative work. This article further outlines the *objectives, principles,* and *techniques* of cooperative design, together with current practical and theoretical trends of the approach.

Scandinavian Heritage

Research projects on user participation in systems development in Scandinavia date back to the 1970s, when new legislation increased possibilities for worker influence. In these projects, workers aided by consultants and researchers explored possible platforms for worker influence on the use of new technology at the workplace. New work practices, focusing on group work and the development of local resources for action, were being shaped and tried out. This action research approach emphasized the active cooperation between researchers and "those being researched," suggesting that researchers need to enter an active commitment with the workers of the organization to help improve their situation. Two further results emerged from these research projects. First, the existing legislation on worker influence was supplemented by technology agreements that gave workers a direct say in the development and use of technology in their workplaces. Second, an extensive series of union education programs emerged—the Norwegian NJMF project (*1*), the Swedish DEMOS, and the Danish DUE project (*2*).

These projects introduced the notion of worker participation in decisions about technology in the 1970s. The rationalistic tradition embedded in computer system development, however, did little to give workers a chance to put forward their own ideas when trying to agree on the introduction of new technology, and the projects proposed alternatives based on people's own *experiences,* providing for them *resources* to be able to *act* in their current situation.

By the early 1980s a new generation of projects was initiated. These projects focused on the design of new kinds of computer support using skill and product quality to push computer system design more toward a user perspective. One example was the Utopia project (*3*), in which computer system developers and researchers collaborated with typographers to help them formulate the ways in which computer technology could be used to enhance their skills and improve the typographical quality of newspapers. Another example was the Florence project (*4*), a cooperative project between computer system developers/researchers and nurses to explore the possible improved use of computer technology in health care. The major practical as well as theoretical achievements of these projects were the experience-based design methods, developed through the focus on hands-on experiences, and emphasizing the need for technical as well as organizational *alternatives.*

Following these large-scale projects, a number of projects continued to explore and develop methods, theories, and perspectives. Characteristics to these projects was that the labor unions played a rather insignificant role, although there was still concern for democracy and organizational conflicts (*5*). Generally there was a distinct focus on the work/use situation, viewing computer system development as a learning process. The projects took place in Denmark, Norway, Sweden, and Finland, and developed further approaches to cooperative prototyping and hands-on experience (*6*), organizational games (*7*), cooperative analysis (*8*), simulations to support learning (*9, 10*), questions of organizational and technical redesign of existing technology (*11, 12*), and product development (*13*).

"Out of Scandinavia"

Since the late 1980s North American human–computer interaction (HCI) research communities have shown a growing interest in obtaining a more active user involvement in system design. This is mirrored in the arrangement of a series of conferences dedicated to the topic "participatory design" (PDC). Moreover, computer–human interaction (CHI) and, computer–supported collaborative work (CSCW) conferences have paper sessions and panels dedicated to PDC and cooperative design issues. A central concern of the PDC conferences (*14–16*) was to import European—and in particular Scandinavian—ideas of user involvement into American settings, in which societal conditions are different. This transformation has not been straightforward, but several designers and researchers in the United States have taken up the challenge and developed thier own approaches (*17–21*). Furthermore, user participation has gained widespread acceptance in the European context as a way of gaining knowledge about work, and various roles for user participation have made their way into the textbooks (e.g., *22, 23*). The main argument for user participation in these contexts is that the quality of the computer application is improved. The main European figure in bringing participatory design "out of Scandinavia" has, however, been Christiane Floyd, who on top of developing her own participatory software engineering approach (*24*) has written extensively about the Scandinavian approaches (*25, 26*).

Objectives

Cooperative design is a particular approach to participatory design, as it makes assumptions about why and how users participate in design. We elaborate on these issues in the following. Cooperative design is distinguished by a number of basic objectives regarding the design process as well as its outcome. (The account given below is partly taken from Ref. *27*).

COMPUTER APPLICATIONS

- When computer applications are brought into a workplace, they should enhance workplace skills rather than degrade or rationalize them.
- Computer applications should be viewed as tools and designed to be under the control of the people using them. They should support work activities, not make them more rigid or rationalized.
- The introduction of computer applications changes the organization of work around them. The design and introduction of computer applications into organizations should focus specifically on the interplay between the computer application and work organizational issues.
- Although computer applications are generally ordered to increase productivity, they also need to be looked at as a means to increase the quality of the results.

THE DESIGN PROCESS

- As is the case with any process taking place in an organization, the design process is a political one and may lead to conflict. Managers who order an application see things differently from the workers who will use it. Different groups of users will need different things from the application, and system designers often pursue their own interests. Conflicts are inherent in the process. If they are ignored, the solution may be less useful and continue to create problems.

- Computer applications that are created for the workplace need to be designed with full participation from the users—both from a democratic point of view and to ensure that competencies central to the design are represented in the design group.
- The design process should highlight the issue of how computers are used in the context of work organization. The practice of users forms the starting point for the design process.
- Encouraging user participation and designing for skill means paying attention to issues that are often left out of the formal specifications, such as tacit knowledge, assumptions that are taken for granted, shared knowledge, and implicit communication.
- Design always takes place between current conditions and future possibilities. The challenge is not to just reproduce the current state of affairs or to invent possibilities without considerations for current work practices, but to explore qualitative new possibilities that remain realizable and appropriate for the current work practice.

Principles

Based on the above objectives, four important principles for cooperative design activities and techniques have developed: cooperating, experimenting, contextualizing, and iterating.

COOPERATING

Cooperative design stresses the issue of cooperation within system development projects. Cooperation stresses two fundamental principles: the "egalitarian" principle, which assumes that all stakeholders within a design process are *juxtapositioned* (all are experts in certain areas and more like novices in others); and the coworking principle, which assumes that a design process is a *learning* process for both computer systems developers and users (*28*).

Cooperative design is seen as the establishment of a new work practice for the duration of a system development project. In this work practice a third principle may unfold, the potential of *multivoicedness,* in which the participants basically address the same issues but from very diverse backgrounds and perspectives (*5, 8*).

EXPERIMENTING

The emphasis on experimentation is an attempt to take seriously the idea that the design process always takes place in the space between new possibilities and current conditions. Experimentation has the dual purpose of inventing the new at the same time as it has to ensure that it is both desirable and realizable for current work practice (*29, 30*).

To facilitate the creation of qualitative new applications and uses, cooperative design makes extensive use of *exploration* (*31*) regarding various possible technologies, their potential uses, and ways of organizing work. Often the exploration takes the concrete form of *gamelike* (*8, 32, 33*) activities to support idea generation by liberating people from too many constraints in current work. In general, cooperative design makes use of very tangible artifacts in these activities (*34*).

The other side of the coin, to ensure that new ideas are or may be embedded within current conditions, is often supported by two principles, both aimed at concretizing and contextualizing design visions. The first is to accomplish experiments with visions, not in a laboratory, but in real work, or when this is inappropriate, by conducting experiments in *simulated* work situations (*9, 35*). The other is *hands-on experience* (*2, 36*) to support users to experience future computer applications in use (i.e., to get hands-on-experience for the future by concretizing the various future possibilities). Mock-ups, prototypes, and various games and simulations are all examples of such concretizations.

CONTEXTUALIZING

Cooperative design takes its starting point in the particular work setting and situations in which the new computer application is to be applied. Cooperative design focuses on these situations in an iterative process of design and use. Furthermore, since use is developing continuously, computer systems development goes on as long as the computer application is in use, and cooperative design specifically aims at dealing with this (*12, 29*).

The constitution of the design situation as well as the situations of use have many social as well as technical aspects. Cooperative design is particularly concerned with the way in which designers and users can be aided in considering and reconsidering the outcome of creating something new, as far as the social setting of use is concerned (*30*).

System development in general, and cooperative design in particular, involve different kinds of participants: professional designers, users, managers, and so on. These participants have a variety of backgrounds, with partly overlapping and partly conflicting interests and concerns. Cooperative design needs to deal with this variety of interests. It is further dependent on such things as the existing and available hardware technology (*37*), and the various groups may have very different ideas of how the future work ought to be supported. Cooperative design proposes that these conditions and conflicts need to be dealt with specifically (*5, 38*).

ITERATING

In design we need to hold on to something not yet known, the future product, as seen from the point of view of design and the future instrument of work as seen from the point of view of use (*38, 39*). Cooperative design argues that this is most preferably done using artifacts that can be experienced by users as well as designers (e.g., through prototypes). Shaping these artifacts gives design a practical purpose, allowing the participants, at least temporarily, to move in a certain direction. This is quite different from the idealized, goal-determined design process prescribed by many design methods, in which the goal (the future computer application) may be determined once and for all at the beginning of the design process, needing only to be refined and detailed through the rest of the process. Designers cooperate with each other and use artifacts as a basis for delegating work. In cooperative design there is a focus on realization early and throughout the process; that is, programming of early prototypes and conversion of example material may appear in early stages, and *qua* cooperation, cooperative design argues for little division of work in the system development process. Recognizing that a certain division of work is unavoidable, the approach advocates overlap between members of the analysis, design, and realization groups. This is in order to compensate for the experience that abstract specifications are insufficient for rendering insight about a computer application and its use context (*38, 40–42*).

Techniques

Since it is a main point in cooperative design that analysis, design, and realization are heavily integrated, and since concrete activities in a system development project contribute to several such objectives, we will in the following section mention a number of techniques for cooperative design without discussing their particular functions. It is a general recommendation of cooperative design that techniques are chosen for the particular needs of particular design situations, not as overall and predetermined schemes.

MOCK-UPS

The idea of mock-up design is to design with simple and inexpensive materials such as paper, cardboard, transparencies, wood, and slides. The technique was developed in the Utopia project as a way in which to encourage active user involvement. Mock-up design is presented by Ehn and Kyng (*43*). Mock-ups share the following characteristics: they encourage users and designers to transcend the borders of reality and imagine what is currently impossible; they support hands-on experience, and thus support user involvement beyond detached reflection; they are understandable, hence there is no confusion between the simulation and the "real thing," they are modifiable by everybody; they are inexpensive, hence many experiments can be conducted without big investments in equipment, commitments, time, and other resources; and finally, they are fun to work with.

METAPHORICAL DESIGN

Metaphorical design is an approach aimed at getting people to talk about and reflect on their daily work in new ways by breaking down the "un-reflected being of the members in an organization" (*44*). The primary means to this end is the use of metaphors. The understanding of the organization in terms of other phenomena is utilized on the grounds that knowledge about these phenomena may become a potential source of inspiration in the design.

FUTURE WORKSHOPS

A future workshop is a structured brainstorming technique developed by Jungk and Müllert (*45*) for citizen groups with limited resources who wanted a say in the decision-making processes of public planning authorities. The idea is to give people the chance to formulate critique, visions, and strategies for change. The use of the future workshop technique for system design is described in Kensing (*46*). The technique is meant to shed light on a common and problematic situation, to generate visions about the future, and to discuss how (parts of) these visions can be realized. Furthermore, a future workshop technique for system development in combination with metaphorical design has been developed (*47*).

DILEMMA GAMES

The purpose of dilemma games is to understand the dynamics in an organization (e.g., what may and may not change; *8*). The primary means is to expose the current work practice to dilemmas—to challenge it. It is accomplished by the participants acting through scenarios that expose dilemmas. It is led by one or more provocateurs who on the basis of a very flexible script introduce scenarios and urge people to take action. The scenarios develop according to the actions chosen by the participants; actions have consequences.

SCENARIO-BASED DESIGN

The idea of scenarios is to use structured textual descriptions to represent a vision of future work *situations* with a new computer system in use. The use of scenarios in system development is discussed in recent papers (*41, 48*). Scenarios are a means to represent work and the context of use of a system, and *not* a system itself. Scenarios can support assessment of alternative designs related to a work practice, and together with prototypes they can serve as a means to establish worklike experiments of emerging designs.

COOPERATIVE PROTOTYPING

Cooperative prototyping is a cooperative design technique in which users are actively involved in the design, evaluation, and redesign of prototypes of a future system. A key point in facilitating such a process is to let users get hands-on experience with prototypes in fluent worklike situations (*35*). It is a cooperative activity between users and designers rather than an activity of designers utilizing the users' more or less articulated requirements. The users' current skills are confronted with new technological possibilities embodied as prototypes in simulated work situations or in a real-use situation. When breakdowns occur, the reasons are discussed, and breakdowns—caused by bad or incomplete design solutions—may rapidly be turned into improved designs "on the spot." Applying flexible tools, the users can participate actively in improving the prototypes.

ORGANIZATIONAL GAMES

An organizational game is a role-playing technique aimed at considering alternative work organizations by playing envisioned work situations and revealing potential problems. The technique is developed by Sjögren and Ehn (*7, 49*), and borrows its concepts and way of thinking from theater. The main ingredients are: *a playground*—a subjective and negotiated interpretation of the work organization in question; the professional *roles* represented by both individual professional ambitions and organizational requirements; the *situation cards* introducing prototypical examples of problematic situations; *commitments* made by individual role players as actions related to a situation card; negotiated *conditions* for these commitments; and finally, an *action plan* for negotiations with the surrounding organization.

REVERSE SPECIFICATION

Design artifacts such as prototypes, mock-ups, scenarios, and various paper-based specifications are used as the basis for implementation. For realization, prototypes and mock-ups need to be analyzed from a technical point of view to break them down into modules and program constructs that can be organized in the target programming environment. This is a kind of "reverse" specification or redesign activity whereby the prototype code and mock-ups are turned into object-oriented specifications that become the application code. To be efficient, this transformation needs computer support in terms of advanced object-oriented case tools (*50, 51*).

FRAMEWORK FOR SCENARIO MAKING AND EXPLORATION IN CONTEXT

In order to maintain focus on the use context, a "tool box" has been developed, which consists of *checklists* addressing social as well as technical issues, *examples,* and an *outline* of how to work with *scenario making* throughout the design process (*30, 52*).

All the tools in the tool box are meant to both speak to and contradict each other to stimulate discussion and dialogue. On the one hand they serve as affordances in that they inform the design process. On the other hand they provide a certain resistance by maintaining focus on the actual use practice from a variety of theoretical and experience-driven perspectives.

The scenarios create the specific anchoring in the use context. They create the context for various games and workshops (future workshops, simulations, organizational games, dilemma games) or for prototypes, whereby users can get their hands on the situation.

From Early Design to Entire Process

In recent years, cooperative design has moved from a core focus on early analysis/design and construction and evaluation of prototypes to a wider concern for the whole system-development process.

A current effort is to extend this focus by supporting active user involvement throughout the entire development process; prototyping experiments that are closely coupled to work situations and use scenarios; by transforming results from early cooperative analysis/design to targeted object-oriented design, specification, and realization; and by designing for tailorability (*53*).

In a sense, cooperative design (as is the case with most other system-development projects) is perpetually situated between ever-changing current conditions and future possibilities. Cooperative design takes the fact that conditions and possibilities change seriously. Possibilities change, for example, due to new developments in hardware and software, price fluctuations, and what is actually learned from work settings. Conditions change due to market shifts, decisions regarding both policies and work practices, our own attempts to improve matters, and so on. The approach tries to take these fluctuations into account as well as actively alter them in a continuous iterative strategy (*29, 54*). In the following we point to three current attempts to inhabit this space between conditions and possibilities.

COUPLING COOPERATIVE DESIGN TO OBJECT ORIENTATION

With a concept borrowed from Brown and Duguid (*55*), it is necessary to provide better means of establishing the context of the design artifacts, or, as it is said, to create more *portable* contexts of representations. Such portable contexts are not just a matter of looking beyond the object, once and for all establishing the context of use; rather, this context of use is continuously changing, in a dialectical relationship with the work practice emerging in the borderland of design and with the development of the computer application itself.

One of the advantages of object-oriented techniques is that many phenomena and concepts related to the users' practice can be mapped to classes and objects in design diagrams, which in turn appear in the user interface and the application code. This enables the developers to discuss design specifications and application code in terms of use-oriented concepts, thus making it easier to trace the objects that will be affected by a design change initiated by users in, for example, a prototyping session. In combination with emerging object-oriented CASE (computer aided software engineering) tools, this offers the potential for enhanced support for iterative development of systems, since the same conceptual framework and notation can be used all the way from analysis to program (*51*).

COOPERATIVE DESIGN AS BRICOLAGE

Design as bricolage is an approach focusing on what can be done "here and now" with available technological possibilities under the given conditions (*54*). Design becomes the enterprise of investigating what bits and pieces should be brought into use; how the bits integrate; what they should be used for, and how; and crucially, whether they enable or confine future developments. This amounts to the design of (organizational and technical) solutions rather than the design of applications, with design extremely closely tied to organizational changes—implementing software solutions also implies implementing who should use them, when, and for what purposes. In that respect, the situation resembles the ones reported on in Bødker et al. (*56*), Simonsen and Kensing (*57*), and Summer and Stolze (*58*).

COOPERATIVE DESIGN AS PRODUCT DEVELOPMENT

Another current direction is the exploration of cooperative design in product development. Recent projects have demonstrated how activities involving specific user organizations may inform general application design aimed for a much wider market and vice versa (*13, 40, 53, 59*). The interplay can be characterized as a series of specific development cycles (e.g., in a range of user organizations) within the development of the generic application. In these projects, *use scenarios and prototypes* with example data from the users' daily work were used as sources both to trigger design ideas and new insights regarding work practice. *Mutual challenging* characterized the interaction between specific cooperative analysis and design activities, as well as general development activities. People working *across boundaries* facilitated this interaction, and prototypes, scenarios, and concise notes were used as *mediating artifacts* rather than comprehensive requirement and design specifications.

REFERENCES

1. K. Nygaard and O. T. Bergo, "Trade Unions: New Users of Research." *Personnel Rev.,* **4**(2), (1975).

2. P. Ehn and M. Kyng, "The Collective Resource Approach to Systems Design," in *Computers and Democracy,* G. Bjerknes, P. Ehn, and M. Kyng, eds. Aldershot, Avebury, England, 1987, pp. 17–57.

3. S. Bødker, et al., "A UTOPIAN Experience: On Design of Powerful Computer-Based Tools for Skilled Graphic Workers," in *Computers and Democracy,* G. Bjerknes, P. Ehn, and M. Kyng, eds. Aldershot, Avebury, England, 1987, pp. 251–278.

4. G. Bjerknes and T. Bratteteig, "Florence in Wonderland," in *Computers and Democracy,* G. Bjerknes, P. Ehn, and M. Kyng, eds. Aldershot, Avebury, England, 1987, pp. 279–295.

5. S. Bødker, "Creating Conditions for Participation: Conflicts and Resources in Systems Design," *Participatory Design Conference: PDC '94,* Computer Professionals for Social Responsibility, Chapel Hill, NC, 1994, pp. 13–20.

6. S. Bødker and K. Grønbæk, "Design in Action: From Prototyping by Demonstration to Cooperative Prototyping," in *Design at Work: Cooperative Design of Computer Systems,* J. Greenbaum and M. Kyng, eds. Lawrence Erlbaum, Hillsdale, NJ, 1991, pp. 197–218.

7. P. Ehn and D. Sjögren, "From System Descriptions to Scripts for Action," in *Design at Work: Cooperative Design of Computer Systems,* J. Greenbaum and M. Kyng, eds. Lawrence Erlbaum, Hillsdale, NJ, 1991, 241–268.

8. P. Mogensen, "Challenging Practice: An Approach to Cooperative Analysis," Ph.D. thesis, Aarhus University, Aarhus, Denmark, 1994.

9. I. Eriksson, R. Hellman, and M. Nurminen, "A Method for Supporting Users' Comprehensive Learning." *Educ. Computing,* **4** (1988).

10. R. Hellman, *Approaches to User-Centered Information Systems,* University of Turku, Turku, Finland, 1989.

11. T. Bratteteig, K. Braa, and L. Øgrim, "Redesign in System Development," in *Proceedings of the 15th*

Information Systems Research Seminar in Scandinavia, University of Oslo, Larkollen, Norway, 1992, pp. 112–126.
12. R. Trigg and S. Bødker, "From Implementation to Design: Tailoring and the Emergence of Systematization in CSCW," *Proceedings of CSCW 94,* ACM Press, Chapel Hill, NC, 1994, pp. 45–54.
13. K. Grønbæk, M. Kyng, and P. Mogensen, "CSCW Challenges: Cooperative Design in Engineering Projects." *Commun. ACM,* **36**(6), 67–77 (1993).
14. S. Kuhn, M. Muller, and J. Meskill, eds., *Proceedings of the Participatory Design Conference,* Boston, 1992.
15. D. Schuler and A. Namioka, *Participatory Design: Principles and Practices,* Lawrence Erlbaum, Hillsdale, NJ, 1993.
16. R. Trigg, S. I. Anderson, and E. Dykstra-Erickson, eds., *Proceedings of the Participatory Design Conference,* Computer Professionals for Social Responsibility: Chapel Hill, NC, 1994.
17. J. Blomberg, L. Suchman, and R. Trigg, "Reflections on a Work-Oriented Design Project," *Participatory Design Conference (PDC'94),* Chapel Hill, NC, Oct. 27–28, 1994, pp. 99–110.
18. J. Blomberg, L. Suchman, R. Trigg, "Back to Work: Renewing Old Agendas for Cooperative Design," in *Computers in Context: Joining Forces in Design,* Dept. of Computer Science, Aarhus University, Aarhus, Denmark, 1995, pp. 1–9.
19. M. J. Muller, "PICTIVE—An Exploration in Participatory Design," *Proceedings of ACM CHI'91 Conference on Human Factors in Computing Systems,* New Orleans, LA, 1991, pp. 225–231.
20. M. J. Muller et al., "Participatory Design in Britain and North America: Responses to the "Scandinavian Challenge," *Proceedings of ACM CHI'91 Conference on Human Factors in Computing Systems,* New Orleans, LA, 1991, pp. 389–392.
21. M. Muller, "PICTIVE: Democratizing the Dynamics of the Design Session," in *Participatory Design—Principles and Practices,* D. Schuler and A. Namioka, eds. Lawrence Erlbaum, Hillsdale, NJ, 1993, pp. 211–238.
22. W. Newman and M. Lamming, *Interactive Systems Design,* Addison-Wesley, Cambridge, MA, 1995.
23. J. Preece et al., *Human-Computer Interaction,* Addison-Wesley, Wokingham, UK, 1994.
24. C. Floyd, F.-M. Reisin, and G. Schmidt, "STEPS to Software Development with Users," in *European Software Engineering Conference '89,* Lecture Notes in Computer Science, vol. 387, Springer-Verlag, Berlin, 1989, pp. 48–64.
25. C. Floyd, "Outline of a Paradigm Change in Software Engineering," in *Computers and Democracy,* Aldershot, Avebury, England, 1987, pp. 191–210.
26. C. Floyd et al., "Out of Scandinavia: Alternative Approaches to Software Design and System Development." *Human-Computer Interact.,* **4**(4), 253–350 (1989).
27. S. Bødker, K. Grønbæk, and M. Kyng, "Cooperative Design: Techniques and Experiences from the Scandinavian Scene," in *Readings in Human-Computer Interaction: Toward the Year 2000,* R. M. Baecker, J. Grudin, and W. A. S. Buxton, eds. Morgan Kaufmann, San Francisco, 1995, pp. 215–224.
28. J. Greenbaum and M. Kyng, *Design at Work: Cooperative Design of Computer Systems,* Lawrence Erlbaum, Hillsdale, NJ, 1991.
29. S. Bødker and P. Mogensen, *Between Possibilities and Conditions: A Two-Level Strategy for System Development,* unpublished manuscript, 1997.
30. S. Bødker and E. Christiansen, "Scenarios as Springboards in Design," in *Social Science Research, Technical Systems and Cooperative Work,* G. Bowker et al., eds. Erlbaum, Mahwah, NJ, 1997, pp. 217–234.
31. C. Floyd, "A Systematic Look at Prototyping," in *Approaches to Prototyping,* Springer-Verlag, Berlin, 1984, pp. 1–18.
32. P. Ehn, *Work-Oriented Design of Computer Artifacts,* Arbetslivscentrum, Stockholm, 1988.
33. P. Mogensen and R. Trigg, "Artifacts as Triggers for Participatory Analysis," *Participatory Design Conference (PDC),* Boston, 1992, pp. 55–62.
34. K. Grønbæk, *Prototyping and Active User Involvement in System Development: Towards a Cooperative Prototyping Approach,* Computer Science Dept., University of Aarhus, Aarhus, Denmark, 1991.
35. S. Bødker and K. Grønbæk, "Cooperative Prototyping: Users and Designers in Mutual Activity," *Internat. J. Man-Machine Stud.,* **34**(3), 453–478 (1991).
36. P. Ehn and M. Kyng, "A Tool Perspective on Design of Interactive Computer Support for Skilled

Workers," *Seventh Scandinavian Research Seminar on Systemeering,* Helsinki School of Economics, Helsinki, 1984, pp. 211–242.

37. L. Mathiassen, *Systemudvikling og Systemudviklingsmetode,* Computer Science Dept., Aarhus University, Aarhus, Denmark, 1981.
38. S. Bødker, "Understanding Representation in Design," *Human-Computer Interaction,* **13**(2), 1998, pp. 107–125.
39. S. Bødker, *Through the Interface—A Human Activity Approach to User Interface Design,* Lawrence Erlbaum, Hillsdale, NJ, 1991.
40. K. Grønbæk and P. Mogensen, "Specific Cooperative Analysis and Design in General Hypermedia Development," *Participatory Design Conference (PDC),* Chapel Hill, NC, 1994, pp. 159–172.
41. M. Kyng, "Making Representations Work," Representations of Work, HICSS Monograph, *Proceedings of the 27th Hawaii International Conference on System Sciences,* Honolulu, 1994, pp. 19–35.
42. M. Kyng, "Creating Contexts for Design," in *Scenario-Based Design: Envisioning Technology in Use,* J. Carrol, ed. Wiley, New York, 1995, pp. 85–107.
43. P. Ehn and M. Kyng, "Cardboard Computers: Mocking-It-Up or Hands-on the Future," in *Design at Work—Cooperative Design of Computer Systems,* J. Greenbaum and M. Kyng, eds. Lawrence Erlbaum, Hillsdale, NJ, 1991, pp. 169–195.
44. K. H. Madsen, "Breakthrough by Breakdown: Metaphors and Structured Domains," in *Systems Development for Human Progress,* H. Klein and K. Kumar, eds. North-Holland, Amsterdam, Holland, 1989, pp. 41–53.
45. R. Jungk and N. Müllert, *Future Workshops: How to Create Desirable Futures,* Institute for Social Inventions, London, 1987.
46. F. Kensing, "Generation of Visions in Systems Development, in *System Design for Human Development and Productivity: Participation and Beyond,* North-Holland, Amsterdam, Holland, 1987, pp. 285–301.
47. F. Kensing and K. H. Madsen, "Generating Visions: Future Workshops and Metaphorical Design," in *Design at Work—Cooperative Design of Computer Systems,* Lawrence Erlbaum, Hillsdale, NJ, 1991, pp. 153–168.
48. J. Carrol, ed., *Scenario-Based design for Human-Computer Interaction,* Wiley, New York, 1995.
49. P. Ehn, B. Mölleryd, and D. Sjögren, "Playing in Reality: A Paradigm Case." *Scand. J. Info. Syst.,* **2**, 101–120 (1990).
50. K. Grønbæk, A. Hviid, and R. H. Trigg, "ApplBuilder—An Object-Oriented Application Generator Supporting Rapid Prototyping," *Fourth International Conference on Software Engineering and Its Applications,* Toulouse, France, Dec. 9–13, 1991, pp. 257–272.
51. J. L. Knudsen et al., *Object-Oriented Software Development Environments—The Mjølner Approach,* Prentice Hall, Englewood Cliffs, NJ, 1993.
52. S. Bødker, E. Christiansen, and M. Thüring, "A Conceptual Toolbox for Designing CSCW Applications," *COOP '95: International Workshop on the Design of Cooperative Systems,* Juan-les-Pins, France, 1995, pp. 266–284.
53. K. Grønbæk, M. Kyng, and P. Mogensen, "Cooperative Experimental System Development—Cooperative Techniques Beyond Initial Design and Analysis," in *Computers in Context: Joining Forces in Design,* Dept. of Computer Science, Aarhus University, Aarhus, Denmark, 1995, pp. 20–29.
54. P. Mogensen and D. Shapiro, "When Survival Is an Issue: PD in Support of Landscape Architecture," *Participatory Design Conference (PDC '96),* Computer Professionals for Social Responsibility, MIT, Cambridge, MA, 1996.
55. J. S. Brown and P. Duguid, "Borderline Issues: Social and Material Aspects of Design." *Human-Computer Interac.,* **9**(1), 3–36 (1994).
56. S. Bødker et al., *The AT-Project: Practical Research in Cooperative Design,* Computer Science Dept., Aarhus University, Daimi, Aarhus, 1993.
57. J. Simonsen and F. Kensing, "Take Users Seriously, but Take a Deeper Look: Organizational and Technical Effects from Designing with an Ethnographically Inspired Approach," *PDC '94—Participatory Design Conference,* Chapel Hill, NC, 1994, pp. 47–58.
58. T. Summer and M. Stolze, "Evolution, Non Revolution: PD in the Toolbelt Era," in *Computers in*

Context: Joining Forces in Design, Dept. of Computer Science, Aarhus University, Aarhus, Denmark, 1995, pp. 30–39.

59. M. Kyng, "Scandinavian Design: Users in Product Development," *Human Factors in Computing Systems, CHI '94, Celebrating Interdependence,* Association for Computing Machinery, 1994, pp. 3–9.

PREBEN HOLST MOGENSEN
SUSANNE BØDKER
KAJ GRØNBÆK

DECISION SUPPORT SYSTEMS

Introduction

Making decisions concerning complex systems (e.g., the management of organizational operations, industrial processes, or investment portfolios; the command and control of military combat units; and the control of nuclear power plants) often strains our cognitive capabilities. Even though individual interactions among a system's variables may be well understood, predicting how the system will react to an external manipulation such as a policy decision is often difficult. What will be, for example, the effect of introducing the third shift on a factory floor? One might expect that this will increase the plant's output by roughly 50 percent. Factors such as additional wages, machine weardown, maintenance breaks, raw material usage, supply logistics, and future demand need also be considered, however, as they all will impact the total financial outcome of this decision. Many variables are involved in complex and often subtle interdependencies, therefore predicting the total outcome may be daunting.

There is a substantial amount of empirical evidence that human intuitive judgment and decision making can be far from optimal, and it deteriorates even further with complexity and stress. Because in many situations the quality of decisions is important, aiding the deficiencies of human judgment and decision making has been a major focus of science throughout history. Disciplines such as statistics, economics, and operations research developed various methods for making rational choices. More recently, these methods, often enhanced by a variety of techniques originating from information science, cognitive psychology, and artificial intelligence, have been implemented in the form of computer programs, either as stand-alone tools or as integrated computing environments for complex decision making. Such environments are often given the common name of *decision support systems* (DSSs). The concept of DSS is extremely broad, and its definitions vary, depending on the author's point of view. To avoid exclusion of any of the existing types of DSSs, we will define them roughly as interactive computer-based systems that aid users in judgment and choice activities. Another name sometimes used as a synonym for DSS is *knowledge-based systems,* which refers to their attempt to formalize domain knowledge so that it is amenable to mechanized reasoning.

Decision support systems are gaining increased popularity in various domains, including business, engineering, the military, and medicine. They are especially valuable in situations in which the amount of available information is prohibitive for the intuition of an unaided human decision maker and in which precision and optimality are of importance. Decision support systems can aid human cognitive deficiencies by integrating various sources of information, providing intelligent access to relevant knowledge, and aiding the process of structuring decisions. They can also support choice among well-defined alternatives and build on formal approaches, such as the methods of engineering economics, operations research, statistics, and decision theory. They can also employ artificial intelligence methods to address heuristically problems that are intractable by formal techniques. Proper application of decision-making tools increases productivity, efficiency, and effectiveness and gives many businesses a comparative advantage over their competitors, allowing them to make optimal choices for technological processes and their parameters, planning business operations, logistics, or investments.

While it is difficult to overestimate the importance of various computer-based tools that are relevant to decision making (e.g., databases, planning software, and spreadsheets), this article focuses primarily on the core of a DSS, the part that directly supports modeling decision problems and identifies best alternatives. We will briefly discuss the characteristics of decision problems and how decision making can be supported by computer programs. We then cover various components of DSSs and the role that they play in decision support. We will also introduce an emergent class of *normative systems* (i.e., DSSs based on sound theoretical principles), and in particular, decision analytic DSSs. Finally, we will review issues related to user interfaces to DSSs and stress the importance of user interfaces to the ultimate quality of decisions aided by computer programs.

Decisions and Decision Modeling

TYPES OF DECISIONS

A simple view of decision making is that it is a problem of choice among several alternatives. A somewhat more sophisticated view includes the process of constructing the alternatives (i.e., developing a list of choice options). A complete picture includes a search for opportunities for decisions (i.e., discovering that there is a decision to be made). A manager of a company may be faced with a choice in which the options are clear (e.g., the choice of a supplier from among all existing suppliers). She may also be faced with a well-defined problem for which she designs creative decision options (e.g., how to market a new product so that the profits are maximized). Finally, she may work in a less reactive fashion and view decision problems as opportunities that have to be discovered by studying the operations of her company and its surrounding environment (e.g., how we can make the production process more efficient). There is much anecdotal and some empirical evidence that structuring decision problems and identifying creative decision alternatives determine the ultimate quality of decisions. Decision support systems aim mainly at this broadest type of decision making, and in addition to supporting choice, they aid in modeling and analyzing systems (such as complex organizations), identifying decision opportunities, and structuring decision problems.

HUMAN JUDGMENT AND DECISION MAKING

Theoretical studies on rational decision making, notably in the context of probability theory and decision theory, have been accompanied by empirical research on whether human behavior complies with the theory. It has been rather convincingly demonstrated in numerous empirical studies that human judgment and decision making is based on intuitive strategies as opposed to theoretically sound reasoning rules. These intuitive strategies, referred to as *judgmental heuristics* in the context of decision making, help us in reducing the cognitive load, but alas at the expense of optimal decision making. Effectively, our unaided judgment and choice exhibit systematic violations of probability axioms (referred to as *biases*). Formal discussion of the most important research results along with experimental data can be found in an anthology edited by Kahneman, Slovic, and Tversky (*1*). Dawes (*2*) provides an accessible introduction to what is known about people's decision-making performance.

One might hope that people who have achieved expertise in a domain will not be subject to judgmental biases and will approach optimality in decision making. While empirical evidence shows that experts indeed are more accurate than novices within their area of expertise, they also seem to be liable to the same judgmental biases as novices and demonstrate apparent errors and inconsistencies in their judgment. Professionals such as practicing physicians have been shown to use essentially the same judgmental heuristics and be prone to the same biases, although the degree of departure from the normatively prescribed judgment seems to decrease with experience. In addition to laboratory evidence, there are several studies of expert performance in realistic settings, showing that it is inferior even to simple linear models [an informal review of the available evidence and pointers to literature can be found in Dawes (*2*)], and so, for example, predictions of future violent behavior of psychiatric patients made by a panel of psychiatrists who had access to patient records and interviewed the patients were found to be inferior to a simple model that included only the past incidence of violent behavior. Predictions of marriage counselors concerning marital happiness were shown to be inferior to a simple model that just subtracted the rate of fighting from the rate of sexual intercourse (again, the marriage counselors had access to all data, including interviews with the couples). Studies yielding similar results have been conducted with bank loan officers, physicians, university admission committees, and so on.

MODELING DECISIONS

The superiority of even simple linear models over human intuitive judgment suggests that one way to improve the quality of decisions is to decompose a decision problem into simpler components that are well defined and well understood. Studying a complex system built out of such components can be subsequently aided by a formal, theoretically sound technique. The process of decomposing and formalizing a problem is often called modeling. Modeling amounts to finding an abstract representation of a real-world system that simplifies and assumes as much as possible about the system, and while retaining the system's essential relationships, omits unnecessary detail. Building a model of a decision problem, as opposed to reasoning about a problem in a holistic way, allows for applying scientific knowledge that can be transferred across problems and often across domains. It allows for analyzing, explaining, and arguing about a decision problem.

The desire to improve human decision making provided motivation for the development of a variety of modeling tools in disciplines of economics, operations research, decision theory, decision analysis, and statistics. In each of these modeling tools, knowledge about a system is represented by means of algebraic, logical, or statistical variables. Interactions among these variables are expressed by equations or logical rules, possibly enhanced with an explicit representation of uncertainty. When the functional form of an interaction is unknown, it is sometimes described in purely probabilistic terms; for example, by a conditional probability distribution. Once a model has been formulated, a variety of mathematical methods can be used to analyze it. Decision making under certainty has been addressed by economic and operations research methods, such as cash flow analysis, break-even analysis, scenario analysis, mathematical programming, inventory techniques, and a variety of optimization algorithms for scheduling and logistics. Decision making under uncertainty enhances the above methods with statistical approaches, such as reliability analysis, simulation, and statistical decision making. Most of these methods have made it into college curricula and can be found in management textbooks. Due to space constraints, we will not discuss their details further.

COMPONENTS OF DECISION MODELS

While mathematically a model consists of variables and a specification of interactions among them, from the point of view of decision making a model and its variables represent the following three components: a measure of preferences over decision objectives, available decision options, and a measure of uncertainty over variables influencing the decision and the outcomes.

Preference is widely viewed as the most important concept in decision making. Outcomes of a decision process are not all equally attractive, and it is crucial for a decision maker to examine these outcomes in terms of their desirability. Preferences can be ordinal (e.g., more income is preferred to less income), but it is convenient and often necessary to represent them as numerical quantities, especially if the outcome of the decision process consists of multiple attributes that need to be compared on a common scale. Even when they consist of just a single attribute but the choice is made under uncertainty, expressing preferences numerically allows for trade-offs between desirability and risk.

The second component of decision problems is available decision options. Often these options can be enumerated (e.g., a list of possible suppliers), but sometimes they are continuous values of specified policy variables (e.g., the amount of raw material to be kept in stock). Listing the decision options is an important element of model structuring.

The third element of decision models is uncertainty. Uncertainty is one of the most inherent and most prevalent properties of knowledge, originating from incompleteness of information, imprecision, and model approximations made for the sake of simplicity. It would not be an exaggeration to state that real-world decisions not involving uncertainty either do not exist or belong to a truly limited class.*

Decision making under uncertainty can be viewed as a deliberation: determining what action should be taken that will maximize the expected gain. Due to uncertainty there is no guarantee that the result of the action will be the one intended, and the best one can hope for is to maximize the chance of the desirable outcome. The process rests on the assumption that a good decision is one that results from a good decision-making process that considers all important factors and is explicit about decision alternatives, preferences, and uncertainty.

It is important to distinguish between good decisions and good outcomes. By a stroke of good luck a poor decision can lead to a very good outcome. Similarly, a very good decision can be followed by a bad outcome. Supporting decisions means supporting the decision-making process so that better decisions are made. Better decisions can be expected to lead to better outcomes.

Decision Support Systems

Decision support systems are interactive, computer-based systems that aid users in judgment and choice activities. They provide data storage and retrieval but enhance the traditional information access and retrieval functions with support for model building and model-based reasoning. They support framing, modeling, and problem solving.

Typical application areas of DSSs are management and planning in business, health care, the military, and any area in which management will encounter complex decision situations. Decision support systems are typically used for strategic and tactical decisions faced by upper-level management—decisions with a reasonably low frequency and high potential consequences—in which the time taken for thinking through and modeling the problem pays off generously in the long run.

There are three fundamental components of DSSs (*3*).

- Database management system (DBMS). A DBMS serves as a data bank for the DSS. It stores large quantities of data that are relevant to the class of problems for which the DSS has been designed and provides logical data structures (as opposed to the physical data structures) with which the users interact. A DBMS separates the users from the physical aspects of the database structure and processing. It should also be capable of informing the user of the types of data that are available and how to gain access to them.
- Model-base management system (MBMS). The role of MBMS is analogous to that of a

*As Benjamin Franklin expressed it in 1789 in a letter to his friend M. Le Roy, "in this world nothing can said to be certain, except death and taxes" (*The Complete Works of Benjamin Franklin,* vol. 10, J. Bigelow, ed. Putnam's, New York, 1887, p. 170).

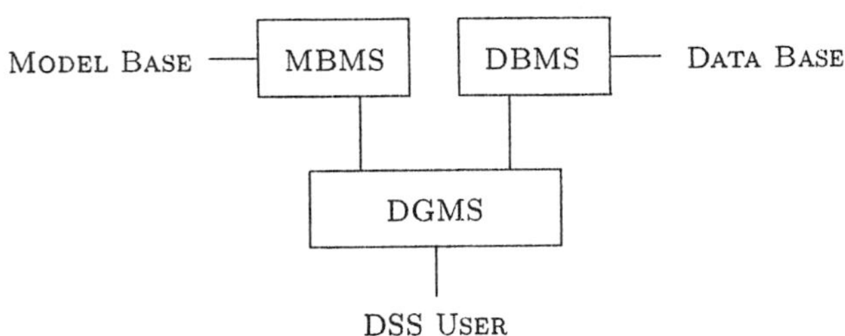

FIGURE 1. *The architecture of a DSS (after Sage, Ref.* 13*).*

DBMS. Its primary function is providing independence between specific models that are used in a DSS from the applications that use them. The purpose of an MBMS is to transform data from the DBMS into information that is useful in decision making. Since many problems that the user of a DSS will cope with may be unstructured, the MBMS should also be capable of assisting the user in model building.

- Dialog generation and management system (DGMS). The main product of an interaction with a DSS is insight. As their users are often managers who are not computer-trained, DSSs need to be equipped with intuitive and easy-to-use interfaces. These interfaces aid in model building, but also in interaction with the model, such as gaining insight and recommendations from it. The primary responsibility of a DGMS is to enhance the ability of the system user to utilize and benefit from the DSS. In the remainder of this article, we will use the broader term *user interface* rather than DGMS.

While a variety of DSSs exist, the above three components can be found in many DSS architectures and play a prominent role in their structure. Interaction among them is illustrated in Fig. 1. Essentially, the user interacts with the DSS through the DGMS. This communicates with the DBMS and MBMS, which screen the user and the user interface from the physical details of the model base and database implementation.

Normative Systems

NORMATIVE AND DESCRIPTIVE APPROACHES

Whether or not one trusts the quality of human intuitive reasoning strategies has a profound impact on one's view of the philosophical and technical foundations of DSSs. There are two distinct approaches to supporting decision making. The first aims at building support procedures or systems that imitate human experts. The most prominent members of this class of DSSs are *expert systems,* computer programs based on rules elicited from human domain experts that imitate reasoning of a human expert in a given domain. Expert systems are often capable of supporting decision making in that domain at a level comparable to human experts. While they are flexible and often able to address complex decision problems, they are based on intuitive human reasoning and lack soundness and formal guarantees with respect to the theoretical reliability of their results. The danger of the expert system approach, increasingly appreciated by DSS builders, is that along with imitating human thinking and its efficient heuristic principles, we may also imitate its undesirable flaws (*4*).

The second approach is based on the assumption that the most reliable method of dealing with complex decisions is through a small set of normatively sound principles of how decisions should be made. While heuristic methods and ad hoc reasoning schemes that imitate human cognition may in many domains perform well, most decision makers will be reluctant to rely on them whenever the cost of making an error is high. To give an extreme example, few people would choose to fly airplanes built using heuristic principles over airplanes built using the laws of aerodynamics enhanced with probabilistic reliability analysis. Application of formal methods in DSSs makes these systems philosophically distinct from those based on ad hoc heuristic artificial intelligence methods, such as rule-based systems. The goal of a DSS, according to this view, is to support unaided human intuition, just as the goal of using a calculator is to aid a human's limited capacity for mental arithmetic.

DECISION-ANALYTIC DECISION SUPPORT SYSTEMS

An emergent class of DSSs known as *decision-analytic DSSs* applies the principles of decision theory, probability theory, and decision analysis to their decision models. Decision theory is an axiomatic theory of decision making that is built on a small set of axioms of rational decision making. It expresses uncertainty in terms of probabilities and preferences in terms of utilities. These are combined using the operation of mathematical expectation. The attractiveness of probability theory, as a formalism for handling uncertainty in DSSs, lies in its soundness and its guarantees concerning long-term performance. Probability theory is often viewed as the gold standard for rationality in reasoning under uncertainty. Following its axioms offers protection from some elementary inconsistencies. Their violation, on the other hand, can be demonstrated to lead to sure losses (*5*). Decision analysis is the art and science of applying decision theory to real-world problems. It includes a wealth of techniques for model construction, such as methods for elicitation of model structure and probability distributions that allow minimization of human bias, methods for checking the sensitivity of a model to imprecision in the data, computing the value of obtaining additional information and presentation of results. (See, for example, Ref. *6* for a basic review of the available techniques.) These methods have been under continuous scrutiny by psychologists working in the domain of behavioral decision theory and have proven to cope reasonably well with the dangers related to human judgmental biases.

Normative systems are usually based on graphical probabilistic models, which are representations of the joint probability distribution over a model's variables in terms of directed graphs. Directed graphs, such as the one in Fig. 2, are known as Bayesian networks (BNs) or causal networks (*7*). Bayesian networks offer a compact representation of joint probability distributions and are capable of practical representation of large models, consisting of tens or hundreds of variables. Bayesian networks can be easily extended with decision and value variables for modeling decision problems. The former denote variables that are under the decision maker's control and can be directly manipulated, and the latter encode users' preferences over various outcomes

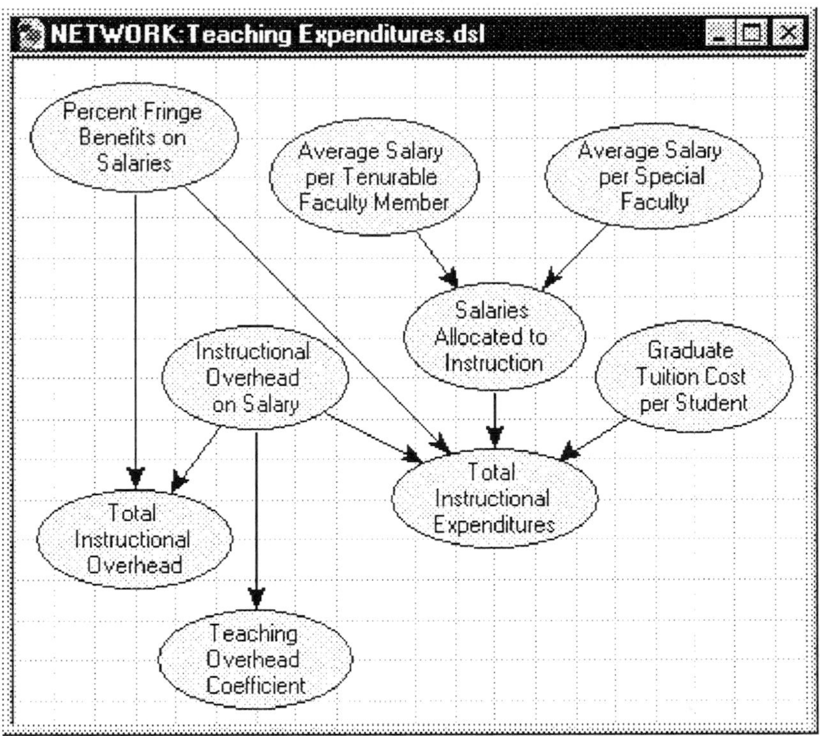

FIGURE 2. *Example of a Bayesian network modeling teaching expenditures in university operations.*

of the decision process. Such amended graphs are known as *influence diagrams* (*8*). Both the structure and the numerical probability distributions in a BN can be elicited from a human expert and are a reflection of the expert's subjective view of a real-world system. If available, scientific knowledge about the system, both in terms of the structure and frequency data, can be easily incorporated in the model. Once a model has been created, it is optimized using formal decision-theoretic algorithms. Decision analysis is based on the empirically tested paradigm that people are able to reliably store and retrieve their personal beliefs about uncertainty and preferences for different outcomes, but are much less reliable in aggregating these fragments into a global inference. While human experts are excellent in structuring a problem, determining the components that are relevant to it and providing local estimates of probabilities and preferences, they are not reliable in combining many simple factors into an optimal decision. The role of a decision-analytic DSS is to support them in their weaknesses using the formal and theoretically sound rules of statistics.

The approach taken by decision analysis is compatible with that of DSSs. The goal of decision analysis is to provide insight into a decision. This insight, consisting of the analysis of all relevant factors, their uncertainty, and the critical nature of some assumptions, is even more important than the actual recommendation.

Decision-analytic DSSs have been successfully applied to practical systems in medicine, business, and engineering.* As these systems tend to naturally evolve into three not necessarily distinct classes, it may be interesting to compare their structure and architectural organization.

- Systems with static domain models. In this class of systems, a probabilistic domain is represented by a large network encoding the domain's structure and its numerical parameters. The network comprising the domain model is normally built by decision analysts and domain experts. An example might be a medical diagnostic system covering a certain class of disorders. Queries in such a system are answered by assigning values to those nodes of the network that constitute the observations for a particular case and propagating the impact of the observation through the network in order to find the probability distribution of some selected nodes of interest (e.g., nodes that represent diseases). Such a network can, on a case-by-case basis, be extended with decision nodes and a value node to support decisions. Systems with static domain models are conceptually similar to rule-based expert systems covering an area of expertise.
- Systems with dynamic decision models. The main idea behind this approach is automatic generation of a graphical decision model on a per-case basis in an interactive effort between the DSS and the decision maker. The DSS has domain expertise in a certain area and plays the role of a decision analyst. During this interaction, the program creates a customized influence diagram, which is later used for generating advice. The main motivation for this approach is the premise that every decision is unique and needs to be looked at individually; an influence diagram needs to be tailored to individual needs (*9*).
- Systems capable of learning a model from data. The third class of systems employs computer-intensive statistical methods for learning models from data (*10–13*). Whenever there are sufficient data available, the systems can literally learn a graphical model from these data. This model can be subsequently used to support decisions within the same domain.

The first two approaches are suited for slightly different applications. The dynamic model generation approach is an attempt to automate the most laborious part of decision making, structuring a problem, so far done with significant assistance from trained decision analysts. A session with the program that assists the decision maker in building an influence diagram is laborious. This makes the dynamic model generation approach particularly suitable for decision problems that are infrequent and serious enough to be treated individually. Because in the static domain model approach an existing domain model needs to be customized by the case data only, the decision-making cycle is rather short. This makes it particularly suitable for those decisions that are highly repetitive and need to be made under time constraints.

The three approaches can be combined in any practical system. A static domain model can be slightly customized for a case that needs individual treatment. Once completed, a dynamic model can be blended into a large static model. Learning systems can support both the static and the dynamic model approach. On the other hand, the learning process can be greatly enhanced by prior knowledge from domain experts or by a prior model.

*At the time of writing, several successful practical systems were already operational. Some examples of applications are described in a special issue of *Communications of the ACM* on practical applications of decision-theoretic methods (vol. 38, no. 3, March 1995).

EQUATION-BASED AND MIXED SYSTEMS

In many business and engineering problems, interactions among model variables can be described by equations which, when solved simultaneously, can be used to predict the effect of decisions on the system, and hence support decision making. One special type of simultaneous equation model is known as the structural equation (SE) model, which has been a popular method of representing systems in econometrics. An equation is structural if it describes a unique, independent causal mechanism acting in the system. Structural equations are based on expert knowledge of the system combined with theoretical considerations. Structural equations allow for a natural, modular description of a system—each equation represents its individual component, a separable and independent mechanism acting in the system—yet the main advantage of having a structural model is, as explicated by Simon (*14*), that it includes causal information and aids predictions of the effects of external interventions. In addition, the causal structure of a structural equation model can be represented graphically (*14*), which allows for combining them with decision-analytic graphical models in practical systems (*15*).

Structural equation models offer significant advantages for policy making. Often a decision maker confronted with a complex system needs to decide not only the values of policy variables but also which variables should be manipulated. A change in the set of policy variables has a profound impact on the structure of the problem and on how their values will propagate through the system. The user determines which variables are policy variables and which are determined within the model. A change in the SEs or the set of policy variables can be reflected by a rapid restructuring of the model and predictions involving this new structure (*16*).

Our long-term project, the Environment for Strategic Planning (ESP), illustrated in Fig. 2 and 3, is based on a hybrid graphical modeling tool that combines SE models with decision-analytic principles. ESP is capable of representing both discrete and continuous variables involved in deterministic and probabilistic relationships. The powerful features of SE models allow ESP to act as a graphical spreadsheet integrating numerical and symbolic methods and allowing the independent variables to be changed at will without having to reformulate the model each time. This provides an immense flexibility that is not afforded by ordinary spreadsheets in evaluating alternate policy options.

User Interfaces to Decision Support Systems

While the quality and reliability of modeling tools and the internal architectures of DSSs are important, the most crucial aspect of DSSs is, by far, their user interface. Systems with user interfaces that are cumbersome or unclear or that require unusual skills are rarely useful and accepted in practice. The most important result of a session with a DSS is insight into the decision problem. In addition, when the system is based on normative principles, it can play a tutoring role; one might hope that users will learn the domain model and how to reason with it over time, and improve their own thinking.

A good user interface to DSSs should support model construction and model analysis, reasoning about the problem structure in addition to numerical calculations and both choice and optimization of decision variables. We will discuss these in the following sections.

SUPPORT FOR MODEL CONSTRUCTION AND MODEL ANALYSIS

User interface is the vehicle for both model construction (or model choice) and for investigating the results. Even if a system is based on a theoretically sound reasoning scheme, its recommendations will be as good as the model they are based on. Furthermore, even if the model is a very good approximation of reality and its recommendations are correct, they will not be followed if they are not understood. Without understanding, the users may accept or reject a system's advice for the wrong reasons and the combined decision-making performance may deteriorate even below unaided performance (*17*). A good user interface should make the model on which the system's reasoning is based transparent to the user.

Modeling is rarely a one-shot process, and good models are usually refined and enhanced as their users gather practical experiences with the system recommendations. It is important to strike a careful balance between precision and modeling efforts; some parts of a model need to be very precise while others do not. A good user interface should include tools for examining the model and identifying its most sensitive parts, which can be subsequently elaborated on. Systems employed in practice will need their models refined, and a good user interface should make it easy to access, examine, and refine its models.

SUPPORT FOR REASONING ABOUT THE PROBLEM STRUCTURE IN ADDITION TO NUMERICAL CALCULATIONS

While numerical calculations are important in decision support, reasoning about the problem structure is even more important. Often when the system and its model are complex it is insightful for the decision maker to realize how the system variables are interrelated. This is helpful in designing creative decision options but also in understanding how a policy decision will impact the objective.

Graphical models, such as those used in decision analysis or in equation-based and hybrid systems, are particularly suitable for reasoning about structure. Under certain assumptions, a directed graphical model can be given a causal interpretation. This is especially convenient in situations in which the DSS autonomically suggests decision options; given a causal interpretation of its model, it is capable of predicting effects of interventions. A causal graph enhances the user interface; the system can refer to causal interactions during its dialogue with the user. This is known to enhance user insight (*18*).

SUPPORT FOR BOTH CHOICE AND OPTIMIZATION OF DECISION VARIABLES

Many DSSs have an inflexible structure in the sense that the variables that will be manipulated are determined at the model-building stage. This is not very suitable for planning the strategic type when both the objectives and methods of achieving them are the subject of the decision-making process. For example, changing policy variables in a spreadsheet-based model often requires that the entire spreadsheet be rebuilt. If there is no support for that, few users will consider it as an option. This closes the world of possibilities for flexible reframing of a decision problem in the exploratory process of searching for opportunities. Support for both choice and optimization of decision variables should be an inherent part of DSSs.

GRAPHICAL INTERFACE

Insight into a model can be increased greatly at the user interface level by a diagram representing the interactions among its components; for example, a drawing of a graph on which a model is based, such as in Fig. 2. This graph is a qualitative, structural explanation of how information flows from the independent variable to the dependent variables of interest. As models may become very large, it is convenient to structure them into submodels, groups of variables that form a subsystem of the modeled system. Such submodels can be again shown graphically with interactions among them, increasing simplicity and clarity of the interface. Fig. 3 shows a submodel-level view of a model developed in our ESP project. Note that the graph in Fig. 2 is an expanded version of the *Teaching Expenditures* submodel in Fig. 3. The user can navigate through the hierarchy of the entire model in her quest for insight, opening and closing submodels on demand.

Summary

Decision support systems are powerful tools integrating scientific methods for supporting complex decisions with techniques developed in information science, and are gaining an increased popularity in many domains. They are especially valuable in situations in which the amount of available information is prohibitive for the intuition of an unaided human decision maker and in which precision and optimality are of importance. Decision support systems aid human cognitive deficiencies by integrating various sources of information, providing intelligent access to relevant knowledge, aiding the process of structuring, and optimizing decisions.

Normative DSSs offer a theoretically correct and appealing way of handling uncertainty and preferences in decision problems. They are based on carefully studied empirical principles underlying the discipline of decision analysis and they have been successfully applied in several practical systems. We believe that they offer several attractive features that are likely to prevail in the long run as far as the technical developments are concerned.

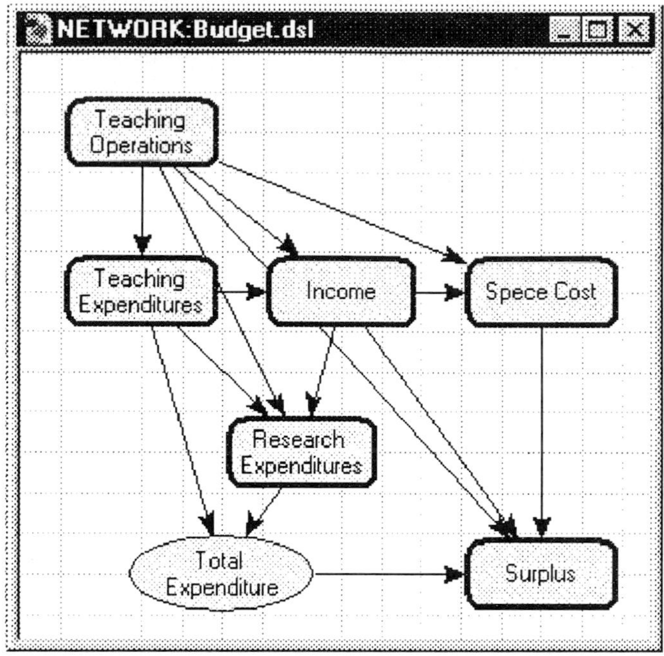

FIGURE 3. *A submodel-level view of a decision model.*

Because DSSs do not replace humans but rather augment their limited capacity to deal with complex problems, their user interfaces are critical. They determine whether a DSS will be used at all and if so, whether the ultimate quality of decisions will be higher than that of an unaided decision maker.

ACKNOWLEDGMENTS

Work on this article was supported by the National Science Foundation under Faculty Early Career Development (CAREER) Program, grant IRI-9624629, by the Air Force Office of Scientific Research under grant F49620-97-1-0225, and by the University of Pittsburgh Central Research Development Fund. Figures 2 and 3 are snapshots of GeNIe, a general purpose development environment for graphical decision support systems developed by the Decision Systems Laboratory, University of Pittsburgh and available at http://www2.sis.pitt.edu/~genie. We would like to thank Ms. Nanette Yurcik for her assistance with technical editing.

REFERENCES

1. D. Kahneman, P. Slovic, and A. Tversky, eds. *Judgment Under Uncertainty: Heuristics and Biases,* Cambridge University Press, Cambridge, U.K., 1982.

2. R. M. Dawes, *Rational Choice in an Uncertain World,* Hartcourt Brace Jovanovich, San Diego, CA, 1988.
3. A. P. Sage, *Decision Support Systems Engineering,* Wiley, New York, 1991.
4. M. Henrion, J. S. Breese, and E. J. Horvitz, "Decision Analysis and Expert Systems." *AI Mag.,* **12**(4), 64–91 (winter 1991).
5. L. J. Savage, *The Foundations of Statistics,* 2nd rev. ed., Dover, New York, 1972.
6. D. von Winterfeldt and W. Edwards, *Decision Analysis and Behavioral Research,* Cambridge University Press, Cambridge, U.K., 1988.
7. J. Pearl, *Probabilistic Reasoning in Intelligent Systems: Networks of Plausible Inference,* Morgan Kaufmann, San Mateo, CA, 1988.
8. R. A. Howard and J. E. Matheson, "Influence Diagrams," in *The Principles and Applications of Decision Analysis,* R. A. Howard and J. E. Matheson, eds. Strategic Decisions Group, Menlo Park, CA, 1984, pp. 719–762.
9. S. Holtzman, *Intelligent Decision Systems,* Addison-Wesley, Reading, MA, 1989.
10. G. F. Cooper and E. Herskovits, "A Bayesian Method for the Induction of Probabilistic Networks from Data." *Machine Learn.,* **9**, 309–347 (1992).
11. D. E. Heckerman, D. Geiger, and D. M. Chickering, "Learning Bayesian Networks: The Combination of Knowledge and Statistical Data." *Machine Learn.,* **20**(3), 197–244 (1995).
12. J. Pearl and T. S. Verma, "A Theory of Inferred Causation," in *KR-91, Principles of Knowledge Representation and Reasoning: Proceedings of the Second International Conference,* J. A. Allen, R. Fikes, and E. Sandewall, eds. Cambridge, MA, 1991, Morgan Kaufmann, San Mateo, CA, pp. 441–452.
13. P. Spirtes, C. Glymour, and R. Scheines, *Causation, Prediction, and Search,* Springer-Verlag, New York, 1993.
14. H. A. Simon, "Causal Ordering and Identifiability," in *Studies in Econometric Method: Cowles Commission for Research in Economics,* W. C. Hood and T. C. Koopmans, eds. Monograph no. 14, Wiley, New York, 1953, Chap. III, pp. 49–74.
15. M. J. Druzdzel and H. A. Simon, "Causality in Bayesian Belief Networks," *Proceedings of the Ninth Annual Conference on Uncertainty in Artificial Intelligence (UAI-93),* Morgan Kaufmann, San Francisco, 1993, pp. 3–11.
16. H. A. Simon, J. R. Kalagnanam, and M. J. Druzdzel, Performance Budget Planning: The Case of a Research University, under preparation, 1999.
17. P. E. Lehner, T. M. Mullin, and M. S. Cohen, "A Probability Analysis of the Usefulness of Decision Aids," in M. Henrion, R. D. Shachter, L. N. Kanal, and J. F. Lemmer, eds. *Uncertainty in Artificial Intelligence,* vol. 5, Elsevier Science, North Holland, Amsterdam, 1990, pp. 427–436.
18. M. J. Druzdzel, "Probabilistic Reasoning in Decision Support Systems: From Computation to Common Sense," Ph.D. thesis, Dept. of Engineering and Public Policy, Carnegie Mellon University, Pittsburgh, Dec. 1992.

MAREK J. DRUZDZEL
ROGER R. FLYNN

DOCUMENT PROCESSING

Introduction

The processes of creating, publishing, and managing documents are undergoing radical changes. In order to assess the validity of this thesis and to better understand the nature of the revolution, it is necessary to establish a framework for analysis. This article takes two perspectives to set the stage. First, an historical analysis attempts to posit the current developments in a larger context. Second, the nature and the magnitude of the changes in several aspects of the technology of document processing are explored. Following these analyses, this article attempts to outline the document-processing revolution. This is done in two parts. First, relevant changes in enabling technologies and information infrastructure are explored. Second, the changes in roles, processes, and products of modern document processing are reviewed.

This article is organized as follows: (1) historical context, (2) the nature and magnitude of the change, (3) enabling technologies and infrastructure, (4) functional changes, and (5) conclusions.

Historical Context

What exactly is happening today? Is this the middle of a revolution or is this much ado about nothing? It has been said that the short-term impact of new technology is overestimated and the long-term impact is underestimated. This section takes two views. The first, a narrower view, positions the changes in the context of the printing or reprographics process. The second view examines the changes in the context of the history of communications.

A NARROW VIEW: REPROGRAPHICS

It is not uncommon to hear the current developments in the area of documents compared to the emergence of the printing press. Eisentstein's book *The Printing Press as Agent of Change* (*1*) provides background for understanding the impact of the printing press. One may view the development of reprographics as marked by four events, beginning with the Gutenberg printing press.

1. Mechanical reprographics
2. Optical reprographics
3. Digital reprographics
4. Ad hoc reprographics

These terms characterize four significant developments in the reprographic process. First, 500 years ago the Gutenberg press signaled the beginning of the era of mechanical reproduction using modular reusable masters. Mechanical reprographics substituted flexible, movable type and mechanical reproduction for human efforts in reproductions; the printing press replaced the scribe.

Optical reprographics represents two distinct revolutions. The first was lithography, the use of photographic technology to make printing plates. For all practical purposes this put an end to mechanical typesetting, causing a significant change in the printing industry. The second was the use of photographic technology coupled with photosensitive dielectrics to give us photo duplication—or "Xeroxing." This made every object in the world a "master" that could be used for the printing process. The revolution here was dramatic. For the first time, virtually anyone could become a printer. The master existing in the copier was infinitely flexible and reusable.

The third revolution, digital reprographics, is somewhat fragmented, and includes the fax machine, laser printers, and the new digital copiers. With the introduction of digital technology, it was no longer necessary that the original have a physical form. If it did have a physical form, the revolution made it possible for the original and the copy to be in different locations.

The most recent reprographic revolution is "ad hoc" reprographics. This term is meant to capture the form of reprographics in which both the master and the copy are electronic. It is characterized by the "printing" of an electronic master to an all-points addressable screen—a computer or TV screen. Ad hoc reprographics is fundamentally different from the earlier stages. No physical resources are consumed. The "document" display is reusable. Neither the master nor the copy may ever exist in a nonelectronic form.

It is interesting to note that even with ad hoc reprographics there is pressure to maintain the traditional printing, publishing, and distributions roles. Part of the attractiveness of CD-ROM is that it maintains a physical object to produce and sell. The media are simply denser and more flexible.

THE BIG PICTURE: COMMUNICATIONS

While the reprographics perspective is helpful, there seems to be something more fundamental and significant happening. A number of authors have suggested that radio and television, which few would deny have had a significant impact on society, have had a profound impact on communications. This can lead one to think about the current revolution as a revolution not in methods of reprographics but in methods of communication. One might postulate the following developments in the communication process:

1. The language revolution
2. The literary revolution
3. The telepresence revolution
4. The metaliteracy revolution

The Oral and Literary Traditions

There is evidence that "humans" have been around for a million years or so (*2*). It is difficult to pinpoint when spoken language developed as a critical means of communication. Ong contends that social interaction has been occurring for the last 30,000 to 50,000 years (*3*). Although it is impossible to date the origin of spoken language, it was clearly millennia before written language. Many scholars refer to this period as the period of the oral tradition. The oldest deciphered written documents are about 6000 years old (*2*). Scholars have identified the development of writing as beginning the literary tradition.

Think about the change in documents—the document-processing revolution—moving first from a prelanguage tradition to language and then from the oral tradition to the written or literary tradition. First, just imagine what kinds of documents existed prior to spoken language. There is not much that easily comes to mind, but there must have been something—the pantomime of the great hunt, the defeat of the great enemy, and so on. These "documents" must have been subject to significant misinterpretation. Little of what constituted the great documents of the day have survived. One might speculate that the creation stories all have some common origin, which seems to be bound to physical objects and dramatic events that could be described without language. Whether these stories predate spoken language is difficult to say. The concepts are surely fuzzy enough and based enough on physical universals—the sun, the Earth, and the stars.

The literary revolution occurred when arbitrary symbols were used to represent spoken language. After 20,000 to 30,000 years of the oral tradition, the development of writing must have caused quite a stir. Echoes of the revolution can be heard to this very day. The revolution must have been cataclysmic. Imagine the court poets arguing over the value of these new scribes. Imagine the ridicule when two scribes used different symbols to represent some utterance. The message in spoken form was easily understood by all. Memory in this frame must have been viewed as a far superior form of communication; the human store could be queried, it was easily understood, and so on. It is not hard to imagine the highly valued court poets claiming that anything recorded in this new way would surely be lost, because even two experts could not agree on how to record a spoken word. Any individual—king to slave—could speak and listen, but only specially trained technologists could read and write. This picture has a modern counterpart. Technological advances never come automatically. Many years after the invention and wide dissemination and acceptance of writing, the advanced Greek society finds one of its brightest luminaries commenting on the technology.

> This invention of yours will produce forgetfulness in the minds of those who learn to use it, by causing them to neglect their memory, in as much as, from their confidence in writing, they will recollect by the external aid of foreign symbols, and not by the internal use of their own faculties.

Many people find this quote by Socrates humorous. It was so long ago and so ludicrous, given the current state of wisdom. Even to this day there are places and situations in which the oral tradition prevails; for example, the notion of eyewitness testimony versus affidavits.

> People had to be persuaded that written documentation was a reliable reflection of concrete, observable events. To the modern mind, the evanescence of the spoken word seems more plastic, quixotic, and undependable than the printed word. To members of a highly oral culture, however, the spoken word was connected to the incontrovertible realities of bodily

> experience, while the written word was a thin, substanceless scratching whose two-dimensionality seemed highly arbitrary (*4,* p. 77).

Socrates had reason to level his criticism. The written word did reduce attention to memory. Written language is a technology to supplement and improve the communication process. The revolutionary change in communication occurred with the virtually unlimited storage capacity and permanence represented by writing. While the literary tradition was accelerated with the development of mass-produced books in the fifteenth century, movable-type printing represents a quantitative change in the technology, not a qualitative change. At the same time, the magnitude of the change caused by the vast reduction in the cost of reproducing materials was significant.

Telepresence

The age of the first literacy continued unchallenged until the late nineteenth century. The invention of the telephone and motion pictures with sound were the early skirmishes in this next revolution. The widespread acceptance of broadcast radio and later television accelerated the change. Some suggest that the technology was giving birth to a second orality and that this new orality would cause a decline in the literary tradition. The decline in the number of general-circulation newspapers was seen as one indication of a reversion from written to spoken sources for current events information.

Television and radio represent something more. Immediate global television broadcast of events ranging from the Olympic games to the war in the Persian Gulf represent something of a return to the preoral tradition. They represent a form of telepresence that can be stored. This recording is in the same form as the original. It is no longer necessary to retell the story; it can be replayed exactly as it happened. This can be very helpful in the analysis of transient events, whether it is Neil Armstrong stepping onto the moon, the assassination of John F. Kennedy, or a human or natural disaster occurring somewhere around the world. We now have the ability to be present to the event; neither the oral nor the written tradition has to be relied upon. In addition, because signals can be stored, the events can be replayed and analyzed repeatedly. There are limits to what is recorded. For film or video, the camera angles and lighting must be correct or there may be important information that is not on the tape. The increased availability of tools to undetectably alter audio tape, photographs, and video raises questions about the reliability of the recordings. Nonetheless, electronic recordings represent a separable tradition that in a sense obviates the need for communication about the event. Within the limits of the recording, it is the event.

The Metaliteracy Revolution

It could be argued that computer-mediated communication is a return to a literary tradition. The proliferation of electronic mail contrasts with the decline in letter writing and an increase in telephone usage. Hypertext is a return to knowledge expressed in a written form. The majority of World Wide Web resources are text- and image-based. This material is highly dynamic; documents are being changed frequently, new documents are added, and old ones are deleted.

In some ways these new documents move beyond simple literacy. On the World Wide Web, the generation and management of links approaches the significance of the documents themselves. This emphasis on linking was virtually nonexistent in the first literacy and represents a kind of metaliteracy. Not only is the message passed on, but recommendations about how to navigate it are passed on as well. This metaliteracy also includes a view of written material that sees it as one alternative for communication. There is increasing use of audio and video documents to supplement text-based documents. This metaliteracy then is characterized by two intertwined developments. First, the communication is now in all the possible forms—symbolic, oral, and telepresence. They may be interwoven at leisure. Beyond this, however, the author can now weave processing instructions into the communication. These enable the receiver to understand how the author developed the communication or allow the receiver to continue to modify and change the document as it is accessed.

The Nature and Magnitude of the Change

Base technologies are what make revolutions possible. In this case, it is both the qualitative and quantitative change in base technologies that are important. This section examines the nature of the underlying changes and the magnitude of those changes.

TRENDS IN TECHNOLOGY

While it is difficult to stay abreast of every development, there are some trends that can be discerned. Key areas of change in the basic technology underlying document processing include digitization, accommodation, standardization, objectification, and integration. Of these, the first two are in our estimation the critical driving technologies of the revolution.

Digitization

Increasingly data are being kept in a digital, instead of analog, form. Perhaps the most common form of digital storage and processing in use today is the laster printer.* The office laser printer transforms a symbolic set of instructions into 8 million bits which are transferred to the paper going through the printer. Each 0 is represented as a black dot on the paper and each 1 is represented as a white dot. The result is the printed page you see in front of you. Another common form of digital information is the audio CD. To create an audio CD, music is sampled about 40,000 times per second

*It may well be that the fax machine is even more ubiquitous and representative of the use of digital representation. The fax machine scans an analog image, compresses the data via a technique that uses run length encoding via a modified Huffman code, transmits the data, decompresses it at the remote end, and prints it.

and the magnitude of the sound wave is represented by a 16-bit number—a value between 0 and 64,000. This means that a CD-audio recording uses 4.8 megabytes of data for every minute of recording.* ISDN offers digital telephone service that provides the user with two lines capable of sending 64,000 bits of information per second—the rate at which all modern phone systems transfer the digital representation of phone conversations. Consumer electronics such as telephone answering machines are available with solid state memory for a digital message instead of a cassette tape. High-definition television (HDTV) is the next major digital technology and it is expected to hit the U.S. market by the year 2000.

Digital data are important in that error correction techniques can be embedded in the representation to allow the data to be self-correcting. This is part of the quality advantage audio CDs (which are digital recordings) have over analog records or tapes. Digital representations of images may be stored at high resolution and displayed at a resolution that is appropriate for the use. There is a trade-off between the resolution and the speed of rendering the image, so different applications may demand different decisions about resolution.

Multipurpose digital signal processing (DSP) integrated circuits are currently being designed to be closely integrated into personal computers (PCs). Some manufacturers are developing motherboards with built-in DSP. The PC DSP provides digital/analog conversion. They replace special-purpose circuitry that is currently used to provide modem, fax, telephone (PC voice mail, fax response, etc.) and sound card functions. Features that were implemented in hardware will be implemented by software, providing for easier maintenance and enhancement.

Accommodation

Computing power has been doubling every two years. Much of this increased power has been used to improve its ease of use; that is, to better accommodate the user. It is interesting to note that the text-based word processor of five years ago had almost all of the capabilities of today's WYSIWYG (what you see is what you get) word processor, yet the WYSIWYG word processor requires a machine that is four to eight times more powerful. Side by side, the functions of the programs seem to operate in about the same human time. Where has all the increased processing power gone? The WYSIWYG program uses all that power to make the word processing functions easier to use. Graphical user interfaces have absorbed almost all of the recent increases in computing power to provide an improved user interface.

One way to understand this is to understand the change that has occurred over the last thirty years. In 1962 the cost of a computer was nearly $1,000,000, and the average professional was making on the order of $10,000. When a conflict arose between the human and the computer, the human lost—they were the less expensive cog in the wheel. Today, when all costs are considered, a professional costs an organization closer to $100,000, while a computer of the same power as the million-dollar computer of 1960 costs about $10,000; the human is now the winner when there is a conflict.

*In reality, compression allows this to be a smaller number, and error correction and format information uses additional space.

The technology of accommodation involves two areas of technology development. The first is the actual interface technologies, the eye phones, the data gloves, the mice and trackballs, and the speech recognition tools. Each of these technological developments is intended to provide an easier, faster, more natural way for a user to input or access data stored in a computer system. Technology is quickly getting to the point at which all of these operate at a level that allows the digital representation to be indistinguishable from the corresponding analog representation, given the normal acuity of the human sensory or motor system in question.

The second aspect of the technology of accommodation has to do with understanding the capabilities of the human component of the information system. The growing body of psychological and biological research is continuing to yield information about how humans process information, and this is being used to improve overall processing speed and efficiency. Take, for example, the theory of preattentive stimuli. Put very simply, this theory says that some stimuli are processed by the sensory system in a massively parallel fashion. Consider, for example, the task of finding a small *t* on a page of newspaper print. This process is not preattentive, and requires that each possibility be processed consciously. On the other hand, finding a red letter on a page of newspaper print can be done in an instant; colors are processed preattentively. The theory is more complex than this, but consider the implications of such a theory for coding information in a search and retrieval task. These kinds of phenomena are the basis of some of the research on navigating information spaces.

Standardization

Mature standards are so widely accepted that they are almost invisible. Standards for traditional document processing have developed over the last 500 years. These standards have included many things: the form of business letters, the process of filing, and the size of stationery. Paper and book sizes are good examples; both come in a variety of sizes, but not an endless one. The effect is that equipment ranging from printing presses to bookshelves can be produced efficiently because there is limited variation to accommodate. Information technology is heading toward mature standards. There are a thousand areas in which standards bodies operate around the world. Even though less than 1 percent of these bodies develop standards for information technology, they are producing about 50 percent of the new standards pages.

Two types of standards are evolving that will significantly impact document-processing productivity. First, technical compatibility standards are emerging that will provide simple and direct machine-to-machine (OSI, MHS, and FTAM)* and program-to-program (SGML and XML) transfers. Second, organizational and industry standards are emerging that will allow for these documents to be viewed coherently

*Information technology standards represent an alphabet soup for most users. Even with the acronyms defined, how these standards make our work easier is not always immediately clear. For the record, the standards mentioned here include the Open Systems Interconnection (OSI), Message Handling Service (MHS), File Transfer and Access Management (FTAM), Standard Generalized Markup Language (SGML) eXtensible Markup Language (XML), Electronic Data Interchange (EDI), and Computer-Aided Acquisition and Logisitics Support (CALS).

(EDI, CALS, etc.). There are also scores of less formal standards in this latter category that need to evolve. For example, organizations need to establish consistent naming conventions and file organizations for the filing of electronic documents. As structural copymarking becomes de rigueur, organizations will need to adopt organizational and industry standards for copymarking of commonly exchanged documents in accordance with metastandards, such as SGML and ODA.

Objectification

Object orientation is a paradigm shift in how computers are programmed to manage data and processes. This shift is significant in two ways. First, related to the development of systems, it represents a recognition of the need to move to a new, more modular view of software. Object-oriented programming is more modular than traditional approaches. This is providing developers with productivity benefits in developing, testing, and maintaining the software. As the cost of software development rises dramatically with the increasing complexity of the software, there is increased emphasis on programmer productivity. Object orientation appears to some to be a means by which we can control this process.

The second impact of objectification relates to the user. Traditionally, data (text, graphics, audio, etc.) were stored independently from the programs that processed the data. One consequence of this separation was that the user had to keep track of the programs that processed data files. For example, there are a dozen different formats for storing PC graphics data. The user had to know which program to use. In the object-oriented approach, the objects contain both the data and "methods," which are the processes that can act on that data. For example, a graphic object might have a "print" method that would render the data in a printable form. Another graphic object with a different format would also have a print method. Now the user only has to know to invoke the print method and no longer cares about the details of the storage format. This provides the user with simpler model of the system.

Integration

Integration is largely the result of technology maturation. For example, maturing DSP technology allows the integration of modem, fax, sound, and computer telephony into one circuit. Integration is manifested through multifunctionality, connectivity, and interoperability.

Multifunctionality is being able to use one advanced item instead of a series of less advanced objects. Many office desks have four terminals on them—telephone, fax, PC, and workstation or mainframe terminal. The trend is toward replacing these with a single multifunction device. Many computers have scanners and printers. A scanner and printer together form a digital copier. A copier with a modem is a fax machine. There have been several commercial products that combine these functions. None has been particularly successful in the marketplace. Performance/quality improvements and price reductions make the promise of a combined personal copier, fax printer, and scanner with a price tag of a few hundred dollars a reasonable expectation in a few years.

This is also a period of rapid integration at the intermachine level. This comes in two forms. First, connectivity is developing beyond the local area network level; it is increasingly important to be connected at the enterprise level. Connections between organizations exist for electronic data interchange (EDI) of business transactions such as purchase orders and invoicing. Electronic funds transfer is well-developed. The Internet and the World Wide Web are promoting new levels of interconnection.

Second, this is the beginning of true interoperability, which goes beyond connectivity. Interoperability allows cooperation between programs running on different computers. For example, a user on one computer might invoke a function that causes a program to run on another computer and have the second computer display the results on the first. Global weather forecasts are the result of massively parallel data-processing efforts. They are ultimately tied together based on the results developed in an independent yet coordinated form on many different kinds of machines all over the world. Similarly, there is increasing use of the information agents "spiders," "worms" and "infobots" that work independently across the network to provide information about what is available.

INFORMATION EARTHQUAKES

While these trends say a lot about what is happening today, many people find it easy to get lost in all the data. One other way to think about the changes that are occurring today is to measure the extent of the changes. It is interesting to think about how much change is being encountered. Changes in storage, transmission, and processing power have been significant. They are so large that they are best measured in orders of magnitude; just like the Richter scale for earthquake intensity, each increase in the number represents a tenfold increase in impact. A rating of one equates to a tenfold increase, a rating of two equates to a hundredfold increase, a rating of three to a thousandfold increase, and so on.

Processing

Information storage and retrieval is at the center of one of the earthquakes. Documents that would fill a library can be searched electronically in minutes. The electronic search can locate information within documents that could not be located by humans in a physical library in any reasonable amount of time. For example, any search that could not be answered based on bibliographical data and abstracts would require reading every document and would be impossible for all practical purposes. This human processing limit drives the need for bibliographic information. Electronic search allows for the storage and retrieval of full text, reducing the need for the analytic surrogates. The U.S. Library of Congress contains about 20 million books. Any word could be located by doing a binary search of an index of these books, and such a search could be completed within forty-two readings of the index (*5,* p. 15). This means the search would be completed in a few milliseconds.

This does not imply that the catalogers, indexers, and librarians are not needed; it does imply a change in their role. Skilled indexers will still be needed to add index terms that do not actually appear within the text. Similarly, a 1965 concordance of Byron's works tooks twenty-five years to develop manually (*5,* p. 2). The 285,000 entries can be generated by a computer in a matter of minutes. While concordance construction will change dramatically, expertise will still be needed in the use of concordances.

Looking at the quake in processing capability, one can make a variety of measurements. Overall the magnitude of the change in information-processing speed via technology between 1950 and the year 2000 is in the range of a magnitude 6 to 7 infoquake.

Storage

Storage media are experiencing similar oder-of-magnitude shocks. The density of memory on silicon chips keeps increasing. The first PCs in the early 1980s contained chips with 16-K bits on a chip. Personal computer memory chips now hold 16 Mb. State-of-the-art chips are now being developed that store 1 GB in a cubic inch. This corresponds to an increase of 1,000 to 62,500 times. Personal computer hard disks have gone from being nonexistent to having multiple gigabyte disks readily available. Similarly, removable media have gone from 360-K floppies to CD-ROM holding about 650 MB, another increase of 1800 times. The current CD-ROMs are the first generation. Enhanced capabilities should be expected. CD video is not yet well implemented, but two hours of CD video are achievable. It is simply now a matter of what standard will be adopted.

Looking at the quake in storage capability, measurements would seem to suggest that from 1950 to the year 2000 the magnitude of the change in information storage capability via technology will be in the range of a magnitude 5 infoquake.

Transmission

Electronic data transmission time is the center of another infoquake. Teletype machines ran at 150 or 300 bits per second (bps). Today, 2400-bps modems are common worldwide, with 28.800-bps modems becoming increasingly common. That is two orders of magnitude over teletype. Basic ISDN offers a fourfold increase over this, to 128,000 bps. This is significant when one considers that to transmit a book with 210 pages, ten images and fifty graphics would take 90 minutes by 2400-bps modem but 31 seconds via basic ISDN.* At ISDN speed, it could be faster to transmit the book to your computer than to find it on a shelf. It would certainly be faster than going to get it from the library. Asynchronous transfer mode (ATM) and frame relay offer bandwidth on demand. It is reasonable to expect serious users will all have the 10,000,000 to 100,000,000 bps network connections many academics currently have on their desktops.

Looking at transmission capability, measurements would seem to suggest that from the 1950 to the year 2000 the magnitude of the change in information transmission capability via technology will be in the range of a magnitude 8 to 9 infoquake. While

*The calculations are based on a book consisting of 210 text pages, each with 9.6 KB of text, ten 120-KB images, and fifty 16-KB graphics.

the transmission infoquake is significant enough in its own right, the co-occurrence of the three infoquakes is truly unprecedented.

Enabling Technologies and Infrastructure

There are a number of technological developments that are essential to a revolution in document processing. There is an effort in the United States at the current time to define these enabling technologies. In some ways this is the major focus of the national information infrastructure effort. A few key enabling technologies are described in this section, including the following:

1. Bit pipes and set-top boxes
2. Electronic currency
3. Network security and reliability
4. Public policy

BIT PIPES AND SET-TOP BOXES

The technical trends discussed above are driving both communications channels and processing devices toward integration, thus while some Americans now have three information lines coming into their houses—one for television, one for voice communication, and one for data—this will change with time. Already, the telephone companies have committed to—and are providing—better-grade communications lines that handle voice and data equally well. Video is not far behind. The various groups working on the national information infrastructure committees are addressing how to connect homes to the network.

A device is needed that provides access to the various kinds of information that can be moved via a digital bit pipe. Early on in the development of ISDN many people felt that the cost of digital phones, an order of magnitude greater than the cost of analog phones, would greatly hamper the extension of digital service. It is true that digital signal-processing capability adds significantly to the cost of a phone, but is only adds marginally to the cost of a PC and it can be used for many other functions in a PC. We will thus see the digital phone emerge as a new service to be provided via our PC, which will also act as an intelligent answering machine, appointment scheduler, videoconferencing device, and so on.

The set-top device has four primary subcomponents. First is the general processing, storage, and memory capabilities that are expected on a rather ordinary desktop device. Second, add the digital signal-processing capability that allows the conversion between digital and analog information, and the result is a phone, scanner, and the guts of a digital television. Third, add an array of connections to the box to allow it to be hooked into the home system. It will thus need a fiber or coax connection to the outside world and internal connections to all the devices in the home that it will feed or that it will integrate. It will need coaxial cable out to the televisions, Ethernet to the other microprocessors in the home, twisted pair out to speakers, and signal-processing lines in from security and fire devices.

The fourth component is the "set" that the device will sit on top of. The notion in the United States is that whatever is built will be a supplement to an existing output device in the home, particularly the television. The assumption is that the device is probably not the television currently in homes, but a digital HDTV. It is interesting to note that some of the same problems that occur with phones and digitization occur with television and digitization. A large home television (30 inches or 76 centimeters) costs $350, while a medium-sized computer monitor costs $1000. In order for an integrated precision output device to be placed into every home, there will have to be some breakthroughs in flat panel digital display technology. These breakthroughs have been accomplished, and they may be made public between the time of this writing and the time you read this. In any case, they are not far away.

All of these capabilities exist today—a wired home can be had for a few thousand dollars from off-the-shelf suppliers to the consumer market. Unfortunately, as of today there is nothing to hook the set-top device to. Remote and computer control devices for electrical outlets, lights, and appliances have been available for years but have yet to achieve significant popularity. This leads to the famous S curve of technology adoption and to the notion of network externality. The S curve of technology adoption indicates that the rate of adoption of a technology is slow in the early and late stages and rapid in the middle.

Network externality is an economic term indicating that the value of a network increases as the number of connections to it increases. An example from cable television illustrates this point nicely. One of Ted Turner's early cable companies was having difficulty attracting advertisers. When cable television had reached 35 percent market saturation, advertisers—Proctor and Gamble in particular—decided that it was a viable medium and started using it for advertising. Once this happened, more people wanted to provide cable channels to get at the available marketing revenues. Once 35 percent saturation was reached, which took about 25 years, an additional 35 percent saturation came in little more than six years. At the same time the number of cable channels swelled from ten to hundreds.

ELECTRONIC CURRENCY

Assuming that the pathways are established, many services can begin to be provided over the information infrastructure, providing that the parties can establish business relationships. This involves the following four subcomponents:

1. Electronic data interchange
2. Secure communications
3. Authentication
4. Electronic currency

The area of EDI is already well developed through the U.S. committee X12 and the international EDIFACT effort. In some industry groups such as banking, aerospace, and automotive, this development is at a reasonable level of maturity. Purchase orders, invoices, and hundreds of other business documents have been designed and are exchanged regularly. There are some minor problems related to system interoperability that have led to the creation of clearinghouses to do format conversions. These are very minor headaches, which are being overcome by additional standardization. The education and library industries are somewhat behind the curve, but this is normal. Progress toward standardized forms for electronic transcripts, proposal formats, overdue notices, and so on will take more time, but these forms are coming.

In the area of security, it is not clear which technologies will win and gain widespread acceptance. Security presents an interesting dilemma. At one level, secure communication can be accomplished today via any of a number of proprietary methods. Unfortunately, if two machines use different schemes they cannot share secure information. They must all agree to the same security method in order for communication to occur, thus within well-defined communities such as defense and banking, the goal has already been achieved. A broader-based public system for general use is needed, however. Added to this, at least in the United States is the demand for a system that can be tapped when a justifiable legal need arises. This debate, known as the "clipper chip debate," has caused significant controversy in the United States.

Third, a means of providing authentication is needed. Authentication verifies a person's identity and establishes that he or she is authorized to make a given transaction. This is important glue in the system. Bank and phone card fraud are already a significant problem in the United States. As the financial system becomes electronic, there needs to be some simple and yet foolproof mechanism for authenticating the user. This is a complex but critical component of the enabling technology.

Finally, there needs to be electronic money itself. A number of people are studying this problem, and the discussions of the characteristics of electronic money are wonderfully complicated. At the core level, the discussion has centered on the fact that money must meet the ACID (for atomic, consistent, isolated, and durable) test used for computerized transactions. This means that whatever form it takes, the money must be

1. Atomic. The payment and the purchase are inextricably linked.
2. Consistent. The amount the buyer pays must be consistent with the amount the seller gets.
3. Isolated. Each transaction should be isolated with no linkage between different transactions.
4. Durable. If the transaction fails in the middle, there should be partial completion and things should roll back.

In addition to these concerns, electronic currency will have to have minimal overhead—the cost of "printing" and processing the money must not add significantly to the cost of the transaction. Electronic money must have reasonable granularity and scalability—that is to say, one must be able to buy cars and candybars. Many people must be able to purchase things electronically at the same time. Electronic money must be trusted. This means that it should be readily accepted. There should not be multiple mutually exclusive forms of money. It should not be possible for someone to make their own money as counterfeiters do now. Similarly, existing money should not be able to be changed in value. Electronic money must hold its value over time; it cannot expire.

The last and perhaps most fascinating feature is related to the isolated nature of the transactions. Part of this has to do with the anonymity of money. When a newspaper is purchased with cash, it is not known who bought it. The physical currency carries no history with it. The technologists are working on similar capabilities for electronic cash. At a simple level, a smart card could take money from a bank account with appropriate authentication and record it on the card. On-card circuitry can then spend that money, debiting the amount on the card without telling the seller anything other than the fact that this card, which is anonymous to the seller, has enough money on it to buy the item in question.

NETWORK SECURITY AND RELIABILITY

The network must be secure at a number of levels. The issue of transaction integrity has already been addressed. This involved the use of a digital signature of some sort to guarantee the validity of the transaction. Security involves a number of other concerns as well. These include the following:

1. Methods to assure that a portal to the network is semipermeable and that it is resistant to unauthorized access.
2. Transmission assurance that the transaction will be delivered only to the proper destination and will not be intercepted or modified en route.
3. Network reliability, survivability, and scalability that will ensure that the message/transaction will be able to get through to the destination without failure; in other words, access will not be affected by catastrophe and network load will not impact performance.

To achieve the first goal, mechanisms are needed to assure that the information does not include Trojan horses and there are no backdoors to the system that cannot be locked and unlocked by the owner. To achieve the second goal, some forms of encryption and authentication are needed. There are also system policies and policing that are required to ensure that other people do not get unauthorized access to the bit pipes.

The last goal makes clear that security also includes assurance that if the transaction is sent it will in fact arrive. This has to do less with the threat of intrusion than it has to do with the reliability of the system. At a simple level, a system needs to have rerouting capabilities to ensure that expected system failures are minimized and localized. This also requires, however, that the system have survivability. Essential services must survive catastrophes such as fires, earthquakes, and typhoons. Finally, these services must be overbuilt to survive extreme use conditions. In the United States this is the Thanksgiving holiday for the transportation system. For the phone system, it is Mother's Day. For the Internet, it might be the demand for copies of the photos of the comet hitting Jupiter or of a war somewhere in the world.

PUBLIC POLICIES

The kind of revolution made possible by these kinds of technologies and infrastructure will be aided or constrained by public policy. These policies will have to do with access, privacy, intellectual property, regulation, and so on. For example, as Samuelson (*6*) has pointed out, copyright policies at heart have to do with establishing financial incentives for authors and publishers that promote societal goals of spreading information and increasing learning. In the United States, access to the National Information Infrastructure (NII) via libraries and schools is a national priority. This kind of public policy will encourage a revolution in how documents are handled. At the same time, some manifestations of new intellectual property regulation seem to ignore the issue of making information more available and appear in some ways to be controlled by special interests looking to keep control of the situation.

Functional Changes

The document-processing revolution that is underway today will make use of this emerging infrastructure. One way to understand what will change is to ask the following three questions:

1. How will the things called documents change?
2. How will the roles of the key players change?
3. How will the processing of these documents change?

Historically, documents have been linear and for the most part atomic. New document forms are emerging that are neither linear nor atomic. More responsibilities are being shifted to the creators and users of documents. The process is being streamlined and the stages of processing are shifting. Each of these areas is examined briefly below.

DOCUMENTS

This section develops a definition for a document, looks at some of the new kinds of documents that are emerging, and takes a particular look at hyperdocuments and active documents.

1. The definition of document
2. The likely new products in the near term
3. Two new document types: hyperdocuments and infobots

The Document Defined

It is interesting that this entity to which so much effort is devoted and which is held so dear is so difficult to define. From an information science point of view, it is essential to develop some definitional clarity to do research in the area. One early effort yielded the following:

> A document is an identifiable entity having some durable form, produced by a person or persons toward the goal of communications; it may take a number of forms, but must have at least one symbolic manifestation that can be comprehended by humans (*7*).

Documents are an essential product in the information age. There was a day a document was a report or a book that consisted predominately of text written by a single author. Things are no longer so simple.

1. Documents include text, graphic, images.
2. Documents may be cohesive (a letter or a report) or disjunctive (a medical record).
3. Documents may be authored by individuals, groups, or organizations.
4. Documents may have a limited life span or be archival.

New Electronic Document Forms

Documents are becoming ever larger and more complex. The support documents for the Boeing 747 weigh as much as the 747. Two copies of the documentation for a new drug application will fill the largest moving van available. Publishing-related expenditures reflect 6 percent to 10 percent of the gross revenues of the Fortune 1000. Over 2 trillion pages were printed in 1986 and nearly 4 trillion were printed in 1990.

What new forms will electronic documents take? There are several clues that may be gleaned from the current situation. Several new forms of documents are emerging, including the following:

1. Custom documents—only what is needed for that customer.
2. On-demand documents—documents only when they are needed.
3. Living documents—the source document is always current.
4. Multimedia documents—the needed mode is used.
5. Distributed documents—the documents is located close to interested parties.
6. Interactive documents—the document exhibits some intelligence.

These various forms of documents overlap, but they can be treated individually for purposes of illustration. The custom document is emerging because of the significantly reduced cost of digital reprographics. It is still true that the cost of mass-produced documents is less than the cost of unique products. It is equally true that the smaller size of custom documents makes them more economical. As an example, consider the cost of the journals on my shelves. The entire journal comes at a lower cost per page than a single copy of the articles I am interested in. However, overall cost of printing one copy of all the interesting articles is less than the cost of the journal containing all the articles. Similarly, copies of advanced textbooks that include only the material I need are likely to include less than the mass-produced versions.

In academia, bulletins and course catalogs are used to specify the rules and regulations that apply to graduate students. At any time the official bulletin fails to reflect the rules and regulations currently in force because the document was printed at some prior date. Living documents are those that have strong version-control features that allow one to print the document as it exists today or as it had existed at a given time.

Multimedia documents are all the rage today, and having experienced the value of being able to switch modes in working with my children I am convinced that they will become even more important. We have only begun to come to understand how to use

There is a need to be sensitive to the human components of the problem and to work to build tools to assist in this process. There are two significant changes in the roles related to documents.

The Author in Control

Historically, document publication has required that the author work with a number of people to create a document—editors to develop the content, graphic artists to lay it out, and printers to make copies. For the most part, computer systems are making it possible for the author to fulfill all these roles. The most dramatic manifestation of this control comes via the emergence of structural copymarking.

Early electronic typesetting embedded codes that indicated specific physical properties for the type (typeface, font, size, line length, leading, etc.). Modern systems have shifted to style sheets and structural copymarking. Structural copymarking indicates the role of the associated text instead of the physical properties. Instead of marking text as "Times Roman bold, 18 point, flush right," the structural copymark might be "major heading." Structural copymarking was implemented in such early systems as Scribe and now appears in leading PC word processors. Definable "styles" and autoformatting capabilities are all examples. WYSIWYG systems have facilitated this shift.

As a consequence of structural copymarking the author can concentrate on the content, and the system will produce aesthetically pleasing output. This can eliminate the intermediaries from copy editors to graphic layout artists to proofreaders. Reducing the intermediaries can reduce the preparation time significantly. In many technical fields, professional communities are concluding that an acceptable editing job done quickly is better than excellent editing done slowly. When the target audience is small and knowledgeable, there is likely to be a high tolerance for minor errors.

The fact that the author can now self-publish has two down sides. First, even with the best system, the author is distracted by these new responsibilities. Even if the author successfully manages to format the document, he or she is doing less authoring and somewhat more designing. Equally critical, the tools are not perfect and there is a risk that the author will not do an adequate job. It is still the case that the results achieved by a professional can far surpass the quality of computer-augmented work.

Interestingly, automation is uncovering some weaknesses in the traditional system. Human copy editors make changes that are not consistent across the entire document. In the editing and review process of a recent book, it became clear that the rule-based component-based document was viewed by the editors as a concrete linear document. Some interesting things were found.

1. Automated aspects of the document were edited repeatedly (e.g., header and footer).
2. In-text changes were made manually rather than by specifying rules. The editor marked every occurrence instead of specifying that all x should be y.
3. Modules that were included multiple times were edited differently at different positions.

Typography is also effected by structural copymarking. Instead of getting a specific typographic design for each document, the documents all have a consistent type. This could be an advantage in creating a consistent image or a disadvantage in settling for a generally acceptable format instead of the best one for each document.

One aspect of the revolution is thus that the author's sphere of influence and responsibility will increase. Authors will in essence be self-publishers, opening up the question of how the reader will be able to distinguish quality work from garbage.

Reader Agents

The electronic document market is just beginning to emerge, but it is already clear that there are several consequences for the consumer. They are not confident about where to look for particular information. There is no way to determine that the desired information is not available. At the present time, Internet searches can be analogous to randomly calling everyone in the phone book. There is pressure to better organize the process.

Most physical products are delivered through a multilevel distribution channel consisting of producers, wholesale distributors, and retail stores. Consumers rely on the retail stores to have the products they need. The retail stores provide a structure for the shoppers. The customer knows (at least in general) what store to purchase a particular type of product from. For example, if you needed car parts, you would go to an automobile parts store, not a food store. Since stores specialize in certain types of products, you would have a reasonable expectation of when to give up looking for an item you could not find. Retail stores in turn rely on the wholesale distributors (and to some extent directly on the producers) to provide the products they will sell. The retailers will select the products they will sell from the full product line offered by the producer through the distributors. The distributors keep the retailers informed of new products in an attempt to get the retailers to sell those products.

We find some of these patterns of supply are beginning on the Internet. There are specialized archives and there are services for such things as archives. Without endeavoring to predict specifics, it is clear that agents will be needed to assist consumers of information. The following are tentative examples of the kinds of direct and indirect agents that will have to find a place on the Web:

1. Information collectors
2. Authorized and recognized repositories
3. Cost-effective Gophers
4. Distributors

Collectors. The network phone books address the difficulty of finding people on the network. They are in some ways remarkable, in other ways quite poor. As the cost of usage, some of the directory services now begin by asking the user to provide information. One has built a directory of a million people this way. This service provides access to information on the million who have registered. In a few years, as the database grows, the service will cease to be free, especially as it becomes accepted as *the* significant place to be listed.

Repositories. There will be both authorized and recognized repositories. An authorized repository might be the official place to leave information of archival value or information with legal implications. For example, to record a property deed, it might have to be deposited with a fee at XYZ location on the web. It will then be guaranteed to be available for twenty years. Similarly, there may be places that are recognized for the quality of their collections—either by virtue of inclusiveness or of selectivity and quality. Whether the supplier or user pays for a piece is hard to determine, but an author may want to submit work to XYZ location because he knows that the site keeps everything on the subject and therefore that is where people look. In addition, the author might put it there because he knows that all of their material is first rate and therefore if they accept his work it will have the characteristic of being considered first rate.

Gophers and Distributors. Imagine that there is a photo of the 1998 America's Cup races from New Zealand that everyone in New York City wants. The cost of moving a million bits from Auckland to New York is $1. If the cost of moving it in New York City is $.10 then it makes sense to open a photo store in New York and have a selection of photos moved there from around the world. If the New York store sells them for $.20 they will make back their investment of a dollar after ten sales. The other side of this coin has to do with distribution. A supplier may ask a distributor to move something to the places where it will sell if it is available locally at reduced cost. The distributor pays to move it to local retailers and gets a commission as copies are sold.

PROCESSES

The processes applied to documents run from creation and dissemination to storage and retrieval. Document processes occur at a number of different levels of detail. For example, creating a document involves the operations of outlining, writing, editing, validating, designing, illustrating, proofing, and displaying. The processes related to accessing them include classifying and organizing them for storage and to formulating queries to retrieve them. This section looks at document processes with an eye to reengineering. In the discussion, the process changes already underway are reviewed.

Reengineering

In *Document Databases* Geoffrey James discusses the fact that while technological innovation is required for a revolution, it is not in itself sufficient.

> Gutenberg's improvement in technology did not by itself cause a revolution in communications. The full impact of his invention was delayed by limitations in the method by which books were produced. Each book was hand crafted to resemble a hand lettered manuscript...The real revolution took place when early forms of mass manufacturing were applied to publications (*10*).

Indeed, there are many who believe that the real revolution related to the book occurred as a result of the efforts of printers such as Aldus Mantius, who introduced new book sizes and typefaces.

Michael Hammer is a work reengineering consultant. In essence, Hammer suggests that cutting fat and automating work processes avoids the critical dimension of what needs to be done. He says that reengineering is the process of "Recognition and breaking away from outdated rules and fundamental assumptions that underlie operations. Unless we change these rules, we are merely rearranging the deck chairs on the Titanic" (*11*).

The document-processing field is replete with processes that might be reengineered. It has been known for years that the retention of information is increased if text is not printed with justified margins and yet informational text is still justified. Computer systems can format most simple documents based on simple rules. Paragraph and sentence spacing can be done automatically if simply left to the system. Still, users persist in doing the physical formatting themselves. Reengineering is a major focus of one of our current research projects called CASCADE (computer-augmented support of collaborative authoring and document editing). Consider some examples from that effort.

1. The processes of logical document structuring and physical document formatting are loosely coupled. Logical document structuring should be able to control and drive document formatting.
2. Entities are referred to directly rather than indirectly, making it necessary to manually change references when locations or numbering are changed by the system.
3. Indices are constructed by hand rather than by the system based on stop words and user removal of inappropriate items.
4. Documents are created from scratch as unique entities rather than developed from templates and modified as needed.

Document processing needs to be reengineered. In general, there are three types of benefits to be gained.

1. Significant savings in the time to produce the document.
2. A reduction in the costs incurred in producing documents, including:
    a. Reduced printing cost because of reduced transportation, waste, and storage costs
    b. Decreased production staff costs
    c. Increased publication value in sales or revenue-related uses
    d. Decreased costs for graphics
3. New opportunities to do such things as
    a. Updated publications on demand and just-in-time publishing
    b. Ability to provide (sell) new services
    c. Customized publications

Processes in Transition

In this section we examine a few trends that are indicative of the kinds of changes taking place in the processing of documents. These include the following:

1. The increase in the revision frequency
2. The ability to print documents on demand
3. The shift to finding by association

Revision Frequency. Electronic editing has increased the frequency of document revision. Indeed, one of the changes that can be noted is the process of making changes to existing documents rather than starting from scratch each time. The document you are reading reflects the merger and extension of ideas from two older documents on the changes in document processing. Historically, the cost of revisions has been high. Today there is virtually no cost. In addition, making changes was very costly when it meant that existing inventory had to be scrapped. If there is no inventory the revision cost is reduced to the work needed to make the logical changes. There are several consequences to this reduced cost.

1. Simple corrections can be easily made.
2. Time-dependent information can be updated frequently.
3. A series of incremental changes can be made instead of major version changes.

This third change is a two-edge sword. With a series of small revisions, how are the readers supposed to know when there are enough changes to merit obtaining a new version? A publisher could announce every small change as "new and improved," hoping to sell more copies of the document. Alternatively, the publisher could withhold any minor updates and only produce infrequent "new editions." In some ways this is analogous to the problems faced by software companies in deciding when to release program patches to fix problems and new versions with new features. A document with frequent revisions is constantly evolving. If a document is required for archival purposes, this raises the issue of what version(s) to retain.

Printing on Demand. Printing on demand is the process of consumers obtaining a document electronically and printing a copy for themselves. This has a profound impact on publishing. It also changes the definitions of archival copies. Traditionally publishers printed documents, creating the plates, putting them on the press, and adjusting the press until good copies were produced. This set-up time can be significant and is not dependent upon the number of copies to be printed once the press is ready. There is therefore a strong incentive to print as many copies as will ever be needed. This spreads the set-up cost over a large number of copies and reduces their average cost. Expressed simply, there are economies of scale in long press runs.

Presses are now available that can take the document via a computer interface, make the plates, and adjust the press without significant operator intervention. Set-up time is reduced but still prohibits economic short press runs. Ultimately, fully electronic printing involves no set-up costs and allows for any number of copies.

There is a more important aspect of printing on demand that has received remarkably little attention to date. Printing on demand shifts production costs from the producer to the consumer. The consumer downloads the electronic document (often paying the communications charges) and consumes his or her own supplies (paper, ink, or toner) and uses his or her own equipment (printer). This transfer of costs has already occurred with faxes. The advertiser sending the fax is causing you to use your supplies and capital to produce its message. This contrasts with "junk" mail advertisements, where the cost is borne primarily by the advertiser.

One of the remaining advantages of mass production in printing has to do with the speed of production. The fastest laser printer just cannot compete with a web press. With network environments this process is changing, however. As a result, the whole process of publishing will be turned inside out. Instead of printing and then disseminating, dissemination will occur first and then printing.

Guided Finding by Association. Since the library at Alexandria, the way to find material has been by looking in an area in which information is stored based on its main focus. All the books on libraries were thus located in the same area. Now there are new ways of locating relevant materials. These methods were first alluded to by Vanevar Bush in an article published at the end of World War II, "As We May Think" (*8*). Hypertext links between documents allow users to navigate between related documents. One problem that results is that people get confused about where they are, where they have been, and where they are going; they are lost in hyperspace. This is particularly likely to occur when the environment is dynamic. Changing connections, updating, and growth increase the user's cognitive load. Users need a guide to assist with routing, selection, and navigation. Just as a teacher serves as a guide to a textbook, the guide would increase the value of the document base.

Conclusions

It is our conclusion that document processing is indeed in a state of revolution. There are orders of-magnitude changes in many areas that have the impact of earthquakes. Basic technology trends, including digitization, standardization, accommodation, and integration, provide a foundation for the revolution. Enabling technologies, including the information infrastructure, electronic currency, security techniques, and intellectual property rights, provide the materials necessary for the revolution. There is a variety of factors that are driving emerging roles for information wholesalers and retailers.

There are changes in products, roles, and processes that also seem to indicate that a revolution is underway. The authoring process has become a logical task, with the computer handling much of the physical design. Being able to download and print documents on demand has led to dissemination followed by printing in contrast to centuries of printing followed by dissemination. Dynamic documents are emerging that change the way we think about these heretofore static artifacts of communication. In concluding, there are two points that merit mention—the economics of documents and the organizations that support that economy.

ECONOMICS OF DOCUMENTS

Economics drives much of what goes on in the world. Fortunately or unfortunately, it is increasingly a fact of life. With the move to an information-based economy and a digital world, many things will move from atoms to bits and those bits will increasingly be treated as commodities. Negroponte has an analysis in his book *Being Digital* (*12*) about the conversion from an economy based on atoms to an economy based on bits. His premise is that where an atom can be replaced by a bit there are advantages to the substitution and they will have an impact on how business is done.

Books and documents are the quintessential examples of the shift from atoms to bits. Where are the new economies of scale in the document business? What are the instances of network externality that are about to emerge? The new bit-based documents will require new hardware and software. Users will have to be attached to a new distribution system. Unlike a physical distribution system however, the costs of the electronic system are decreasing. As the start-up costs of joining the network go down, by the rules of network externalities, it can be expected that users and providers in this new environment will achieve economies of scale. When selling physical goods, the store must invest in inventory for each item sold, and each item uses up shelf space in the store. There is therefore a significant marginal cost for each item carried. The document market has a marginal cost of "stocking" a document that is close to the cost of the disk space consumed. The additional cost for each item sold is almost zero. If the document seller receives revenue for every document sold and his or her marginal cost is very low, there is a tremendous incentive to increase sales volume. Physical retail is driven to larger stores by economies of scale that reduce marginal cost. Document retail has a low marginal cost and will be driven to maximize revenue.

Current information providers are analogous to small mom-and-pop retailers. With decreasing start-up costs, more and more providers are entering the market. Economics provides an argument for increasing size. Customer service (know where to look and when to stop looking) will further drive the consolidation into stronger wholesalers and retailers of electronic documents.

PEOPLE, TECHNOLOGY AND ORGANIZATIONS

There are significant unknowns about the process of introducing technology in a workplace and in a culture. The process can become destructive or at the very least nonproductive if it is not handled well.

At the Institute for Research on Interactive Systems (IRIS) at the Rand Corporation, Bikson and others have been studying the process of introducing technology in the workplace: "We found that site to site variations in the success of implementing new technologies were more fully explained by differences in the implementation process itself than by differences in the systems or in the organizations" (*13*).

Among the specific findings were the following:

1. Better implementation is achieved if social as well as technical issues are addressed during implementation.
2. Satisfaction and production increased when learning to use the computer is supported.
3. Implementation is more successful when users feel capable of exerting a substantive, positive influence on the spread of technology.
4. Implementation succeeds when the software is suited to user needs.
5. Implementation succeeds when the program is modifiable by the user.

In *In the Age of the Smart Machine: The Future of Work and Power* (*4*), Shoshana Zuboff traces the long history of automation. The application of power technology to the production process is automation. She reviews the impact of Frederick Taylor and the industrial engineers who developed the time motion and document-flow studies. They are the people that took the holistic joy out of finishing the job you started. In essence, they are the people who created word-processing pools and piecework. They are the people who said anyone can type anything for anybody; it is simply an I/O process.

Zuboff says that the introduction of the computer has caused something new to occur. Where the steam engine caused automation, the computer causes information. Rather than automating, we are informating. More important, while the industrial revolution was characterized by piecework and the fragmentation of work, the information revolution may well be characterized by informated control of the overall process once again. As an example, the use of computers has made it possible for a single individual to control the paper-making process in a very large plant.

The task then is to make use of this new technology in a way to help people help organizations. What is needed is a new way to think about people and organizations. In the informated organization

> Members can be thought of as being arrayed in concentric circles about a central core, which is the electronic data base... On the innermost ring, nearest to the core, are those who interact with information on a real-time basis. They have responsibility for daily operations (*4,* p. 396).

REFERENCES

1. E. Eisentstein, *The Printing Press as Agent of Change,* Cambridge University Press, Cambridge, MA, 1979.

2. V. Fromkin, and R. Rodman, *An Introduction to Language,* Harcourt Brace College Publishers, Fort Worth, 1993, p. 22.

3. W. J. Ong, *Orality and Literacy,* Methuen, London, 1982, p. 2.

4. S. Zuboff, *In the Age of the Smart Machine: The Future of Work and Power,* Basic Books, New York, 1988.

5. I. H. Witten, A. Moffat, and T. C. Bell, *Managing Gigabytes,* Van Nostrand Reinhold, New York, 1994.

6. P. Samuelson, "Legally Speaking: Copyright and Digital Libraries." *Commun. ACM,* **38**(4), 15–21, 110 (April 1995).

7. M. Spring, *Electronic Printing and Publishing: The Document Processing Revolution,* Marcel Dekker, New York, 1990, p. 8.

8. V. Bush, "As We May Think." *Atlantic Monthly,* **176,** 101108 (July 1945).

9. M. Spring and M. Jennings, "Virtual Reality and Abstract Data: Virtualizing Information." *Virt. Real. World,* **1**(1), c–m (spring 1993).

10. G. James, *Document Databases,* Van Nostrand Reinhold, New York, 1984, p. 9.

11. M. Hammer, "Reengineering Work: Don't Automate, Obliterate." *Harvard Bus. Rev.,* **90**(4), 104112 (July/Aug. 1990).

12. N. Negroponte, *Being Digital,* Knopf, New York, 1995.

13. T. Bikson, B. Gutek, and D. Mankin, *Implementing Computerized Procedures in Office Settings,* Rand Institute for Research on Interactive Systems, R3077NSF/IRIS, Santa Monica, CA, p. v.

MICHAEL B. SPRING
JEFFREY D. CAMPBELL

ELECTRONIC RECORDKEEPING

Introduction

The increasing use of computer technology and information systems to support communications and business processes is transforming the way that many organizations and individuals create and maintain records. Electronic recordkeeping is concerned with the policies, practices, and technologies that enable organizations and individuals to create and retain reliable and authentic electronic records, eliminate unnecessary paper records, and satisfy organizational needs and legal requirements for evidence and memory.

Records are documents in any form created or received by an organization or individual in the normal course of business and kept because they provide evidence of policies, procedures, actions, or decisions. Electronic records are records created or captured and retained in electronic form. They can exist in many different formats (such as word processing documents, spreadsheets, data files and databases, graphics, digital audio files, and hypertext), and are stored on a variety of computer-readable media, including magnetic tapes, diskettes, optical disks, and magnetic disks. Some electronic records resemble traditional paper documents because they use highly structured electronic forms to standardize their contents and appearance. Innovations in information technology have also spawned new types of documents.

Electronic mail, hypertext, and multimedia documents are examples of new record formats that do not have antecedents in paper-based recordkeeping practices. Electronic records are not directly readable by the human eye. Storage, retrieval, and viewing of electronic records depends upon the availability of computer hardware and software capable of reading, interpreting, and presenting the records. The complex dependencies between information systems and electronic records complicate the management and control of electronic records.

Evolution of Electronic Recordkeeping

The concept of electronic recordkeeping is relatively recent. Large corporations and government agencies started to use computers for complex calculations, research, and accounting during the 1950s, and by the 1970s they relied on automated systems to process many routine transactions. Most early computer systems, however, produced a paper copy that was filed and kept as the "record copy." Although the concept of the "paperless office" was introduced in the late 1970s, organizations have only gradually shifted from paper-based to electronic recordkeeping systems. A combination of technical, social, and cultural factors may explain the lag between the introduction of information technology and its extensive use for recordkeeping. Concerns about the authenticity and legality of electronic records have persisted and some organizations have been reluctant to depend solely on electronic recordkeeping systems until their reliability could be demonstrated. Few common off-the-shelf software products readily support recordkeeping without some customization for each specific application. Solutions to the technical, organizational, and legal issues have not kept pace with advances in information technology (*1*).

A number of technological and organizational changes since the 1970s have served as catalysts for electronic recordkeeping. Improvements in office systems, the decentralization of computing services, and the development of much more complex applications facilitated the integration of information systems into everyday work and communications. Networking made it possible for users to retrieve records directly from an online repository and to view them on a dedicated terminal or personal workstation. With the growth and popularity of E-mail, electronic messages superseded internal memos as the preferred mode of internal communication in many organizations. Today, some organizations use the World Wide Web as their primary means for information dissemination, rely on an intranet for internal recordkeeping, and conduct most external transactions through electronic data interchange (EDI). Although many organizations still maintain hybrid paper and electronic recordkeeping systems, more and more organizations are seeking systems and methods for electronic recordkeeping.

Significance of Electronic Records

Records serve many useful functions in organizations. Organizations rely on their recordkeeping systems to coordinate group activities, track resources, establish precedents, monitor performance, and maintain consistency and continuity. Records help people remember details that are too numerous or too complex to recall and to find information about events, transactions, and decisions that occurred in the past. People who are removed from an event, either temporally or spatially, rely on records for a summary or replica of what transpired. Records play an important role in ensuring accountability when individuals or institutions are entrusted with the authority and responsibility to act on behalf of others. Public records, for example, enable private citizens and oversight bodies to monitor the actions and decisions of government agencies and elected officials. Financial records are used to protect funds from fraud, misuse, and embezzlement. Records are an important component of organizational memory and learning. The recorded memory of an organization, found in its paper and electronic files, constitutes an important organizational resource that can be exploited to trace and analyze past practices, maintain continuity when personnel changes, and determine precedents for decisions (*2*).

Organizations and individuals create and maintain some records because they are required to comply with external recordkeeping requirements. Laws, regulations, and institutional policies require organizations to create and keep certain records, dictate the acceptable forms and formats for records, and establish minimum retention periods. The concept of formal, established mandates for recordkeeping found in statutes, regulations, policies, and professional practice guidelines, is called the warrant for recordkeeping (*3*). Each business process or type of transaction has specific recordkeeping requirements that determine the exact contents of records, their routing or distribution, the access points for further retrieval, and their retention. Efforts to compile comprehensive collections of recordkeeping requirements have identified thousands of requirements applicable to specific businesses, regulated organizations, professional practitioners, and individuals. Several reference sources exist to assist organizations in the identification of recordkeeping requirements (*4, 5*).

Accurate and reliable records are especially important in litigation. Revised federal rules governing discovery—the process through which defendants in a case must turn over relevant records to the plaintiffs—permit broad searches of electronic files and storage systems. Records that are inaccurate or unreliable can harm a defendant's case, while the inexplicable absence or destruction of records can lead to allegations of tampering with evidence. Increasingly, electronic records are used to satisfy recordkeeping requirements, and they may be admissible as evidence in legal proceedings.

Most societies recognize the historical and cultural significance of certain records that are organized formally into archives. In data processing, the term archives refers to long-term storage areas, often on magnetic tape, for backup copies of files or files that are no longer in use (*6*). For archivists and records managers, archives are defined more narrowly as the records of an organization, person, or institution with continuing value (*7*). Archives offer insights into historical trends and provide people with a link to their past. Electronic records must fulfill all of the organizational, legal, communicative, and cultural purposes that traditional formats of records have served for centuries.

Benefits and Challenges of Electronic Recordkeeping

Organizations and individuals create and keep records in electronic form because there are distinct advantages to electronic recordkeeping. The storage capacity of digital media far exceeds that of paper and microfilm. Electronic records, if organized in a consistent structure and adequately indexed, are much more accessible than paper documents. Organizations can use sophisticated search and retrieval routines to identify specific documents and deliver them to the requester's E-mail address or online work space.

Electronic recordkeeping systems also integrate the processes of records creation and use with the normal workflow of business processes. Systems for electronic commerce and EDI allow organizations to conduct business transactions with little human intervention in the computer-to-computer exchange of information. Local area networks, groupware, and enterprisewide intranets allow everyone involved in a business process to communicate electronically and share electronic files. Such processes often eliminate the need for most intermediate paper documents and may eliminate paper records entirely.

Until recently organizations could fall back on printing out records and storing them in established filing systems. Today many records are retained in electronic form because there is no other technical or economical option. Some digital repositories store such vast quantities of records that printing them on paper would take weeks or even months. Emerging forms of documents, such as hypertext and multimedia, cannot be printed or stored on paper without significant losses of functionality and information. Finally, many electronic records are more useful if they are delivered in a computer-processable format that can be analyzed, edited, and manipulated.

The special attributes of electronic records and the lack of experience with this new form of recordkeeping present challenges for the management and control of electronic records. The reliability and authenticity of electronic records may be questioned because electronic records are easy to alter without leaving a trace of tampering. Electronic recordkeeping systems are subject to human and technological failures, which can result in significant losses of important records. If a system fails, an organization may lose access to vital information that is essential for ongoing operations until the system is restored, and if the system does not have adequate backup, information may be lost forever. Computer viruses and malfunctioning software can produce erroneous results or alter the contents of electronic records.

Many organizations are accumulating vast quantities of electronic records in the normal course of business because their information systems have a great capacity to collect and store information. The accumulation of large volumes of private and public records in electronic form raises concerns about the impact of electronic recordkeeping on personal privacy. Organizing large volumes of digital information into manageable electronic recordkeeping systems that will satisfy the demands of both day-to-day operations and future access and retrieval is another significant challenge.

Electronic records also are more difficult to maintain and preserve for the long term because they are stored on magnetic or optical media, which are much more fragile than traditional recording and storage media. High-quality paper stored under proper conditions can last for more than 100 years, and archival quality microfilm has a life expectancy of 500 years. By contrast, even under ideal conditions, the upper limit for magnetic tape is thirty years (*8*). Some optical media may last longer, but optical media have also been known to fail after a relatively short period of time. The storage media used for electronic records are subject to rapid deterioration and catastrophic loss when the entire contents of a single tape or disk become irretrievable. Recovery procedures are expensive at best, and there is no guarantee that information stored on media that fail can be recovered.

The rapid rate of technological obsolescence is a serious problem for organizations that wish to retain their records in electronic form. Devices, processes, and software for recording and storing information are being replaced with new products and methods on a regular three- to five-year cycle, driven primarily by market forces. Many new software products provide backward compatibility with earlier versions to facilitate the transfer of records from a system that is being phased out to a new system. Migration is more difficult when backward compatibility spans only one or two versions of the software and when organizations build customized applications to meet specific requirements. Not all records have to be retained long enough to require migration, but many organizations are facing considerable expense and the potential loss of records when they migrate from legacy systems to contemporary system architectures (*9*). The "year 2000 problem" is a potent example of what happens when system developers fail to consider the requirements for long-term uses of software and records. In this context, long term does not refer to a specific period of time; it means long enough to be concerned with the impact of changing technologies on continuing access and use of records.

Electronic Recordkeeping Methods and Best Practices

The increasing reliance on electronic records for organizational, technological, and financial reasons makes it imperative to develop robust and affordable solutions to the challenges of electronic recordkeeping. Organizations can use a combination of policy, standards, system design methodologies, best practices, and emerging technologies to create and maintain effective electronic recordkeeping systems. The goal of electronic recordkeeping is to ensure that records kept in electronic form are reliable and authentic, that they capture an accurate and complete record of a transaction or event, and that they are available, understandable, and usable now and in the future. Because most information systems were not designed explicitly to maintain records, functionality has to be added to systems to address the security, authenticity, access, and maintenance requirements for electronic records (*10*).

AUTHENTICITY

The key to authenticity of electronic records is the ability to demonstrate that a particular record was created at a specific date and time, that is has not been altered since, and that it is the only record of the transaction or issue in question (*11*). Without adequate precautions, an individual with motivation and some knowledge of information systems can easily change the contents or dates of records, add or delete records from the system, and forge signatures. Maintaining authenticity and reliability of electronic records begins with effective security, including controls over which users have permission to create, alter, or delete records. Even the best-designed security system may not be adequate to prevent fraud by insiders or to stop determined unauthorized users from gaining access to the system.

A number of techniques have been developed to enhance the authenticity of records by providing additional levels of verification. One approach attaches a unique time and date stamp to each record and then uses cryptography to calculate a unique identifier, or hash code, for each record. Digital signatures work in much the same way, by assigning a unique code for the signatory of the document and calculating a hash code for its contents. Another method to prevent changes to electronic records uses a separately designed electronic filing system or repository to segregate records from the active information-processing environment. Permission to access records in the repository is severely restricted, all attempts to access it are logged, and the functions that permit alteration of documents are disabled. If there is a need to edit, annotate, or redact information from a record after it has been filed in the repository a copy of the original is made and a new record is returned to the active information-processing system for updating (*12*). Some organizations use trusted third parties who have no interest in altering records to provide certificates of authenticity and repository or archiving services.

RELIABILITY AND ACCURACY OF RECORDS

Effective recordkeeping systems, whether manual or automated, depend on the implementation of good system design principles. Well-designed systems that are tested regularly and that provide methods for checking and verifying the accuracy of records produce more reliable records than systems that are designed and used in an arbitrary or ad hoc manner. Controls that monitor input and output processes, hardware and software performance, and security help to assure that the records generated by a system are accurate and reliable. These controls should be an integral part of any well-managed system, built into a system when it is developed, embedded in operating policies and procedures, and implemented through ongoing training and support.

To be effective, electronic recordkeeping systems must be used at all times in the normal course of business by individuals who are authorized to create, edit, file, and delete records. Electronic recordkeeping systems should have audit trails that log all access to the system and all changes to records so that attempts to tamper with records are detectable. Systems that are not used consistently and that lack adequate controls over the creation, maintenance, and use of records cannot produce reliable and authentic records.

ORGANIZATION AND DESIGN OF ELECTRONIC RECORDKEEPING SYSTEMS

Organizations that carry out several different functions or support several core business processes will need multiple electronic recordkeeping systems, each of which has specific recordkeeping requirements associated with it. The degree of security required, the volume and formats of records that must be stored, access and retrieval needs, and the length of time that records must be retained all depend on the operational needs and external requirements associated with each organizational function or business process. Designing an electronic recordkeeping system therefore requires a careful analysis of the records-creating process, the immediate and long-term needs for access to records, and any external recordkeeping requirements. An important consideration is the point at which a record should be captured and filed in the repository or filing system. In routine transactional systems, a record of each transaction should ordinarily be captured when the transaction is completed, signed, and time/date stamped. Many processes have more complex documentation requirements. The design of a new product or the development of a new policy, for example, may go through many iterations, in which proposals, draft documents, comments, and revisions provide important evidence of the decisions leading to the final product design or policy. Version control is an important element in systems in which multiple iterations of a document are retained so that users can distinguish final products from previous drafts. To avoid the accumulation of vast stores of disorganized digital information, records must be segregated from other forms of electronic communications and classified, arranged, indexed, and stored for future reference. Electronic recordkeeping systems should be capable of linking together all of the records pertaining to a particular transaction, case, client, or event. Hybrid systems that produce records in both paper and electronic formats should provide linkage between related paper and electronic records.

technology for recordkeeping purposes, delineate the processes and methods necessary to ensure accuracy and authenticity of electronic records, specify provisions for quality control, storage, and retention, and set parameters under which access to electronic records is permitted or denied. Electronic records policies should also spell out the roles and responsibilities of management, systems administration staff, and end users for the creation, maintenance, protection, and release of electronic records.

STANDARDS

Records created using systems that comply with widely adopted international standards for encoding, compression, content representation, file transfer and access, and storage are much more amenable to long-term retention and maintenance than records that are stored in uncommon or proprietary formats. ASCII and Unicode (ISO 10646) are the preferred standards for encoding text and data. The tagged image file format (TIFF), joint photographic expert group (JPEG), and International Telecommunications Union (ITU) are widely adopted standards for the representation and compression of images. Other commonly recommended standards include the standard generalized mark-up language (SGML; ISO 8879), for representing the logical structure of textual documents, and Document Style Semantics and Specification Language (DSSSL) (ISO/IEC 10179:1995), for specifying document formatting and transformation in a platform-independent manner. The portable document format (PDF) from Adobe has some potential for storing and distributing electronic records because PDF files cannot be altered without PDF creation software. Although it is widely used, PDF is a proprietary format. Several consortia are developing standards for interoperability across repositories and among the various hardware and software components of recordkeeping systems (*15*).

Future Prospects

Information technologies, standards, policies, and best practices are evolving gradually to support electronic recordkeeping. Some regulated industries, financial services, and government agencies have designed sophisticated electronic recordkeeping systems to cope with large volumes of records and strict requirements for accuracy, completeness, accessibility, and privacy protection. Continued improvements in the capacity and performance of digital storage media, adoption of standards for open systems and interoperability, and better support for recordkeeping requirements in commonly available software may make electronic recordkeeping an affordable, reliable, and effective alternative to traditional media for many organizations and individuals. Ultimately, the effectiveness of electronic recordkeeping systems will not depend on technology developments alone. The transition from paper to electronic recordkeeping is likely to be incremental and slow. Institutional policies, recordkeeping practices, individual skills and habits, and cultural assumptions all lag behind the capabilities of the technology.

REFERENCES

1. R. Cox, "The Record: Is It Evolving?" *Records Retriev. Rep.*, **10**, 1–16 (March 1994).
2. E. W. Stein, "Organizational Memory: Review of Concepts and Recommendations for Management," *Internet J. Info. Mgt.*, **15**, 17–32 (1995).
3. W. Duff, "Increasing the Acceptance of Functional Requirements for Electronic Evidence," *Archives Mus. Informatics*, **10**(4), 326–351 (1996).
4. D. S. Skupsky, *Recordkeeping Requirements*, Information Requirements Clearinghouse, Denver, 1988.
5. "Literary Warrant," Functional Requirements for Evidence in Recordkeeping, University of Pittsburgh, School of Information Sciences, <www.lis.pitt.edu/~nhprc/>.
6. *Dictionary of Computer Words*, Houghton Mifflin, Boston, 1993, p. 9.
7. L. J. Bellardo and L. L. Bellardo, comps., *A Glossary for Archivists, Manuscript Curators, and Records Managers*, Society of American Archivists, Chicago, 1992, p. 3.
8. G. R. Ashton, ed. *Storage Technology Assessment Final Report*, National Media Lab, technical report RE-0016, Minneapolis, Aug. 1994, p. 105.
9. M. L. Brodie and M. Stonebraker, *Migrating Legacy Systems*, Morgan Kaufman, San Francisco, 1995.
10. D. Bearman, *Electronic Evidence*, Archives & Museum Informatics, Pittsburgh, 1994, pp. 34–70.
11. L. Duranti, "Reliability and Authenticity: The Concepts and Their Implications," *Archivaria*, **39**, 5–10 (1995).
12. U. Anderson, "Short Version of the Sesam Report," *Proceedings of the DLM-Forum on Electronic Records*, Brussels, 1997, pp. 175–189.
13. "Metadata Specification," Functional Requirements for Evidence in Recordkeeping, University of Pittsburgh, School of Information Sciences, P. Hsburgh, <www.lis.pitt.edu/~nhprc/>, Sept. 18, 1996.
14. *Preserving Digital Information*, Report of the Task Force on Archiving Digital Information, Commission on Preservation and Access, Washington, DC, May 1, 1996, p. 5.
15. P. Le Cerf, L. de Bremme, and R. Schockaert, "Standards for Electronic Document Management," *Proceedings of the DLM-Forum on Electronic Records*, Brussels, 1997, pp. 217–222.

MARGARET HEDSTROM

EXPERT AND KNOWLEDGE-BASED SYSTEMS

Definitions and Terminology

EXPERT SYSTEM

An *expert system* (ES) is a software tool that is based on artificial intelligence (AI) techniques. Originally intended to simulate and perhaps replace human reasoning in various settings, ESs now typically embody the more modest goal of applying approaches derived from the study of human intelligence to assist in tasks such as real-time diagnosis and troubleshooting, manufacturing and process control, financial analysis, and data interpretation. The term expert system, which perhaps overstated the capabilities of earlier systems by implying that expert human behavior could be captured and reproduced in a computer system, is thus giving way to the more generic term *knowledge-based system.*

KNOWLEDGE-BASED SYSTEM

A knowledge-based system (KBS) can incorporate one or more of the computational reasoning techniques developed in AI research. Historically, ESs were synonymous with *rule-based systems,* which represented human expertise as a series of IF-THEN rules that linked a description of the problem to its eventual solution. An ES also typically was a stand-alone software tool, perhaps requiring specialized computer hardware, which communicated little, if at all, with conventional information systems (ISs) and software.

Although the rule-based paradigm still predominates in KBSs, there is increasing use of more flexible knowledge representations in KBSs, including objects and frames, case-based reasoning, neural networks, data analytic and statistical reasoning, and fuzzy logic. Depending on the problem domain and application, a KBS is often a hybrid system that combines several knowledge representation schemes. A KBS may also be *embedded* in other mainstream applications, allowing the use of AI reasoning techniques to be used in conjunction with traditional information processing. Embedding a KBS in an IS environment allows the KBS to retrieve and store information in shared databases and to communicate with users via standard interfaces.

"INTELLIGENT" DECISION SUPPORT SYSTEMS

Knowledge-based systems are sometimes termed *intelligent decision support systems* (IDSSs). A *decision support system* (DSS) is a tool that assists a decision maker in formulating and solving complex problems. Generally a DSS provides a user with a database and a data model. The data model can serve as the basis for manipulating the data, performing sensitivity and what-if analyses, and exploring alternative scenarios and model assumptions.

The definition of DSS is general enough that it is possible to consider ESs and KBSs as DSSs. From a design perspective, however, a DSS is primarily intended to facilitate data analysis by a human, and leaves the role of interpretation and decision making to the user. Expert systems and KBSs are explicitly intended to have proactive reasoning capabilities and to be capable under proper conditions of assuming a portion of the interpretation and decision-making role.

There are ways in which ESs/KBSs clearly fit within the broader definition of a DSS. Every DSS is equipped with a model that manipulates data, typically numeric data. The knowledge and reasoning capabilities of an ES/KBS also result from a model that manipulates data, although the data manipulated by the model that provides the "intelligence" of an ES/KBS is not limited to numeric quantities. The perspective of an ES/KBS as an extended DSS is consistent with the view of an ES/KBS as an "intelligent assistant." An ES/KBS might, for example, provide what-if analyses to the human decision maker based on its own manipulations of the data model and its own inherent reasoning capabilities.

DISTINGUISHING AN EXPERT SYSTEM FROM OTHER SYSTEMS

Although ESs/KBSs share a number of capabilities with traditional applications, they also tend to exhibit certain characteristics that differentiate them from other software. Buchanan and Smith (*1*) describe several characteristics that define a stereotypical expert system. Ideally, an ES/KBS should

- Use *domain-specific* knowledge in addition to general knowledge
- Reason with *symbolic* (conceptual) as well as numeric knowledge
- Employ heuristic methods (i.e., the plausible methods or rules of thumb often used by human problem solvers) as well as algorithmic methods (i.e., the certain or deterministic procedures found in traditional software)
- "Perform well" in its domain or problem area; that is, generate accurate and useful solutions in a reasonable amount of time
- Be capable of explaining its knowledge and its rationale for proposed solutions
- Be "flexible," which means that it can be modified and expanded by adding to and deleting from its knowledge base without the need for rewriting the program itself

The first three characteristics are derived from an ES's roots in AI methodologies and, as Buchanan and Smith note, define an ES as an AI program. The last three are related to its output, interface, and organization, and are important to the design and implementation of a viable system.

Waterman (*2*) draws similar distinctions between ESs/KBSs and conventional applications, focusing primarily on knowledge. He suggests that the accumulation and codification of knowledge that is both explicit and accessible characterizes an ES/KBS. Unlike traditional systems, the knowledge base of an ES/KBS can provide a type of institutional memory drawn from the collective experience of various experts and specialists in an organization [also called "private"—or unpublished—knowledge by Hayes-Roth et al. (*3*)]. Furthermore, structured knowledge retained in an ES/KBS can form the basis for an explanation of the system's output, although processing and presenting an explanation in a way that effectively informs a human may itself require an ES. An ES/KBS is an implementation of a problem-solving theory or model, one that is capable of explaining an answer by describing the pathways in the model leading from problem description to solution.

All of this notwithstanding, the distinction between ESs/KBSs and conventional systems is more ambiguous than it might appear. Buchanan and Smith (*1*), for example, note that the ES/KBS attributes they list can be found to some extent in any "well-designed" software. Conversely, not all ESs/KBSs tend to exhibit all of the attributes listed, particularly the last three, which relate to system performance. Some systems perform better, explain better, and are more flexible than others.

The distinction between an ES/KBS and other types of software systems has become even more blurred in the 1990s, as two trends in AI, which began in the late 1980s, have continued. First, the relative number of stand-alone ESs is declining, and second, AI/ES/KBS technology is being integrated into conventional systems. As the basis characteristics of ESs/KBSs increasingly become a part of traditional applications, AI-

TABLE 1

Problem Types Addressed by Expert Systems

Interpretation	Construction
Diagnosis: Determining the cause of system problems from observed symptoms	*Design:* Configuring/placing components under constraints
Instruction: Diagnosing and correcting student performance	*Planning:* Designing plans to achieve goals
Monitoring: Comparing observed events to expectations	*Prescription:* Proposing solutions to an observed problem
Prediction: Inferring likely outcomes from current observations	*Simulation:* Modeling causal interactions and interdependencies among system components
Selection: Identifying and choosing a solution from a set of possibilities	*Repair:* Executing a plan of action to achieve an identified solution
Debugging: Prescribing solutions for diagnosed problems	

Source: Adapted from Refs. *15, 1, 3.*

related technologies and approaches are beginning to predominate over the implementation of independent ES/KBS.

PROBLEM TYPES

The types of generic problems they are intended to solve also distinguish ESs/KBSs. Buchanan and Smith (*1*) suggest that problems most appropriate to ES/KBS approaches fall into the following two broad categories:

- *Interpretation* of data for situation assessment
- *Construction* of a solution, given an imposed set of constraints

The two categories, in turn, can be further decomposed into a number of subcategories. (See Table 1.)

Interpretation and construction tasks occur in a wide variety of problem domains. For example, problems of *interpretation,* and corresponding KBSs designed to address them, are related to the following:

- Medical diagnosis
- Equipment troubleshooting
- Preventive maintenance of monitored systems
- Data interpretation
- Credit authorization
- Fraud detection

Similarly, ESs/KBSs address problems of *construction* in the following areas:

- Configuration
- Scheduling

- Network and database design
- Capital budgeting

In real applications, problem areas are rarely so easily partitioned. Most of the areas included under "problems of construction" contain aspects of interpretation as well. An intelligent scheduling system, for example, requires an assessment of the current situation, including resources and imposed constraints, before it can begin to construct a schedule that conforms to stated goals. Other areas are even less easily classified. The solutions to problems of therapy management in medicine, industrial process control, machine translation, and financial auditing require extensive amounts of both interpretation and construction.

Buchanan and Smith (*1*) identify other characteristics of real-world problems that tend to further complicate attempts at classification. First, the solution spaces of some problems are sufficiently small that an ES/KBS can identify the list of possible solutions and consider each in turn. Other solution spaces are much larger or even infinite, requiring the generation of a set of alternative solutions by a method other than explicit enumeration. Second, some problem domains are static, allowing a program to consider a "snapshot" of the current situation. Other domains are dynamic, requiring the program to monitor the situation and to respond to changes in it. Third, some problems are relatively simple, and can be solved by people with little expertise in the problem domain. Other problems are more complex, and require extensive expertise and/or experience in the area.

The difficulty in characterizing problem areas underscores an important aspect of ES/KBS development. Typically an ES/KBS is designed to address the task at hand, utilizing whatever techniques are required to understand the problem and to provide a solution to it. In other words, there is a fundamental linkage between the *type of problem* and the *method* used to solve it (*1*).

Finally, the nature of the domain and the type of problem have great bearing on the success or failure of an implemented ES/KBS. Likelihood of success is enhanced when (1) the problem is narrowly defined and well understood, and (2) the list of possible solutions is also well-defined, unambiguous, and static.

Architectures and Knowledge Representation

RULE-BASED SYSTEMS

As currently defined, expert systems began in the 1970s with the development of *rule-based* systems, and for some time thereafter rule-based systems and ESs were considered synonymous. The basic paradigm of rule-based systems outlines (1) how knowledge is represented as a set of rules and factual knowledge (i.e., the *knowledge base*), and (2) how the system reasons about its knowledge in the process of solving problems (i.e., the *inference engine*). The goal of the early so-called *first-generation* systems was to provide an inference engine that could be made independent of the knowledge requirements of any individual domain, thereby allowing ESs to be constructed for various types of problems, but still conforming to a common developmental approach.

Knowledge Base

In a rule-based system, a knowledge base consists of the following:

- A *working memory*: any number of facts or assertions about the state of the world
- A *rule base*: a set of IF-THEN rules

Working Memory. Although there are several ways to represent factual information in a rule-based system, a common method is the use of *predicate calculus.* In a predicate calculus scheme, an assertion is an *atomic formula* containing a predicate (a statement that can only be either "true" or "false") and one or more arguments, as follows:

(predicate {*arguments*})

For example:

(useful *this-encyclopedia*) should return TRUE.

First-order logic uses operators or functions in addition to predicates, because functions can "return" values other than TRUE or FALSE. In a human resources domain, useful functions, and what they would return when applied to an individual, might include the following:

(occupation *John Programmer*)—John's occupation is programmer
(employed-by *John ABC-Corp*)—John is employed by ABC Corp.

Such formulas provide for a standard representation of information in a knowledge base, which then can be matched to a set of associated rules.

Rule Base. A rule is structured as a link between the conjunction of one or more *antecedents* (clauses on the left-hand side of the rule) and a set of *consequents* (clauses on the right-hand side of the rule), as follows:

IF <antecedent 1> THEN <consequent 1>

IF <antecedent 2> AND <antecedent 3> THEN <consequent 2>

The antecedent of a rule is an assertion describing the observed or inferred state of the world, while the consequent can be either of the following:

- *A conclusion or inference drawn from an assertion:*
  IF (paid-by John ABC-Corp)—John is paid by ABC Corp.
  AND (office-location John ABC-Corp)—John's office is at ABC Corp.
  AND <other qualifications for employment>
  THEN (employed-by John ABC-Corp)—John is employed by ABC Corp.
- *An action to be taken:*
  IF (employed-by John ABC-Corp)
  THEN <Invoke procedure to withhold taxes from John's paycheck>.

Inference Engine

The inference engine is the mechanisms by which facts are matched to rules and rules are linked together to form a series of conclusions and possible actions. Consequents are proven from antecedents through a principle of logic called *modus ponens,* which takes an assertion (A is true) and a rule (If <A is true> then <B is true>), and derives a new assertion from the relationship (B is true).

Because rules are intended to match specified facts in working memory and (perhaps) to add new facts, the structure of rules is consistent with the representation of facts in working memory. Assuming that a first-order logic representation is used, a rule could take the general form

IF (function {arguments}) AND (function {arguments}) AND...

THEN (function {arguments} AND...

Drawing from the example above:

IF (occupation John Programmer) AND (employed-by John ABC-Corp)

THEN (lives John Pittsburgh)

(i.e., If John is a programmer and works for ABC-Corp, then he lives in Pittsburgh).

If the following facts reside in working memory:

(occupation John Programmer), and

(employed-by John ABC-Corp),

then by invoking the rule and matching on these facts in the antecedent, the following conclusion can be drawn:

(lives John Pittsburgh).

Although this rule allows the system to derive useful conclusions, it applies only to John and therefore is much too specific to be of any practical use. Separate rules would have to be provided for each programmer employed by ABC Corp. As a result, rules tend to be defined in more general terms, utilizing *pattern variables* instead of specific entities. A pattern variable will match *any* entity sharing the other characteristics of the assertions described in a rule. For example, the rule above can be recast using a pattern variable as follows:

IF (occupation ?x Programmer) AND (employed-by ?x ABC-Corp)

THEN (lives ?x Pittsburgh).

In this new incarnation of the rule, the pattern variable ?x represents *anyone.* Note how the use of a pattern variable changes the intent and scope of the original rule. Instead of focusing exclusively on John, the rule now states that all programmers employed at ABC Corp. live in Pittsburgh. The rule can be used to derive conclusions using any set of facts that match the pattern. The reasoning mechanism for doing this is called *unification,* which is a process of inferring the value of pattern variables from the values of other facts in a rule or rule chain.

Continuing the example above, the conclusion we reached before about John (lives John Pittsburgh) can be derived from the same initial facts, but this time using the general rule. The facts match the antecedent of the rule as follows:

IF (occupation ?x Programmer) AND (employed-by ?x ABC-Corp)

(occupation John Programmer)   (employed-by John ABC-Corp).

Because the patterns match, the pattern variable takes on the value "John," and the rule is instantiated (meaning all the variables are replaced with specific values) as follows:

IF (occupation John Programmer) AND (employed-by John ABC-Corp)

THEN (lives John Pittsburgh)—{*where ?x = 'John'*}.

The power of this type of representation, however, lies in its applicability to any number of other facts in the knowledge base. For example, if the following facts reside in working memory:

(occupation John Programmer)
(occupation Susan Programmer)
(occupation Jim Programmer)
(occupation Sean Programmer)
(employed-by John ABC-Corp)
(employed-by Susan ABC-Corp)
(employed-by Jim XYZ-Corp)
(employed-by Sean ABC-Corp)

then by invoking the general rule and matching on these facts, all of the following conclusions can be drawn from the single, general rule:

(lives John Pittsburgh)
(lives Susan Pittsburgh)
(lives Sean Pittsburgh)

Rules can be connected into a type of branching-tree structure, or network, by associating the consequent in a rule to the antecedent in other rules, as follows:

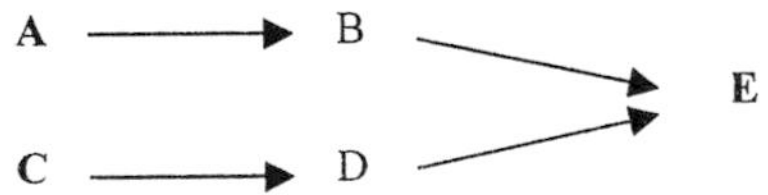

FIGURE 1. *An abstract rule-based reasoning chain.*

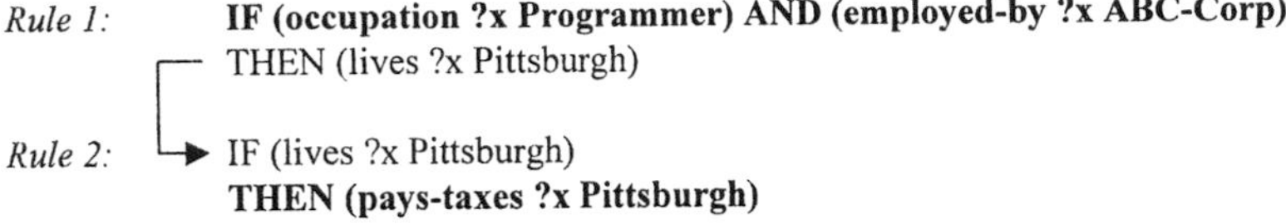

FIGURE 2. *Propagation of reasoning from two linked rules.*

IF A THEN B,

IF C THEN D, and

IF B and D THEN E.

The tree structure illustrating the above three rules is shown in Fig. 1. The figure shows that assertion E can be inferred from an observation of assertions A and C by following the linkages between the first two rules and the third one. In the example above, adding another rule produces a similar type of reasoning chain, through which one can infer that if someone is a programmer and is employed at ABC Corp, then that person must pay taxes in Pittsburgh. (See Fig. 2.)

The direction of the reasoning illustrated above—that is, navigating either from left to right or from right to left in Fig. 1 (or top to bottom or bottom to top in Fig. 2)—is an aspect of the *control structure* used by the inference engine. The control structure can take one of the following three approaches:

1. Forward chaining
2. Backward chaining
3. A combination of forward and backward chaining

In *forward chaining,* the reasoning is data-driven. The system begins with information about the state of the world, then reasons forward through the set of rules, from antecedent to consequent, until some conclusion is reached (or the system runs out of rules). The inference engine begins by collecting rules having an antecedent that is consistent with the state of the world; that is, their left-hand sides can be instantiated with at least one set of values based on the facts currently in working memory. Note that a single rule might be instantiated several times. In situations in which more than one rule has a matching antecedent, the inference engine uses a *conflict resolution* strategy, which is a heuristic intended to select a rule that is most appropriate to the current situation. For example, it might select a rule that is most specific (i.e., has the most number of assertions in its antecedent), or one that has not been selected subsequent to any other candidate rule (i.e., is the least recently selected rule).

Once a rule is selected, it is "fired," meaning that any conclusions in its right-hand side are asserted into working memory and any consequent actions are carried out. The cycle then begins again, with the collection of rules that now match the updated working memory, the selection of a single rule, and the firing of that rule. The result is a propagation of inferred assertions in working memory produced by a forward navigation—that is, from antecedent to consequent—through a chain of rules (in Fig. 1, from A to B; in Fig. 2, from the first rule to the second rule). The process continues until some predefined goal is achieved or until no rule matches the state of the world and therefore none can be selected.

As suggested in Fig. 2, forward chaining would match existing facts in working memory [e.g., (*occupation John programmer*) (*works John ABC-Corp*)] with the antecedent of the first rule, which then would store its consequent in working memory (*lives John Pittsburgh*). In turn, the antecedent of the second rule would match the new fact, which would cause the rule to fire and store *its* consequent in working memory, thereby concluding that John pays taxes in Pittsburgh (*pays-taxes John Pittsburgh*) through forward chaining. This is a trivial example; if there were additional rules having matching antecedents, they would continue to fire and the process would continue until all matching rules were exhausted.

In *backward chaining,* the reasoning is hypothesis- or goal-driven, and the direction of inference is reversed (e.g., in Fig. 1 from E to A and B, in Fig. 2 from the second rule to the first). Backward chaining begins with an ordered collection of potential hypotheses from the consequents of rules identified as *terminal* rules. If one of the consequents matches a fact in working memory, then the hypothesis is proven immediately, without the need for any additional reasoning. If there is not an initial match, however, the inference engine attempts to prove the consequent's assertion in each of the retrieved rules by searching for working memory facts that match the antecedent of the consequent's rule. If a match can be found in one of the retrieved rules, the hypothesis is proven through *modus ponens.*

In Fig. 2, a simple backward-chaining reasoner would attempt to prove the hypothesis that John pays taxes in Pittsburgh by first determining if that fact currently exists in working memory. It doesn't, so the reasoner would then attempt to determine whether the hypothesis could be proven indirectly—in this case via the second rule. The hypothesis will be true if the second rule is true, and the second rule is true if the clauses on its left-hand-side can be matched up to facts in working memory. It reasons backward to discover whether the fact in the antecedent of the second rule (*lives John Pittsburgh*) exists in working memory. Because it does not, the reasoner continues, attempting to prove whether John lives in Pittsburgh by searching for rules having (*lives John Pittsburgh*) as a consequent. Because rule 1 is the only candidate, the reasoner attempts to match the left-hand side of rule 1 against existing facts in working memory. This time, the facts (*occupation John programmer*) and (*works John ABC-Corp*) match the antecedents of rule 1, which makes the consequent of rule 1 true, which in turn makes the left-hand side of rule 2 true, thereby proving indirectly the consequent of rule 2, and verifying the hypothesis that John lives in Pittsburgh.

If the antecedent in a rule does not match a fact in working memory, a backward-chaining inference engine tries to prove the antecedent's assertion by retrieving rules having the assertion as a consequent, and attempting to prove the antecedents in each of the retrieved rules. The inference engine continues navigating backward through the rules until (1) it is able to prove an assertion that in turn will prove a terminal hypothesis through some chain of related rules, or (2) the inference engine is not able to retrieve any more rules.

The choice between forward and backward chaining depends on the task and the type of problem (*4*). In general, when a large number of potential conclusions and pathways for reaching them can be generated from a set of facts in working memory, then *backward chaining should be used* in order to scope the search process. On the other hand, when the number of conclusions and pathways that can be generated from the data is relatively small, then *forward chaining should be used.* In some cases, *a dual strategy can be employed,* using forward chaining to generate a set of hypotheses from the available data, which then can be tested using backward chaining.

The choice of control structure may also depend on how the system designer wishes the system to interact with an end user. The designers of MYCIN, an important early rule-based medical ES, sought to avoid natural language input of data from a physician, choosing instead to control the session by asking questions about the patient (*5*). The hypothesis-driven approach afforded by backward chaining allowed the developers to use such an interface. On the other hand, the task of configuring computer system components generally depends on preexisting information about customer requirements and technical constraints (*6*). This, in combination with the ability to break the configuration task into a series of milestones that constrain potential outcomes, argues for a forward-chaining approach.

FRAME-BASED/OBJECT-ORIENTED SYSTEMS

A *frame* includes both declarative and procedural knowledge within a single data structure (*7*), and generally is used to enhance the representational capabilities of an ES knowledge base. With the incorporation of frames, ESs evolved into what are termed *second-generation* systems.

Knowledge Representation

A frame-based representation is similar to an object-oriented representation. A frame is a model of some entity in a system allowing the various data elements describing the entity to be collected and encapsulated in a single, somewhat heterogeneous structure. In the standard definition of a frame object, each data element is stored within an *attribute* or *slot* defined for the frame.

Frames and objects are a convenient modeling paradigm because they tend to reflect the way people think about the world. Consider, for example, how an employee in a company might be represented in a frame-based system. An employee would have a name, a position, a department, a telephone number, and so on. Those data elements can be stored inside a frame structure, as shown in Fig. 3.

Access to the individual attributes stored directly in the frame provides a certain level of knowledge about a person. Because the data are encapsulated within the

Employee:	
Attribute	*Value*
Name	John Smith
Position	Systems Analyst
Department	Information Systems
Telephone	555-1234

FIGURE 3. *An example of a frame, showing slots and values.*

frame object, each attribute has meaning only within the context of the frame itself; that is, a reasoning agent cannot retrieve an attribute without also indicating the object to which the attribute is connected. For example, if <John Smith> is used to represent the frame object and its data elements, the values of individual attributes can be retrieved as follows:

(Position *of* <John Smith>) = 'Systems Analyst', and

(Department *of* <John Smith>) = 'Information Systems'.

Additional knowledge comes from linkages between the frame object and other constituents of the frame-based system; that is, additional knowledge about the object described in a frame can be inferred from the following:

1. The frame's position in some type of classification hierarchy (*generalization/specialization*)
2. The frame's linkages to other objects (*aggregation*).

A frame-based system is organized into a hierarchy of related concepts (*classes* or *parents*) to which individual frame objects are connected. A frame object in turn is defined as an *instance* of one or more classes. For example, assume that John Smith is an instance of the *employee* class, in that he is a specific, real-world example of the abstract concept of "employee." Knowing that John Smith is an employee allows a reasoning agent to infer, by determining the attributes of the employee class, what information about John Smith is potentially available or discoverable.

In turn, the employee class can be linked to any number of other classes or parents further up in the hierarchy. For example, because an employee is generally a person, a reasoning agent can infer a number of facts about an employee in addition to those stored directly in the frame object. In a frame-based system, a hierarchy might be defined as shown in Fig. 4.

Each entity relates to its parent through a generalization/specialization link (*is-a*). Because each entity inherits attributes and perhaps values from each of its parents, an object is actually a compendium of attributes and values collected from each of its superordinate structures in the hierarchy. The *John Smith* frame, for example, inherits attributes and values not only directly from the employee class, but also indirectly from the person class. John Smith, unless specified otherwise, assumes the charac-

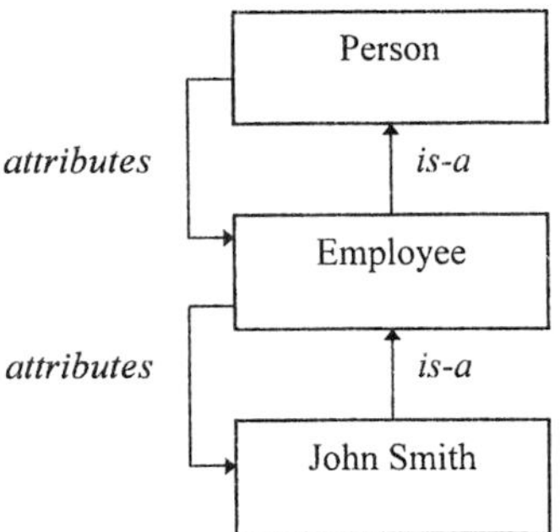

FIGURE 4. *Linking frames through generalization/specialization.*

Employee:	
Attribute	***Value***
Name	John Smith
Position	Systems Analyst
Department	
Telephone	555-1234

has-a

Department:	
Attribute	***Value***
Name	Information Systems
Location	Building-A
Manager	
Unit	Corporate

has-a ....

FIGURE 5. *Linking frames through aggregation.*

teristics of a person as well. He sleeps, consumes food, becomes ill, and so on. Knowing that John Smith is an employee allows the reasoning agent (1) to also assume, unless informed otherwise, that he has personlike characteristics, and (2) to reason from that assumption.

Linkages between a frame and other frame objects also enhance reasoning. For example, the department assigned to the John Smith object, *information systems,* might be a separate object that defines all of the characteristics of a department. (See Fig. 5.) Knowledge related to John Smith is enhanced by *aggregating* information in the John Smith object with information in the information systems object (via a "*has-a*" link). As shown, the aggregation process may include the object representing the manager of the IS department, and perhaps other objects as well. As with generalization/specialization, aggregation is constrained only by the number of relationship (or links) defined in the knowledge base.

Procedural Attachment

Data-driven procedures, or daemons, that are linked to attributes or slots in individual frames, enhance the inherent reasoning capabilities of frame-based systems. Using data-driven procedures can help reduce the size of a knowledge base by limiting the need for redundant information, and can help maintain the integrity of a knowledge base by linking related information. Daemons generally fall into one of the following three categories:

1. *If-needed* procedures—which execute when a process requires information from a slot but the slot is empty. An if-needed procedure can be invoked to retrieve the required information.
2. *If-added* procedures—which execute when data are placed in the slot. An if-added procedure can be used to propagate data flows to other slots and/or frames or to invoke reasoning chains that might be dependent on a value contained in the slot.
3. *If-removed* procedures—which execute when data are cleared from the slot.

In the employee example above, adding a new value for the department slot could execute an if-added procedure attached to the slot. The procedure could then attempt to obtain other information dependent on a change of department, such as a telephone number. If the department location is required but the associated slot in the department is empty, an if-needed procedure might be invoked to find a value for it. Finally, an if-removed procedure could execute whenever information in an employee's name slot is deleted. The procedure could be responsible for ensuring that data in the remaining slots of the frame as well as all linkages to other frames are updated to reflect the employee's changed status.

COMBINING RULES AND FRAMES

Rules and frames can be consolidated into reasoning systems that are able to use the inferencing capabilities of both. The consolidation can take each of the following two forms:

1. Rules can reference frame slot values and linkages.
2. Frame slots can contain embedded rules.

Referencing Frame Structures in Rules

A frame-based knowledge representation can enrich the information available to a rule-based system, particularly the rules and facts used to drive the system's inference engine. In a conventional rule-based system, facts in a knowledge base are assertions about the state of the world derived from either concrete observations or inferences drawn from those observations. When the elements of a frame-based representation are introduced, the structure of the assertions can explicitly or implicitly assume the characteristics of frames. Individual rules therefore must be structured to match against such an enhanced style of representation, which includes the following:

- References to frame objects and attributes
- References to conceptual linkages between frames, including is-a and has-a relationships
- References to attached procedures (more on this in the following section)

Rules can incorporate a frame-based approach in a number of ways. For example

IF (<attribute-name> *of* <frame1> *is* <value1>)

THEN (<attribute-name> *of* <frame2> *is* <value2>),

IF (<frame1> is-a <frame2>) AND (<attribute-name> *of* <frame1> *is* <value1>)

THEN (<attribute-name> *of* <frame2> *is* <value2>), and

IF (<frame1> has-a <frame2>) AND (<attribute-name> *of* <frame2> *is* <value2>)

THEN (<function1> <argument-1> <value3>).

For example

IF (?x is-a Department) AND (Unit *of* ?x *is* 'Corporate')

THEN (location *of* ?x *is* 'Building-A'), and

IF (?x is-a Employee) AND (works ?x Pittsburgh)

THEN (pays-taxes ?x Pittsburgh).

The last rule indicates that frames and predicate-argument entities can be combined in a single knowledge base and referenced collectively in a single rule.

Embedding Rules in Frame Slots (Rule-Based Procedural Attachment)

Any of the types of attached procedures described in the previous section can be implemented in rule-based form, relying on forward- or backward-chaining inferencing mechanisms rather than encoded algorithms to respond to changes in slot values. For example, retrieval of the IS department location in an if-needed procedure (as described above) can be accomplished through backward-chaining pattern matching. The goal state is attached to the location slot as an if-needed procedure.

Find: (Location *of* <information systems department> *is* ?y)

The inference engine would attempt to determine the location by finding rules matching the goal state and then using those rules along with other facts in the knowledge base to instantiate the pattern variable (?y). For example, the consequent of the following rule matches the pattern:

IF (?x is-a Department) AND (Unit *of* ?x *is 'Corporate')*

THEN (location *of* ?x *is* 'Building-A').

If the following facts are present or can be inferred in the knowledge base

(<Information Systems Department> is-a Department, and

(Unit of <Information Systems Department> is 'Corporate'),

then the antecedent of the rule matches the knowledge base, and the consequent (along with the location) can be inferred as follows:

(location of <Information Systems Department> is 'Building-A').

VARIATIONS ON KNOWLEDGE-BASED SYSTEMS

There are a number of alternative and complementary approaches to rule- and frame-based systems. A brief overview is provided in order to familiarize the reader with the important current and emerging technologies associated with ESs/KBSs. The reader should refer to the resource listing at the end of this article for sources providing more comprehensive information about each area.

Fuzzy Logic Systems

Fuzzy logic is a method for representing the inherent uncertainty and ambiguity in the real world. Unlike traditional computer systems, including standard rule- and frame-based systems, fuzzy logic systems are capable of reasoning about nebulous concepts such as *tall/short, hot/cold,* and *old/young.* In a practical sense, such concepts do not have strict definitions. For example, there is no single point of delineation separating tall and short. Instead, a height of six feet might be considered "fairly tall," seven feet might be considered "unquestionably tall," three feet might be considered "not tall at all," and so on.

Values in a fuzzy logic system are represented in terms of their *degree of membership* in a fuzzy set, usually expressed as a number between 0 and 1. In the "tall" fuzzy set, for example, a person six feet in height might be assigned a degree of membership of 0.7, the seven-foot person might be assigned 1.0, and the three-foot person might be assigned 0.0. Degrees of membership also determine the result of combining individual items using logical operators such as *AND, OR,* and *NOT.* Consider the following expression:

A is tall *AND* A is young.

Assume that person A has a height of six feet (degree of membership = 0.7) and is fifty years old (degree of membership in the *young* set = 0.1). The truth value of the conjunctive expression in turn has its own degree of membership, which by convention is the *minimum* of the constituent degrees of membership (i.e., 0.1). If the expression were a disjunction (A is tall *OR* A is young), the function would take the *maximum* of the degrees of membership (i.e., 0.7).

The key to fuzzy logic reasoning is the ability to construct rules containing fuzzy constructs, such as the following:

IF ?x is high and ?y is low THEN ?z is low, and

IF ?x is high and ?y is high THEN ?z is high.

The net output of both rules is determined by various fuzzy set reasoning algorithms. In general, the algorithms combine the elements of the antecedent of each applicable rule, derive a fuzzy result for the consequent of each rule, and then consolidate all of the fuzzy results into a single (fuzzy) solution, which is likely to have a membership value somewhere between *low* and *high.*

Fuzzy logic was developed in the United States in the mid-1960s (*8*), but did not become popular until the Japanese began to commercialize it in the 1980s and early 1990s. With the success of a number of Japanese applications, it now has generated widespread interest in North America and Europe as well. Fuzzy systems have been implemented in a number of areas, including process control, data analysis, robotics, telecommunications monitoring, consumer electronics, and financial systems.

Case-Based Reasoning Systems

Case-based reasoning (CBR) systems retain knowledge in the form of *cases,* which are structured models of prior experience. A case can store any number of attributes describing (1) the characteristics of prior situations, (2) problems faced in those situations, (3) methods used to try to solve the problems, (4) the state of the world following the implementation of the methods (i.e., the outcome), (5) a determination of the success or failure of those methods, and—perhaps—(6) a determination of why the methods succeeded or failed (*9–11*). Case-based reasoning systems reason by analogy, attempting to relate the characteristics of a current situation to prior experience. Their goal is to find a similar case that can be used to solve the current problem—typically by adapting the solution methods used in a previous case so that the methods and their rationales conform to the current state of the world.

As in other forms of KBSs, CBR systems can address various types of both interpretation and construction problems. For example, to diagnose a patient experiencing the symptoms of heart failure (interpretation), a CBR system can retrieve the records of other patients who have experienced similar symptoms and can select (and then test) the differential diagnoses of the best matches. Likewise, a military planning CBR system could select prior cases containing similar battlefield configurations and choose the strategy most closely related to the current situation—perhaps with some modifications to account for any differences found (construction). Currently, CBR systems are used extensively in help-desk applications, in which prior cases, in the form of hundreds or perhaps thousands of accumulated problem reports, provide a basis for solving end-user problems in a variety of areas.

Proponents of CBR systems argue that they offer several advantages over traditional rule-based systems (*11*). First, CBR systems can *learn* by accumulating and indexing new cases into an evolving knowledge base. A traditional rule-based system retains only what has been programmed into it. Second, CBR systems are capable of relating a problem to a partial match of its knowledge base (i.e., it finds the best fit and

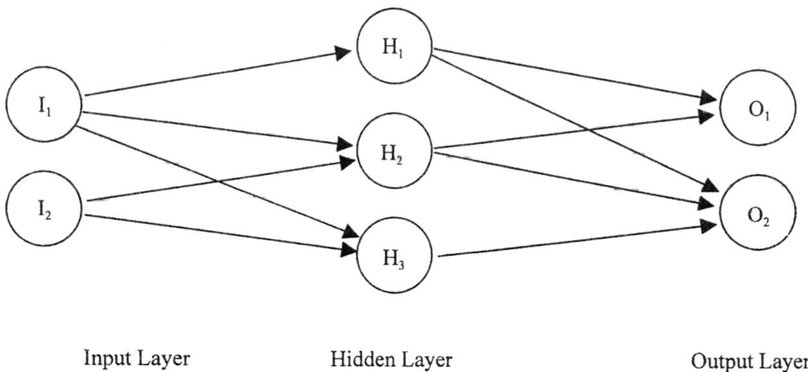

FIGURE 6. *A small neural network.*

adapts it). Rule-based systems tend to demand an exact match on a rule before the rule can fire. Finally, knowledge acquisition from a human expert can be made simpler, primarily because recounting stories of past experiences is much easier than attempting to delineate all of the rules of thumb required to solve problems.

On the other hand, case-based systems are not appropriate for all situations. In some task domains, general knowledge, in the form of heuristic rules, might be more accessible than cases. Rules are simply abstractions of experience, induced from compilations of (perhaps) numerous separate cases. In many circumstances, the rules can remain long after the cases from which they were derived are forgotten. To the degree that this occurs, the knowledge acquisition process will tend to focus on rules rather than cases.

Neural Network Systems

Neural network (or connectionist), systems depart significantly from the symbolic approaches to ES/KBS development of rule-, frame-, and case-based systems. Neural networks simulate human cognition by modeling the inherent parallelism of neural circuits found in the brain, generally in the form of mathematical models of how the circuits function. The models typically are composed of a layer of *input* nodes, one or more layers of intermediate (or *hidden*) nodes, and a layer of *output* nodes.

As shown in the small neural network of Fig. 6, behavior propagates from values set in the input nodes, continues through the hidden layer(s), and results in the establishment of values in the output layer. Generally the value of a node in one layer is a nonlinear function of the weighted sum of the values of nodes in an adjoining layer. In Fig. 6, for example, the value of output node O_2 is a function of nodes H_1, H_2, and H_3

$$v(O_2) = f\left[\sum_{i=1}^{3} w(H_i)v(H_i)\right]$$

where v is the *value* of the output node and w is the *weight* assigned to each input.

Typically a neural net is trained by providing it with a set of inputs and corresponding outputs from which it can learn pattern associations. In the *back-propagation* algorithm, the network propagates inputs through the network, derives a set of output values, compares the computed output to the provided (corresponding) output, and calculates the difference between the two numbers (i.e., the error). If a difference exists, the algorithm proceeds backward through the hidden layer(s) to the input layer, adjusting the weights between connections in an attempt to minimize the calculated error. When the error is minimized, the network retains the set of weights used to associate the input pattern with some desired output—such as an interpretation, classification, or prediction—derived from the pattern.

Neural network systems offer certain inherent advantages over traditional rule-based systems. Given a sufficient number of training sets, neural nets are capable of *learning* general patterns and of *distinguishing* between objects belonging to general classes. When presented with a pattern or object that it has never seen, the back-propagation algorithm can map the pattern onto some classification by interpreting it in the context of the existing set of connections and weights. Given enough examples of the letter *Z,* for example, a neural net system can accept a variation in the font or size of the letter, and still recognize the letter as a Z.

A neural network's inductive learning capability allows it to perform inexact matching—to find a best fit for some set of input data. As a result, neural networks are well suited to classification tasks that are inherently fuzzy—that is, tasks that generally are simple for humans but traditionally difficult for computers. Successful neural network applications include character, speech, and handwriting recognition, telecommunications monitoring, criminal activity monitoring and detection, and market analysis and classification of buying patterns. Neural networks also comprise an important constituent of *data mining,* which attempts to find interesting and useful patterns in (generally) large repositories of data. (See the section Resource Listing at the end of this article for more information on data mining.)

Neural networks are not appropriate for every application for several reasons. First, knowledge that is inherently symbolic, such as heuristic rules or cases, doesn't lend itself to representation in a neural network. A neural network application is most appropriate when available knowledge resides implicitly in a data repository and not in the brains of human beings. Second, neural networks can be time-consuming to train, particularly if the training data set is large. Finally, because the knowledge is stored as connections and weights rather than as symbols, neural networks generally are poor at explaining how and why they arrived at a particular result.

Decision-Tree/Rule-Induction Systems

Like neural networks, decision-tree systems are capable of automated learning—that is, discovering general concepts and patterns from input data. Decision-tree systems deal primarily with *symbolic* data, however, and they construct data patterns in the form of *rules.* They accept as input data that can be represented in tabular form. The data are used to construct a decision tree that leads from a description of each

Attribute: *'Occupation'*	Attribute: *'Employed-by'*	Classification: *'Lives'*
Programmer	ABC-Corp	Pittsburgh
Programmer	XYZ-Corp	Morgantown
Analyst	ABC-Corp	Morgantown

FIGURE 7. *Sample tabular data used for rule induction.*

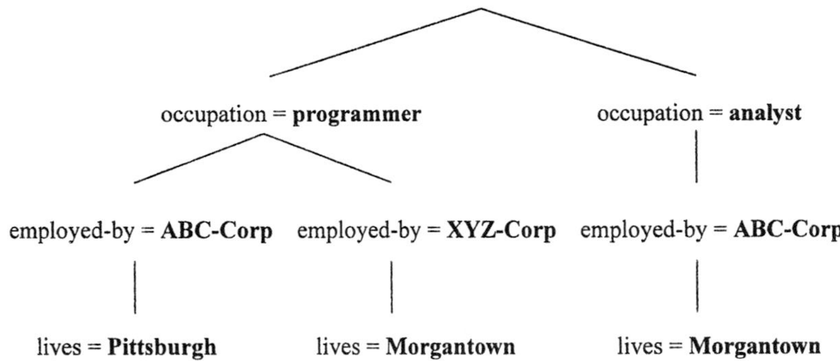

FIGURE 8. *A decision tree constructed from tabular data.*

data attribute to some associated classification. The decision tree then can be used to generate rules. For example, if the information in Fig. 7 were available in the corporate database, the decision tree shown in Fig. 8 could be constructed from it.

From the decision tree, in turn, the following rules can be induced:

1. IF occupation = programmer AND employed-by = ABC-Corp
   THEN Location = Pittsburgh.
2. IF occupation = programmer AND employed-by = XYZ-Corp
   THEN Location = Morgantown.
3. IF occupation = analyst AND employed-by = ABC-Corp
   THEN Location = Morgantown.

Most rule-induction systems attempt to make the rules more efficient by (1) removing unnecessary antecedents from rules (note that in rule 3, adding "employed-by" is not necessary for determining the location), and (2) removing unnecessary rules that share a common consequent and replacing them with a *default rule* that is fired when no other rule applies. (Note that rules 2 and 3 could be replaced with a rule that states: If no other rule applies, the location is Morgantown.)

Rule-induction systems are most appropriate when data are available and can be structured to conform to the requirements of a decision-tree representation. Similar to neural networks, such systems are used in classification and prediction applications, and may be appropriate for data-mining tasks.

Genetic Algorithms

Genetic algorithms (GAs) use search and optimization techniques that mimic the biological mechanisms of reproduction and natural selection. Genetic algorithms belong to a family of related technologies that are referenced by various names, including *genetic programming, evolutionary algorithms, evolutionary programming, evolution strategies,* and *classifier systems* (*12*). In searching for a solution, GAs employ the following three-step iterative process:

1. *Selection*—choose which of the members of the current generation will be copied to the next generation, based on an *objective function* that reflects the relative utility or value of each feature (i.e., its contribution toward a solution).
2. *Crossover*—select two of the chosen members, and based on some randomizing function, select some subset of attributes within each member. Exchange the selected attributes between the members—creating two new members of the current generation.
3. *Mutation*—modify one or more of the attributes in one or more of the members prior to further selection and crossover.

The process continues until convergence criteria are satisfied (i.e., until a solution is found). For example, consider the search for a schedule that satisfies the constraints of an organization or department. A schedule will have a number of *attributes*—employees scheduled, task(s) assigned, time-of-day allotments, and so on. A GA would approach this problem by generating a set of candidate schedules, selecting individual candidates from the set, and then modifying the candidates by crossover and mutation of individual schedule attributes. In each cycle, the schedules of the new generation are tested to determine how close they are to a solution. Poor schedules are selected out, while the better ones are retained for the next cycle. When a schedule from a new generation satisfies the imposed constraints, the search is finished.

Proponents of the technology argue that GAs are inherently more robust than traditional AI search methods; that is, they remain efficient and effective across a broad range of problems. Genetic algorithm applications have been developed in a number of commercial areas, including data mining, telecommunications network design, and scheduling. The technology is still new, however, and the solutions provided by GAs generally must be closely examined by human intermediaries (*13*).

Hybrid and Embedded Systems

A major trend of ES/KBS implementation in the 1990s is the integration of multiple technologies within single applications. Integration has taken the following two forms:

1. Multiple ES/KBS paradigms, such as those described above, are being combined with stand-alone AI applications.
2. ES/KBS technology is being added to or embedded within conventional industrial and scientific applications.

The first type of integration includes such hybrid systems as fuzzy neural networks, rule-enhanced neural networks, fuzzy GAs, rule induction using neural networks, and rule/case-based systems. A number of ES/KBS development environments include facilities for developing applications utilizing several different representations (*14, 15*).

In the second type of integration, ES/KBS modules participate within the existing IS infrastructure of an organization by (1) retrieving and storing information in existing organizational databases rather than maintaining their own data, (2) communicating with users through standard interfaces shared by other applications, (3) communicating directly with other applications through procedure calls or other mechanisms, and (4) communicating indirectly with other applications through messaging, data storage, or other means (*16*).

Knowledge-Based System Development

Traditionally, ESs/KBSs are designed and constructed using a process of *knowledge engineering* undertaken by a specialized systems analyst known as a *knowledge engineer.* Knowledge engineering is a systems development methodology similar to those used to construct conventional applications. Compatibility with the approach employed for standard ISs is important, particularly given the current tendency of fielding an ES/KBS as an integral component of a larger application or suite of applications, each of which must be developed and implemented in the context of the overall system.

Knowledge engineering encompasses all of the individual tasks required for the construction of an ES/KBS, which includes the following:

1. *Problem identification and characterization:* Description of the specific problem to be addressed by the system, including the following:
   a. *The type of problem*—diagnosis, prediction, simulation, planning, etc.
   b. *The problem domain*—disease management, nurse scheduling, equipment troubleshooting, etc.
2. *Requirements analysis:* Identification of system users and determination of the form and substance of the information the system must present to the user in order to provide a viable solution.
3. *Knowledge acquisition:* Identification, collection, and modeling of information required for the ES/KBS knowledge base. The information can come from the following:
   a. *Written documentation*—technical reports, company literature, books, notes.
   b. *A repository of data,* either in written or electronic form.
   c. *Human experts,* whose knowledge is generally elicited through interviewing and observational techniques. A knowledge engineering tends to focus on both the expert's corpus of domain knowledge and the expert's style of reasoning and problem solving.
4. *Program development:* Incorporation of acquired knowledge within an ES/KBS using a development tool or programming language. (More on this below.)
5. *Installation and testing:* Comparison of ES/KBS output with performance criteria (i.e., system verification and validation).

Two caveats concerning the above list deserve mention. First, because of the often exploratory nature of the process, ES/KBS development is not as sequential and rigid as the list above might imply. Instead, developers normally use an iterative, prototyping approach, looping through the general process and returning periodically to tasks that are incomplete. During the program development task, for example, the developer might return to a user to verify that the output of the program conforms to the user's expectations. Program coding also might reveal gaps in the knowledge base, requiring that the developer engage in additional knowledge acquisition before continuing. The possibility of loops in the program development process makes estimating project durations a challenge.

Second, although the general tasks enumerated above are a part of any ES/KBS development effort, the *specific* nature of the process is dependent on the type of problem and characteristics of the task domain, as well as on the knowledge representation scheme(s) and technology used to implement the system. For a rule-based representation, for example, the emphasis is on identifying and constructing knowledge from rules. When knowledge is to be represented using cases, the emphasis is on obtaining enough cases, and ones that will describe the full range of possible problem instances. For systems that rely on mathematical optimization, such as neural networks and GAs, the focus is less on a human expert and more on obtaining a sufficiently large repository of information from with the ES/KBS can derive patterns.

PROGRAMMING LANGUAGES AND DEVELOPMENT TOOLS

Many first- and second-generation ESs were developed on specialized (and expensive) computer hardware running development software, often based on the programming language Lisp. Later, however, the development and implementation of ESs/KBSs expanded to encompass other hardware platforms and programming environments, and the need for so-called special-purpose Lisp machines disappeared (as did many of the companies that produced them). Today ESs/KBSs are developed on a wide variety of computing platforms, from microcomputers to mainframes, and in a variety of development tools (or *shells*) and programming languages.

The choice of a development environment depends on the nature of the problem, as well as on the resources that are available. There are tools targeted to the development of rule-based systems, frame/object systems, case-based systems, fuzzy logic systems, neural networks, and combinations of those paradigms within a single tool. (See Refs. *14* and *15*). All or part of a system also can be implemented in a general-purpose programming language. The most popular languages for ES/KBS development include Lisp (which is most conductive to modeling the symbolic knowledge inherent in most human reasoning), C/C++, and Smalltalk, although an ES is an ES because of its functionality, not its implementation. There are no conceptual barriers to developing an ES/KBS in *any* language; ES/KBS systems have been developed in APL, FORTRAN, COBOL, BASIC, Pascal, and other ostensibly "traditional" programming languages.

Resource Listing

The goal of this article is to provide the reader with a high-level review of major areas and issues of ES/KBS design, development, and implementation. The resource listing provided in this section points to other sources of information that provide more detail about specific areas. Because of the rapid pace of change in AI theory and practice, the Internet sites and conference proceedings cited here help the reader to stay current in the field.

Note that the Internet-based *frequently asked questions* (FAQ) documents referenced below contain extensive and up-to-date listings of books, journals, and conferences related to each area, and therefore are highly recommended.

GENERAL EXPERT SYSTEMS

Books and Review Articles

A large number of introductory and overview books describing ESs and KBSs are available. Buchanan and Shortliffe (*5*), Hayes-Roth et al. (*3*), and Waterman (*2*) are excellent introductory texts written during the golden age of ESs. Winston (*4*) and Dean et al. (*17*) have written more recent books on general AI principles, but include extended discussions of ES/KBS principles as well.

Awad (*18*), Kasabov (*19*), and González and Dankel (*20*) discuss knowledge engineering and ES/KBS development. Holsapple and Whinston (*21*) describe ESs/KBSs in the context of their role as DSSs.

Durkin (*15*) discusses the current state of ES/KBS implementation. Wong and Monaco (*22*) review the types of domains and generic problems of ES/KBS deployed in various domains.

Periodicals/Journals

The leading journals for which ES/KBS research, development, and implementation is a primary component include *IEEE Intelligent Systems, AI Magazine, Expert Systems, Expert Systems with Applications, AI Expert, ACM SIGART Newsletter,* and *Knowledge Engineering Review.*

Organizations

Major AI/ES/KBS organizations throughout the world include the *American Association of Artificial Intelligence* (AAAI), the *Canadian Society of Computational Studies of Intelligence,* the *European Coordinating Committee on AI* (ECCAI), the *Japanese Society for Artificial Intelligence* (JSAI), the *Australian Computer Society's Committee for Artificial Intelligence and Expert Systems,* and *Sociedad Mexicana de Inteligencia Artificial.* In addition, the *IEEE Computer Society* and the *Association for Computing Machinery* (ACM; including the *Special Interest Group on Artificial Intelligence,* or *SIGART*) have significant involvement in the field.

Conferences

Leading conferences for ES/KBS study include the *National Conference on Artificial Intelligence* (organized by the AAAI), the *International Joint Conference on Artificial*

Intelligence (IJCAI), *Innovative Applications of Artificial Intelligence* (IAAI), the *World Congress on Expert Systems,* and the *IEEE Conference on Artificial Intelligence for Applications.*

Internet

The *Expert Systems Shells Frequently Asked Questions* (FAQ; *14*) document provides a timely discussion of ES development tools (*shells*). It also includes an extensive list of pointers to other sources of information on ES/KBS. It is posted periodically to the *comp.ai.shells* newsgroup, and can also be retrieved from other World Wide Web (WWW) and File Transfer Protocol (FTP) sites.

In addition, there are a number of WWW and FTP sites and newsgroups dedicated to AI and ES/KBS. Most of the major AI organizations and conferences have Web sites, as do the leading educational and corporate organizations. Carnegie-Mellon University, for example, maintains the *CMU Artificial Intelligence Repository,* a Web site containing a comprehensive collection of technical information about AI, as well as links to related AI sites (*www.cs.cmu.edu/Groups/AI/html/repository.html*).* The AAAI has an extensive array of resources and links available at its Web site (*www.aaai.org*). The main newsgroup dedicated to communication of AI issues is *comp.ai,* which in turn has a number of subtopics.

SPECIFIC AREAS

Although many of the sources above include the various subareas within ES/KBS, there also are a number of sources dedicated specifically to each area. This list focuses on the more recent ones.

Fuzzy Systems

The *Fuzzy Systems FAQ* (*23*) is posted monthly to the *comp.ai.fuzzy* newsgroup. It is a regularly updated compendium of information on fuzzy systems, and contains pointers to bibliographies and other information. The IEEE holds an annual conference (*IEEE Conference on Fuzzy Systems*), and also publishes a journal (*IEEE Transactions on Fuzzy Systems*), each of which is a good source of current work in the area. There also are numerous books on fuzzy systems. (For example, see Refs. *24* and *25.*)

Case-Based Reasoning

Recent books by Leake (*26*), Kolodner (*27*), and Shank and Riesbeck (*28*) provide good overviews of the field. In addition, there are a number of dedicated conferences and workshops focusing on CBR, including the *International Conference on Case-based Reasoning* (ICCBR), the *European Workshop on Case-based Reasoning* (EWCBR), as well as the IJCAI, U.K., and German workshops on CBR. Several CBR

*Note that Internet addresses, particularly those referencing specific files, often are quite volatile.

research organizations and companies also provide Internet Web sites containing information and resource listings. (For example, see the Web site at *www.iccbr.org.*)

Neural Networks

This is a vast area of interest. The *Neural Networks FAQ* (*29*) is posted monthly to the *comp.ai.neural-nets* newsgroup, and includes much more information than can be summarized here. In brief, there are a number of conferences on neural networks [including the *Neural Information Processing Systems* (NIPS) conference, and the *International Conference on Artificial Neural Networks* (ICANN)], as well as numerous dedicated or related journals (e.g., *IEEE Transactions on Neural Networks, Neural Networks,* and *Neural Computation*) and books. (For example, see Refs. *29–32.*) The *International Neural Network Society* is another good source of current information and activity in the field.

Decision Tree/Rule Induction

See Quinlan (*33*) for a discussion of rule-induction techniques based on ID3 and C4.5. Michalski et al. (*34, 35*) and Winston (*4*) also contain descriptions of decision trees and rule-induction techniques.

Genetic Algorithms

The Evolutionary Computation FAQ (*12*) is posted monthly to the *comp.ai.genetic* newsgroup. The FAQ organizes its bibliography, including books and journal articles, by topic and level of difficulty, and therefore is recommended as a starting point for the novice reader. Introductory sources include Refs. *36–39.* Journals in the field include *Evolutionary Computation* and *IEEE Transactions on Evolutionary Computation.* The major conferences include the *International Conference on Genetic Algorithms,* the *Annual Conference on Evolutionary Programming,* and the *IEEE Conference on Evolutionary Computation.*

Machine Learning

Resources in the broad domain of machine learning can point the reader to additional information in the areas of neural networks, CBR, decision tree/rule induction, and GAs. The reader should refer to the various books (e.g., Refs. *34, 35, 40–42*), journals (e.g., *Machine Learning*), and conferences (e.g., the *International Conference on Machine Learning,* the *European Conference on Machine Learning*) dedicated to this area. There also are a number of organizational Internet Web sites dedicated to machine learning information and resources. (Pointers are contained in the AAAI and CMU Web sites.)

Data Mining

Information resources in this area are growing rapidly. The *Knowledge Discovery Mine* Web site at *www.kdnuggets.com* is a comprehensive source of current activity in the field. In addition, the annual *International Conference on Knowledge Discovery and Data Mining,* and the journals *Data Mining and Knowledge Discovery* and *Intelligent Data Analysis* provide current information on the state of research and implementation in the field. [See also Fayyad et al. (*43*), Piatetsky-Shapiro et al. (*44*), and Frawley et al. (*45*).]

REFERENCES

1. B. G. Buchanan and R. G. Smith, "Fundamentals of Expert Systems," in *Handbook of Artificial Intelligence,* A. Barr, P. R. Cohen, and E. A. Feigenbaum, eds. Addison-Wesley, Reading, MA, 1989, pp. 149–192.

2. D. A. Waterman, *A Guide to Expert Systems,* Addison-Wesley, Reading, MA, 1986.

3. F. Hayes-Roth, D. A. Waterman, and D. B. Lenat, "An Overview of Expert Systems," in *Building Expert Systems,* F. Hayes-Roth, D. A. Waterman, and D. B. Lenat, eds. Addison-Wesley, Reading, MA, 1983.

4. P. H. Winston, *Artificial Intelligence,* Addison-Wesley, Reading, MA, 1997.

5. B. G. Buchanan and E. H. Shortliffe, *Rule-Based Expert Systems: The Mycin Experiments of the Stanford Heuristic Programming Project,* Addison-Wesley, Reading, MA, 1984.

6. J. McDermott, "R1: The Formative Years," *AI Mag.,* **2**, 21–29 (1981).

7. M. Minsky, "A Framework for Representing Knowledge," in *Psychology of Computer Vision,* P. H. Winston, ed. MIT Press, Cambridge, MA, 1975.

8. L. A. Zadeh, "Fuzzy Sets." *Info. Control,* **8**, *338–353 (1965).*

9. J. L. Kolodner, "Improving Human Decision Making Through Case-Based Decision Aiding." *AI Mag.,* **12**, 52–68 (1991).

10. J. L. Kolodner, "An Introduction to Case-Based Reasoning." *AI Rev.,* **6**, 3–34 (1992).

11. S. Slade, "Case-Based Reasoning: A Research Paradigm." *AI Mag.,* **12**, 42–55 (1991).

12. J. Heitkoetter and D. Beasley, "The Hitch-Hiker's Guide to Evolutionary Computation: A List of Frequently Asked Questions (FAQ)," USENET: comp.ai.genetic, 1995 (available via anonymous FTP from rtfm.mit.edu:/pub/usenet/news.answers/ai-faq/genetic/).

13. Price Waterhouse World Technology Centre, "Intelligent Systems and Artificial Intelligence," in *Technology Forecast: 1996,* Price Waterhouse, Menlo Park, CA, 1995.

14. M. Kantrowitz, E. Horstkotte, and C. Joslyn, "Answers to Frequently Asked Questions about Expert System Shells," USENET: comp.ai.shells, 1997 (available via anonymous FTP from cs.cmu.edu:/user/ai/pubs/faqs/expert/).

15. J. Durkin, "Expert Systems: A View of the Field." *IEEE Exp.,* **11**, 56–63 (1996).

16. F. Highland, "Embedded AI." *IEEE Exp.,* **9**, 18–20 (1994).

17. T. Dean, J. Allen, and Y. Aloimonos, *Artificial Intelligence: Theory and Practice,* Benjamin Cummings, Redwood City, CA, 1995.

18. E. M. Awad, *Building Expert Systems: Principles, Procedures, and Applications,* West, Saint Paul, MN, 1996.

19. N. K. Kasabov, *Foundations of Neural Networks, Fuzzy Systems, and Knowledge Engineering,* MIT Press, Cambridge, MA, 1995.

20. A. J. González and D. D. Dankel, *The Engineering of Knowledge-Based Systems: Theory and Practice,* Prentice Hall, Englewood Cliffs, NJ, 1993.

21. C. W. Holsapple and A. B. Whinston, *Decision Support Systems: A Knowledge-Based Approach,* West, Saint Paul, MN, 1996.

22. B. K. Wong and J. A. Monaco, "Expert System Applications in Business: A Review and Analysis of the Literature (1977–1993)." *Info. Mgt.,* **29**, 141–152 (1995).

23. M. Kantrowitz, E. Horstkotte, and C. Joslyn, "Answers to Frequently Asked Questions about Fuzzy

Logic and Fuzzy Expert Systems," USENET: comp.ai.fuzzy, 1997 (available via anonymous FTP from cs.cmu.edu:/user/ai/pubs/faqs/fuzzy).

24. R. R. Yager and L. Zadeh, *Fuzzy Sets, Neural Networks, and Soft Computing,* Van Nostrand Reinhold, New York, 1994.
25. B. Kosko, *Neural Networks and Fuzzy Systems,* Prentice Hall, Englewood Cliffs, NJ, 1992.
26. D. B. Leake, *Case-Based Reasoning: Experiences, Lessons and Future Directions,* MIT Press, Cambridge, MA, 1996.
27. J. Kolodner, *Case-Based Reasoning,* Morgan Kaufmann, San Mateo, CA, 1993.
28. R. C. Schank and C. K. Riesbeck, *Inside Case-Based Reasoning,* Lawrence Erlbaum, Hillsdale, NJ, 1989.
29. W. S. Sarle, "Answers to Frequently Asked Questions about Neural Networks," USENET: comp.ai.neural-nets, 1997 (available via anonymous FTP from ftp.sas.com/pub/neural).
30. J. A. Anderson, *An Introduction to Neural Networks,* MIT Press, Cambridge, MA, 1995.
31. L. Fausett, *Fundamentals of Neural Networks: Architectures, Algorithms, and Applications,* Prentice Hall, Englewood Cliffs, NJ, 1994.
32. D. E. Rumelhart and J. L. McClelland, *Parallel Distributed Processing,* MIT Press, Cambridge, MA, 1986.
33. J. R. Quinlan, *C4.5: Programs for Machine Learning,* Morgan Kaufmann, San Mateo, CA, 1993.
34. R. S. Michalski, J. G. Carbonell, and T. M. Mitchell, *Machine Learning: An Artificial Intelligence Approach,* vol. 1, Morgan Kaufmann, San Mateo, CA, 1983.
35. R. S. Michalski, J. G. Carbonell, and T. M. Mitchell, *Machine Learning: An Artificial Intelligence Approach,* vol. 2, Morgan Kaufmann, San Mateo, CA, 1986.
36. M. Gen and R. Cheng, *Genetic Algorithms and Engineering Design,* Wiley, New York, 1997.
37. J. H. Holland, "Genetic Algorithms." *Sci. Am.,* **267**, 66–72 (1992).
38. J. R. Koza, *Genetic Programming: On the Programming of Computers by Means of Natural Section,* MIT Press, Cambridge, MA, 1992.
39. D. E. Goldberg, "The Genetic Algorithm: Who, How, and What Next?" in *Adaptive and Learning Systems,* K. S. Narenda, ed. Plenum, New York, 1986.
40. T. M. Mitchell, *Machine Learning,* McGraw-Hill, New York, 1997.
41. P. Langley, *Elements of Machine Learning,* Morgan Kaufmann, San Francisco, 1996.
42. J. W. Shavlik and T. G. Dietterich, *Readings in Machine Learning,* Morgan Kaufmann, San Mateo, CA, 1990.
43. U. M. Fayyad, G. Piatetsky-Shapiro, P. Smyth, and R. Uthurusamy, *Advances in Knowledge Discovery and Data Mining,* AAAI Press, Menlo Park, CA, 1996.
44. G. Piatetsky-Shapiro, C. J. Matheus, P. Smyth, and R. Uthurusamy, "KDD-93: Progress and Challenges in Knowledge Discovery in Databases." *AI Mag.,* **15**, 77–82 (1994).
45. W. J. Frawley, G. Piatetsky-Shapiro, and C. J. Matheus, "Knowledge Discovery in Databases: An Overview." *AI Mag.,* **13**, 57–70 (1992).

William E. Spangler
Jerrold H. May

A FRAMEWORK FOR KNOWLEDGE DISCOVERY IN DATABASES

Introduction

In recent years, the volume of data has been increasing far faster than the number of tools and techniques for processing the data, thereby preventing us from fully utilizing these databases. There have been several reports on the development of new tools for extracting different kinds of knowledge from databases, including diagnostic rules, rules for expert systems, and rules for semantic query optimization (*1–16*).

Modern database technology involves processing a large volume of data in databases in order to discover new knowledge. Knowledge discovery is defined as the nontrivial extraction of implicit, previously unknown, and potentially useful information from data (*5–15*). Many organizations have started to develop or employ tools to discover knowledge from databases. For example, banks are analyzing data to find better rules for credit assessment. Similarly, several systems [e.g., (*16, 17*)] have been developed to discover knowledge from medical databases.

Several tools have recently been developed for knowledge discovery in databases. DataLogic/R (Reduct Systems; *18*) is an example of such tool. Based on the mathematical concepts called "rough sets," DataLogic/R discovers rules from a database that help users to decide how to categorize entities in the databases. The Information Discovery System (IDIS; *19–21*) also processes the databases to discover new knowledge in the form of rules.

Databases contain a variety of patterns, but few of them are of much interest. A pattern is interesting not only to the degree to which it is accurate but to the degree to which it is also useful with respect to the end user's knowledge and objectives (*9, 56*). A critical issue in knowledge discovery is how well the database is created and maintained. Real-world databases present difficulties as they tend to be dynamic, incomplete, redundant, inaccurate, and very large. Naturally, the efficiency of the discovery process and the quality of the discovered knowledge are strongly dependent on the quality of data. Subsequently, the databases have to be cleaned before the actual discovery process takes place in order to avoid discovering incomplete, inaccurate, redundant, inconsistent, and uninteresting knowledge.

In this article we describe a framework in which available database tools and techniques can be applied to large, real-world databases in discovering new knowledge in the form of rules. Such discovered rules could help users to improve their understanding of the organizational data, potentially leading to more efficient operational, tactical, and strategical use of data. In addition, the discovered rules could be used as the basis for rule-based knowledge bases for expert systems and decision support systems development. The framework illustrated in Fig. 1 includes the following main components:

1. Data quality improvement tools. Anomaly detection tools (*19–21*), logical database design tools (*20, 23, 24*), and the relational query language SQL (*25–27*) can be used to detect inconsistencies that might exist in the database. For very large real-world data-

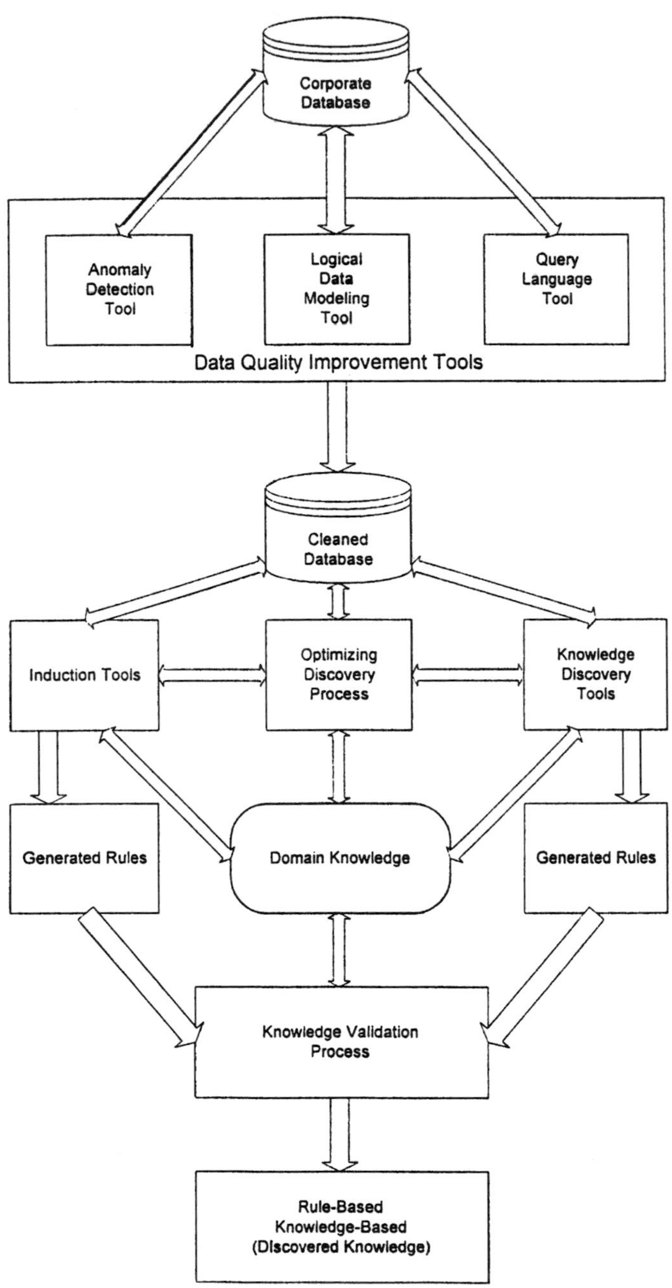

FIGURE 1. *A framework for knowledge discovery in databases.*

bases the combination of these tools can provide a better environment for automatic knowledge acquisition. To discover useful knowledge from the databases, we need to provide clean data to the discovery process. Most large databases have redundant and inconsistent data and missing data fields and/or values as well as data fields that are not logically related and that are stored in the same data relations. Data quality improvement tools can remove most of these problems, thereby increasing the chance of producing consistent, accurate, and meaningful rules by the induction/discovery tools.

2. Discovery tools.
   a. Induction tools such as LogicGem (*1*) and First Class (*28, 29*) can be used to transform data to optimized sets of rules.
   b. Knowledge discovery tools such as IDIS (*19–21*) and Knowledge Seeker (*30*) can operate on data to discover implicit relationships that might exist among attributes and present them in the form of rules. Also, these tools are able to analyze data to detect data anomalies (i.e., attributes that have abnormal values).

   Induction and discovery tools can both be used independently to generate rules. Induction tools seem to be very effective for small data sets with few attributes where attributes are independent of each other and all of the attributes are involved in the decision-making process. Knowledge discovery tools, on the other hand, are very useful in handling a large volume of data with many interrelated attributes. In addition, discovery tools enable users to guide the discovery process by focusing on selected attributes as well as to verify any piece of knowledge that has been acquired through traditional knowledge acquisition techniques. In general, the induction and discovery tools can complement each other. They use different algorithms, both to identify the hidden patterns and relationships in the databases and to generate rules. Subsequently, application of both of these tools, when appropriate and possible, can reduce the chance of missing any decision-making rules from the databases.

   Knowledge discovery has been done primarily on the operational relational databases in which the most recent and detailed data about the organization are stored. Summary and historical data (which are essential for accurate and complete knowledge discovery) are generally absent in the operational databases. Rule discovery based on just the detailed (most recent) data is neither accurate nor complete. In addition, the design of an operational relational database is based on the normalization technique, which is not suitable for effective knowledge discovery. A data warehouse is an ideal environment for rule discovery since it contains the cleaned, integrated, detailed, summarized, historical, and meta data (*15, 31–33*).

3. Optimization process. This process is used to focus the search for interesting patterns as well as to minimize the search efforts.

   While the available discovery tools are promising, they are limited in many ways. Some databases are so large that they make the discovery process computationally expensive. The problem of searching for all possible relationships in a database is non-polynomial (NP) hard (*14, 34, 35*). The vastness of the data forces the use of techniques for focusing on specific portion of the data, which requires some additional information about the form of data and constraints on it. This information, known as domain or background knowledge, can be defined as any information that is not explicitly presented in the data (*7, 12, 13, 36–39*). In a medical database, for example, the knowledge "male patients cannot be pregnant" is considered to be domain knowledge. A knowledge discovery in a database system must be able to represent and appropriately use domain knowledge in conjunction with the application of discovery algorithms. Domain knowledge assists knowledge discovery by focusing the search (*12–14, 37–39*). We should be careful in using domain knowledge to narrow the search in a database, however, in order to avoid blocking the discovery of unexpected knowledge.

4. Validation process. This process is used to make sure that the discovered knowledge is accurate, consistent, and nonredundant.

   The set of discovered rules has to be verified for its accuracy (the rules portray the database), consistency (no redundant or contradictory rules), and usefulness (rules showing the decision-making process) for the knowledge base being developed. Currently there is no tool available to accomplish this. The knowledge verification process can use the feedback from the domain expert as well as the available domain knowledge specific to the application being considered for expert system development.

In the following sections, we describe the utilities, capabilities, and limitations of the tools and techniques identified in the framework for knowledge discovery in databases. In the next section we look at data quality issues and describe different tools and techniques in order to remove redundancies and inconsistencies from the databases being considered for discovery. In the following section we look at the knowledge discovery process and show the shortcomings of rule discovery on operational relational databases and explain how and why a data warehouse can provide an effective environment for discovering accurate, complete, consistent, and meaningful rules. In the section after that we describe different schemes to optimize the discovery process by focusing the search for interesting patterns. The subsequent section discusses different schemes to validate the discovered knowledge for accuracy, consistency, and completeness. In the final section we provide some future directions for knowledge discovery in databases.

DATA QUALITY IMPROVEMENT TOOLS

Each database has its own character, reflecting the types of data it contains. The first step in understanding a database is understanding what the tables and fields are and what types of data they contain. In large databases it is often unclear as to what the fields signify and what type and range of values they contain. For instance, if one has a field such as "age," one may hazard a reasonable guess about the range of values it contains. For a field such as "complaint," however, one does not know, for example, the number of complaints or the most frequent complaint.

In knowledge discovery there is a critical dependency on how well a database is characterized and how consistently the existing and discovered knowledge is evolved. Real-world databases present difficulties due to the nature of their contents, which tend to be dynamic, incomplete, redundant, and very large. Data can be incomplete either because of the absence of values in individual record fields or because of the complete absence of data fields necessary for certain discoveries. In relational databases, the problem occurs frequently because the relational model dictates that all records in a relation must have the same fields, even if values are nonexistent for most records (*25–27*). Consider, for instance, a hospital database with fields for a wide range of laboratory tests and procedures. In general, only a few of these fields would be filled in for any given patient. Incomplete or missing fields in relations could lead to a meaningless discovery. In addition, data often recur in multiple places within a database. A common form of a redundancy is a functional dependency in which a field is defined as a function of other fields; for example, Profit = Sales – Expenses. The problem with redundant information is that it can be mistakenly discovered as knowledge, even though it is usually not interesting to the knowledge engineer.

The quality of information interpretation and discovery depends on the quality of the data. The quality (or lack of) and vastness of the data in real-world databases represent the core problems for knowledge discovery. Overcoming the data quality problem requires the use of the tools to detect anomalies, to clean up the anomalies, and to refine the logical database design if necessary.

ANOMALY DETECTION TOOL

There are many types of errors (anomalies) that can occur in a database, ranging from a simple data entry error (e.g., age of employee entered as 135 instead of 35) to a poor logical database design (e.g., unrelated attributes grouped in a relation). Some measures of data quality may be enforced by using anomaly detection tools. In general, an anomaly detection tool has the following tasks:

1. It finds anomalous data items and unusual patterns by itself. Deterministic checks find obvious mistakes (e.g., inputting an invalid value for an attribute) and probabilistic checks look for unlikely values.
2. It enforces integrity constraints that are maintained separately from databases and application programs by using rules.

In an anomaly detection tool such as Database/Supervisor (*20, 21*), the user can define constraints in the form of rules. For instance, consider the following rule:

IF department = "sales" THEN salary > 30000

If the rule in a constraint is completely specified, then for each record that satisfies the IF condition, anomaly detection can check whether the THEN part is also satisfied. Anomaly detection will report all the records that satisfy the IF condition, but fail the THEN part. This type of checking is useful when we know the relationships between database fields, and these relationships can be represented as rules.

IDIS (*19*) is another anomaly detection tool (in addition to being a rule discovery tool) that can look for anomalies by means of the following:

Scalar analysis: Calculating average values for scalar fields and looking for values that fall beyond the tolerance levels.

Nonscalar analysis: Calculating occurrence frequencies and looking for values that occur too seldom or too frequently.

Correlation analysis: Finding unusual correlations between values in pairs of scalar fields.

Constraint enforcement: Allowing the user to define constraints on his table using if-then combinations. IDIS can look for invalid data in the table using these integrity constraints.

Although anomaly detection tools can identify many sources of errors in a database, they do not have the capability to identify the flaws in the underlying logical design of a database. There are, however, specific logical database design tools that one can use in order to develop better logical database design or to improve an existing logical database design.

Example 2: Detecting Contradictory Data

In general, most contradictory data can be prevented by enforcing functional dependencies when adding rows to the relation. When the relationship already exists, however, the following query could be used for every value of the left side of a dependency for a relation to identify any contradiction. Consider the following SQL statement based on Fig. 3:

```
CREATE VIEW R1 AS   SELECT UNIQUE Type-of-disease   FROM Medication
WHERE Prescription = "Take excedrin"
INTERSECT
CREATE VIEW R2 AS   SELECT UNIQUE Type-of-disease   FROM Medication
WHERE Prescription <> "Take Excedrin"
```

If the result of the INTERSECT is empty, then contradictory data exist in the relation, causing the generation of contradictory rules.

Example 3: Detecting Redundant Data

If primary key constraint is enforced, then there would be no duplication of rows in a relation and thus no redundant rules will be generated based on that relation; otherwise, the following SQL query could be used to check a relation for possible redundancy:

```
CREATE VIEW R3 AS   SELECT *   FROM relation-name
CREATE VIEW R4 AS   SELECT UNIQUE *   FROM relation-name
```

If $R_3 - R_4 \neq R_3$, then there is redundancy. If $R_3 - R_4 \neq 0$, then redundant data are found in R_3; otherwise, redundant data are found in R_4.

The database administrator should use SQL on the database (whether it already exists or is being designed and developed) in order to detect and avoid any data inconsistencies. Such use would result in a more accurate and maintainable database. In addition, if such a database is used to acquire knowledge for expert system development either with induction tools or knowledge discovery tools, the generated set of rules will be more maintainable and less inconsistent.

Discovery Tools

There have been significant developments in the creation of tools for extracting additional knowledge from databases—a process known as knowledge discovery. Knowledge discovery is defined as the nontrivial extraction of implicit, previously unknown, and potentially useful information from data (*5–7, 14, 20, 21, 40*). Knowledge discovery processes the database in order to uncover interesting features in the database based on user-defined measures of interest. It includes the identification of relationships that would have gone undetected without specialized approaches to discovery. In general, the discovered knowledge is represented as a set of if-then rules.

Current induction/knowledge discovery tools employ different discovery schemes, including classification, characteristics, association, and sequence. An understanding of these schemes is essential in order to use the right discovery tool on the database being explored for automatic knowledge acquisition. In the following, we briefly describe these discovery schemes. The reader is referred to Refs. *4, 20, 29,* and *41–43* for a detailed discussion of these schemes.

Discovery systems have been applied to real databases in medicine, computer-aided design, the stock market, and many other areas. The type of rule or pattern that exists in the database depends on the domain. A discovered rule can be either a qualitative rule or a quantitative rule, where the former does not associate quantitative information, whereas the latter does (*4, 7, 20, 41, 42*). For example, the statement the salaries of professors of sciences are high is a qualitative rule, while the statement the salaries of 60 percent the professors of arts are high is a quantitative rule. A quantitative rule provides statistical information about the rule, which facilitates quantitative reasoning, incremental learning, and learning in the presence of noise and exceptions. Scientific data are likely to have quantitative patterns. If the experiment is properly controlled to deal with only one cause, then usually a single pattern exists in data. The collected data in business databases, on the other hand, typically reflect the uncontrolled real world, in which many different causes overlap and many patterns are likely to exist simultaneously. The eventual use of the pattern determines the approach to finding it.

From another point of view, a discovered rule can be either a classification rule or a characteristic rule. A classification rule is an assertion that discriminates the concepts of one class from others (*4, 7, 20, 41*). For example, to distinguish one disease from others, a classification rule summarizes the symptoms that distinguish this disease from others. In general, given a set of records, each containing a number of attributes, a set of tags (representing classes of records), and an assignment of a tag to each record, a classification function examines the set of tagged records and produces descriptions of the characteristics of records for each of the classes. For example, consider the credit card analysis application. The customer record can be tagged with good, medium, or poor. A classification function can examine these tagged records and generate an explicit description of each of these classes. Such a classifier would produce a description of the set good customers as those with "Income over $40,000, between the age of 40 and 55, and live in X neighborhood." Decision trees have been used for classification in order to simplify the search for rules (*3, 22, 42, 44, 45*). This approach does not function efficiently when data are inconclusive, however, or when there are a few positive data and many more negative data.

A characteristic rule is an assertion that characterizes the concept satisfied by all of the relevant data in the database (*4, 7, 20, 41*). For example, the symptoms of a particular disease can be summarized as a characteristic rule. In general, a characteristic description describes what the records in a class share in common among themselves. In most learning from examples, the examples undergoing discovery are partitioned into positive and negative sets. Since a relational database does not store negative data in general, however, there are usually no explicitly specified negative examples. When discovering a characteristic rule, one should note that there are no negative examples for specialization, and the generalization on the data should be performed cautiously to avoid overgeneralization.

Other less frequently used discovery schemes include the association rule and the

AC-Input	Secondary-Voltage	Filter-Output	Regulator-Output	Result
OK	OK	Normal	Zero	Open Regulator
OK	OK	Low	Low	Bad Capacitor
OK	OK	Zero	Zero	Bad Rectifier
OK	Zero	Zero	Zero	Bad Fuse
OK	OK	Normal	High	Short Regulator

FIGURE 4. *A sample matrix for hypothetical power supply.*

sequence rule. An association rule is an assertion that associates different attributes of a database; that is, given a collection of items and a set of records, each of which contains some number of items from the given collection, an association function can find rules such as "70 percent of all the records that contain items A, B, and C also contain items D and E" (*4, 7, 29, 41, 46*). In a market application, we may find that "30 percent of the time that a specific brand of toaster is sold, customers also buy a set of kitchen mitts and matching cover sets."

A sequential function will analyze a collection of related records and will detect frequently occurring patterns over time (*29*). For example, a sequential function may discover a rule that "60 percent of the time when stock X increased its value by at most 10 percent over a 5-day trading period and stock Y increased its value between 10 and 20 percent during the same period, then the value of stock Z also increased in a subsequent week."

INDUCTION TOOLS

Induction tools (*3, 43–45, 47–50*) build a rule base for an expert system from a set of examples that describe (1) a series of attributes or conditions that describe each example, and (2) the result or consequence that occurred given those attributes. The examples are entered into a spreadsheetlike matrix in which each column represents either an attribute of the examples or the result that derives from the attributes. Each row describes a different example. Figure 4 displays a matrix of examples for a hypothetical power supply troubleshooting expert system. The induction tool generates the rules from the matrix. A sample rule generated by such a tool would be the following:

IF Filter-Output = "Zero" AND Secondary-Voltage = "Zero"
THEN solution = "Bad Fuse"

Induction tools have their basis on the Quinlan ID3 algorithm, which generates a decision tree to classify data (*42, 47, 48, 50, 51*). Figure 5 shows a decision tree generated by the induction tool 1st-Class (*28, 29*), which uses the Quinlan's ID3

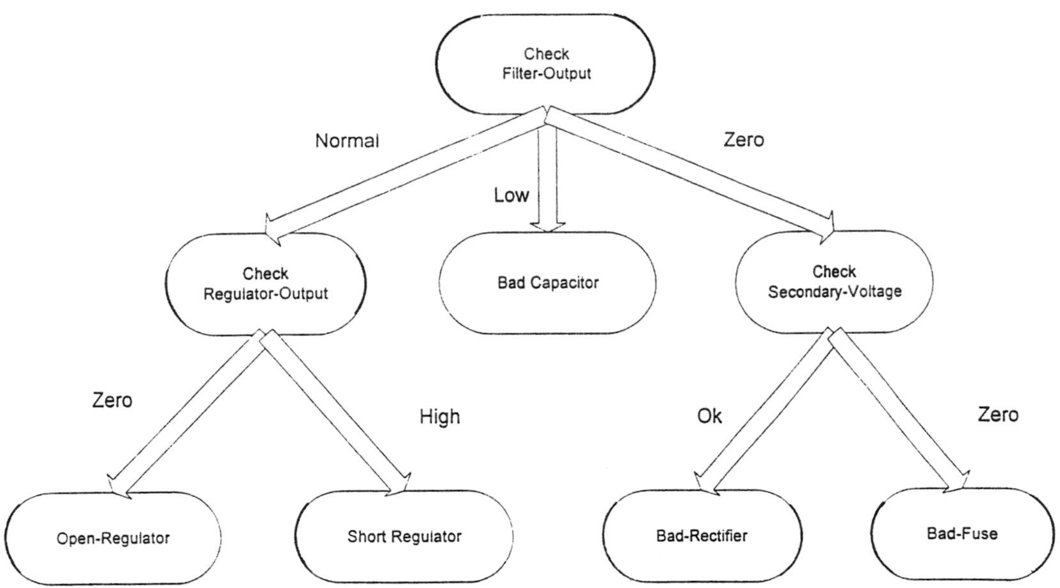

FIGURE 5. *Decision tree (based on Fig. 4).*

algorithm for optimizing the rule from the cases. This algorithm determines which factors are most useful in discriminating among possible variable values in order to reach a conclusion. At times this algorithm discards some variables because they do not assist in the selection of paths to follow in the decision tree. For example, the AC-input variable in Fig. 4 does not contribute to the results and therefore it is removed from the generated rules.

The primary advantage of an induction tool is its ease of use. Creating the matrix of attributes and results is simple, thus minimizing the complex and time-consuming knowledge acquisition phase. In many applications (e.g., medicine, business), the decision-making data are already available in the form of a matrix. Inductive techniques are most used for classification tasks. For example, as a form of classification, diagnosis fits under this category. In general, induction tools are most helpful in the development of small systems in which an expert acts as his own knowledge engineer. They are very effective in handling small numbers of attributes and values in a matrix. When expert systems are being constructed, the database administrator can use the database to create examples for an induction tool. The induction tool matrix can be produced automatically and efficiently from queries. In some cases, the database can be augmented with additional data acquired from the domain expert.

Induction tools have several shortcomings that are worthwhile to mention. First, they can only operate on a single data relation (or matrix). It is impossible to directly apply them to databases in which several interrelated data relations exist. This problem can be solved, however, by joining all the data relations to create a single relation, although it may be too large to be processed by induction tools efficiently.

Second, the interrelationships among attributes cannot be shown in the matrix. The restriction that attributes have to be independent of each other may not be appropriate for some applications. Furthermore, for system expansion, the matrix representation may require the entire rule set to be modified if new attributes are added to the decision-making process. Similarly, when the database is expanded, there is no capability in induction tools to do an incremental generation of rules. The expanded data relation has to be processed in its entirety to generate a new set of rules. Finally, induction tools based on ID3 algorithm do not do well with noisy data. Specifically, the tree becomes overly complicated in order to account for the noisy instances. A related problem is that it cannot deal with inconclusive data—that is, when they are no rules that classify all possible examples correctly using only the available attributes. If unguided, ID3 can easily get into error and generate a large decision tree that makes little sense.

KNOWLEDGE DISCOVERY TOOLS

Tools specifically designed for knowledge discovery have recently been released. These tools differ substantially in the types of problems they are designed to address and in the ways in which they work. DataLogic/R (*18*) is a PC-based package. DataLogic/R uses "rough sets," an offshoot of fuzzy logic, that helps the user ferret out rules characterizing the data in the database and that suggests how to make decisions on categorizing the data for optimum analysis. Datalogic/R provides pattern recognition, modeling, and data analysis techniques that discover new knowledge in the form of rules. In general, it is able to deal with uncertainty in data, to analyze hidden facts in data, to represent new knowledge in a rule format, and to create models for prediction and classification. DataLogic/R has demonstrated success in applications such as consumer survey analysis, process control measurement, substance toxicity identification, insurance analysis, and fault detection (*18*).

IDIS:2 (IntelligenceWare; *19*) also generates possible rules for explaining relationships among variables. It uncovers information based on questions no one thought to ask by posing a hypothesis and then testing it for accuracy and relevancy. It concludes with a list of rules in two- and three-dimensional hypermedia graphs. Guided by the user, IDIS uses induction to assign weights to attributes used in the rules. It finds suspicious entries and unusual patterns automatically, including data items that violate correlations, extreme boundary items, and items that are beyond normal standard deviations. IDIS has been used in areas as diverse as financial analysis, marketing, scientific discovery, quality control, medical discovery, and manufacturing (*19, 52*). It induces classification rules, generalized rules with intervals, and inexact rules. The induction method may be guided by the user with the assignment of weights to attributes. A generated rule can be saved as a constraint and then used along with the anomaly detection facility in order to find the values and exceptions that violate a specific rule. In addition, ad hoc queries can be used to verify simple, human-generated hypotheses. In effect, ad hoc queries are a method of knowledge verification. We have done several experiments on the car relation (Fig. 6), with twenty-six attributes and 205 records, using the IDIS discovery tool on a 486 IBM-compatible PC. We were interested in discovering the relationship between the highway mileage

Relation Car:

CAR (Symboling, Losses, Make, Fuel-Type, Aspiration, Doors, Body, Drive, Engine-Loc, Wheel-Base, Length, Width, Height, Weight, Engine-Type, Cylinders, Engine-Size, Fuel-Sys, Bore, Stroke, Compress, Horse-Power, Peak-RPM, City-MPG, High-MPG, Price)

Generated Rules:

Rule 1: If Fuel-Type = "gas" AND 0< = Horse-Pwr < = 156 Then 16 < = High-MPG < = 43

Rule 2: If Fuel-Type = "gas" AND Cylinder = "four" AND 61< =Engine-Size < =161
Then 16 < = High-MPG < =39

Rule 3: If Aspiration = "std" AND Cylinder ="four" AND 3< =Stroke< =4
AND 7< =Compress < =9 Then 27 < =High-MPG < =37

Rule 4: If Drive = "fwd" AND Cylinder = "four" AND 61< =Engine-Size < =122
AND 3< =Stroke < =4 Then 30 < =High-MPG < =46

FIGURE 6. *Data relation CAR and a set of rules discovered by IDIS tool in finding the factors affecting highway mileage.*

and the rest of the attributes. Figure 6 shows some sample rules generated using the IDIS discovery tool.

Similar to induction tools, knowledge discovery tools also suffer from some shortcomings. First, they, too, operate on a single data relation to generate the rules. For databases with several interrelated relations, the relevant data relations are to be joined in order to create a single relation. Second, the discovery tools do not have a direct facility to perform incremental rule generation when the database is expanded. The previously generated rules, however, can be defined as constraints and run against the expanded database to see if newly added records contradict or confirm the previously generated rules or cause the generation of a new set of rules. Finally, a major concern in using the discovery tools is related to the consistency and accuracy of the generated rules. With very large real-world databases consisting of many attributes and lots of records, the ability of these tools to generate useful and accurate rules in a timely fashion becomes an issue. The following discussions show the problems associated with IDIS discovery based on the car data relation in Fig. 6. Similar problems have been noted on other discovery tools as well.

1. The discovery process was too slow. It took a week to generate more than 1000 rules. The reason was that the discovery process had to consider all possible combinations of attributes even though some of them were inappropriate (e.g., the price of the car, which is not related to highway mileage).
2. Some of the generated rules were uninteresting and/or known facts. For example, the tool

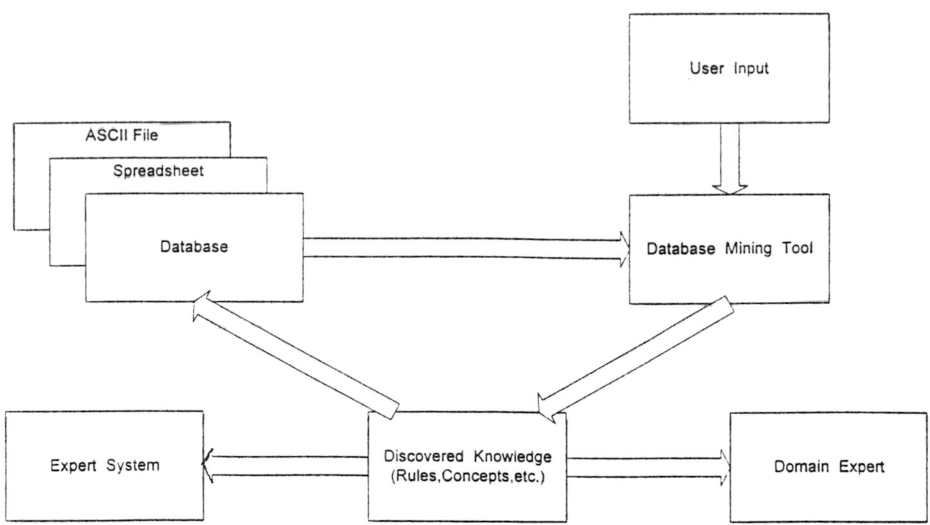

FIGURE 7. *A database mining and discovery environment.*

discovered that "the smaller the engine-size, the better High-MPG," which is a trivial discovery since it is a known fact (or a domain knowledge). Similarly, the tool discovered that "the more expensive the car, the better High-MPG," which seems to be uninteresting since there is no relationship between the price of the car and the highway mileage.

3. Some of the discovered rules were redundant. In general, databases have redundant attributes that could lead to the discovery of redundant rules. In the car relation, for example, we have the attribute engine-size, which is the same as Bore*Stroke*Cylinders. The discovery tool discovered rules relating the highway mileage to engine size and highway mileage to bore, stroke, and cylinders. The rules relating highway mileage to bore, stroke, and cylinders thus appear to be redundant.

Some of the above problems can be removed by using the available domain knowledge (e.g., the smaller the engine size, the better the high MPG; or the price of the car is not related to high MPG) in the discovery process (*38, 39*). Current discovery tools are lacking the ability to represent domain knowledge and use them automatically in discovering the rules, however. The use of domain knowledge is handled manually by eliminating any irrelevant attributes from consideration in the discovery process when defining a particular discovery case.

There is no single approach to knowledge discovery; however, a generalized approach described in Fig. 7 includes several key steps, including the following:

- Identify an extensive database that is to be analyzed.
- Decide whether you wish to use a tool to test your own hypotheses on what knowledge may be contained in the database or whether you wish the tool to generate a hypotheses for you.
- Select an appropriate tool.
- Generate and test hypotheses.
- Validate the discovered knowledge.

- Utilize the discovered knowledge by integrating it into corporate expert systems usage and into expert practice or by refining the database for more effective future action.

The database manager can assist in the use of these tools in several ways. The first is to acquire and experiment with knowledge discovery tools to better understand their uses and limitations. Often data will have to be reformatted in order to be processed efficiently. Also, this manager will have to be aware of knowledge acquisition efforts underway so knowledge engineers can be alerted to the presence of data that bear on the development of their system.

PROBLEMS WITH KNOWLEDGE DISCOVERY IN OPERATIONAL RELATIONAL DATABASES

Most knowledge discovery has been done on the operational relational databases. An operational database stores the detailed data. In addition, the goal of the relational databases is to provide a platform for querying data about uniquely identified objects. Such uniqueness constraints are not desirable in the knowledge discovery environment, however. In fact, they are harmful, since from a data mining point of view, we are interested in the frequency with with which objects occur (*7*). In the following, we discuss two main problems associated with knowledge discovery in relational databases; namely, the possibility of discovering incorrect and incomplete knowledge from operational relational databases.

Incorrect Knowledge Discovery from Relational Databases

In general, summary data are never found in the operational environment. Without discovery process on summary data, we may discover incorrect knowledge from detailed operational data. Discovering rules based just on current detail data may not depict the actual trends in data. The problem is that statistical significance is usually used in determining the extent of interest of the patterns (*34*). Statistical significance alone is often insufficient to determine a pattern's degree of interest. A "5 percent increase in sales of product X in the western region," for example, could be more interesting than a "50 percent increase of product X in the eastern region." In the former case, it could be that the western region has a larger sales volume than the eastern region, and thus its increase translates into greater income growth.

The following example, adapted from Ref. *53,* shows that we can discover incorrect knowledge if we only look at the detailed data. Consider Table 1, in which the goal of discovery is to see if product color or store size has any effect on the profits. Although the data are not extensive, they show the points.

Assume we are looking for patterns that tell us when profits are positive or negative. We should be careful when we process this table using such discovery methods as simple rules or decision trees. These methods are based on probability, which make them inadequate for dealing with influence within aggregation (summary data). A discovery scheme based on probability may discover the following rules from Table 1:

Rule 1: IF Product Color = Blue Then Profitable = No CF = 75%

TABLE 1

Sample Sales Data

Product	Product color	Product price	Store	Store size	Profit
Jacket	Blue	200	S1	1000	-200
Jacket	Blue	200	S2	5000	-100
Jacket	Blue	200	S3	9000	7000
Hat	Green	70	S1	1000	300
Hat	Green	70	S2	5000	-1000
Hat	Green	70	S3	9000	-100
Glove	Green	50	S1	1000	2000
Glove	Blue	50	S2	5000	-300
Glove	Green	50	S3	9000	-200

Source: Ref. 53.

TABLE 2

Sample Sales Data

Product	Product color	Product price	Store	Store size	Profit
Jacket	Blue	200	S1	1000	-200
Jacket	Blue	200	S2	5000	-100
Jacket	Blue	200	S3	9000	100
Hat	Green	70	S1	1000	300
Hat	Green	70	S2	5000	-1000
Hat	Green	70	S3	9000	-100
Glove	Green	50	S1	1000	2000
Glove	Blue	50	S2	5000	-300
Glove	Green	50	S3	9000	-200

Source: Ref. 53.

Rule 2: IF Product Color = Blue and Store Size > 5000 Then Profitable = Yes CF = 100%

The results indicate that blue products in larger stores are profitable; however, they do not tell us the extent of profits that can go one way or another. Now, consider Table 2, in which the third row in Table 1 is changed. Rules 1 and 2 are also true in Table 2; that is, Tables 1 and 2 produce the same results with respect to the probability of the patterns being discovered. This is not true when we look at Tables 3 and 4, however, which are the summary tables based on Tables 1 and 2, respectively. Table 3 tells us that blue is profitable and Table 4 tells us it is not; that is, in the summary tables, the probability behavior of these detailed tables begins to diverge and thus produce different results. We should be careful when we analyze the summary tables since we may get conflicting results when the discovered patterns from the summary tables are compared with the discovered patterns from detailed tables. In general, the probabilities are not enough when discovering knowledge from detailed data; we need the summary data as well.

Similarly, if we look at Tables 1 and 2, we may discover that

TABLE 3

Summary Sales (Based on Table 1)

Product color	Profit
Blue	6400
Green	1000

TABLE 4

Summary Sales (Based on Table 2)

Product color	Profit
Blue	-500
Green	1000

If Product Color = Green Then Profitable = No CF = 60% (3 records out of 5)

but both summary Tables 3 and 4 tell us that green products are profitable. One possible explanation for such differences in the result is that the summary tables do not have all the information. In fact, it is the green products in small stores that are profitable.

The above discussion indicates that we cannot discover accurate knowledge if we only process the detailed data or just the summary data. We need to combine probability computations with aggregations in order to avoid discovering contradictory knowledge. It is suggested that multidimensional data mining is the right approach to take (*7*).

Incomplete Knowledge Discovery from Relational Databases

The traditional database design method is based on the notions of functional dependencies and lossless decomposition of relations into third normal forms. This decomposition of relation is not useful with respect to knowledge discovery, however, because it hides dependencies among attributes that might be of some interest. To provide maximum guarantee that potentially interesting statistical dependencies are preserved, the knowledge discovery process should use universal relations (*25, 27*) as opposed to normalized relations. In the following example we show that knowledge discovery on normalized relations may not reveal all the interesting patterns.

Consider the relations sales and region adapted from Ref. *7* in Fig. 8, which are in third normal form. Figure 9 shows the universal relation, which is the join of the two tables in Fig. 8. From Fig. 9 we can discover that there is a relationship between the average price of the house and the type of products purchased by people. Such a relationship is not that obvious in the normalized relations in Fig. 8. This example shows that knowledge discovery on "well-designed" (i.e., 3NF) databases according to the normalization techniques could lead to incomplete knowledge discovery.

Sales

Client Number	Zip Code	Product Purchased
1111	11111	Wine
2222	22222	Bread
3333	11111	Wine
4444	33333	Wine
5555	44444	Wine

Region

Zip Code	City	Average House Price
11111	Paris	High
22222	Peking	Low
33333	New York	High
44444	Moscow	High

FIGURE 8. *Relational Database in 3NF (from Ref. 7).*

Sales/Region

Client Number	Zip Code	City	Average House Price	Product Purchased
1111	11111	Paris	High	Wine
2222	22222	Peking	Low	Bread
3333	11111	Paris	High	Wine
4444	33333	New York	High	Wine
5555	44444	Moscow	High	Wine

FIGURE 9. *Universal relation, join of the tables in Fig. 8 (from Ref. 7).*

KNOWLEDGE DISCOVERY IN THE DATA WAREHOUSE ENVIRONMENT

As we showed in the previous sections, knowledge discovery in operational relational databases could lead to inaccurate and incomplete discovered knowledge. The operational data contain the most recent data about the organization and are organized for fast retrieval as well as for avoiding update anomalies. Summary data are not generally found in the operational environment. In addition, metadata (i.e., description of the data) are not complete. Rule discovery does not mean analyzing details of data alone. To understand the deep knowledge regarding the decision-making process for expert system development, it is critical that we perform pattern analysis on all sources of data, including summarized and historical data.

Without first warehousing its data, an organization has lots of information that is not integrated and has little summary information or history. The effectiveness of knowledge discovery on such data is limited. The data warehouse provides an ideal environment for effective knowledge discovery. Applications suitable for knowledge discovery (e.g., medicine, finance) are information-rich and have a changing environment (*2, 31, 32, 37*). The following factors are important:

- Volume: There should be a sufficient number of cases.
- Complexity: The more attributes (fields) there are, the more complex the application.
- Quality: Error rates should be relatively low.
- Accessibility: Data should be easily accessible; accessing data or merging data from different sources increases the knowledge discovery process time.
- Change: Although dealing with change is more difficult, it can be more rewarding, since the application can be automatically and regularly retrained on up-to-date data.

A data warehouse environment supports these factors. Basically, data warehousing is the process of extracting and transforming operational data into informational data and loading them into a central data store or warehouse. A data warehouse environment integrates data from a variety of source databases into a target database that is optimally designed for decision support. A data warehouse includes (*2, 7, 31, 32*) integrated data, detailed and summary data, historical data, and metadata. Each of these elements enhances the knowledge discovery process.

Integrated data: When data are moved from the operational environment into the data warehouse, they assume a consistent coding convention (e.g., gender data are transformed to *m* and *f*. Without integrated data, we have to cleanse the data before the process of knowledge discovery can be effective; that is, keys have to be reconstituted, encoded values reconciled, structures of data standardized, and so on. Integrated data could remove any redundancies and inconsistencies that we may have on data, thus reducing the chance of discovering redundant and inconsistent knowledge.

Detailed and summarized data: Detailed data (e.g., sales detail from 1992 to 1993) are necessary when we wish to examine data in their most granular form. Very low levels of detail contain hidden patterns. At the same time, summarized data ensure that if a previous analysis is already made we don't have to repeat the process of exploration. Summary data (e.g., highly summarized monthly sales by product line 1981–1993; lightly summarized weekly sales by subproduct 1985–1993) are detailed data that are summarized for specific decision-support requirement. Summary tables can provide efficient access to large quantities of data as well as help reduce the size of the database. Summarized data contain patterns that can be discovered. Such discovered patterns can complement the discovery on operational/detail data by verifying the patterns discovered from the detailed data for consistency, accuracy, and completeness.

Historical data: Processing only very recent data (detailed or summarized) can never detect trends and long-term patterns in the data. Historical data (e.g., product sales for 1982–1991) is essential in understanding the true nature of the patterns representing the data. The discovered knowledge should be correct over data gathered for a number of years, not just the recent year.

Metadata: Metadata are used to describe the content of the data (e.g., description of the tables; fields; constraints; data transformation rules, such as profit = income – cost; and domain knowledge, such as male patients can not be pregnant). In addition, metadata are used to define the context of the data. When data are being explored over time, context becomes as relevant as content. Raw content of data becomes very difficult for exploration when there is no explanation for the meaning of the data. Metadata can be used to identify the redundant and inconsistent data (when data are gathered from multiple data sources), thereby reducing the chance of discovering redundant and inconsistent knowledge.

There are several benefits in rule discovery in a data warehouse environment.

1. The rule discovery process is able to examine all the data in some cohesive storage format. There is a repository or directory (metadata) of enterprise information. This will enable the users or tools to locate the appropriate information sources. To allow an effective search of data, it is important to be aware of the relationships between them as well as all the information that is stored in the system. Rules discovered from only part of the business data produce potentially worthless information. Rule discovery tools actually need to be able to search the warehouse data, the operational data, the legacy data, and any distributed data on any number of servers.
2. A major issue in rule discovery in an operational database environment is whether or not the data are clean. As explained above, the data have to be verified for consistency and accuracy before the discovery process. In a data warehouse environment, however, the validation of the data is done in a more rigorous and systematic manner. Using metadata, many data redundancies from different application areas are identified and removed. In addition, a data-cleansing process is used in order to create an efficient data warehouse by removing certain aspects of operational data (e.g., low-level transaction information) that slow down the query times (*2, 7, 31, 32*). The cleansing process will remove duplication and reconcile differences between various styles of data collection.
3. Operational relational databases built for online transaction processing are generally regarded as unsuitable for rule discovery since they are designed for maximizing transaction capacity and typically have many tables in order not to lock out users. Also, they are normalized to avoid update anomalies. Data warehouses, on the other hand, are not concerned with the update anomalies since an update of data is not done. This means that at the physical level of design we can take liberties to optimize the access of data, particularly in dealing with the issues of normalization and physical denormalization. Universal relations can be built in the data warehouse environment for the purposes of rule discovery, which could minimize the chance of detecting hidden patterns.

There are several issues and concerns in rule discovery in a data warehouse environment.

1. We should be careful when processing a universal relation since it could mistakenly lead to discovering a known fact (i.e., a functional dependency; FD). Note that when we denormalize the relations (joining them) to create the universal relation, we will have redundancies, because of the functional dependencies among attributes. For example, consider the universal relation sales/regions in Fig. 9. A discovery system may discover that

   $$\text{If Zip Code} = 11111 \text{ Then City} = \text{Paris}$$
   $$\text{If City} = \text{Paris Then AverageHousePrice} = \text{High}$$

   The above rules indicate that there are relationships between zip code and city and between city and averagehouseprice. These relationships, however, do not represent new discovery since they are in fact the given functional dependencies that are true.
2. Databases to support management control and strategic levels of an organization usually contain summarizations of data from operational (most recent and detailed data) databases. Summarized data contain patterns that can be discovered as noted above. Such discovered patterns can complement the discovery on operational data and verify

Student (Stid, Stname, Address, Major)

Course (Course#, Title, Instructor-name)

Instructor (Instructor-name, Office#)

Registration (Stid, Course#, Grade)

FIGURE 10. *Part of the university relational schema.*

Major	College	Dean	No-of-students	Average-gpa
cs	CAS	Miller	200	3.1
is	CAS	Miller	180	2.9
math	CAS	Miller	120	2.7
stat	CAS	Miller	145	3.4
physics	CAS	Miller	85	2.7
chemistry	CAS	Miller	60	3.2
art	CAS	Miller	220	3.4
ee	Engineering	Brown	155	2.9
mechanical	Engineering	Brown	140	2.6
...				
...				

FIGURE 11. *A summarized relation based on majors in colleges.*

the patterns discovered from the detailed data for consistency, accuracy, and completeness.

In general, summarized data are represented as relational tables. These tables may need to be normalized to avoid all the anomalies found in operational databases. Consider the university relational scheme in Fig. 10. We may be interested only with grade summaries by department or major. For example, the summarized data of grades by major would be represented by major-grades (major, no-of-students, average-gpa). This relation is in 3NF (*26*). Note that average-gpa is functionally dependent on major, although it is mathematically related to no-of-students. The summary table major-grades is created from the student and registration tables of Fig. 10.

To remove redundancies, we should always see if it is possible to have normalized relations, even for summarized tables. For example, consider the major-college-grades relation in Fig. 11. Since it is very likely that each college has only one dean, the attribute dean is functionally dependent on the attribute college. The major-college-grades relation is not in 3NF. An unnormalized summary table could lead to discovering knowledge that is a known fact (e.g., an FD). For instance, we may discover from the above relation that if college =CAS then dean = Miller. The relationship between College and Dean is a functional dependency (which is always true), however, and not a new discovery. The unnormalized relation can be put in 3NF to remove the redundancies (created due to the functional dependencies between attributes) as maj-grades (major, college, no-of-students, average-gpa) and college-info (college, dean).

GENERAL PROBLEMS AND ISSUES IN KNOWLEDGE DISCOVERY

Knowledge discovery systems rely on databases to supply the raw data for input, and this raises problems in that databases tend to be dynamic, incomplete, noisy, and large. Other problems arise as a result of the adequacy and relevance of the data stored (*7, 12, 13, 37*).

Limited information: A database is often designed for the operational environment. Its purposes are different from knowledge discovery and sometimes the attributes that would simplify the discovery task are not present, nor can they be requested from the real world. Inconclusive data cause problems. It may be impossible to discover significant knowledge about a given domain (e.g., medicine) if some attributes essential to knowledge about the application domain are not present in the data. For example, we cannot diagnose malaria from a patient database if the data do not contain the patients' red blood cell counts.

Noise and missing values: Databases normally contain errors. Attributes that rely on subjective or measurement judgments can give rise to errors, causing some examples to even be misclassified. Missing data can be treated by discovery systems by simply discarding missing values, omitting the corresponding records, or inferring missing values from known values. Statistical methods can also be used to treat problems of noisy data and separate different types of noise.

Uncertainty: Uncertainty refers to the severity of the errors and the degree of noise in the data. Data precision is an important consideration in a discovery system.

Size, updates, and irrelevant attributes: Databases are generally dynamic in that their contents are changing as data are added, modified, or deleted. Care must be taken to assure that the discovered rules are up to date and consistent with the most current data. Another issue is the degree of relevance of the attributes involved in the current focus of discovery. For example, height and diagnosis may not be causally related if the discovery focus deals with liver disease, but they may be casually related for physiotherapy.

External data: There may be cases in which the discovered patterns based on the internal organizational data cannot be justified or explained. Such patterns can only be explained by additional external data that are not available in the operational data or data warehouse associated with an enterprise. For example, we may discover a steady decline in sales of a given product line over the past two months. At the same time, the company's other products are doing well and overall revenues and profits are up in all regions. One reason for the drop of the product could be that a major price-driven marketing push by a competitor was made with regard to its own product line. Such information may not be available in our system. The point is that the operational and/or data warehouse deals almost exclusively with traditional internal data within the organization.

Optimization of the Knowledge Discovery Process

Modern database technologies process large volumes of data to discover new knowledge. Some large databases make discovery computationally expensive. Additional knowledge, known as domain or background knowledge, can often guide and restrict the search for interesting knowledge. Domain knowledge has been used in different aspects of knowledge discovery in a few systems. For example, Meta-Dendral (*11, 54*) uses domain knowledge (knowledge of chemistry) heavily for both hypothesis (representing the knowledge to be discovered) generation and testing. Prospector (*11, 54*) uses its domain (geological) knowledge in the same areas as Meta-Dendral. RX (*16, 17*) employs a little domain knowledge for generating correlations in its medical database, but uses more domain knowledge for testing.

Although the use of domain knowledge in knowledge discovery has been mentioned by researchers (*12–14, 37, 46*), the literature does not have any detailed discussions regarding the use of domain knowledge in different aspects of knowledge discovery. In this article, we discuss the areas in which domain knowledge can be used to reduce the search time in discovering knowledge from databases. In particular, we look at the use of domain knowledge in the following areas:

1. To reduce the size of the databases
2. To optimize the hypotheses, which represent the interesting knowledge to be discovered
3. To optimize queries used to prove the hypotheses
4. To verify possible contradictory rule discovery
5. To avoid possible redundant rule discovery

DOMAIN KNOWLEDGE

Domain or background knowledge can be defined as any information that is not explicitly presented in the database (*13, 14, 38, 39*). In a medical database, for example, the knowledge "male patients can not be pregnant" or "male patients do not get ovarian cancer" is considered to be domain knowledge since it is not contained in the database directly. Similarly, in a business database, the domain knowledge "customers with high income are good credit risks" may be useful even though it is not always true. Other types of knowledge, such as interfield knowledge (e.g., experience and salary being positively correlated) and interinstance knowledge, can be related to data, but they are more related toward the semantics of the domain (*14, 46*).

Domain knowledge originates from many sources. A data dictionary is the most basic form of domain knowledge (*8, 14, 46*). Typical information in the data dictionary includes the types of attributes, sizes of attributes, names of attributes, meaning of each attribute, format, constraints, domain of attribute, usage statistics, access control, and mapping definitions (*25, 26*). Additional information about the specific analysis objectives may come from the domain expert [although it may be generated automatically from the database (*36, 46*)] and can assume many forms. A few examples include (*46*): lists of relevant fields on which to focus for discovery purposes; definition of new fields (e.g., age = current-date - birth-data); lists of useful classes or categories of fields or records (e.g., revenue fields: profits, expenses); generalization hierarchies (e.g., A is-a B is-a C); and functional or causal models.

Formally, domain knowledge can be represented as $X \Rightarrow Y$ (meaning X implies Y), where X and Y are simple or conjunctive predicates over some attributes in the database. For example, consider the following relations, which are part of a medical database:

Patient(Patient #, name, age, place of birth, ...)
Medical-History(Patient #, disease, medication, effects, . . .)

Assume that we are trying to discover whether drug X has any effects on patients who have malaria. The available domain knowledge includes "people born in U.S. and Europe have had malaria vaccine in their childhood," and "people who had malaria vaccine cannot get malaria," which can be represented as follows:

(Birthplace = Europe/USA) ⇒ (malaria vaccination = yes)
(Malaria vaccination = yes) ⇒ (getting malaria = no)

It is also possible to derive domain knowledge from a set of given domain knowledge. For instance, through transitive dependency, one could establish a new domain knowledge as "People born in U.S. and Europe can not get malaria," which can be represented as

(Birthplace = Europe/USA) ⇒ (getting malaria = no)

Let DK be the set of all domain knowledge available for a database. We define DK^+, the closure of DK, as: $DK^+ = DK \cup \{ DDK_i \mid DDK_i \text{ is implied by } DK \}$; that is, the set of all domain knowledge consists of those defined by the domain expert and those that can be derived from the defined domain knowledge. The derivation process can be accomplished by using augmentation and transitive rules, the same way used to operate on functional dependencies in a database (*25, 26*).

USING DOMAIN KNOWLEDGE FOR KNOWLEDGE DISCOVERY

Knowledge discovery is the process of extracting implicit, previously unknown, and potentially useful information from the databases (*14, 31, 55*). In practice, however, some databases are so large that even the fastest algorithms for rule discovery can be too expensive to apply to all data. There are several approaches that can be utilized in order to minimize the search efforts. In the first approach, the size of the database can be reduced by eliminating the attributes that do not participate in the discovery. Ziarko (*56*) uses the theory of rough sets for the identification and the analysis of data dependencies or cause-effect relationships in databases. He demonstrates how to evaluate the degree of the relationship and identify the most critical factors contributing to the relationship. Identification of the most critical factors allows for the elimination of irrelevant attributes prior to the generation of rules describing the dependency.

Limiting the number of fields alone may not sufficiently reduce the size of the data set, in which case a subset of records must be selected. In the second approach, we can apply the discovery algorithms to a random sample of data. The rules discovered in a sample can be invalid on the full data set, however. Piatetsky-Shapiro (*40*) presents a formal statistical analysis for estimating the accuracy of sample-derived rules when applied to a full data set.

Finally, in the third approach (taken by the author), additional information called domain knowledge (*8, 13, 14, 46*) can be used to guide and constrain the search for interesting knowledge. The search time can be minimized by reducing the size of the database, optimizing the hypothesis that represents the knowledge to be discovered, and optimizing queries that are used to process the data to prove the hypothesis.

Using Domain Knowledge to Reduce Database Size

Domain knowledge can be used to reduce the size of the database that is being searched for discovery by eliminating data records that are not needed for discovery. Consider a medical database in which simple domain knowledge could be "male patients cannot be pregnant." If the knowledge to be discovered is "whether drug X has effects on pregnant patients," domain knowledge can be used to reduce the size of database by eliminating the records for male patients from consideration. Other domain knowledge (e.g., "female patients under 12 or above 65 cannot be pregnant") can be applied to further reduce the size of the database. To formalize the process, assume that the set of domain knowledge is represented as follows:

$$DK = \{ (\text{sex} = \text{female}) \Rightarrow (\text{pregnancy} = \text{yes}), (\text{age} > 12) \Rightarrow (\text{pregnancy} = \text{yes}), (\text{age} < 65) \Rightarrow (\text{pregnancy} = \text{yes}), \ldots\ldots \}.$$

The initial hypothesis (note that the actual hypothesis for discovery may include other attributes of the patients; e.g., race and weight) can be represented as a rule as follows:

IF pregnancy = Yes AND drug taken = X THEN Effects = Yes.

The database reduction algorithm can apply the domain knowledge to the initial hypothesis to create a set of constraints. Basically, for each condition in the hypothesis the reduction algorithm searches the set of domain knowledge. If the condition is found to be in the Y part of a domain knowledge, then the X part of the domain knowledge is selected as a constraint. The set of constraints can then be used to create an SQL statement to be executed in order to produce the reduced database. For the above hypothesis, the following SQL statement can be created and executed to produce the reduced database:

```
Select* FROM Patient-File Where sex = 'female' AND age > 12 AND age < 65
Into Reduced-Patient-File
```

Database Reduction Algorithm:

Begin

Let $C = \{C_k \mid k=1,\ldots,n\}$, where C_k is a condition in the premise of the hypothesis, and n is the number of conditions.

Let DK = set all of all domain knowledge, such that $\{ (C_i,C_j) \mid C_i \Rightarrow C_j, i \neq j \}$;

Let N = set of constraints to be used to reduce the database, initialized to 0

For k = 1 to n do

If C_k in $C = C_j$, such that (C_i,C_j) in DK Then $N = N \cup \{C_i\}$

End.

Using Domain Knowledge to Optimize Hypothesis

In addition to reducing the size of the database, domain knowledge can be used to define an optimal hypothesis by eliminating unnecessary conditions in the hypothesis, thereby reducing the search time for discovering interesting knowledge from the database. A discovery process can be guided by specifying the criteria to focus on, although it may be set to move freely through the database to find any pattern or relationship. For each pattern or relationship to be discovered, one would (*20, 21*) do the following:

1. Form hypotheses
2. Make some queries to the database
3. View the result and modify the hypotheses if needed
4. Continue this cycle until a pattern merges

This task can be automated with a discovery module, which can repeatedly query the database until knowledge is discovered. Initially hypotheses can be formed by domain experts (or by the discovery system automatically) and should aim toward one specific concept. The basic form of representing a hypothesis is the rule representation

IF Premise THEN Conclusion

where premise is a set of conditions (or criteria). ANDed together, defined by the domain expert to focus the search, and the conclusion will be the discovered knowledge when the premise is satisfied by the database. Generally speaking, there may be some interdependency between or among conditions that implies that some conditions can be implied by others. Of course, these dependencies can be identified by domain knowledge. Subsequently those conditions that can be implied by others may be removed from the hypothesis (since they provide no additional information in knowledge discovery), resulting in a faster discovery process. The following algorithm shows the process for eliminating the unnecessary conditions in a hypothesis:

Hypothesis Optimization Algorithm:
Begin
Let DK be the set of all defined domain knowledge; such that $\{ (C_i,C_j) \mid C_i \Rightarrow C_j, i \neq j \}$;
Let DK^+ be the closure of DK;
Let C be the set of all conditions in the premise of the hypothesis;
For every (C_i,C_j) in DK^+ do
if $C_i \in C$ and $C_j \in C$ then $C = C - C_j$;
End.

To show how the algorithm works, consider the CAR1 data relation in Fig. 12. A collection of cars is described in terms of such attributes as overall length (SIZE), number of cylinders (CYL), presence of a turbocharger (TURBO), type of fuel system (FUELSYS), engine displacement (DISPLACE), compression ratio (COMP), POWER, type of transmission (TRANS), WEIGHT, and mileage (MILEAGE; *56*). Suppose we are interested in factors affecting high car mileage. The full functional dependency means that the mileage of a car is affected by interactions of all or some possible causes represented by attributes contained in the CAR1 relation. A discovery system (or a domain expert) may start with the following hypothesis represented as a rule:

IF SIZE = subcompact AND CYL = 4 AND TURBO = no AND FUELSYS = efi
AND DISPLACE = small AND COMP = high AND POWER = medium
AND TRANS = manual AND WEIGHT = light THEN MILEAGE = high

The set of domain knowledge may include the following:

(SIZE = subcompact) ⇒ (WEIGHT = light); (TURBO = no) ⇒ (POWER = medium)

SIZE	CYL	TURBO	FUELSYS	DISPLACE	COMP	POWER	TRANS	WEIGHT	MILEAGE
compact	6	yes	efi	medium	high	high	auto	medium	medium
compact	6	no	efi	medium	medium	high	manual	medium	medium
compact	4	yes	efi	medium	high	high	manual	light	high
compact	6	no	efi	medium	medium	medium	manual	medium	medium
compact	6	no	2-bbl	medium	medium	medium	auto	heavy	low
compact	6	no	efi	medium	medium	high	manual	heavy	low
subcompact	4	no	2-bbl	small	high	low	manual	light	high
compact	4	no	2-bbl	small	high	low	manual	medium	medium
compact	4	no	2-bbl	small	high	medium	auto	medium	medium
subcompact	4	no	efi	small	high	low	manual	light	high
subcompact	4	no	efi	medium	medium	medium	manual	medium	high
compact	4	no	2-bbl	medium	medium	medium	manual	medium	medium
subcompact	4	yes	efi	small	high	high	manual	medium	high
subcompact	4	no	2-bbl	small	medium	low	manual	medium	high
compact	4	yes	efi	medium	medium	high	manual	medium	medium
compact	6	no	efi	medium	medium	high	auto	medium	medium
compact	4	no	efi	medium	medium	high	auto	medium	medium
subcompact	4	no	efi	small	high	medium	manual	medium	high
compact	4	no	efi	small	high	medium	manual	medium	high
compact	4	no	2-bbl	small	high	medium	manual	medium	medium
compact	6	no	efi	medium	high	high	manual	medium	medium

FIGURE 12. *A sample CAR1 data relation.*

By applying domain knowledge to the initial hypothesis, conditions 7 (POWER = medium) and 9 (WEIGHT = light) can be removed from the hypothesis. The discovery system will evaluate the hypothesis with respect to actual data and may remove additional irrelevant conditions from the hypothesis in discovering knowledge.

We have done several runs on the CAR1 relation using a microcomputer-based knowledge discovery tool called IDIS (*19*). Figure 13 shows the rules generated by IDIS when all conditions are applied. In the second run, we eliminated the WEIGHT condition because of the existence of domain knowledge (e.g., SIZE implies WEIGHT). Except for rule 2 in Fig. 13, the rest of the rules have been generated in the

Rule 1: CF = 100.00 %	Rule 2: CF = 100.00 %	Rule 3: CF = 100.00 %
MILEAGE = "high"	MILEAGE = "high"	MILEAGE = "high"
IF SIZE = "subcompact"	IF WEIGHT = "light"	IF FUELSYS = "efi"
		and DISPLACE = "small"
Rule 4: CF = 100.00 %	Rule 5: CF = 100.00 %	Rule 6: CF = 100.00 %
MILEAGE = "high"	MILEAGE = "high"	MILEAGE = "high"
IF CYL = "4"	IF CYL = "4"	IF CYL = "4"
and TURBO = "yes"	and FUELSYS = "efi"	and TURBO = "no"
and COMP = "high"	and POWER = "medium"	and FUELSYS = "efi"
		and TRANS = "manual"

FIGURE 13. *Rules generated by IDIS tool based on the CAR1 relation in Fig. 12, with mileage as the goal and the rest of attributes as conditions.*

second run. We note that rule 2 seems to be another domain knowledge and not a new discovery.

In the third run, the POWER condition was removed using the domain knowledge (e.g., TURBO implies POWER). Except for rule 5 in Fig. 13, the rest of the rules have been generated in the third run. Note again that if we replace the POWER condition with the TURBO condition, then rule 5 becomes a subsumption of rule 6 (a redundant discovery), therefore the absence of rule 5 in the third run is not an indication of blocking the unexpected discovery.

Finally, in the fourth run, the WEIGHT and POWER conditions have both been removed from the initial hypothesis. All the rules in Fig. 13 have been generated, except for 2 and 5. The absence of rules 2 and 5 does not mean the blocking of unexpected discovery, as explained in the second and third runs above.

Using Domain Knowledge to Optimize the Query Used to Prove a Hypothesis

To discover patterns, a discovery system forms the hypotheses, make queries to the database, views the result, and modifies the hypotheses if needed. This process continues until a pattern emerges. A major component of a discovery system is the database interface. Raw data are selected from the DBMS (using queries) and then processed by the extraction algorithms that produce the discovered patterns. The queries can be posed in SQL, a standard query language for many relational databases (*25–27*). The DBMS interface is where database queries are generated. Domain knowledge can be used to optimize a query used to prove a hypothesis. For example, consider the following data relations in a database:

employee(E#,Ename,title,experience,seniority)
money(title,seniority,salary,responsibilities)

Assume the knowledge to be discovered is “What are the criteria for an employee to earn more than $50,000.” An expert may suggest that experience and seniority are the two criteria contributing to having a salary exceeding $50,000. The hypothesis may be represented as the following rule:

IF has experience AND has seniority THEN earn more than 50000.

To prove (or disprove) the hypothesis, a discovery system may execute the following SQL statement:

```
Select experience,seniority From employee E,money M
Where salary > = 50000 AND E.title=M.title AND E.seniority=M.seniority.
```

Now, assume that we have the following domain knowledge:

Only level-1 and level-2 managers have a salary more than 50000, represented as:
(title = level-1) ⇒ (salary > = 50000), (title = level-2) ⇒ (salary > = 50000)

We can use this domain knowledge to minimize our search by eliminating the unnecessary join operation. Basically, for each condition in the hypothesis, the query optimization algorithm searches the set of domain knowledge. If the condition is found to be in the Y part of the domain knowledge, then the X part will replace the condition, and the unnecessary join operation will be removed from the query. The optimized SQL statement for the above example would be

```
Select experience,seniority From employee Where title = level – 1 or title = level – 2
```

The following algorithm shows the process for the optimization of the query used to prove or disprove a hypothesis:

Query Optimization Algorithm:
Begin
Let C = $\{ C_k \mid k=1,\ldots,n\}$, where C_k is a condition in the Where Clause of the SQL statement used to prove(or disprove) the hypothesis, and n is the number of conditions.
Let DK = set of all domain knowledge; such that $\{ (C_i,C_j) \mid C_i \Rightarrow C_j, i \neq j \}$;
For every domain knowledge (C_i,C_j)
If C_k in C = C_j Then Replace the condition C_k with C_i;
Remove the unnecessary join condition from the SQL statement;
End.

Using Domain Knowledge to Avoid Possible Contradictory Rule Discovery

Rules are contradictory when they have the same conditions and different mutually exclusive conclusions. The following rules are contradictory:

Rule 1: If Car Model = Honda AND Cylinders = 4 Then Mileage = High
Rule 2: If Car Model = Honda AND Cylinders = 4 Then Mileage = Low

Domain knowledge can be used to avoid generating contradictory rules. Consider our CAR1 relation in Fig. 12 (with the added attributes car model and car year). Suppose one is interested to find out whether or not car model and cylinders have any relationships with highway mileage. Without using domain knowledge, our discovery system could discover the above rules. Assume we have the available domain knowledge that cars produced after 1980 have special features that cause better performance and better mileage. We could use the domain knowledge to define a more accurate hypothesis in order to avoid generating rules that seem to be otherwise contradictory. The basis idea is to expand the hypothesis by adding more conditions based on the available domain knowledge. The process is to examine the set of available domain knowledge and find any of them that involve the goal defined for the discovery. In the above example, let's assume we have the following domain knowledge:

(Car Year > 1980) ==> (Mileage = High).

Subsequently, we (or the discovery system) should include the car year attribute in the hypothesis. Then we may get the following rules that do not seem to be contradictory:

Rule 1: If Car Model = Honda AND Cylinders = 4 AND Car Year > 1980 Then Mileage = High
Rule 2: If Car Model = Honda AND Cylinders = 4 AND Car Year < = 1980 Then Mileage = Low

Using Domain Knowledge to Avoid Possible Redundant Rule Discovery

Databases normally contain redundant data and definitions that could lead to discovering redundant rules. The redundant data and definitions are generally different syntactically. For instance, consider the CAR relation in Fig. 6. The relation contains the attributes engine-size, bore, stroke, and cylinder, among others. The redundant attribute engine-size is defined as: engine-size = bore * stroke * cylinder. In our discovery experiment, we defined the High-MPG as the goal and the rest of the attributes as the premise. The discovery tool IDIS discovered rules relating the engine-size to High-MPG as well as rules relating bore, stroke, cylinder to High-MPG. Obviously, the discovered rules based on engine-size and bore, stroke, cylinder are syntactically different, but they are semantically identical.

We can define the redundant information in the database as domain knowledge and apply it in the discovery process in order to avoid generating rules that are syntactically different but semantically equivalent. Before knowledge discovery, the user (or the discovery system) should check the available domain knowledge to find domain knowledge that has attributes involved in the discovery hypothesis. If there is such domain knowledge, then the attributes in one side of the domain knowledge should be included in the discovery process. For the above CAR relation, we could use the engine-size attribute or the bore, stroke, cylinder attributes in the discovery process; the choice depends on whether we are looking to generate more general rules or more detailed rules.

The advantage of using this process is not only a gain in avoiding redundant rules, but also in generating rules that are more meaningful. In our experiment, IDIS generated rules for the High-MPG based on engine-size and bore alone and engine-size and stroke alone, which do not seem to be meaningful, since none of the attributes bore, stroke, or cylinder by itself has any connection with engine-size.

We should note that the discussion is the expansion of the hypotheses optimization process given above. We created a separate section for clarity, however.

EVALUATION OF USING DOMAIN KNOWLEDGE

Experimental Results

We have done several experiments on the CAR relation in Fig. 6. We were interested to discover the relationship between the highway mileage and the rest of the attributes. The following discussions show our findings, both with and without using domain knowledge on the CAR relation. We should note that the current discovery tools are lacking the ability to represent domain knowledge and use them automatically in discovering the rules. The use of domain knowledge is handled manually by eliminating any irrelevant attributes from consideration in the discovery process when defining a particular discovery case.

Results Without Using Domain Knowledge.

1. The discovery process was too slow. It took a week to generate more than 1,000 rules. The reason was that the discovery process had to consider all possible combinations of attributes, even though some of them were inappropriate (e.g., price of the car, which is not related to highway mileage).
2. Most of the generated rules were not interesting and/or were known facts. For example, the tool discovered that "the smaller the engine-size, the better High-MPG," which is a trivial discovery since it is a known fact (or a domain knowledge). Similarly, the tool discovered "the more expensive the car, the better High-MPG," which seems to be uninteresting since there is no relationship between the price of the car and the highway mileage.
3. Some of the discovered rules were redundant. Generally databases have redundant attributes that could lead to the discovery of redundant rules. In the car relation, for example, we have the attribute engine-size, which is the same as bore*stroke*cylinders. The discovery tool discovered rules relating the highway mileage to engine-size and highway mileage to bore, stroke, and cylinders. The rules relating highway mileage to bore, stroke, and cylinders thus appear to be redundant.

Results Using Domain Knowledge. In this experiment we have eliminated some of the attributes (e.g., price, doors) from consideration in the discovery process based on the available domain knowledge. Some of the domain knowledge included the following:

- The smaller the engine-size, the better the High-MPG.
- The lighter the car, the better the High-MPG.
- The price of the car is not related to High-MPG.
- Engine-size = Bore * Stroke * Cylinders.

When domain knowledge was used, the discovery process was very fast. (It took 3 hours.) Also, the generated rules were fewer but more interesting and nontrivial. In other experiments, as noted above, our runs did not show any blocking of unexpected discovery when domain knowledge was used.

Avoid Blocking Unexpected Discovery

The main purpose of using domain knowledge is to bias the search for interesting patterns. This can be achieved by focusing the discovery on portions of the data. The benefits are greater efficiency and more relevant discoveries. Too much reliance on domain knowledge, however, may unduly constrain the knowledge discovery and block unexpected discovery by leaving portions of the database unexplored.

Consider the following hospital data relation:

hospital(p#,pname,age,diagnosis,drugs,effects,...)

Assume that the knowledge to be discovered is "the effects of drug X on patients with heart disease" and the domain knowledge is "People under 20 don't have heart disease." This domain knowledge helps us to reduce the size of our database by eliminating the records for patients under 20. Suppose the discovered knowledge is

Drug X has such and such effects on people with heart disease.

If we avoid using domain knowledge, the knowledge discovery system may find a more reasonable result, such as

Drug X has these effects on people over 20 with heart disease
and these effects on people under 20 with heart disease

Excluding this domain knowledge during discovery may help to classify the data more efficiently. For example, our data may support the conclusion that drug X has different effects on people under 20 and over 20. Due to the elimination of part of the database (records for patients under 20), however, the discovery scheme just can't find enough data to support this. In another example, if we use the domain knowledge "male patients do not get breast cancer" for the hypothesis "effects of drug X on patients with breast cancer," we may never discover that male patients can have breast cancer (an unexpected discovery, as found in Ref. *57*).

There are several things that we can do to improve the effective use of domain knowledge in knowledge discovery and to avoid blocking the unexpected discovery. First, the domain expert can assign a confidence factor to each domain knowledge and uses it only if the confidence factor is greater than a specified threshold. The assignment of a confidence factor to domain knowledge depends on how close the domain knowledge is to the established facts. For instance, given the known facts, such domain knowledge as "male cannot be pregnant" should get a higher confidence factor than domain knowledge that "Female over 65 and under 12 may not be pregnant," as the former can medically be proved to be true whereas in the latter case there may be a slight chance that females under 12 or above 65 can get pregnant. The domain expert needs to define a mechanism to calculate the confidence factor of domain knowledge that is derived from the given domain knowledge.

Second, rarely is discovered knowledge true across all the data. It is important to represent and convey the degree of certainty to decide how much confidence the system or user should put into a discovery. Certainty involves several factors, including the integrity of the data, the size of the sample on which the discovery is performed, and perhaps the degree of support from available domain knowledge (*13, 14, 38*). If the size of the database is reduced too drastically after using some domain knowledge, we may therefore consider using less domain knowledge (or none) in order to avoid blocking unexpected discovery results; otherwise knowledge is discovered that does not have a high enough confidence factor to be considered interesting.

Third, using too much domain knowledge can produce a specialized discovery scheme that can be more efficient than any general scheme in its domain, but will not be useful outside its domain (*13, 14, 38*). Domain knowledge can be used more effectively by developing a general scheme for knowledge discovery and then augmenting it with the specific domain knowledge (*14*). The interface (integration of the general-purpose discovery scheme and domain knowledge) may require developing a set of rules that can recommend when and how much of the domain knowledge to use in different phases (e.g., creating the hypothesis, querying the database, modifying the hypothesis) of the general-purpose discovery scheme. The hypothesis optimization algorithm given above, for example, can be part of such an interface and can automatically be applied to every hypothesis generated by the general-purpose discovery scheme. The interface should have a mechanism for reducing the size of the database (if possible) by using all the available domain knowledge efficiently (e.g., perhaps by using the criteria explained in this section and other criteria). The reduced database should be provided to the general-purpose discovery scheme for knowledge discovery.

Validation of the Discovered Knowledge

Databases contain a variety of patterns, but few of them are of much interest. A pattern is interesting not only to the degree to which it is accurate but is useful with respect to the end user's knowledge and objectives (*40, 46*). In addition, databases include redundancy, which could lead to discovering redundant knowledge. Also, databases are normally incomplete, thus discovered knowledge may be inconsistent and inaccurate.

Most knowledge discovery is performed on an operational relational database environment, which is not well suited for knowledge discovery. First, operational databases lack the summary data. Without discovery process on summary data, we may discover incorrect knowledge from detailed operational data (*53*). Second, the operational relational databases are designed based on the normalization techniques in order to avoid update anomalies (*26, 27*). Normalized tables are not good for knowledge discovery, however, since they lose some of the hidden patterns as a result of the normalization process (*7*).

Much research in knowledge discovery has focused on ways of extracting interesting patterns from databases; there has been no discussion on the validation of the discovered knowledge. A key aspect of any discovery system should be to ensure that the discovered knowledge is consistent, accurate, and complete, particularly when incremental discovery from the database is employed. The basic idea is to subject each discovered rule or pattern to a series of tests that determine its suitability as discovered knowledge. The main tests for consistency include redundancy, subsumption, and contradiction. In this article, we look at validation of knowledge discovery in databases. In particular, we consider the possibility of using domain knowledge in validating the discovered knowledge.

KNOWLEDGE BASE INCONSISTENCY

As noted above, there is a possibility of discovering incorrect and incomplete knowledge from operational relational databases. In the following, we describe other types of inconsistent knowledge, including redundant, subsuming, contradictory, and uninteresting knowledge, which may also be discovered from the operational relational databases.

Redundant knowledge: Information often recurs in multiple places within a database. A common form of redundancy is a functional dependency in which a field is defined as a function of other fields; for example, profit = sales − expenses. The problem with redundant information is that it can be mistakenly discovered as knowledge even though it is usually not interesting to the end user. The discovered knowledge may contain redundancy when two pieces of knowledge are exactly the same (rules having the same premises and conclusions) or semantically equivalent (*40, 46*). In addition, the discovered knowledge may indeed be a previously known fact (i.e., domain knowledge) rather than a new discovery. Consider the CAR relation in Fig. 6. We have done several experiments on the CAR relation. We were interested in discovering the relationship between the highway mileage and the rest of the attributes. Some of the discovered rules were redundant. In general, databases have redundant attributes that could lead to the discovery of redundant rules. In the CAR relation, for example, we have the attribute Engine-Size, which is the same as bore*stroke*cylinders. The discovery tool discovered rules relating the highway mileage to engine-size and highway mileage to bore, stroke, and cylinders, thus the rules relating highway mileage to bore, stroke, and cylinders appear to be redundant.

Subsuming Knowledge: Discovered knowledge could be a subsumption of knowledge (i.e., rules having the same conclusion, but one rule having more conditions). For instance, consider the following rules discovered from the CAR relation where the goal was engine-size and the conditions were bore, stroke, and cylinders attributes:

Rule 4: CF = 84.88% "61" < = "Engine-Size" < = "161" IF "0" < = "Bore" < = "4"
Rule 16: CF = 100.00% "61" < = "Engine-Size" < = "161"
IF "Cylinders" = "four" AND "0" < = "Bore" < = "4"

Rule 4 is a subsumption of rule 16. In fact, the above rules may not accurately represent the real knowledge since the engine-size cannot be determined by bore or (bore and cylinders) without the stroke attribute.

Contradictory Knowledge: There is a possibility of contradictory knowledge being discovered from a database. Consider the following rules discovered from the CAR relation:

Rule 29: CF = 100.00% "16" < = "High-MPG" < = "54" IF "61" < = "Engine-Size" < = "326"

Rule 30: CF = 99.00% "16" < = "High-MPG" < = "50" IF "61" < = "Engine-Size" < = "234"

Rule 31: CF = 96.34% "16" < = "High-MPG" < = "43" IF "61" < = "Engine-Size" < = "183"

The above rules indicate that the smaller the engine-size, the lower the High-MPG, contrary to the domain expert's knowledge. One possible reason is that the relation does not have accurate data or the High-MPG may be dependent on other factors, such as the existence of a turbocharger in addition to the engine-size of the car. Another possibility for the contradiction is when two rules have the same conditions, but different conclusions that are mutually exclusive.

Uninteresting knowledge: As we noted, databases contain a variety of patterns, with few being of much interest. A pattern is interesting to the degree that it is useful with respect to the user's knowledge and objectives. In our knowledge discovery of the CAR relation, some of the generated rules were uninteresting and/or known facts. For example, the tool discovered that "the smaller the weight, the better the High-MPG," which is a trivial discovery since it is a known fact (or domain knowledge)—similarly, the discovered rule "the more expensive the car, the better the High-MPG," which seems to be uninteresting since there is no relationship between the price of the car and its highway mileage. The following rule was also discovered, which could be interesting:

CF = 86.84% 28 < = High-MPG < = 39 IF Fuel-Type = "gas" AND Drive = "fwd"
AND Cylinder = "four" AND 61 < = Engine-Size < = 120

APPROACHES TO VALIDATION OF THE DISCOVERED KNOWLEDGE

Discovered knowledge has to be validated to assure its accuracy and consistency. One possible scheme for knowledge validation is to include the discovered knowledge in the database to see whether or not it is correct by observing its interaction with the existing data (*14, 40*). A discovered rule is inconsistent with the database if an example exists in the database that satisfies the condition part of the rule, but not the conclusion part (*34, 58*). A knowledge base is inconsistent with the database if there is an inconsistent rule in the knowledge base. A knowledge base is incomplete with respect to the database if an example exists in the database that does not satisfy the condition part of any consistent rule.

For example, suppose we discover the following rules in an incremental knowledge discovery scheme:

R1: (Feet = web) --- > (Gives-milk = no)
R2: (Feet = claw) --- > (Gives-milk = yes)
R3: (Feet = hoof) --- > (Gives-milk = yes)

Now, suppose that a new example for a platypus is added to the database.

(Feet = web) (Ears = external) (Eats = meat) (Gives-milk = yes) (Flies = unable) (Swims = well).

We can see that rule R1 is inconsistent with platypus because a platypus has webbed feet but gives milk, and that the knowledge base is incomplete because neither R2 nor R3 covers platypus.

Another scheme is to use statistical techniques in order to prove or disprove the newly discovered knowledge (*40*). When databases are very large, with records in the millions, a complete analysis of all the data for knowledge discovery may not be feasible. Discovery algorithms must then rely on some form of sampling, whereby only a portion of the data is considered. The resulting discoveries in these cases are necessarily uncertain. The discovered rules from a sample database can be invalid on the full database. Statistical techniques, however, can measure the degree of uncertainty. They can also be used to determine how much additional sampling would be required to achieve a desired level of confidence in the results. Piatetsky-Shapiro (*40*) presents a formal statistical analysis for estimating the accuracy of sample-derived rules when applied to a full database.

As we noted, most knowledge discovery is performed on operational relational databases. Operational databases contain basically the most current detailed data about the organization. As we showed above, knowledge discovery on operational relational databases can lead to inaccurate and incomplete knowledge discovery. The third scheme is to use summary data to validate the discovered rules from the detailed operational databases. Summary data can provide efficient access to large quantities of data as well as help reduce the size of the database. Summarized data contain patterns that can be discovered. Such discovered patterns can complement the discovery on operational/detail data by verifying the patterns discovered from the detailed data for consistency, accuracy, and completeness. In general, if the results (discovered rules) from the detailed data and summary data are the same, then we have more confidence on the knowledge discovered from the detailed data.

The fourth scheme is to use domain knowledge (*14, 39, 46*) to validate the discovered knowledge. This is the approach that we are considering. The discovered knowledge is checked to see whether it contradicts available domain knowledge. In some cases there may not be any applicable domain knowledge to be used for evaluation. If it does exist, however, and if domain knowledge contradicts discovered knowledge, then either the domain knowledge or the discovered knowledge (or both) is wrong. If the discovered knowledge does not contradict the domain knowledge, then we may have some confidence in its accuracy.

VALIDATION OF DISCOVERED KNOWLEDGE BASED ON DOMAIN KNOWLEDGE

Domain knowledge can be used to test the validity of the discovered knowledge. In general, domain knowledge can be used to verify whether contradictory discovered knowledge is indeed contradictory or if possibly consistent discovered knowledge is in fact accurate or inaccurate. Also, domain knowledge can be used to verify whether or not we discovered redundant and incomplete rules.

Validating Possibly Contradictory Rules

Domain knowledge can be used to verify whether contradictory discovered rules are indeed contradictory or accurate. Consider our CAR1 relation in Fig. 12 (with the added attributes car model and car year). Suppose one is interested to find what affects the High-way mileage. A discovery system may discover the following knowledge:

Rule 1: If Car Model = Honda AND Cylinders = 4 Then Mileage = High
Rule 2: If Car Model = Honda AND Cylinders = 4 Then Mileage = Low

At first glance it seems like the two discovered rules are contradictory, however, we have the available domain knowledge that cars produced after 1980 have special features that cause better performance and better mileage. Domain knowledge thus verifies that the discovered knowledge is accurate rather than contradictory.

Name	Age	Drug X Administered	Side Effect	Has condition Improved
John	45	No	None	Neutral
Cathy	68	Yes	None	Yes
Paula	50	Yes	Yes	Yes
Peter	55	Yes	Yes	Yes
Charles	25	Yes	Yes	Yes
Dechter	40	Yes	Yes	No
Freuder	75	Yes	Yes	Yes
Bemon	60	Yes	None	Yes
Freude	53	No	None	Neutral
Doyle	40	Yes	Yes	Yes
Dhar	57	Yes	None	Yes
Montanari	35	No	None	Neutral
Mittal	46	No	None	Yes
Nadel	24	Yes	Yes	No

FIGURE 14. *Patient's data.*

Validating Possibly Consistent Rules

Domain knowledge can be used to test whether possibly consistent discovered knowledge is accurate. For example, consider the patient's data relation in Fig. 14. Assume that domain knowledge is "Taking drug X does not deteriorate heart disease" and the knowledge discovered from the patient's data is "Drug X improves one's heart condition, although it has some side effects." To test the validity of this discovered knowledge, we could see if it contradicts domain knowledge. If it does, then either domain knowledge is wrong or the discovered knowledge is wrong. In the above example, the discovered knowledge does not contradict domain knowledge, but goes one step beyond it by saying that the effect of drug X (e.g., anacin) on a heart condition is not bad but good. The fact that domain knowledge does not contradict discovered knowledge assures the validity of discovered knowledge with a confidence factor of x percent.

Validating Possibly Redundant Rules

Databases normally contain redundant data and definitions that could lead to discovering redundant rules. The redundant data and definitions are generally different syntactically. For instance, consider the CAR relation in Fig. 6. The relation contains the attributes engine-size, bore, stroke, and cylinder, among other attributes. The redundant attribute engine-size is defined as: engine-size = bore * stroke * cylinder. In our discovery experiment, we defined High-MPG as the goal and the rest of the attributes as the premise. The discovery tool IDIS discovered rules relating the Engine-Size to High-MPG as well as rules relating bore, stroke, cylinder to High-MPG. Obviously, the discovered rules based on engine-size and bore, stroke, cylinder

TABLE 7

Summary Sales (Based on Table 5)

Product	Product color	Profit
Jacket	Blue	-400
Hat	Green	-800
Glove	Blue	-300
Glove	Green	1800

Case 4: There are cases in which the discovered knowledge from summary tables is based on statistically significance knowledge. For example, from Table 5 we may discover that:

If Product Color = Green Then Profitable = Yes CF = 40% (2 records out of 5)

From Table 7, which is a summary table based on Table 5, we discover that the green product is profitable, say, CF = 50% (1 record out of 2). If the discovered knowledge from detailed and summary tables support each other with different confidence factors, then additional information from other sources (perhaps from the domain expert, if possible) is needed to verify the accuracy of the discovered knowledge.

Validating Possibly Incomplete Rules

As noted above, in operational relational databases there is a possibility that some knowledge is not discovered as a result of the normalization. Every decomposition involves a potential information loss that has to be analyzed and quantified, and traditional techniques from statistics and machine learning (minimum description length) can be used (7).

The chance of having complete or incomplete knowledge discovery depends on the discovery process. If the knowledge discovery process uses the universal relation, then we could provide the maximum guarantee that potentially interesting statistical dependencies are preserved. In case of normalized relations, it depends on how the discovery process is performed on multiple relations. For instance, if the discovery process works on relations independently we may never discover that there is a relationship between average house price and the product purchased in the relations of Fig. 8.

One possible scheme for validating the completeness or incompleteness of the discovered knowledge is to analyze the discovered rules (known as statistical dependencies) with the available functional dependencies (known as domain knowledge). If new dependencies are generated that are not in the set of discovered rules, then we have incomplete knowledge discovery. For example, processing the sales relation in Fig. 8 we may discover that if Zip Code = 11111 then Product Purchased = Wine with some confidence. We call this a statistical dependency, which indicates that there is a correlation (with some confidence) between the zip code and the product purchased by people. Now, consider the region relation in Fig. 8, in which the given dependencies are Zip Code ---> City and City ---> Average House Price, which gives the derived new functional dependency Zip Code ---> Average House Price due to the transitive dependency. By looking at the discovered statistical dependency and the new derived functional dependency (or a given dependency in general), one may deduce (with some confidence) that there is a relationship between the average house price and the product purchased. If our discovery process does not generate such a relationship, then we have incomplete knowledge discovery, which is the consequence of working on normalized relations as opposed to universal relations. The main issue in the validation process is then to generate all the statistical dependencies. Foreign key detection algorithms that are used in reversed engineering of databases along with a special query mechanism can be used to detect statistical dependencies (7).

TESTING MECHANISM

The following two main steps can be suggested for validating the set of discovered knowledge:

Step 1: The set of discovered knowledge R (represented as rules) is tested against itself for possible redundancy, subsumption, and contradiction. Traditional schemes for testing rule-based knowledge bases can be applied (*58*). The basic idea is to check every discovered rule in R with the rest of the discovered rules in R for inconsistency. There are several issues to consider in our testing mechanism. First we need to recognize that rules (knowledge in general) may syntactically be different but semantically identical. Second, heuristic methods should be employed in order to avoid searching the entire set of discovered knowledge, possibly by classifying the set of discovered knowledge. Finally, the identified inconsistent rules need to be analyzed in order to decide whether we have anomalies in our database or whether our discovery mechanism is inadequate.

Step 2: The set of discovered knowledge R is tested against the set of available domain knowledge DK. For every discovered rule, if it is the same (syntactically or semantically) as any domain knowledge, then we have redundancy, and the discovered rule must be eliminated. If the discovered rule contradicts (syntactically or semantically) domain knowledge, then it should be eliminated. It is only when a discovered rule does not contradict the available domain knowledge or some domain knowledge complements a discovered rule that we have some confidence in the validity of the discovered rule as being new knowledge. Finally, if a discovered rule does not exist in the set of the available domain knowledge, then we may have new knowledge, which could be verified by domain experts (if possible). In general, we should be concerned with the confidence that we have on the available domain knowledge in order to avoid eliminating a valid discovered rule in the testing process. For instance, if domain knowledge is (patient-sex = male) ------> (pregnancy = No) and if the discovered rule is [If patient-sex = male Then pregnancy = Yes], then we have a discovered rule that is inconsistent with the available domain knowledge and should be eliminated because we have high degree of confidence with the available domain knowledge. In general, the domain expert can assign a confidence factor to each domain knowledge and uses it only if the confidence factor is greater than a specified threshold. The assignment of a confidence factor to domain knowledge depends on how close the domain knowledge is to the established facts. The domain expert needs to define a mechanism to calculate the confidence factor of domain knowledge that is derived from the given domain knowledge.

Conclusion and Future Direction

Current database technology involves processing a large volume of data in databases in order to discover new knowledge. Several tools have been developed for automatic extraction of the interesting patterns from databases. Databases are full of patterns, but few of these patterns are of much interest. In addition, databases are normally incomplete and exhibit redundancy, which could lead to discovery of knowledge that is inconsistent or redundant. Furthermore, the high volume of the databases makes the discovery process computationally expensive. Subsequently, a discovery system should validate the discovered knowledge for its consistency and accuracy.

We described a framework that knowledge engineers can use to process databases and generate rules or to detect data anomalies, if necessary. In particular, we discussed the relational normalization tool and language, induction tools, and knowledge discovery tools. Through the use of these tools, one can efficiently translate knowledge provided in a database to the format of a rule-based system. The techniques described here are intended to provide some additional tools and to initiate the search for other knowledge acquisition mechanisms related to database utilization.

We showed that rule discovery in operational relational databases could lead to incomplete and inaccurate discovery. Relational databases are normalized in order to prevent update anomalies. In addition, operational databases contain mainly the most recent and detailed data. We need an environment in which the detailed data as well as the summary and historical data are provided in order to have an effective discovery process. Data warehouses seem to be the answer. Most organizations have already started to build their own data warehouses. Knowledge discovery in a data warehouse environment has a better chance of producing accurate, consistent, complete, and meaningful rules since data warehouses support clean, integrated, detailed, summarized, and historical data, as well as metadata. Each of these elements is essential in order to have a viable knowledge discovery process.

Databases become larger and they continue to contain incomplete and inaccurate data, which makes knowledge discovery more difficult. Domain knowledge can be used to provide some assistance in different aspects of knowledge discovery. We have discussed the benefits using domain knowledge to constrain the search when discovering knowledge from databases. Domain knowledge can be used to reduce the search by reducing the size of the databases, reducing the size of the hypotheses by eliminating unnecessary conditions from the hypotheses, and removing unnecessary operations from a query that is used to process the data to prove (or disprove) the hypotheses.

We looked at the validation aspect of the knowledge discovery in databases. The basic idea is to subject each discovered rule or pattern to a series of tests that determine its consistency and accuracy. We discussed the possibility of using domain knowledge to validate the discovered knowledge. We showed that domain knowledge can be used to verify whether contradictory discovered knowledge is indeed contradictory or whether possibly consistent discovered knowledge is in fact inaccurate. One possible scheme is to validate the discovered knowledge to see whether or not it contradicts the available domain knowledge. (In some cases there may not be any applicable domain knowledge to be used for evaluation.) If it does, then either domain knowledge or the discovered knowledge (or both) is wrong. If the discovered knowledge does not contradict domain knowledge, then we may have some confidence in its accuracy. More research is needed in developing techniques for validating discovered knowledge. Some have suggested the use of statistical techniques, and others have proposed the inclusion of the discovered knowledge in the databases. An alternative as well as complementary approach is to use domain knowledge to verify the discovered knowledge. Currently we are studying mechanisms for gathering domain knowledge (i.e., both from domain experts and from automatic generation of domain knowledge from databases). Also, we are developing formal algorithms for validating the discovered knowledge for redundancy, subsumption, and contradiction.

The problem with the use of domain knowledge in knowledge discovery is the likelihood of blocking unexpected discovery. This may happen as a result of using too much domain knowledge, which may result in a large reduction of data in the database or in the conditions in the hypothesis. Subsequently the discovered knowledge may not generate high enough confidence to be considered interesting. We defined some guidelines in order to use domain knowledge effectively to avoid some of the above problems. In particular, we suggested assigning confidence factors to domain knowledge and using them when these confidence factors are high enough based on the user's specification. In addition, we recommended using domain knowledge when its use does not lead to a major reduction in the databases in order to avoid having few sample data for discovery or missing interesting data. Finally, domain knowledge should be used as a separate and supplemental resource to a general knowledge discovery system to make these systems more efficient and yet domain-independent, rather than being used directly in developing the general methods for knowledge discovery. Currently we are studying this aspect of domain knowledge utilization in the discovery process.

In the future the described induction/database discovery tools as well as the techniques for the knowledge discovery process, optimization, and validation need to be expanded in order to handle the following problems:

1. Because updates are frequently encountered in many databases, a flexible database discovery tool should allow discovery to be performed incrementally on database updates. Incremental discovery avoids restarting the costly discovery process from scratch on database updates (*46*).
2. If the relevant data are spread over several relations, join operations should be performed on these relations to collect relevant data before the discovery tool is applied. In many cases the separate relations of a relational database can be logically joined by constructing a universal relation (UR) (*26, 27*). A UR is either computed and stored, or if too large, logically represented through a UR interface. A discovery tool should be able to interact with the UR interface and treat the database as a single, flat file (though perhaps inefficient). As a result, existing induction/discovery tools can be readily applied to relational databases by treating each record in the UR as a single training instance.
3. Although a relational database stores a large amount of data, usually only a portion of it is relevant to a specific discovery task. Obviously preprocessing must be performed to extract and group the task-relevant data from a database before generalization. The preprocessing can be viewed as a relational query that takes a discovery request as a retrieval command to search for the necessary sets of data from the database and group them according to the discovery task (*50*). Future discovery tools should be able to look at the nature of data and available domain knowledge in order to automatically produce the retrieval command to search for the relevant data to be processed by the discovery tool.
4. We need to define precisely the significance and role of the domain knowledge in knowledge discovery identifying the sources and mechanism of acquiring domain knowledge from domain experts or from automated discovery tools. We also need to consider knowledge representation and manipulation in the discovery process so that domain

knowledge can be used effectively. Furthermore, we need to define other mechanisms to guarantee unblocking of the unexpected discovery when using domain knowledge to narrow the search in the databases. Finally, we should see how domain knowledge can be used to make the discovered knowledge more understandable to end users.

REFERENCES

1. D. Baker, "A Truly Intelligent CASE Tool—Using Logic Gem to Develop an Expert System." *PC AI,* vol. 3, no.4 (1989).
2. R. Barquin and H. A. Edelstein, *Building, Using, and Managing the Data Warehouse,* Prentice-Hall PTR, Englewood Cliffs, NJ, 1997.
3. J. Giarrantanto and G. Riley, *Expert Systems—Principles and Programming,* PWS-Kent, Boston, MA, 1989.
4. J. Han, Y. Cai, and N. Cercone, "Data-Driven Discovery of Quantitative Rules in Relational Databases." *IEEE Trans. Knowl. Data Eng.,* **5**(1), (1993).
5. E. Simoudis, "Reality Check for Data Mining." *IEEE Exp.,* **11**(5), (1996).
6. D. Vasant and A. Tuzhilin, "Abstract-Driven Pattern Discovery in Database." *IEEE Trans. Knowl. Data Eng.,* **5**(6), (1993).
7. P. Adriaans and D. Zantinge, *Data Mining,* Addison-Wesley, Reading, MA, 1996.
8. R. Agrawal, T. Imielinski, and A. Swami, "Database Mining: A Performance Perspective." *IEEE Trans. Knowl. Data Eng.,* **5**(6), (1993).
9. R. J. Brachman, T. Khabaza, W. Kloesgen, G. Piatetsky-Shapiro, and E. Simoudis, "Mining Business Databases." *CACM,* **39**(11), (1996).
10. R. J. Brachman and T. Anand, "The Process of Knowledge Discovery in Databases," in *Advances in Knowledge Discovery and Data Mining,* U. M. Fayyad, G. Piatetsky-Shapiro, and P. Symth, eds. AAAI Press/the MIT Press, Menlo Park, CA, 1996.
11. B. G. Buchanan and E. A. Feigenbaum, "Dendral and Meta-Dendral: Their Applications Dimension." *AI,* **11**(1), (1978).
12. U. Fayyad, "Data Mining and Knowledge Discovery: Making Sense Out of Data." *IEEE Exp.,* **11**(5), (1996).
13. U. M. Fayyad, G. Piatetsky-Shapiro, P. Symth, "From Data Mining to Knowledge Discovery: An Overview," in *Advances in Knowledge Discovery and Data Mining,* U. M. Fayyad, G. Piatetsky-Shapiro, and P. Symth, eds. AAAI Press/the MIT Press, Menlo Park, CA, 1996.
14. W. J. Frawley, G. Piatetsky-Shapiro, and C. J. Matheus, "Knowledge Discovery in Databases: An Overview." *AI Mag.,* **14**(3), (1992).
15. W. H. Inmon, "The Data Warehouse and Data Mining." *CACM,* **39**(5), (1996).
16. R. L. Blum, "Induction of Causal Relationships from a Time-Oriented Clinical Database: An Overview of the RX Project," *Proceedings of the Second National Conf. on Artificial Intelligence,* Pittsburgh, 1982.
17. R. L. Blum, "Discovery Confirmation and Incorporation of Causal Relationship from a Large Time-Oriented Clinical Database: The RX Project." *Computers Biomed. Res.,* **15** (1982).
18. A. Szladow, "Datalogic/R—Mining the Knowledge in Databases." *PC AI,* **7** (1993).
19. *IDIS: The Information Discovery System User's Manual,* IntelligenceWare, Los Angeles, 1994.
20. K. Parsaye, M. Chignell, S. Khoshafian, and H. Wong, *Intelligent Data Base and Automatic Discovery,* Neural and Intelligent Systems Integration, edited by B. Soucek and the IRIS Group, Wiley, New York, NY, 1991.
21. K. Parsaye and M. Chignell, *Intelligent Database Tools and Applications—Hyperinformation Access, Data Quality, Visualization, Automatic Discovery,* Wiley, New York, NY, 1993.
22. D. DeSalvo and J. Liebowitz, *Managing Artificial Intelligence and Expert Systems,* Yourdon, New York, 1990.
23. O. Owrang, M. Mehdi, and W. G. Gunartna, "A Logical Design Tool for Relational Databases." *IEEE MICRO,* **9**(3), (1989).
24. *SILVERRUN-RDM: A Software Engineering Tool for Designing Relational Data Schema,* General Reference Manual, CSA Computer Systems Advisor, Woodcliff Lake, New Jersey, 1995.
25. C. J. Date, *An Introduction to Database Systems,* 5th ed., vol. 1, Addison-Wesley, Reading, MA, 1990.
26. D. Maier, *The Theory of Relational Databases,* Computer Science Press, Rockville, MD, 1983.
27. J. D. Ullman, *Principle of Database Systems,* Computer Science Press, Rockville, MD, 1982.
28. T. Wes and W. Hapgood, *1st Class Instruction Manual: Programs in Motion,* AI Corp., Wayland, MA, 1994.

29. F. Zahedi, *Intelligent Systems for Business: Expert Systems with Neural Networks,* Wadsworth, Belmont, CA, 1993.
30. *Angoss Knowledge Seeker for Windows: Version 3.0 User's Guide,* Angoss Software International, Turonto, CA, 1994.
31. J. Bischoff and T. Alexander, *Data Warehouse—Practical Advise from the Expert,* Prentice-Hall, Englewood Cliffs, NJ, (1997).
32. M. E. Meredith and A. Khader, "Designing Large Warehouses." *Database Prog. Des.,* vol. 9, no. 1 (1996).
33. K. Parsaye, "Data Mines for Data Warehouses." *Database Prog. Des.,* (supplement), **9** (1996).
34. J. Hong and C. Mao, "Incremental Discovery of Rules and Structure by Hierarchical and Parallel Clustering," in *Knowledge Discovery in Databases,* AAAI/MIT Press, Menlo Park, CA, 1991, pp. 177–194.
35. J. M. Long, E. A. Irani, J. R. Slagle, and POSCH Group, "Automating the Discovery of Causal Relationships in a Medical Records Database," in *Knowledge Discovery in Databases,* AAAI Press/MIT Press, Menlo Park, CA, 1991, pp. 465–476.
36. R. H. L. Chiang, T. M. Barron, V. C. Storey, "Extracting Domain Semantics for Knowledge Discovery in Relational Databases," *AAAI Workshop on Knowledge Discovery in Databases,* 1994, pp. 299–310.
37. U. Fayyad, G. Piatetsky-Shapiro, and P. Symth, "The KDD Process for Extracting Useful Knowledge from Volumes of Data." *CACM,* **39**(11), (1996).
38. O. Owrang, M. Mehdi, and F. Grupe, "Using Domain Knowledge to Guide Database Knowledge Discovery." *Exp. Syst. Appl.,* **10**(2), (1996).
39. O. Owrang and M. Mehdi, "The Role of Domain Knowledge in Knowledge Discovery in Databases." *Microcomputers Appl.,* **16**(1), (1997).
40. G. Piatetsky-Shapiro, "Discovery, Analysis, and Presentation of Strong Rules," in *Knowledge Discovery in Databases,* AAAI Press/MIT Press, Menlo Park, CA, 1991, pp. 229–247.
41. V. Dhar and A. Tuzhilin, "Abstract-Driven Pattern Discovery in Databases." *IEEE Trans. Knowl. Data Eng.,* **5**(6), (1993).
42. J. R. Quinlan, "Induction of Decision Trees." *Machine Learn.,* **1**(1), (1986).
43. A. D. Shapiro, *Structured Induction in Expert Systems,* Turing Institute, Glasgow, Scotland, 1987.
44. E. Frenzel Jr., *Understanding Expert Systems,* Howard W. Sams, New York, 1987.
45. P. Harmon, R. Mau, and W. Morrissey, *Expert System—Tools and Applications,* Wiley, New York, 1988.
46. C. J. Matheus, P. K. Chan, and G. Piatetsky-Shapiro, "Systems for Knowledge Discovery in Databases." *IEEE Trans. Knowl. Data Eng.,* **5**(6), (1993).
47. R. Keller, *Expert System Technology—Development and Application,* Yourdon, New York, 1994.
48. J. Keyes, "Branching to the Right System: Decision-Tree Software." *AI Exp.,* volume 5, no. 3 (1990).
49. K. Pederson, *Expert Systems Programming—Practical Techniques for Rule-based Systems,* Wiley, New York, 1989.
50. P. Smyth and R. M. Goodman, "An Information Theoretic Approach to Rule Induction from Databases." *IEEE Trans. Knowl. Data Eng.,* **4**(4), (1992).
51. B. M. E. Moret, "Decision Trees and Diagrams." *ACM Comp. Surv.,* **14** (1982).
52. G. Piatetsky-Shapiro, "Knowledge Discovery in Real Databases: A Report on the International Joint Conference on Artificial Intelligence 1989 Workshop." *AI Mag.,* **11** (1991).
53. K. Parsaye, "OLAP & Data Mining—Bridging the Gap." *Database Prog. Des.,* **10**(2), (1997).
54. M. G. Walker, "How Feasible Is Automated Discovery?" *IEEE Exp.,* **2**(2), (1987).
55. R. Uthurusamy, "From Data Mining to Knowledge Discovery: Current Challenges and Future Directions," in *Advances in Knowledge Discovery and Data Mining,* U. M. Fayyad, G. Piatetsky-Shapiro, and P. Symth, eds. AAAI Press/MIT Press, Menlo Park, CA, 1996, pp. 561–569.
56. W. Ziarko, "The Discovery, Analysis, and Presentation of Data Dependencies in Databases," in *Knowledge Discovery in Databases,* AAAI Press/MIT Press, Menlo Park, CA, 1991, pp. 195–209.
57. J. Hayward, *Hormones and Human Breast Cancer,* Springer-Verlag, Berlin, 1970.
58. M. M. Owrang, M. C. Frame, and L. R. Medsker, "Testing for Inconsistencies in Rule-Based Knowledge Bases." *Exp. Syst. Appl.,* EXPERSYS-90, 281–286 (1990).

M. MEHDI OWRANG O.

AN INTELLIGENT DICTIONARY HELP SYSTEM

Introduction

The Intelligent Dictionary Help System (IDHS) is a monolingual (explanatory) dictionary system (*1, 3*). Its design was conceived from the study of questions that human users would like to have answered when consulting a dictionary. The fact that it is intended for people instead of automatic processing distinguishes it from other systems dealing with the acquisition of semantic knowledge from conventional dictionaries. The system provides various access possibilities to the data, allowing the deduction of implicit knowledge from the explicit dictionary information. IDHS deals with reasoning mechanisms analogous to those used by humans when they consult a dictionary.

The starting point of IDHS is a dictionary database (DDB) built from an ordinary French dictionary. Definitions have been analyzed using linguistic information from the DDB itself and interpreted to be structured as a dictionary knowledge base (DKB). As a result of the parsing, different lexical-semantic relations between word senses are established by means of semantic rules (attached to the patterns); these rules are used for the initial construction of the DKB.

Once the acquisition process has been performed and the DKB built, some enrichment processes have been executed on the DKB in order to enhance its knowledge about the words in the language. Besides, the dynamic exploitation of this knowledge is made possible by means of specially conceived deduction mechanisms. Both the enrichment processes and the dynamic deduction mechanisms are based on the exploitation of the properties of the lexical-semantic relations represented in the DKB (*6*).

The analysis of the definitions has been done after some empirical studies on the data contained in the DDB (*7*). The analysis mechanism is mainly based on hierarchies of phrasal patterns (*5*), with some extensions. The parser has been implemented, and integrated with the DDB so that the definitions are directly obtained from the DDB and the different parses resulting from the analysis are recorded in it. Obviously the DDB itself has played the role of lexicon for the parser. The methodology used in the process of construction of the hierarchies is briefly explained.

An overview of IDHS is given in the following section. The section after that presents the process of constructing the DKB. The knowledge representation model and the enrichment mechanisms are fully described in the subsequent sections. The section that follows describes some inferential aspects of the system. Some figures about the size and contents of the prototype built are shown in the next section. In the section after that, some perspectives and derived works undertaken to deal with multilingual dictionary help environments are outlined. The final section presents some conclusions.

The IDHS Dictionary System

The IDHS is a dictionary help system intended to assist a human user in language

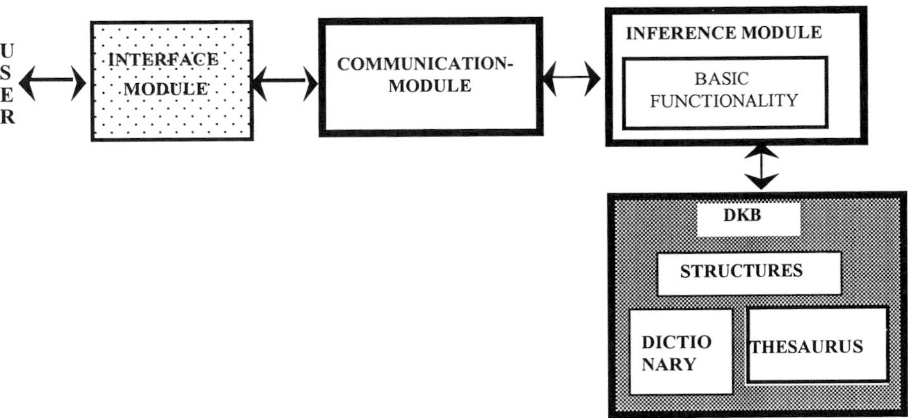

FIGURE 1. *Basic architecture of IDHS.*

comprehension or production tasks. The architecture of IDHS includes the following four modules:

- The *dictionary knowledge base,* which represents the knowledge extracted from the dictionary by means of frame structures. It has been organized in different submodules, and will be explained in more detail below.
- The *inference module,* which facilitates the inferencing capabilities of the system. The basic functionality is part of this module. More precise explanations are given below.
- The *communication module,* which on the one hand interprets the questions posed by the user and translates them to the internal representation, and on the other hand translates the answer of the system into a comprehensible text.
- The *interface module,* which permits friendly communication with the user.

The first two modules and a simple schema of the communication module have been specified and a prototype implemented (*4*). The last module is not the focus of the work presented here.

Figure 1 shows the general architecture presented.

The system provides a set of functions that have been inspired by the different reasoning processes a human user performs when consulting a conventional dictionary. Some of the functions implemented include definition queries, a search of alternative definitions, differences, relations and analogies between concepts, a thesaurus-like word search, and verification of concept properties and interconceptual relationships (*8, 9*).

For instance, a definition request, Demande de Définition (DDEF), takes as input a concept, an explanatory level, a dictionary, and a language, giving as output a definition, but it has different levels of explanations: textual (the result is just the text associated to that definition), local (the answer gives the networklike representation of the textual definition), and inherited (it produces the networklike representation of the textual definition plus other relations deduced from the concept hierarchy). The following examples are definition queries for the meaning of *wasp* in the LPPL French dictionary, but the requested explanatory levels are different: *textual* in the first example, *local* in the second, and *inherited* in the third.

User.- DDEF (|guêpe I 1|, textual, LPPL, French, ?D)
The user asks for the definition of wasp in French with "textual" as explanatory-level
System.- D= 'insecte hyménoptère à aiguillon'

U.- DDEF (|guêpe I 1|, local, LPPL, French, ?D)
Definition of wasp in French with "local" as explanatory-level

S.- D= (and	(|guêpe I 1|	HYPERONYME	|insecte I 1|)
	(|guêpe I 1|	CARACTERISTIQUE	|hyménoptère I 1|)
	(|guêpe I 1|	POSSESSION	|aiguillon I 1|)

Wasp is an hymenopterous insect with sting.

U.- DDEF (|guêpe I 1|, inherited, LPPL, French, ?D)
Definition of wasp in French with "inherited" as explanatory-level

S.- D= (and	(|guêpe I 1|	HYPERONYME	|insecte I 1|)
	(|guêpe I 1|	CARACTERISTIQUE	|hyménoptère I 1|)
	(|guêpe I 1|	CARACTERISTIQUE	|articuler I 1#m|)
	(|guêpe I 1|	POSSESSION	|aiguillon I 1|)
	(|guêpe I 1|	POSSESSION	|patte I 1#n|)
	(|guêpe I 1|	HYPONYME	|frelon I 1|)
	(|guêpe I 1|	POSSESSEUR	|guêpier I 1|))

Wasp is an articulated hymenopterous insect with sting and legs, a bumblebee is a wasp, and a wasp's nest has wasps.

The next example will show the effects of the thesaurus-like search of concepts Recherche thésaurique (RTHS). This function takes as input an expression of constraints, a dictionary, and a language, and returns the list of concepts that meet the constraints stated. Examples follow.

U.- RTHS((and (?X HYPERONYME |instrument I 1|)
(?X OBJECTIF |mesurer I 1|))
LPPL, French, ?X, ?LC)
The user asks for nouns in French that are tools used for measurement
S.- LC=(|baromètre I 1|, |dynanomètre I 1|, |telemètre I 1|)

U.- RTHS((and (?X HYPERONYME |consumer I 1|)
(?X AGENT |feu I 1|)),
LPPL, French, ?X, ?LC)
The user asks for verbs in French for to consume with agent fire
S.- LC=(|brûler I 1|, |calciner I 1|)
to burn, to blacken.

In summary, IDHS can be seen as a repository of dictionary knowledge apt to be accessed and exploited in several ways. The system has been implemented using a knowledge engineering environment (KEE).

All the knowledge represented in IDHS has been acquired from a conventional dictionary by means of parsing dictionary definitions using Natural Language Processing (NLP) techniques. Two different steps were distinguished when building the DKB. First is the extraction of the information from the dictionary and its recording into a relational database—the DDB. This DDB was the starting point in order to create the object-oriented DKB, in step 2 (see Fig. 2) that is the support of our deduction system.

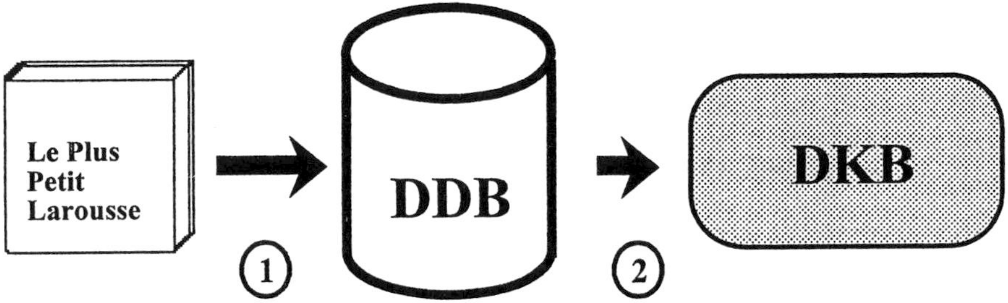

FIGURE 2. *From the MRD to the DKB.*

Focusing on step 2 (construction of the DKB from the DDB), two phases are distinguished. First, information contained in the DDB is used to produce an initial DKB. General information about the entries obtained from the DDB (POS, usage, examples, etc.) is conventionally represented—attribute-value pairs in the frame structure—while the semantic component of the dictionary (i.e., the definition sentences) has been analyzed and represented as an interrelated set of concepts. In this stage the relations established between concepts could still in some cases be of lexical-syntactic nature. In a second phase, the semantic knowledge acquisition process is completed using the relations established in the initial DKB. The purpose of this phase is to perform lexical and syntactical disambiguation, showing that semantic knowledge about hierarchical relations between concepts can be determinant for this.

Building the Dictionary Knowledge Base

The starting point of this system is a small monolingual French dictionary (*Le Plus Petit Larousse,* Librairie Larousse, Paris, 1980). This dictionary consists of nearly 23,000 senses related to almost 16,000 entries. Each entry contains the following components: POS, meaning definition or cross-references to synonyms, marks of discourse domain usage, examples (14% of entries), and so on. Among the definitions, 74 percent have four words or fewer. The average number of words per definition is 3.27.

The dictionary was recorded in a relational database (the DDB). This DDB is the basis of every empirical study that has been developed in order to design the final representation for the intelligent exploitation of the dictionary. The information attached in the DDB to each word occurrence in meaning descriptions was completed, following a mainly automatic tagging process. Every definition word occurrence was attached to its canonical form (homograph and sense numbers included when possible). Figure 3 shows two different entries and the information associated in the database to their definition words.

The definition sentences—that is, the semantic component of the dictionary—have been analyzed in the process of transformation of the data contained in the DDB to produce the DKB. The analysis mechanism used is based on hierarchies of phrasal

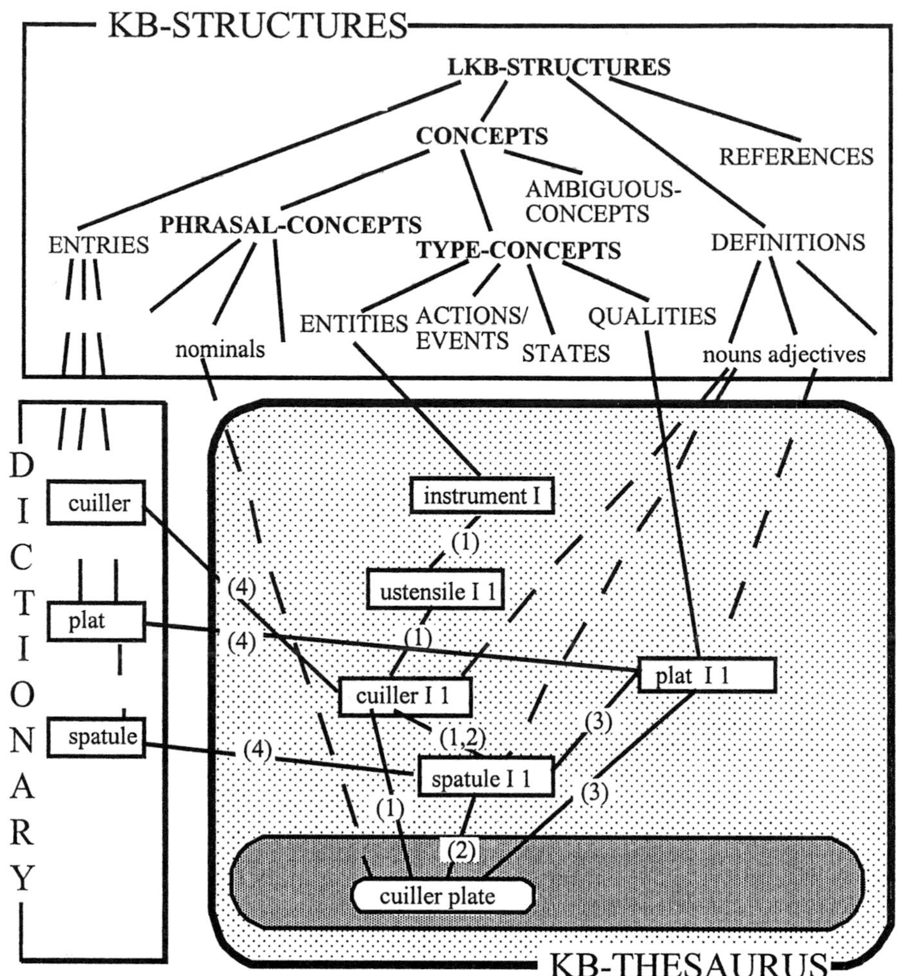

FIGURE 4. *The dictionary knowledge base.—SUBCLASS link; ---MEMBER-OF link (instance). (1) Taxonomic relation: HYPERNYM/HYPONYM; (2) specific (metalinguistic) relation: SORTE-DE/SORTE-DE+INV (KIND-OF/KIND-OF+INV); (3) CARACTERISTIQUE/CARACTERISTIQUE+INV (PROPERTY/PROPERTY+INV) relation; (4) MOTS-ENTREE/SENS (ENTRY-WORD/WORD-SENSE) relation; (English gloss: cuiller = spoon, cuiller plate = flat spoon, plat = flat, spatule = spatula, ustensile = instrument).*

KB-STRUCTURES: THE METAKNOWLEDGE

This KB reflects the hierarchical organization of the knowledge included in the DKB.

We will focus on the LKB-STRUCTURES class, which defines the data types used in KB-DICTIONARY and KB-THESAURUS, and which organizes the units belonging to these KBs into a taxonomy.

Slots defined in KB-STRUCTURES have associated aspects such as the value class and the inheritance role determining how values in children's slots are calculated. Each lexical-semantic relation—represented by an attribute or slot—has its own inheritance role. For instance, the inheritance role of the CARACTERISTIQUE relation states that every concept inherits the union of the values of the hypernyms for that relation, while the role defined for the SYNONYMES relation inhibits value inheritance from a concept to its hyponyms.

The subclasses defined under LKB-STRUCTURES are the following:

- ENTRIES, which groups dictionary entries belonging to KB-DICTIONARY
- DEFINITIONS, which groups word senses classified according to their POS
- REFERENCES, concepts created in KB-THESAURUS due to their occurence in definitions of other concepts ("definitionless")
- CONCEPTS, which groups under a conceptual point of view word senses and other conceptual units of KB-THESAURUS

The classification of conceptual units under this last class is as follows:

- *TYPE-CONCEPTS* correspond to Quillian's "type nodes" (*10*); in fact, this class is like a superclass under which every concept of KB-THESAURUS is placed. It is further subdivided into the classes ENTITIES, ACTIONS/EVENTS, QUALITIES, and STATES, which classify different types of concepts.
- *PHRASAL-CONCEPTS* is a class that includes concepts similar to Quillian's "tokens"—occurrences of type concepts in the definition sentences. Phrasal concepts are the representation of phrase structures that are composed of several concepts with semantic content. A phrasal concept is always built as a subclass of the class that represents its head (the noun of a noun phrase, the verb of a verb phrase, etc.), and integrated in the conceptual taxonomy. Phrasal concepts are classified into NOMINALS, VERBALS, ADJECTIVALS, and ADVERBIALS.
  For instance, |plante I 1#3| is a phrasal concept (see Fig. 5), subclass of the type concept |plante I 1|, and represents the noun phrase *une plante d'ornement* (*an ornamental plant*).
- Finally, the concepts that after the analysis phase are not yet completely disambiguated (lexical ambiguity), are placed under the class *AMBIGUOUS-CONCEPTS,* which is further subdivided into the subclasses HOMOGRAPHE (e.g., |faculté ? ?|), SENSE (|panser I ?|), and COMPLEX (|donner I 5/6), in order to distinguish them according to the level of ambiguity they present.

The links between units in KB-THESAURUS and KB-DICTIONARY are implemented by means of slots tagged with the name of the link they represent. These slots are defined in the different classes of KB-STRUCTURES.

The representation model used in the system is made up of the following two levels:

- *Definitory level,* in which the surface representation of the definition of each sense is made. Such morphosyntactic features as verb mode, time, and determination are represented by means of facets attached to the attributes. The definitory level is implemented using *representational attributes.* Examples of this kind of attribute are: DEF-SORTED, DEF-QUI, CARACTERISTIQUE, and AVEC.
- *Relational level,* which reflects the relational view of the lexicon. It supports the deductive behavior of the system and is made up of *relational attributes,* which may eventually contain deduced knowledge. These attributes, defined in the class TYPE-CONCEPTS, are the

implementation of the interconceptual relations: ANTONYMES, AGENT, CARACTERISTIQUE, SORTE-DE, CE-QUI, and so on.

KB-DICTIONARY: FROM WORDS TO CONCEPTS

This KB contains the links between each dictionary entry and its senses. (See link 4 in Fig. 4.)

KB-THESAURUS: THE CONCEPT NETWORK

KB-THESAURUS stores the concept network that is implemented as a network of frames. Each node in the net is a frame that represents a conceptual unit: one-word concepts and phrasal concepts.

The arcs interconnect the concepts and represent lexical-semantic relations; they are implemented by means of frame slots containing pointers to other concepts. Hypernym and hyponym relations have been made explicit, making up a *concept taxonomy.* These taxonomic relations have been implemented using the environment hierarchical relationship in order to get inheritance automatically.

For example, the represenation of the following definition:

géranium I 1: *une plante d'ornement*

requires the creation of two new conceptual units in THESAURUS, one which corresponds to the definiendum, and the phrasal concept, which represents the noun phrase of the definition. Moreover, the units that represent *plante* and *ornement* are also to be created (if they have not been previously created because of their occurrence in another definition).

Let us suppose that three new units are created: |géranium I 1|, |plante I 1#3|, and |ornement I 1|. Attributes in the units may contain facets (attributes for the attributes) used in the definitory level to record such aspects as determination and genre, but also to establish the relations between definitory attributes with their corresponding relational or to specify the certainty that the value in a representational attribute has to be "promoted" to a corresponding relational. (See the case of the slot DE in |plante I 1#3| below.)

The following shows the composition of the frames of these three units at the definitory level of representation (slots are in small capitals, whereas facet identifiers are in italics):

|géranium I 1|
MEMBER.OF: NOMS
GROUPE-CATEGORIEL: NOM
CLASSE-ATTRIBUT: INFO-GENERALE
TEXTE-DEFINITION: "une plante d'ornement"
CLASSE-ATTRIBUT: INFO-GENERALE
DEF-CLASSIQUE: |plante I 1#3|
CLASSE-ATTRIBUT: DEFINITOIRES
DETERMINATION: UN
GENRE: F
RELATIONNELS-CORRESPONDANTS: DEFINI-PAR

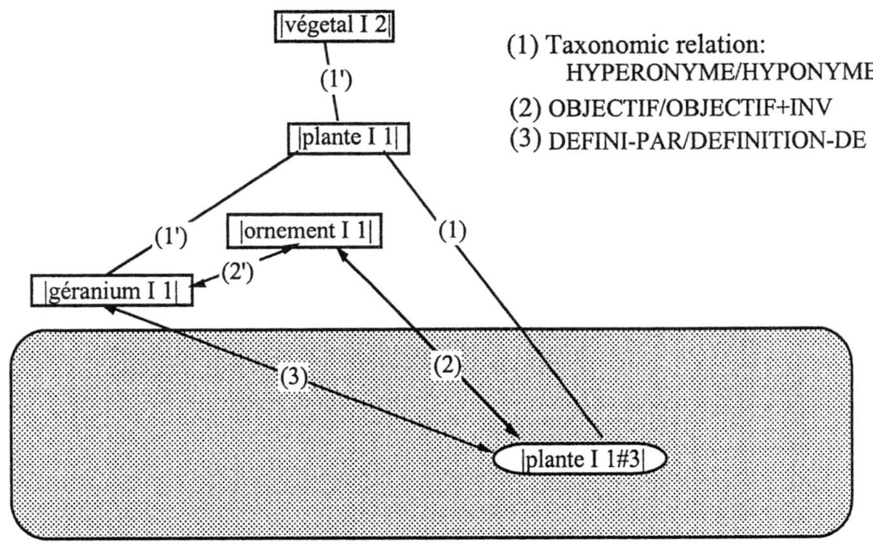

FIGURE 5. *Relational view of the concept |géranium I 1| (in the THESAURUS net); (English gloss: DEFINI-PAR = defined by, DEFINITION-DE = definition of, géranium = geranium, ornement = ornament, plante = plant, végetal = vegetable).*

|plante I 1#3|
SUBCLASS.OF: |plante I 1|
MEMBER.OF: NOMINALES
TEXTE: "plante d'ornement"
CLASSE-ATTRIBUT: INFO-GENERALE
DE: |ornement I 1|
CLASSE-ATTRIBUT: SYNTAGMATIQUES
RELATIONNELS-CORRESPONDANTS: ORIGINE, POSSESSEUR, MATIERE, OBJECTIF
OBJECTIF: 0.9

|ornement I 1|
MEMBER.OF: REFERENCES

Before showing the representation of these units at the relational level, it has to be said that after the initial DKB has been built some deductive procedures have been executed (e.g., deduction of inverse relationships, and taxonomy formation). In other words, in Fig. 5, in which the relational view is presented, the relations deduced by these procedures are also represented.

The conceptual units in THESAURUS are placed in two layers (see Fig. 5), recalling the two planes of Quillian (*10*). The upper layer corresponds to type concepts, whereas phrasal concepts are placed in the lower one. Every phrasal concept is placed in the taxonomy directly (depending on its nuclear concept), as a hyponym of it.

It is interesting to note in the figure the relation of *conceptual equivalence* established between |géranium I 1| and |plante I 1#3| (link labeled 3). These units in fact represent the same concept, because |plante I 1#3|, standing for *une plante d'ornement,* is the definition of |géranium I 1|.

The frame of |géranium I 1| at the relational level of representation takes the following aspect, once the relational attributes have been (partially) completed:

|géranium I 1|
SUBCLASS.OF: ENTITIES, |plante I 1|
MEMBER.OF: NOMS
GROUPE-CATEGORIEL: NOM
CLASSE-ATTRIBUT: INFO-GENERALE
TEXTE-DEFINITION: "une plante d'ornement"
CLASSE-ATTRIBUT: INFO-GENERALE
DEF-CLASSIQUE: |plante I 1#3|
CLASSE-ATTRIBUT: DEFINITOIRES
DETERMINATION: UN
GENRE: F
RELATIONNELS-CORRESPONDANTS: DEFINI-PAR
DEFINI-PAR: |plante I 1#3|
CLASSE-ATTRIBUT: RELATIONNELS
INVERSES-CORRESPONDANTS: DEFINITION-DE
OBJECTIF: |ornement I 1|
CLASSE-ATTRIBUT: RELATIONNELS
INVERSES-CORRESPONDANTS: OBJECTIF+INV

Let us now give another example, the case of two definitions stated by means of two different sterotyped formulae belonging to the lexicographic metalanguage. Many verbs in the LPPL are defined by means of a formula beginning with *rendre,* and many nouns with one beginning with *qui.* The definitions selected for this example correspond to the entries *publier I 1* and *ajusteur I 1,* which are represented at the definitory level using the metalanguage attributes DEF-RENDRE and DEF-QUI, respectively.

publier I 1: *rendre public* (*publish: to make public*)
ajusteur I 1: *qui ajuste des pièces de métal* (*metalworker: who adjusts pieces of metal*)

The frame corresponding to |pulier I 1| is the following:

|publier I 1|
MEMBER.OF: VERBES
GROUPE-CATEGORIEL: VERBE
CLASSE-ATTRIBUT: INFO-GENERALE
TEXTE-DEFINITION: "rendre public"
CLASSE-ATTRIBUT: INFO-GENERALE
DEF-RENDRE: |public I 1|
CLASSE-ATTRIBUT: DEFINITOIRES
RELATIONNELS-CORRESPONDANTS: RENDRE

where it can be seen that no phrasal concept is involved because the link (DEF-RENDRE) is established directly between |publier I 1| and |public I 1|. In the case of the definition of *ajusteur I 1,* however, two phrasal concepts are created: the attribute DEF-QUI points to the phrasal concept |ajuster I 1#1|, representing *ajuster des pièces de métal,* and this phrasal concept in turn has a syntagmatic attribute (OBJET) pointing to a nominal that represents *pièce de métal.* Let us show the frames involved in this last case:

|ajusteur I 1|
MEMBER.OF: NOMS
GROUPE-CATEGORIEL: NOM
CLASSE-ATTRIBUT: INFO-GENERALE
TEXTE-DEFINITION: "qui ajuste des pièces de métal"
CLASSE-ATTRIBUT: INFO-GENERALE
DEF-QUI: |ajuster I 1#1|
CLASSE-ATTRIBUT: DEFINITOIRES
MODE: IND
ASPECT: NT
TEMPS: PRES
PERSONNE: 3
RELATIONNELS-CORRESPONDANTS: QUI

|ajuster I 1#1|
SUBCLASS.OF: |ajuster I 1|
MEMBER.OF: VERBALES
TEXTE: "ajuster des pièces de métal"
CLASSE-ATTRIBUT: INFO-GENERALE
OBJET: |pièce I 1#2|
CLASSE-ATTRIBUT: SYNTAGMATIQUES
DETERMINATION: UN
NOMBRE: PL
RELATIONNELS-CORRESPONDANTS: THEME

|pièce I 1#2|
SUBCLASS.OF: |pièce I 1|
MEMBER.OF: NOMINALES
TEXTE: "pièce de métal"
CLASSE-ATTRIBUT: INFO-GENERALE
DE: |métal I 1|
CLASSE-ATTRIBUT: SYNTAGMATIQUES
RELATIONNELS-CORRESPONDANTS: ORIGINE, POSSESSEUR, MATIERE, OBJECTIF
MATIERE: 0.9

Frequently phrasal concepts represent "unlabeled" concepts (i.e., they indeed represent concepts that do not have a significant in the language). For instance, there is not, at least in French, a verbal concept meaning *ajuster des pièces de métal* or a noun meaning *pièce de métal.* This is not the case of the phrasal concepts that are linked to type concepts by means of the relation DEFINI-PAR/DEFINITION-DE, however, because there the phrasal concept is in fact another representation of the concept being defined. (See the example of the definition of *géranium I 1* above.) In the representation model proposed in this work, phrasal concepts denote concepts that are typically expressed in a periphrastic way and that do not necessarily have any corresponding entry in the dictionary.*

Another interesting point related to the creation of these phrasal concepts is the maintenance of direct links between a concept and all the occurrences of this concept

*This could be very interesting also, in the opinion of the authors, in a multilingual environment; it is possible that in another language the concept equivalent to that which has been represented by the phrasal concept |pièce I 1#2| has its own significant, a word that denotes it. In this case, the phrasal concept-based representation may be useful to represent the equivalence between both concepts.

in the definition sentences of other concepts. It gives, in fact, a virtual set of usage examples that may be useful for different functions of the final system.

Enrichment Processes Performed on the DKB

In this section the enrichment processes accomplished on the DKB are explained. Two phases are distinguished: (1) the enrichment obtained during the construction of the initial DKB, and (2) where different tasks concerning mainly the exploitation of the properties of synonymy and taxonymy have been performed.

ENRICHMENT OBTAINED DURING THE CONSTRUCTION OF THE INITIAL DKB

KB-THESAURUS itself, represented—as a network—at the relational level, can be considered an enrichment of the definitory level because, while the DKB was built, the following processes were performed:

- Values coming from the definitory level have been promoted to the relational level.
- Values coming from the unit representing the definiens have been transferred to the corresponding definiendum unit.
- The maintenance of the relations in both directions has been automatically guaranteed.
- The concepts included in REFERENCES have been directly related to other concepts.
- The taxonomy of concepts has been made explicit, thus obtaining value inheritance.

SECOND PHASE IN THE ENRICHMENT OF THE DKB

Several processes have been carried out in order to infer new facts to be asserted in the DKB.* The enrichment obtained in this phase concerns the following two aspects:

- Exploitation of the properties of synonymy (symmetric and transitive)
- Enlargement of the concept taxonomy based on synonymy

Another aspect that has been considered to be exploited in this phase is disambiguation. The use of the lexical-semantic knowledge about hierarchical relations contained in the DKB can be determinant in order to reduce the level of lexical and syntactical ambiguity.† Heuristics based on the taxonomic and synonymic knowledge obtained previously have been considered in this phase. Some of them have been designed, implemented, and evaluated in a sample of the DKB.

---

*By means of rules fired following a forward chaining strategy.

†Lexical ambiguity comes from the definitions themselves; syntactical ambiguity is due mainly to the analysis process.

Inferential Aspects: Dynamic Deduction of Knowledge

Dynamic acquisition of knowledge deals with the knowledge not explicitly represented in the DKB and captured by means of specially conceived mechanisms that are activated when the system is to answer a question posed by the user (*8*). The following aspects are considered:

- Inheritance (concept taxonomy).
- Composition of lexical relations.
- Links between concepts and relations. Users are allowed to use actual concepts to denote relationships (and not only primitive relations).
- Ambiguity in the DKB; treatment of remaining uncertainty.

Some aspects concerning to the second point will be discussed in the following.

In IDHS, the relationships among the different lexical-semantic relations can be easily expressed in a declarative way. It is the way of expressing these relationships that is called the *composition of lexical relations.* From an operative point of view, this mechanism permits the dynamic exploitation—under the user's requests—of the properties of the lexical relations in a direct manner. It is, in fact, a way of acquiring implicit knowledge from the DKB.

The declarative aspect of the mechanism is based on the definition of triples: each triple expresses a relationship among different lexical-semantic relations. These triples have the form $(R_1 R_2 R_3)$, where R_i represents a lexical relation.* The operative effect of these declarations is the dynamic creation of transitivity rules based on the triples stated. The general form of these rules is the following:

$$\text{if } X\ R_1\ Y \text{ and } Y\ R_2\ Z \text{ then } X\ R_3\ Z$$

When the value(s) of the attribute R_3 is (are) asked, a reading demon (attached to the attribute) creates the rule and fires the reasoning process with a backward-chaining strategy. The deduced facts, if any, will not be asserted in the background of the DKB, but in a temporary context.

For instance, the problem of transitivity in meronymic relations (*11, 12*) can be easily expressed by stating the triple (PARTIE-DE PARTIE-DE PARTIE-DE), and not stating, for instance, (PARTIE-DE MEMBRE-DE PARTIE-DE), thus expressing that the transitivity in the second case is not true. Examples of other triples that have been stated in the system are the following:

- Combination of meronymic and nonmeronymic relations:
  (PARTIE-DE LOCATIF LOCATIF)
  (LOCATIF HYPERONYME LOCATIF)
  (MEMBRE-DE HYPERONYME MEMBRE-DE)
- Combination of relations derived from the definition metalanguage:

*The result of the transitivity rule that will be created will be the deduction of values for the R_3 attribute. The triples are stored in a facet of R_3.

(CARACTERISTIQUE QUI-A POSSESSION)
(OBJECTIF CE-QUI OBJECTIF)

Explicit rules of lexical composition can be used when the general form of the triples is not valid. These rules are used following the same reasoning strategy.

The following is the rule derived from the last triple and one instance of it. By means of this rule instance, the fact that the purpose of a *géranium* is the action of *orner* is deduced from the definitions of *géranium* and *ornement*:

```
if   X OBJECTIF Y and   ;;;  the objective of X is Y (entity)
     Y CE-QUI Z         ;;;  Y "est ce qui" Z (action)
then  X OBJECTIF Z      ;;;  the objective of X is Z (action)

if   |géranium I 1| OBJECTIF |ornement I 1| and
     |ornement I 1| CE-QUI |orner I 1|
then  |géranium I 1| OBJECTIF |orner I 1|
```

The Prototype of IDHS: Size and Contents of the DKB

The prototype obtained after the construction of the DKB contains an important subset of the source dictionary. The quality of the semantic knowledge extracted from the DDB is conditioned by the size of definitions in the dictionary. In our case definitions are short, and many of them use no more than one, two, or three synonyms.

KB-DICTIONNAIRE contains 2400 entries, each one representing one word. KB-THESAURUS contains 6130 conceptual units; 1738 units of these are phrasal concepts. In this KB there are 1255 ambiguous concepts. Once the initial construction phase was finished, 19,691 relational arcs—interconceptual relationships—had been established. After the enrichment processes, the number of relational links have been incremented up to 21,800 (10.7% more). It has been estimated that using the mechanism of lexical composition, the number of interconceptual relations could reach an increment of between 5 and 10 percent.*

Manual evaluation of a meaningful sample of 100 concept-relation-concept triples from the enriched KB-THESAURUS gave us a correctness rate of 90 percent (under a 95% confidence rate given by the size of the sample).

Concerning the deduction of semantic knowledge, two considerations arise. First, the use of dubious lexical rules such as the transitivity of synonymy has led to some errors in the prototype. Second, lexical ambiguity restricts deduction, because we make ambiguous concepts stop deduction both in the enrichment process and in lexical composition. Lexical disambiguation is not a trivial issue, and is receiving much attention in recent research. Our group has developed a knowledge-based technique for lexical disambiguation of free-running text (*13*), which is now being applied to dictionary definitions.

---

*Considering only the set of triples declared until now.

Perspectives: A Multilingual Dictionary Help System

Currently a multilingual environment is being designed on the basis of different dictionaries. MLDS (multilingual dictionary system, an extension of IDHS) is conceived as an intelligent help system for human translations (*14, 15*), where two monolingual dictionaries (French and Basque) constitute the KB along with a bilingual dictionary that establishes equivalence-links among concepts from the monolingual dictionaries. This allows the system to enrich its functionality, as will be shown next.

As a result of our analysis of translators' needs the functions have been classified according to three main activities: source text understanding, object text generation, and the search for translation equivalents. The functions included in the monolingual dictionary help system (IDHS) give an answer to the two first activities, while searching for translation equivalents would correspond to the specific functionality of the multilingual dictionary help system.

There are some well-known problems with lexical gaps when (1) there is no single word in the target language to express the source concept, which can be solved giving *phrasal concept equivalents,* and when (2) the source concept does not appear as an entry in the bilingual dictionaries. In this case, in order to express that the concept in the result is *more general* or *more specific* than the source concept, set operators as ⊇ and ⊆ can be used.

In the first two examples below there is no problem when translating the concept |*accusatif I 1*| or |*coup_de_bec I 1*| from French into Basque. In the third and fourth examples, |*pattar I 1*| and |*txakolin I 1*| are not in the bilingual dictionary, so the system gives the closest concept from the monolingual dictionary and indicates whether it is more or less specific. In the last example there is no single word to say *abere* (domestic animal) in French, therefore a phrasal concept is returned.

T. - EQUIV ((|accusatif I 1|, ,), Basque, gram, ?LP)
S. - LP = ((akusatibo I 1|, ,))

T. - EQUIV ((|coup_de_bec I 1|, ,), Basque, common, ?LP)
S. - LP = ((|mokokada I 1|, ,))

T. - EQUIV ((|pattar I 1|, ,), French, common, ?LP)
S. - LP = ((⊆, |eau-de-vie I 1|, ,))

T. - EQUIV ((|txakolin I 1|, ,), French, common, ?LP)
S. - LP = ((⊇, |vin I 1|, ,))

T. - EQUIV (|(abere I 1|, ,), French, common, ?LP)
S. - LP = ((animal I 1#n|, ,))
where |animal I 1#n| represents "domestic animal".

Conclusions

A methodology for the extraction of semantic knowledge from a conventional dictionary has been described. This extraction is founded on a systematic study of dictionary definitions. A parser based on phrasal pattern hierarchies has been implemented and used in that study.

The method followed in the construction of the hierarchies needed by the parser is based on an empirical study on the structure of definition sentences. The results of its application to a real dictionary has shown that the parsing method is particularly suited to the analysis of short definition sentences, as it was the case of the source dictionary.

As a result of this process, the characterization of the different lexical-semantic relations between senses—which is the basis for the proposed DKB representation schema—has been established.

A frame-based knowledge representation model has been described. This model has been used in an intelligent dictionary help system to represent the lexical knowledge acquired automatically from a conventional dictionary.

The characterization of the different interconceptual lexical-semantic relations is the basis for the proposed model and it has been established as a result of the analysis process carried out on dictionary definitions.

Several enrichment processes have been performed on the DKB—after the initial construction—in order to add new facts to it; these processes are based on the exploitation of the properties of lexical-semantic relations. Moreover, a mechanism for acquiring—in a dynamic way—knowledge not explicitly represented in the DKB is proposed. This mechanism is based on the composition of lexical relations.

The general objective of IDHS is to assist a human user in language comprehension or production tasks. As a particular application, IDHS has been used in the design and implementation of a computerized translation-oriented dictionary that helps human translators in choosing suitable target lexical units that correspond with those that are in the source text (*15*). A new lexical KB was constructed for Basque following the same architecture, and the IDHS functionality was enriched with the treatment of knowledge about the process of lexical translation.

REFERENCES

1. X. Artola, "HIZTSUA: Hiztegi-sistema urgazle adimendunaren sorkuntza eta eraikuntza/Conception d'un système intelligent d'aide dictionnariale (SIAD)," Ph.D. thesis. University of the Basque Country UPV-EHU, Donostia, 1993.

2. X. Artola and F. Evrard, "Dictionnaire intelligent d'aide à la compréhension," *Actas IV Congreso Int. EURALEX'90* (Benalmádena), Biblograph, Barcelona, 1992, pp. 45–57.

3. E. Agirre, X. Arregi, X. Artola, A. Díaz de Ilarraza, K. Sarasola, and A. Soroa, "Constructing an Intelligent Dictionary Help System." *Natural Lang. Eng.,* **2**(3), 229–252 (1996).

4. E. Agirre, X. Arregi, X. ARtola, A. Díaz de Illarraza, F. Evrard, and K. Sarasola, "Intelligent Dictionary Help System," in *Applications and Implications of Current Language for Special Purposes Research,* vol. I, M. Brekke, Ø. Andersen, T. Dahl, J. Myking, eds. Fagbokforlaget, Bergen, Norway, 1994, pp. 174–183.

5. H. Alshawi, "Analysing Dictionary Definitions," in *Computational Lexicography for Natural Language Processing,* in B. Boguraev and T. Briscoe, eds. Longman, New York, 1989, pp. 153–169.

6. E. Agirre, X. Arregi, X. Artola, A. Díaz de Ilarraza, F. Evrard, and K. Sarasola, "Lexical Knowledge Representation in an Intelligent Dictionary Help System," *Proc. of COLING'94,* Kyoto, Japan, 1994, pp. 544–550.

7. E. Agirre, X. Arregi, X. Artola, A. Díaz de Ilarraza, F. Evrard, and K. Sarasola, "A Methodolgy for the

Extraction of Semantic Knowledge from Dictionaries Using Phrasal Patterns," *Proc. of IBERAMIA'94,* Caracas, Venezuela, 1994, pp. 263–270.

8. X. Arregi, X. Artola, A. Díaz de Ilarraza, F. Evrard, and K. Sarasola, "Aproximación funcional a DIAC: Diccionario inteligente de ayuda a la comprensión," *Proc. SEPLN,* vol. 11, 1991, pp. 127–138.
9. E. Agirre, X. Arregi, X. Artola, A. Díaz de Ilarraza, F. Evrard, and K. Sarasola, "IDHS, MLDS: Towards Dictionary Help Systems for Human Users," in *Semantics and Pragmatics of Natural Language: Logical and Computational Aspects,* K. Korta and J. M. Larrazabal, eds. ILCLI, Donostia (Basque country), 1995, pp. 167–188.
10. M. R. Quillian, "Semantic Memory," in *Semantic Information Processing,* M. Minsky, ed. MIT Press, Cambridge, MA, 1968, pp. 277–270.
11. C. A. Cruse, *Lexical Semantics,* Cambridge University Press, Cambridge, 1986.
12. M. E. Winston, R. Chaffin, and D. Herrmann, "A Taxonomy of Part-Whole Relations." *Cog. Sci.,* **11**, 417–444 (1987).
13. E. Agirre and G. Rigau, "Word Sense Disambiguation Using Conceptual Density," *Proc. of COLING'96,* Copenhagen, 1996.
14. X. Arregi, "ANHITZ: Itzulpenean laguntzeko Hiztegi-sistema eleanitza" ("ANHITZ: Multilingual Dictionary Help System for Translation Tasks"), Ph.D. thesis, University of the Basque Country UPV-EHU, Donostia, 1995.
15. E. Agirre, X. Arregi, X. Artola, A. Díaz de Ilarraza, H. Patel, K. Sarasola and A. Soroa, "A Computerised Translation-Oriented Dictionary," *Proc. of NLP+IA/TAL+AI 96,* University of Moncton, Moncton, Canada, 1996.

BIBLIOGRAPHY

Agirre E., X. Arregi, X. Artola, A. Díaz de Ilarraza, and K. Sarasola, "Lexical-Semanatic Information and Automtic Correction of Spelling Errors," in *Semantics and Pragmatics of Natural Language: Logical and Computational Aspects,* K. Korta and J. M. Larrazabal, eds. ILCLI, Donostia (Basque Country), 1995, pp. 157–166.

Amsler, R. A. "A Taxonomy for English Nouns and Verbs," *Proc. 19th Annual Meeting ACL,* Stanford, 1981, pp. 133–138.

Arango Gaviría, G, *Une approache pour amorcer le processus de compréhension et d'utilisation du sens des mots en langage naturel.* Thèse de 3éme cycle (Paris VI), Publications du Groupe de Recherche Claude François Picard, 1983.

Boguraev, B and T. Briscoe, eds., *Computational Lexicography for Natural Language Processing,* Longman, New York, 1989.

Byrd, R. J., N. Calzolari, M. S. Chodorow, J. L. Klavans, M. S. Neff, O. A. Rizk, "Tools and Methods for Computational Lexicography." *Computa. Ling.,* **13**(3–4), 219–240 (1987).

Calzolari, N., "Machine-Readable Dictionaries, Lexical Data Bases and the Lexical System," Proc. COLING, Standford University, Stanford, 1984, p. 460.

Calzolari, N. and E. Picchi, "Acquisition of Semantic Information from an On-Line Dictionary," *Proc. COLING,* Budapest, 1988, pp. 87–92.

Chodorow, M. S. and R. J. Byrd, "Extracting Semantic Hierarchies from a Large On-Line Dictionary," *Proc. ACL,* 1985, pp. 299–304.

Chouraqui, E and E. Godbert, "Représentation des descriptions définies dans un réseau sémantique," *Actes 7ème Congrès Reconnaissance des Formes et Intelligence Artificielle* (AFCET-INRIA, Paris), 1989, pp. 855–868.

Copestake, A., "An Approach to Building the Hierarchical Element of a Lexical Knowledge Base from a Machine-Readable Dictionary," *First Int. Workshop on Inheritance in NLP,* Tilburg, Holland, 1990.

van den Hurk, I. and W. Meijs, "The Dictionary as a Corpus: Analyzing LDOCE's Definition-Language." *Corpus Ling. II,* 1986, 99–125.

Litkowsky, K. C., "Models of the Semantic Structure of Dictionaries." *Amer. J. Computa. Ling.,* **81**, 25–74 (1978).

Markowitz, J., T. Ahlswede, and M. Evens, "Semantically Significant Patterns in Dictionary Definitions," *Proc. 24th Annual Meeting ACL,* New York, 1986, pp. 112–119.

McRoy, S., "Using Multiple Knowledge Sources for Word Sense Discrimination." *Computa. Ling.*, **18**(1), (1992).

Pazienza, M. T. and P. Velardi, "A Structured Representation of Word-Senses for Semantic Analysis," *Proc. 3rd European Conference ACL*, Copenhagen, 1987, pp. 249–257.

Tsurumaru, H., T. Hitaka, and S. Yoshida, "An Attempt to Automatic Thesaurus Construction from an Ordinary Japanese Language Dictionary," *Proc. COLING*, Bonn, 1986, pp. 445–447.

Vossen, P., W. Meijs, and M. den Broeder, "Meaning and Structure in Dictionary Definitions," in *Computational Lexicography for Natural Language Processing*, Longman, New York, 1989, pp. 171–192.

Wilks, Y., D. Fass, G. Cheng-Ming, J. E. McDonald, T. Plate, and B. M. Slator, "Providing Machine Tractable Dictionary Tools." *Machine Transl.*, **5**, 99–154 (1990).

ENEKO AGIRRE
XABIER ARREGI
XABIER ARTOLA
ARANTZA DIAZ DE ILARRAZA
KEPA SARASOLA
AITOR SOROA
FABRICE EVRARD

INTELLIGENT WEB SEARCH AGENTS

Information Retrieval on the Web

We identified four generations of information retrieval tools that assist people in searching the World Wide Web. The first generation of information retrieval tools was designed for use with bibliographic databases. The first generation provided access to references to the end documents rather than to the documents themselves, and indexing and searching were thus applied to document surrogates, such as titles or abstracts. These tools require considerable human effort to collect, arrange, code, and annotate the various resources. A primary benefit of the first generation of tools is providing users with easy browsing capabilities. The second generation of tools attempts to collect and index resources as an automated function. Automatic collection and indexing reduces the amount of human effort. The ability to search through massive amounts of information and locate the desired information for the user is the primary benefit of the second generation of tools. The third generation deals with World Wide Web meta-search engines, such as Harvester and MetaCrawler. The fourth generation involves new ideas such as search agent technology currently being developed to search for information on the Web. In this article we discuss search agents and introduce the characteristics of our intelligent Web search agent. We begin with Web search engines.

The opinion and assessments in this paper are solely those of the authors and do not reflect the views of Bell Atlantic Network Services, Inc., the U.S. Air Force, or the U.S. government.

WEB SEARCH ENGINES

Web search engines have two components: collection and search. The collection part roams the Internet, primarily visiting Web sites and file servers. It brings back the resources (often an abstract instead of the entire resource), indexes the materials it brought back, and creates a database. The search component concerns the provision of information to the end user, and is an interface between the user and the indexed database of resources.

There are two schools of thought regarding whether to add user-controlled search options to a search service in an attempt to acquire more relevant documents. Many software designers of relevance-ranking systems suggest that searchers first allow the search algorithms to do their best without interference. They recommend throwing as many related terms at the search engine as possible to give it a chance at interpreting the query.

The strategy of throwing many related terms at the search engine may work well for some queries, but not for all. We have found that adding more terms to a query can skew the results in such a way that the search engine software interprets an unintended concept as central to a user's interest. Furthermore, most modern search engines utilize a thesaurus of similar terms; therefore, throwing many related terms at the search engine may be an unnecessary effort by the human being. Later in this article we introduce the idea of an autonomous software component that among other things can assist the user in selecting additional query terms.

Web search engines can be widely encompassing or narrowly specialized. Each of them has unique content, unique interface, a set of rules for searching, and different displays for search results. To perform an exhaustive search, users often utilize multiple resources, necessitating familiarity with the different interfaces and searching rules. Fortunately, there are tools that overcome the difficulties of having to learn multiple interfaces and searching rules. These tools are referred to as metasearch engines.

METASEARCH ENGINES

Unlike the individual search engines, metasearch engines do not have their own databases—nor do they collect Web pages, accept universal resource locator additions, or classify or review Web sites. Instead, they send queries simultaneously to multiple Web search engines. Some metasearch engines, such as SavvySearch, try to maximize the likelihood of finding good links while holding resource consumption to a minimum by ranking the available search engines for how well they respond to the terms in the query and dispatching the query only to the top-ranked search engines. Many metasearch engines integrate search results, eliminate duplications, and rank the results through their own criteria.

Metasearch engines are not designed for exhaustive searches. Most metasearch engines only make use of the top ten to 100 hits from each of the search engines they contact. While this is sufficient for most searches, individual search engines must be consulted if a user must search all of the hits and cannot reformulate the query to avoid a large number of hits.

We recommend the use of metasearch engines when a user is looking for a particular resource or a specific answer to a question. For these purposes, the metasearch engine seems more likely to return the relevant resource. We recommend searching multiple individual search engines when a user desires to see every resource that covers a particular topic. In order to answer the question of when to select between a metasearch engine and an exhaustive search of individual search engines, we suggest the use of search agents.

Search Agents

An agent is a powerful and ubiquitous abstraction for performing advanced information retrieval on the Web. By using search agents, we can hide the details of the complex technology underlying the Internet and the many resources the agent accesses. By making the technology transparent, we are more likely to succeed in our goals of focusing on the user's needs and improving the relevancy of the information being retrieved.

The pervasive interactive style for today's computers is direct manipulation; point at the icon, click on it, drag it, and drop it. Several studies have remarked upon the productivity and timesaving benefits of "point-and-click" interfaces for human users and the marketplace has certainly agreed. In a similar vein, who would want to spend days and weeks looking through hundreds of networks with millions of potentially useful items? Experts in artificial intelligence propose search techniques to resolve these problems. Intelligent background processes that can successfully clone their users' goals and carry them out should result in major savings of human effort and productivity. Indirectly managing agents could potentially result in greater productivity savings then personal computer users experienced when they switched from text commands to point-and-click graphical user interfaces.

Users delegate to the search agent the tasks of determining where to find the information and how to retrieve it. There are many different possible methods agents may use and many different resources they may contact in their search for an answer. There are a number of specialized search agents already performing on the Web. BargainBot is an interactive search agent that simultaneously searches multiple bookstores for the details of particular books. Electronic commerce is considered by many to be the future of the Internet.[1] The presence of effective search agents to locate competing products and the lowest available price will be crucial to commerce over the Web.[2]

Some agents can adapt to their environment. The environment in which an agent has to interact can be described in several different ways. It can be accessible vs. inaccessible; deterministic vs. non-deterministic; episodic vs. nonepisodic; static vs. dynamic; and discrete vs. continuous.[3] The agents can learn from their experience, via machine learning, knowledge discovery, statistical techniques, and through communication with other agents and knowledge repositories. The common object request broker architecture (CORBA) can assist agents in adapting to their environment by providing access to knowledge that is stored in ontology agents (defined in subsection

"Ontology" below) and through other services such as naming services, trader services, and broker services.

Other agents know how to recognize the user's underlying goals and intentions, and react to unexpected situations in a robust manner. In other words, intelligent agents are able to both represent and reason about a number of things that are essential in determining if information is relevant to a user. The agent can reason about such topics as beliefs about what the user wants, services available from other agents and ontologies, intentions about its own future plan to satisfy the users' needs, perceptions, and desires about future states (i.e., goals).

We refer to software agents with the above features as intelligent Web search agents.

Intelligent Web Search Agents

We define an intelligent Web search agent as an autonomous, goal-directed process that is situated in, is aware of, and reacts to its World Wide Web environment. It uses standard languages and protocols to cooperate and collaborate with other agents (software or human) to accomplish its tasks. Intelligent Web search agents process and "understand" information, both on the level of individual documents or objects as well as collectionwide.

Although highly desirable, the design and implementation of intelligent agents for searching the Web is full of technical challenges. In designing these agents, we must touch upon a number of thorny information retrieval issues. Some of these issues are relevance feedback, interfaces and browsing, distributed information retrieval, multimedia retrieval, and routing and filtering. Fortunately, agent technologies and artificial intelligence techniques are potentially applicable to many of these issues.[4] Intelligent Web search agents employ statistical approaches for deriving metadata from information that are particularly interesting for analyzing text objects, such as n-grams and latent semantic indexing. N-grams involve fragmenting a word into a sequence of strings of n adjacent characters, and then estimating the similarity between a pair of words by the similarity between the corresponding sets of n-grams. Latent semantic indexing is a technique that uses the singular value decomposition of a parallel document collection to obtain term factor representations, which are comparable across all the languages of the collection.[5]

Let us consider the problem of efficiently extracting from the amazingly fast-growing collection of documents available in the hypertext markup language (HTML), which was created to display data for humans to read. It was never meant for data mining. The "knowledge" on a Web page is in a human-readable language (usually English), laid out with tables, graphics, and frames in ways that we as humans comprehend visually. Proponents of extended markup language (XML) claim that Web page authors will be able to annotate their Web documents with machine-readable knowledge, so that intelligent Web search agents can compile a knowledge base from Web pages.

The central component of a knowledge-based agent is its knowledge base. A knowledge base is a set of representations of facts about the world. Our intelligent Web search agent has a knowledge base represented by facts and rules in the C-language integrated production system inference engine. A knowledge-based agent has a learning capability if its knowledge base may be increased with new information it acquires as a result of its own actions.

Stuart Russell and Peter Norvig suggested that "an agent is anything that can be viewed as perceiving the environment through sensors and acting upon the environment through effectors."[6] A human agent has "eyes, ears, and other agents for sensors" and "hands, legs, mouth, and other body parts for effectors." Similarly, an intelligent Web search agent may have Web browsers, Java input screens, and interfaces to commercial search engines for sensors and includes inference engines, Java output screens, and Web page parsers for effectors. The effectors for an intelligent Web search agent are acting on the state space of the search engines and the outcome tables of the planning level.

A rational agent is "one that does the right thing." The measurement criteria of an intelligent Web search agent may be difficult to quantify, given the size of the domain of the World Wide Web and the difficulties of natural language parsing and searching. Moreover, computer scientists have argued over the meaning of relevance in information retrieval for over forty years without arriving at a conclusion. What is necessary, then, is not to attempt to reach some imaginary nirvana called "relevance"; rather, what is necessary is to predefine some set of procedures and standards and then judge the agent by whether or not it adheres to those procedures and standards. In doing so, we recognize that these particular procedures may not obtain the most relevant documents for an individual user. By standardizing our approach, however, we attempt to provide consistent and improving results over the long run.

ONTOLOGY

At the core of our approach lies the concept of ontology. An ontology in the domain of artificial intelligence describes an explicit specification of some topic and a set of relationships among the terms in that domain. It is a formal, declarative representation that includes the vocabulary for referring to terms in the subject area and the logical statements that describe the terms.[7] When an agent requests additional information regarding a particular domain of knowledge, the agent requests this information from an ontology agent. If the active agent discovers new knowledge about its world, it may send this knowledge to the ontology agent to add to the ontology.

WEB SEARCH AGENT ONTOLOGY

For the purposes of knowledge sharing, we designed a hierarchical structure to simplify the ontological relationships within our chosen domain. The two most prominent parts of the hierarchy are the Web page ontology (see Table 1) and the Web search agent ontology (see Table 2). The Web search agent ontology inherits

TABLE 1

Web Page Ontology

Structure	Hypertext markup language
Structural attributes	Meta, link, titles, image captions
Content	Alphanumeric data, organized in word form

TABLE 2

Web Search Agent Ontology

Agent goal	Return multiple Web pages in order of "relevance"
Keywords	Words identified as likely to increase "relevance" if found in Web page
Keyword search list	List of words likely to increase "relevance" if found on the same Web page
Special relationships	Two or more keywords located within a predefined distance of each other
Knowledge base	Collection of statistics of knowledge items related to the subject matter
Web page	Incorporates concepts found in the Web page ontology

much of its content from the Web page ontology. Likewise, the Web page ontology inherits much of its content from the metaclasses above it, such as the multimedia document class and the language constructs class.

Our proposed ontology describes the knowledge domain for the intelligent Web search agent. In particular, we focused on categories that our Web pages could fall into, as well as the relationships between those categories. We also focused on data, which could be used to specify the nature of the relationships. For instance, a document with metadata is likely to be more relevant than a document that lacked metadata (holding all other characteristics equal). Close proximity of related words could further increase the potential importance of the document.

An Intelligent Web Search Agent Prototype

The goals of our intelligent Web search agent are to produce a refined and distilled subject-matter search of the Web, given certain inputs and tolerance criteria prepared in advance of the search. It uses an objective approach to indicate a different presentation order of the various pages returned from a search engine. Also, a reduced list of "relevant" Web pages on a topic is returned. The rule-based inference engine keeps track of the descriptive statistics for each page and may give contingency-based recommendations up the planning chain, depending on the nature of those statistics.

Stuart Russell and Peter Norvig suggest that an agent is a program working within a given architecture and that each agent type has within its framework or makeup percepts, actions, goals, and its environment.[8] The percepts of our intelligent Web search agent are typed words. Its actions are to print suggestions and initiate search criteria on the Web, and its goals are to distill and aggregate given subject matter on

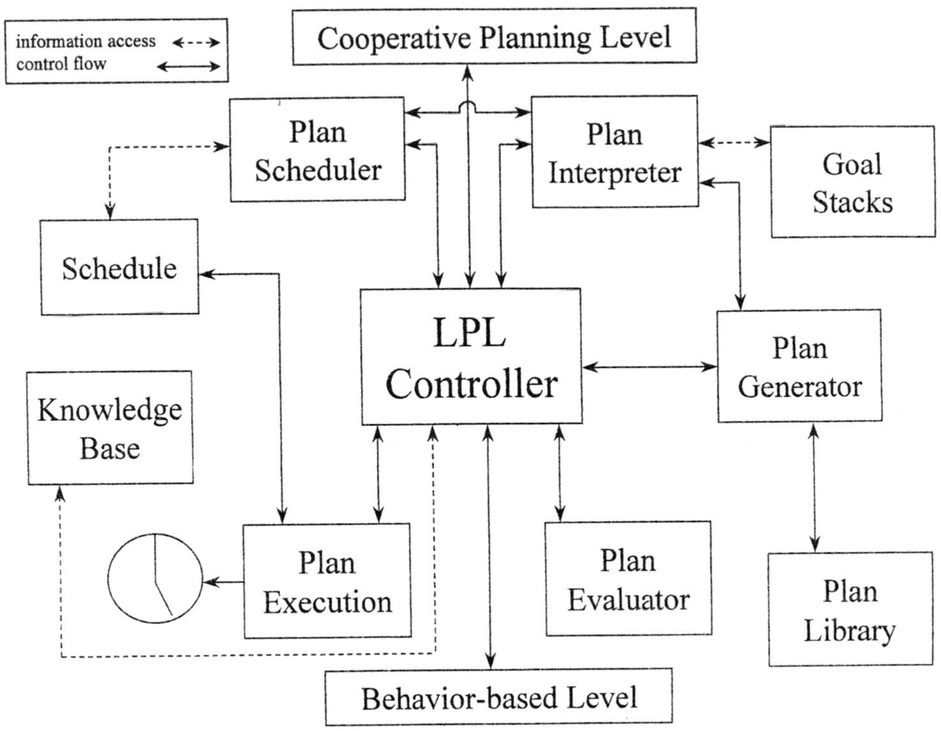

FIGURE 1. *Jörg Müller's Local Planning Layer*

the Web. Its environment is the domain of Web pages and related commercial search engines.

The design for our intelligent Web search agent was inspired by Jörg Müller's robotic world. In his book, *Design of Intelligent Agents: A Layered Approach,* he describes robotic agents in an active-world loading-dock scenario that have to react in real time using limited resources and an incomplete knowledge about the world. He presents the integration of agent interaction in planner-reactor architecture using a control architecture that defines interactions among three layers: the behavior-based, the local planning, and the cooperative planning layers. Building on a heritage of distributed artificial intelligence and the knowledge query and manipulation language, Müller deals with coordination and cooperation among distributed intelligent agents, where communication plays an important role in their interaction. He created a layered architecture with hybridization between a reactive system approach and a deliberative systems approach. He chose to avoid a pure reactive system approach because he did not want to limit the scope of goal-directed behavior. He declined a pure deliberative systems approach because of the danger of intractable general-purpose reasoning mechanisms. His integration of reactive behavior and rational planning model supports reactive, goal-directed, and interacting agents that present control layers and a knowledge base that supports different abstraction levels of knowledge as well as a control structure among the layers. His control architecture uses as general design decisions the following: layered control, layered knowledge base, bottom-up activation, and top-down execution. The design of the knowledge base of his agent has three layers: the world model, the mental model, and the social model, which reflect the informational state of the situations as well as the beliefs and the goals of the individual agent. The behavior of his agents results from the interplay among the individual control layers (Fig. 1).[9]

Müller designed his local planning layer, as seen in Fig. 1, to produce a sequence of actions to achieve a goal or task that has been presented to the agent. The planner, guided by domain knowledge, searches for a sequence of operator applications in a state space, and given a problem description, attempts to return a plan. Plans are selected, interpreted, scheduled, and executed in the control cycle of the local planning layer. In each control loop, one interpretation step is done for each plan stack; the agent determines what action to execute next. The planner commits to schedule the intention structure and the implementing actions of the agent. The local planning layer of his agent uses the agent's capabilities of planning to pursue its local goals. It can access the world model layer of the agent knowledge base to obtain information about the world. The local planning layer receives upward activation requests by the behavior-based layer, while commitments of execution of procedural patterns are posted down to the behavior-based layer.

IMPLEMENTATION STRATEGY

We designed the intelligent Web search agent as a hierarchical structure to distill and aggregate information found on the World Wide Web. Our implementation strategy, as displayed in Fig. 2, includes the following chain of events:

- Solicit a subject
- Use search engines to acquire related Web pages
- Parse Web pages to examine their structure
- Prepare the parsed words for input-fact format
- Derive ontological knowledge into a collection of rules
- Run inference engine rules over the input-facts
- Produce recommendations based on the relevance rankings

A demonstration of the proposed agent structure was limited to a select knowledge domain. The user entered into his browser the topic for which he sought information. The Java applet then formatted and uploaded the information to the server-based intelligent agent. The agent contacted the metasearch engine MetaCrawler. This in turn contacted at least ten other search engines. After receiving a list of possible relevant sites, the agent contacted the individual Web sites, downloading their respective contents. The agent then used the parser, the thesaurus, and the stemmer to reduce the number of terms. The agent then attempted to match the terms with relevant keywords from the knowledge domain. After discovering keywords, the agent determined whether or not those keywords had special significance within each document.

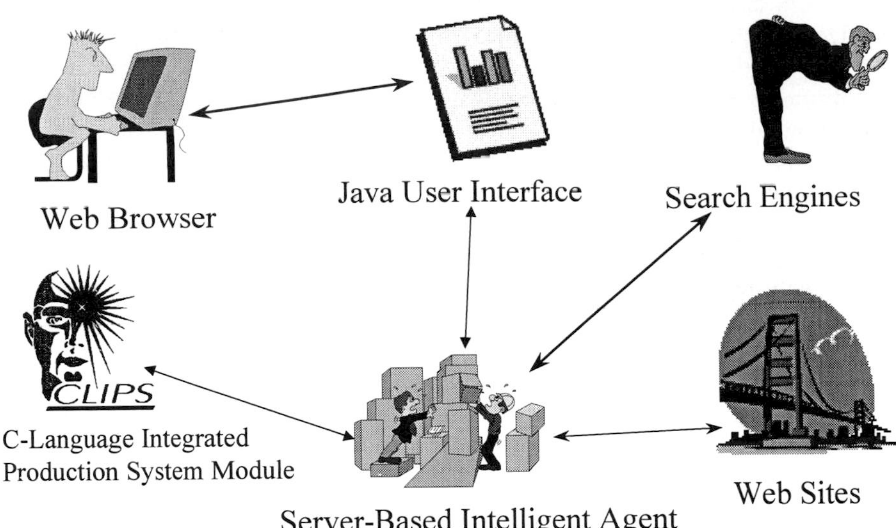

FIGURE 2. *Intelligent web search agent.*

Each document had a corresponding truth table indicating the presence or absence of keywords and their possible special status, as determined by their ontology. We defined the "relevance" of one document as being potentially greater if more significant elements were present in the document. The documents were then organized in order of potential relevance. They were displayed to the user, along with their individual truth tables.

USER INTERFACE

The user opens up his Web browser and accesses our Web page. The user attempts to retrieve information by entering a word phrase into the Java applet interface module through his browser. The Java user interface then transmits his request to the planning level controller of the server-based intelligent agent.

As seen in Fig. 3, the user submits a topic to the agent through his browser. In the particular case of Fig. 3, the user accesses Microsoft Internet Explorer, enters the universal resource locator for our Web page, and chooses a topic. In this particular case, the user chose to retrieve information on the topic ontology. The Java applet then transmitted the user's request to the server-based intelligent agent.

After the server-based intelligent agent finishes processing the user's request, the results are then handled by the Java output applet (as seen later in Fig. 6).

PLANNING LEVEL

We established modest goals for our intelligent Web search agent. We wanted the planning level to be able to recognize prepared input words, which are the data on

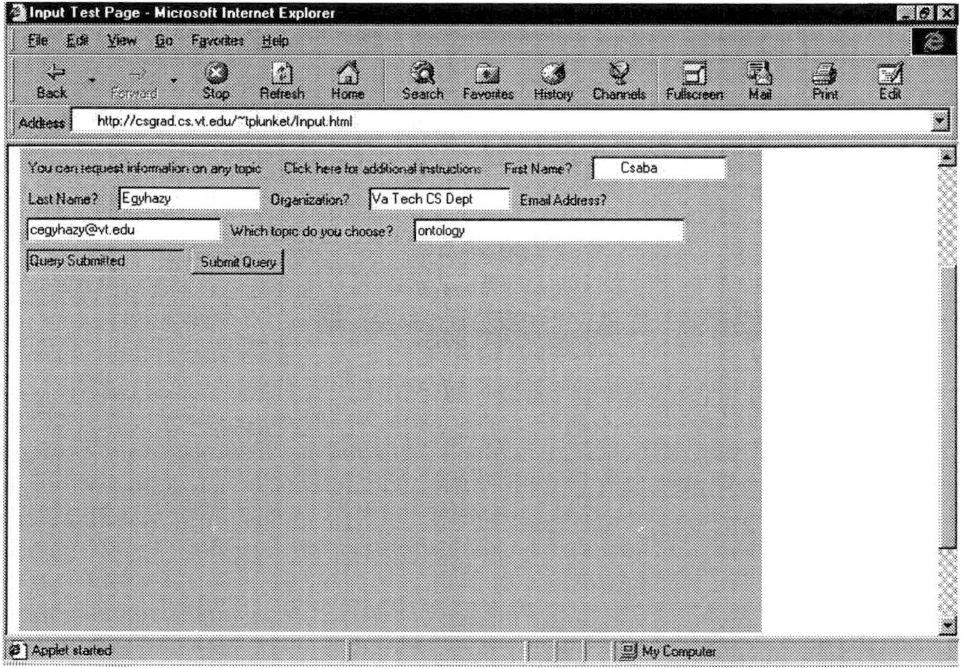

FIGURE 3. *Input Test Page of Intelligent Web Search Agent*

which the inference engine could be applied, prepare some truth tables that could be passed upward, and recommend updated search criteria on the given subject.

Figure 4 focuses on the planning level to simplify the conceptual abstraction of our working model. The interaction characteristics could easily be extended upward to the feedback loop level and downward to the search engine interface level.

The planning level controller is central to the planning level of the architecture. Unlike Müller's architecture, our cycle of control is more state-related than temporal-related. After a condition (or series of conditions) is recognized in the pages that are examined, a recommendation can be passed up to the feedback loop level. Access to the knowledge base is achieved through the defined rules in the inference engine and its interfaces to the other modules. We use the thesaurus and stemmer to expand the search capabilities to cover similar and related word phrases. In the search iteration generator, we analyze word phrases and the context in which they appeared in the search history. After further analysis utilizing the thesaurus and stemmer, we generate a search plan that may recommend additional search iterations.

The ontology has collections of various statistics or item frequency triggers on several words or knowledge items that are related to the subject matter under consideration. It is also supplemented with a thesaurus, which could broaden or refine the current search criteria. A recommendation may go up to the feedback loop level to incorporate the broadened criteria in a separate or expanded search of the Web. The

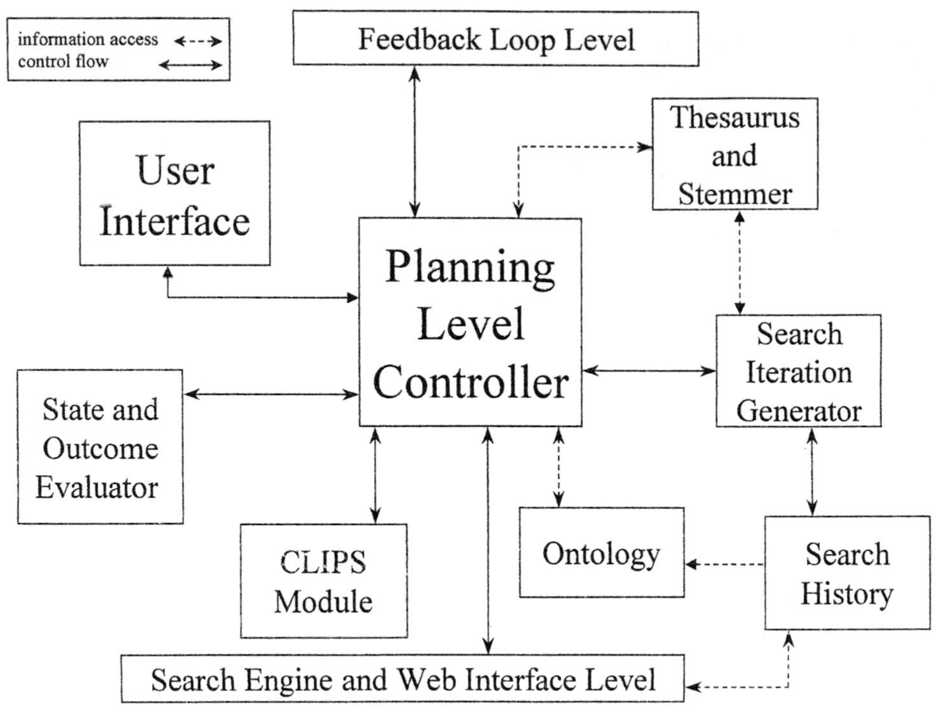

FIGURE 4. *Intelligent Web Search Agent Planning Level*

derived relationships could then be incorporated into the knowledge base for future cycles of searches on the subject matter.

We have given value to word or subject matter frequency as reinforcing criteria to the search. Furthermore, we have given additional value to whether or not

- The keyword or subject matter phrase was incorporated into a metaword field of the document
- The keyword was incorporated into a Web link structure
- The keyword was part of an image title, caption, or file name
- The keywords were in close proximity to additional keywords or subject matter

When predefined goals are met in the analysis of the truth table, subsequent actions are triggered. The context and types of criteria related to the goal activation triggers influence plan selection. Related but subtly differing plans could be activated, based on the context of the is-meta, the is-link, the is-image, and the is-proximate criteria associated with the prepared lists of words as facts.

The outcome evaluator module analyzes the results of the search and recommends whether or not to pursue an additional iteration of the search through the feedback loop level. Alternatively, the agent may decide to present the search results to the user at this point. If so, the state evaluator will transform the fact relationships into truth-table format for display to the user, as seen in Fig. 5.

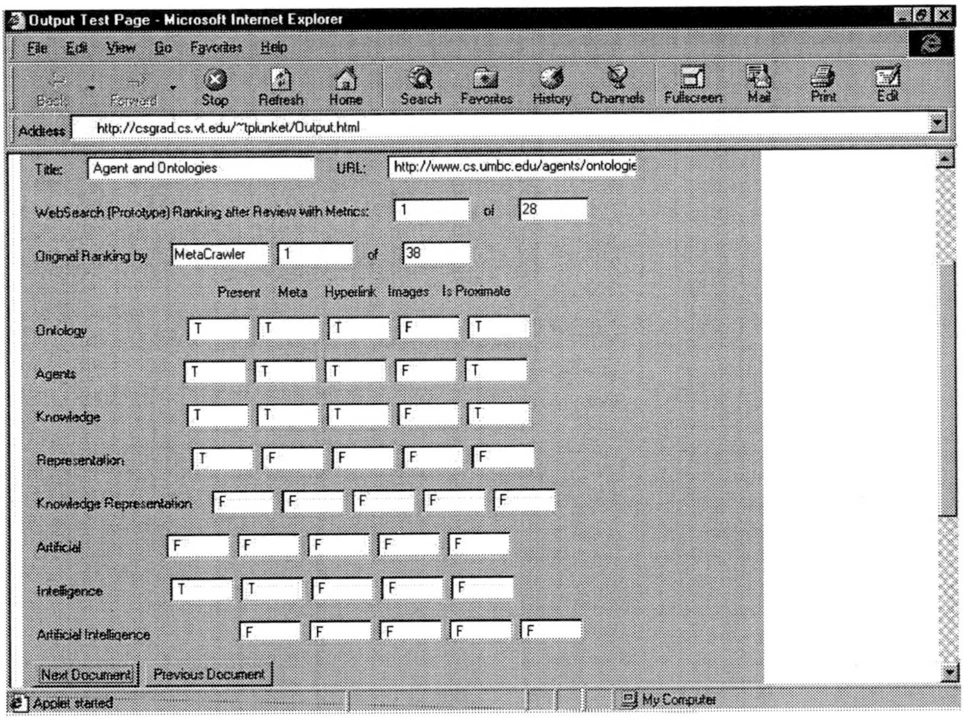

Output Test Page - Microsoft Internet Explorer
File Edit View Go Favorites Help
Back Forward Stop Refresh Home Search Favorites History Channels Fullscreen Mail Print Edit
Address http://csgrad.cs.vt.edu/~tplunket/Output.html
Title: Agent and Ontologies
URL: http://www.cs.umbc.edu/agents/ontologie
WebSearch (Prototype) Ranking after Review with Metrics: 1 of 28
Original Ranking by MetaCrawler 1 of 38
Present Meta Hyperlink Images Is Proximate
Ontology T T T F T
Agents T T T F T
Knowledge T T T F T
Representation T F F F F
Knowledge Representation F F F F F
Artificial F F F F F
Intelligence T T F F F
Artificial Intelligence F F F F F
Next Document Previous Document
Applet started
My Computer

FIGURE 5. *Output Test Page of Intelligent Web Search Agent*

In Fig. 5, the output test page presents the title and universal resource locator of the retrieved page, the original ranking by the commercial meta-engine MetaCrawler, the postprocess ranking, and the truth-table relationships. Navigation buttons allow the user to see the individual results for each Web page that the intelligent Web search agent was able to contact. In the particular case of this retrieval, both our agent and MetaCrawler ranked the "agent and ontologies" Web site at *www.cs.umbc.edu* as potentially the most relevant. When navigating through the series of documents, individual Web pages have different rankings between the two series. MetaCrawler had ranked thirty-eight pages; our intelligent Web search agent eliminated ten of those pages because the Web sites were either duplicative or inaccessible.

INFERENCING C-LANGUAGE INTEGRATED PRODUCTION SYSTEM MODULE

The C-language integrated production system (CLIPS) module provides the inferencing capability for our knowledge base. This rules-based inference engine was a key component in our project. We created rule- and fact-based inference code where the engine analyzed and matched the keywords and various aspects of the Web pages. The facts and rules that are inputs into the inference engine are represented on the planning level diagram by the knowledge base. The inference engine applies those rules to the input and sends the output to the outcome evaluator.

CLIPS is an expert system shell developed by NASA. CLIPS is broadly available[10] as freeware for educational purposes through the Client Server Systems Branch of the NASA/Johnson Space Center.[11]

The CLIPS structure is divided between the paradigms and the constructs. The CLIPS rules paradigm supports the expert system structure by implementing the rules in our ontology. The CLIPS pattern paradigm supports pattern recognition by identifying frequencies of particular words and relations in documents. The CLIPS procedural paradigm supports the logic within the planning level by implementing the interrelationships of the various modules. The object paradigm supports object-oriented programming concepts of abstraction, encapsulation, inheritance, polymorphism, and dynamic binding.[12]

The CLIPS constructs are an essential part of the production system, as seen in Fig. 6. The Deffacts construct imports a list of facts into the system for processing. The ontology defines the rules that describe how to solve the problem, and these rules are imported into the planning level by the Defrule construct. The rules execute or do not execute based on the existence of facts or objects. The Defmodule constructs provide supports for the modular development and execution of the knowledge base for the planning level controller. The Deffunction constructs perform the distillation and

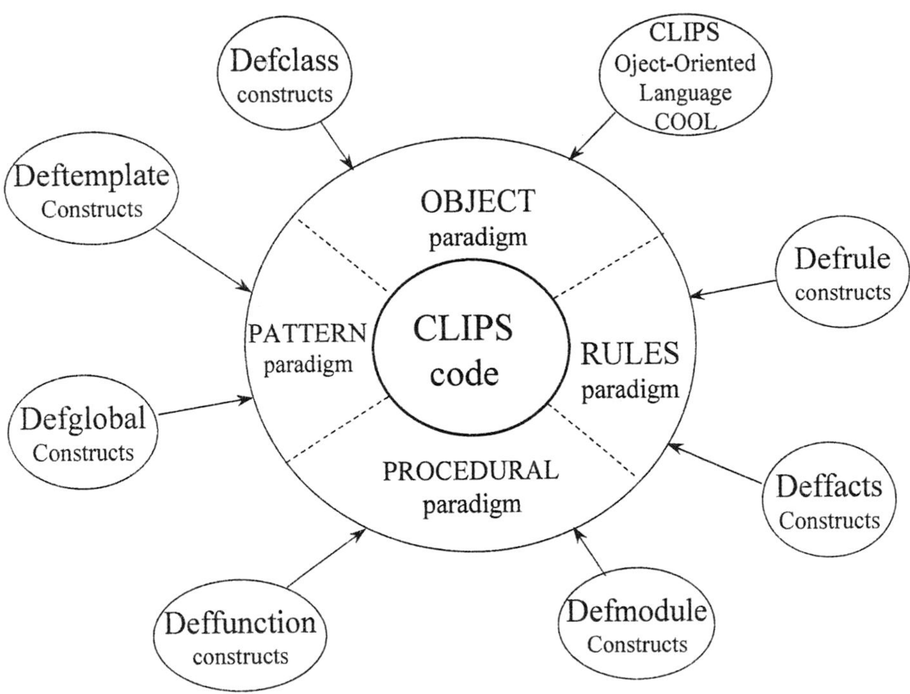

FIGURE 6. *C-Language integrated production system.*

aggregation actions in the module. The remaining constructs affect some of the interrelationships among the modules within the planning level.

SEARCH ENGINE AND WEB INTERFACE LEVEL

Another vital component of the intelligent Web search agent is the search engine and Web interface level. This level of the intelligent Web search agent will contact MetaCrawler or other search engines to acquire a list of Web sites. Subsequently the intelligent Web search agent will contact these Web pages individually to parse text and other hypertext markup language constructs in preparation for input fact format.

FEEDBACK LOOP LEVEL

The purpose of the feedback loop level is to add intelligence to the agent's behavior in its world. The feedback loop level may receive a recommendation from the planning level controller to obtain enhanced criteria for the ontology, such as additional keywords or value-added criteria, which could either change the relative values of the individual Web pages or generate additional searches of the Web. The feedback loop level can choose to accept or ignore the recommendations of the planning level controller. Furthermore, the intelligent Web search agent may implement iterative searching based on expanded criteria in order to refine the subject matter under consideration.

Conclusions

We believe that many knowledge-acquisition tasks will be easier to perform when aided by intelligent Web search agents. This belief is based on our experience in comparing the quality and time difference of the results of unassisted searches with agent-assisted searches.[13] Moreover, the agent paradigm should be easier to extend to new capabilities than previous information retrieval technologies because of its intrinsic object-oriented nature and the associated benefits of software reuse.

We feel that further research in the field of intelligent Web search agents will achieve significant results in allowing users to more efficiently acquire the information they seek from the World Wide Web. Future work may include the extension of the server-based intelligent agent querying capabilities to include semiautonomous multilevel subject-matter query capability and an augmented ability to distill and refine subject matter.

REFERENCES AND NOTES

1. O. Etzioni and M. Perkowitz, "Adaptive Web Sites: An AI Challenge," *Proceedings of the 1997 International Joint Conference on Artificial Intelligence,* Morgan Kaufmann, San Francisco, 1997, propose that Web servers should analyze user request patterns and use these data to dynamically restructure their pages to fulfill user needs.
2. Some examples of commercially available desktop agent software include Web Ferret and Copernic.

3. S. Russell and P. Norvig, *Artificial Intelligence: A Modern Approach,* Prentice Hall, Englewood Cliffs, NJ, 1995, p. 46.
4. The Intelligent Software Agents group at Carnegie Mellon is developing WebMate, a personal Web agent integrating parallel search techniques, relevance feedback, similarity-fetching, and off-line browsing.
5. T. K. Landaur and M. L. Littman, "Fully Automatic Cross Language Document Retrieval Using Latent Semantic Indexing," *Proceedings of the Sixth Conference of UW Center for the New OED and Text Research,* Waterloo, Ontario, 1990, pp. 31–38.
6. See Ref. 3, p. 31ff.
7. T. R. Gruber, "A Translation Approach to Portable Ontologies." *Knowl. Ac.,* **5***(2), 199–220 (1993).*
8. See Ref. 6.
9. J. Müller, *The Design of Intelligent Agents: A Layered Approach,* Springer, London, 1996.
10. *CLIPS,* version 6.0, can be found at the Carnegie Mellon University Intelligence Repository at www.cs.cmu.edu/afs/cs/project/ai-repository/ai/areas/expert/systems/clips.
11. C. Giarratano, *CLIPS User's Guide,* Version 6.05, (unpublished, available at Web Site, ref. 10) 1997.
12. *CLIPS Reference Manual, Volume 1: Basic Programming Guide,* Version 6.05, (unpublished, available at Web Site, ref. 10) 1997.
13. Future plans call for rigorously evaluating the statistics for this methodology.

DAVID M. THOMPSON
CSABA J. EGYHAZY
THOMAS K. PLUNKETT, JR.

LOGIC DESIGN

Introduction

DEVICES AND TECHNOLOGIES

The switching elements used in modern electronics are diodes and transistors, and the AND, OR, and NOT gates are constructed using these. These three gates represent the most basic building blocks in digital circuits. Other more complex circuits are created by connecting these devices in different ways. Examples are the NAND and NOR gates, flip-flops, registers, adders, multipliers, decoders, and microprocessors. To be able to interface with the analog world, analog to digital and digital to analog (ADA) converters are required. These, however, are outside our immediate scope.

The basic logic components can in fact be magnetic devices or even mechanical devices with the logic functions performed by jets of air or liquid (Fig. 1). The switching elements, or the two-state devices, can be simple mechanical switches, relays, or valves, although at present diodes and transistors are almost always used. We must not forget that electronic devices require a power supply of some kind. Figure 1 shows a selection of gates representing different technologies. Since the 1960s, gates have become available as standard integrated circuits (ICs) known as chips. Standard

ICs are available with gates, flip-flops, counters, registers, read only memories (ROMs), random access memories (RAMs), and so on. In fact, ICs may contain anything from one or a few gates (SSI) up to the equivalent of hundreds of thousands of gates (VLSI). Mass production, miniaturization, and standardization means that the number of transistors per IC has increased from tens in the early 1960s to tens of millions in the 1990s. The cost per unit component, on the other hand, has decreased by about the same factor over the same period of time.

The materials employed in the fabrication of these devices are semiconductors. In the early days, germanium (Ge) was used. Nowadays, it is mainly silicon (Si), although a compound known as gallium arsenide (GaAs) is gaining popularity in some specialized applications. GaAs has a high electron mobility and thus results in a higher speed than silicon devices. Its high speed and radiation hardness make it suitable for military and space applications where cost is not a major consideration. Different materials and different technologies result in a wide selection of logic families to suit different applications, each with its advantages and disadvantages.

Silicon devices can be divided into two main categories, depending on the type of transistor used, namely, bipolar and metal oxide semiconductors (MOS). The bipolar family includes transistor transistor logic (TTL), emitter coupled logic (ECL), and integrated injection logic (I^2L) devices. The TTL is the most popular and has a number of subdivisions offering various trade-offs between power dissipation and speed. Generally, the TTL and ECL devices are fast but dissipate more power. This is

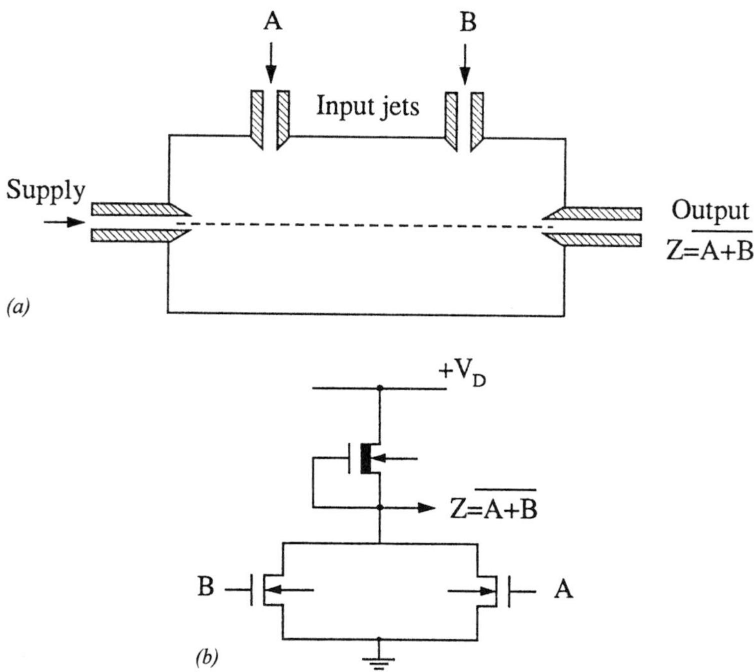

FIGURE 1. *Samples of gates from different technologies. (a) fluid NOR gate; (b) NMOS NOR gate; (c) TTL NAND gate; (d) CMOS NAND gate.*

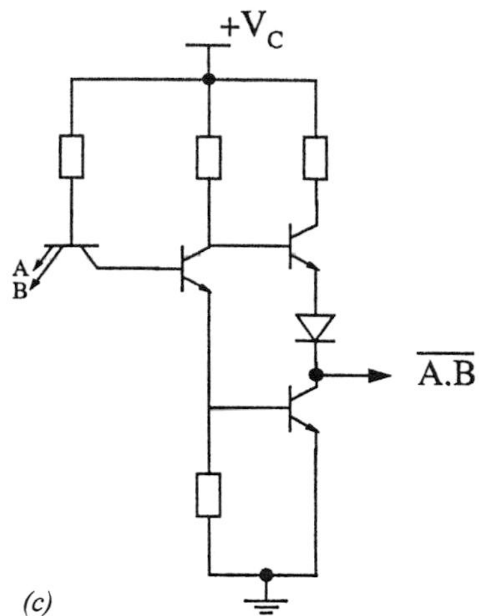

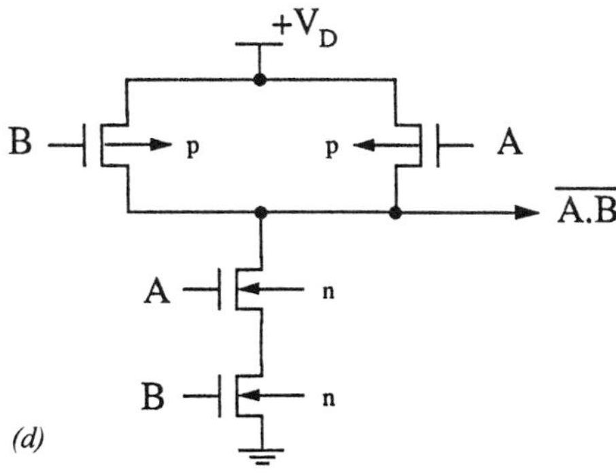

FIGURE 1. (continued).

particularly true for ECL. Except for the I²L, bipolar devices employ resistors as well as transistors, and thus have lower packing density. Depending on their value and the technology used, a resistor may occupy five to ten times the area of a transistor.

Metal oxide semiconductors are subdivided into PMOS, NMOS, and CMOS, depending on whether they use a p-channel transistor, an n-channel transistor, or both. None of these employs resistors. The CMOS technology employs both p- and n-type transistors, a factor that results in low density compared to NMOS. PMOS devices employ p-type transistors in which the carriers are holes rather than electrons. They are therefore slow and not widely used at present. Generally MOS devices have low power dissipation and good noise immunity. CMOS devices in particular are designed to be compatible with TTL devices. Further, their low power dissipation and tolerance to power supply variations make them suitable for battery-operated products.

BOOLEAN LOGIC

Binary operations used in digital circuits, including digital computers, are based on Boolean algebra and are implemented by logic circuits. To understand Boolean algebra and its applications, certain definitions and basic theorems must be introduced.

The basic Boolean operations are the AND, OR, and NOT (complement). NAND, NOR, and exclusive OR (EXOR) can be derived from the first three operations. In digital systems, inputs, outputs, or in fact any variable can be in one of two distinct states—true or false, high or low, and so on. In what follows, symbols 1 and 0 are used to indicate high and low voltage levels, respectively. This is known as positive logic. Although other symbols may used, 1 and 0 are convenient in digital electronic circuits to represent the two voltage levels of 5 and 0 volts that are commonly (although not always) used. The most widely used operations and their symbols are summarized in Table 1. Note that although two inputs are shown, AND, OR, NAND, and NOR can in theory have any number of inputs. It can be seen that the (.), (+), (–), and (⊕) are used to represent AND, OR, complement, and EXOR, respectively. The (.) is sometimes omitted. Table 2 summarizes the most important Boolean postulates and theorems, assuming switching variables *A, B,* and *C.* The last two are known as De Morgan's theorems.

TABLE 1

Operations and their symbols.

INPUTS A B	NOT $\overline{A}$	AND $A.B$	OR $A+B$	NAND $\overline{A.B}$	NOR $\overline{A+B}$	EXOR $A \oplus B$
0 0	1	0	0	1	1	0
0 1	1	0	1	1	0	1
1 0	0	0	1	1	0	1
1 1	0	1	1	0	0	0

TABLE 2

Boolean postulates and theorems.

$\overline{0} = 1$	$A+A = A$
$\overline{1} = 0$	$A+1 = 1$
$0.0 = 0$	$A+0 = A$
$0.1 = 0$	$A+\overline{A} = 1$
$1.1 = 1$	$A.B = B.A$
$0+0 = 0$	$A+B = B+A$
$0+1 = 1$	$A+A.B = A(1+B) = A$
$1+1 = 1$	$A.B+A.C = A(B+C)$
$A.A = A$	$A+B+C = (A+B)+C = A+(B+C)$
$A.1 = A$	$A+\overline{A}.B = \overline{A}.B+A(1+B) = \overline{A}.B+A+A.B$
$A.0 = 0$	$= A+B(\overline{A}+A) = A+B$
$A.\overline{A} = 0$	$\overline{A+B} = \overline{A}.\overline{B}$
$\overline{\overline{A}} = A$	$\overline{A.B} = \overline{A}+\overline{B}$

Combinational Circuits

Logic circuits can be divided into the following two main categories:

1. Combinational circuits, in which the output(s) at any time depend(s) on the inputs at that time.
2. Sequential circuits, in which the output(s) at any time depend(s) on the present as well as past inputs.

COMBINATIONAL LOGIC BASED ON THE INCLUSIVE_OR

The design of a combinational circuit normally starts by a statement specifying the logical behavior of the circuit. From this statement a truth table is derived to indicate the state of the output(s) for all possible input combinations. It is possible that certain input combinations do not occur or that it does not matter whether they do or not. These are known as don't care conditions and are represented by X on the truth table. The don't cares can be used as 1's or 0's, whichever gives a simpler solution. Boolean

TABLE 3

Truth table.

A	B	C	D	PASS	FAIL	TIE
0	0	0	0	0	1	0
0	0	0	1	0	1	0
0	0	1	0	0	1	0
0	0	1	1	0	0	1
0	1	0	0	0	1	0
0	1	0	1	0	0	1
0	1	1	0	0	0	1
0	1	1	1	1	0	0
1	0	0	0	0	1	0
1	0	0	1	0	0	1
1	0	1	0	0	0	1
1	0	1	1	1	0	0
1	1	0	0	0	0	1
1	1	0	1	1	0	0
1	1	1	0	1	0	0
1	1	1	1	1	0	0

equations are then derived, simplified if possible, and implemented using suitable devices. The simplification is only carried out if it is required to minimize the hardware used. This can be achieved using Boolean algebra for small problems. Generally it is more convenient to use Karnaugh maps (K-maps) for functions with up to six variables. If the number of variables is greater than six, such tabular techniques as the Quine-McCluskey method are used. For large logic expressions, it would be desirable to program the Quine-McCluskey method. Quine-McCluskey is particularly suitable for computer implementation and logic functions of up to about fifteen variables.

Normally logic expressions are given as a sum of products as follows:

$$f(x) = \sum_{i=0}^{2^n-1} a_i m_i = a_0 m_0 + a_1 m_1 + \ldots + a_r m_r$$

where m_i are the minterms, $a_i \in \{0,1\}$, and $r = 2^n - 1$ and $a_i = 1$ or 0 to indicate the presence or absence of a minterm, respectively. Minterms are product terms containing all variables in either true or complemented form.

Suppose that it is necessary to design a circuit to indicate pass, fail, or tie when four members of a panel vote for or against a particular test. The members register their votes by the flick of a switch to the yes or no positions. Let the four members be represented by four variables (A, B, C, and D). A yes vote gives a high voltage signal (1), while a no note gives a low voltage signal (0). First a truth table is drawn as shown in Table 3. From the truth table, the following expressions are derived:

$$\text{Pass} = \overline{A}BCD + A\overline{B}CD + AB\overline{C}D + ABC\overline{D} + ABCD$$

$$\text{Fail} = \overline{A}\,\overline{B}\,\overline{C}\,\overline{D} = \overline{A}\,\overline{B}\,\overline{C}D + \overline{A}\,\overline{B}C\overline{D} + \overline{A}B\overline{C}\,\overline{D} + A\overline{B}\,\overline{C}\,\overline{D}$$

$$\text{Tie} = \overline{A}\,\overline{B}CD = \overline{A}B\overline{C}D + \overline{A}BC\overline{D} + A\overline{B}\,\overline{C}D + A\overline{B}C\overline{D} + AB\overline{C}\,\overline{D}$$

These expressions are in sum of products form. A direct implementation of these three output expressions requires sixteen 4-input AND gates plus two 5-input OR gates, plus one 6-input OR gate. If, however, the expressions are entered in K-maps and simplified as shown in Fig. 2 and it is recognized that a tie is neither a pass nor a fail (Fig. 2c shows that the expression for tie does not simplify),

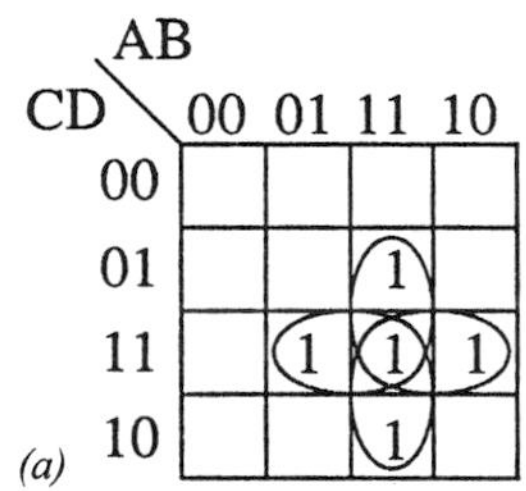

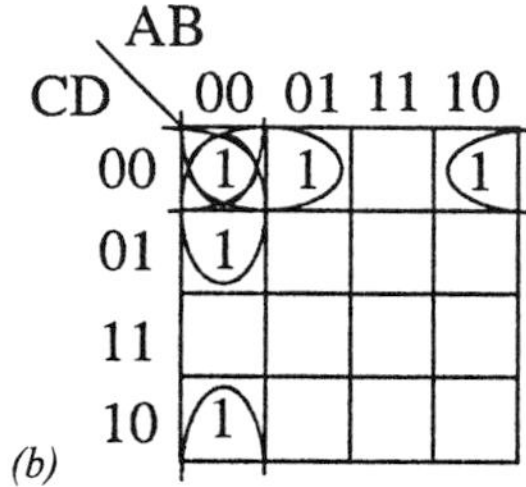

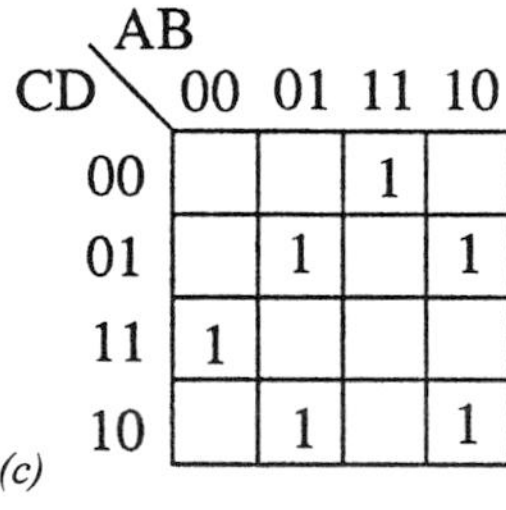

FIGURE 2. *Karnaugh maps and circuit for voting system. (a) K-map for pass; (b) K-map for fail; (c) K-map for tie; (d) logic circuit.*

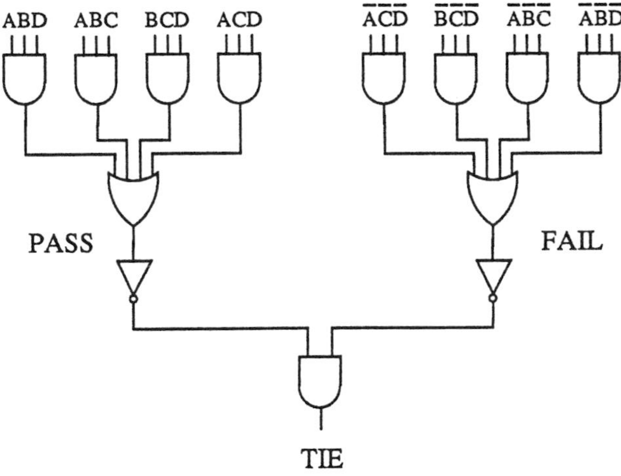

FIGURE 2. (continued).

i.e., Tie = NOT Pass AND NOT Fail,

then the following is obtained

$$\text{Pass} = ABD + ABC + BCD + ACD$$

$$\text{Fail} = \overline{A}\,\overline{C}\,\overline{D} + \overline{A}\,\overline{B}\,\overline{C} + \overline{B}\,\overline{C}\,\overline{D} + \overline{A}\,\overline{B}\,\overline{D}$$

$$\text{Tie} = \overline{\text{Pass}}\,.\,\overline{\text{Fail}}$$

The final circuit in Fig. 2 requires eight 3-input AND gates plus two 4-input OR gates plus two inverters (NOT gates) and one 2-input AND gate, a total of thirteen small gates as compared to nineteen larger gates.

As will be explained below, such equations are commonly realized using programmable logic devices (PLD) such as a programmable logic array (PLA) or a programmable array logic (PAL).

COMBINATIONAL LOGIC BASED ON THE EXCLUSIVE_OR

Combinational logic circuits can also be described in terms of Reed-Muller (RM) expansions. These expansions make use of modulo-2 operations where Galois fields over binary numbers GF(2) are employed.

The basic components used in these circuits are the AND and EXOR gates. It is generally accepted that functions that do not produce efficient solutions using Boolean techniques tend to have efficient solutions using RM techniques and vice versa. Further, RM circuits are easier to test. For any two-valued variable A, $\dot{A}$ is used to represent a logic variable in its true or complemented form. The following can be seen from the definition of the EXOR:

$$
\begin{aligned}
1 \oplus \dot{A} &= \overline{\dot{A}} \\
0 \oplus \dot{A} &= \dot{A} \\
\dot{A} \oplus \dot{A} &= 0 \\
\dot{A} \oplus \dot{A} &= 1 \\
1 \oplus 1 &= 0 \\
\dot{A}(1 \oplus \dot{B}) &= \dot{A} \oplus \dot{A}\dot{B} \\
g \oplus g\dot{A} &= g\overline{\dot{A}} \text{ where } g \text{ is any Boolean function}
\end{aligned}
$$

The associative, distributive, and commutative laws also hold, hence

$$
\begin{aligned}
A \oplus (B \oplus C) &= (A \oplus B) \oplus C = A \oplus B \oplus C \\
A\ (B \oplus C) &= (AB \oplus AC) \\
A \oplus B &= B \oplus A
\end{aligned}
$$

RM expansions can be derived from Boolean equations. Consider the following two variable expressions:

$$f(A_2A_1) = a_0\overline{A}_2\overline{A}_1 + a_1\overline{A}_2A_1 + a_2A_2\overline{A}_1 + a_3A_2A_1$$

Since $m_1.m_j = 0$ for all values of i and j $(i \neq j)$, the OR can be replaced by the EXOR, hence

$$f(A_2A_1) = a_0\overline{A}_2\overline{A}_1 \oplus a_1\overline{A}_2A_1 \oplus a_2A_2\overline{A}_1 \oplus a_3A_2A_1$$

If each $\overline{A}_i$ is replaced by $(A_i \oplus 1)$, the following is obtained:

$$f(A_2A_1) = b_0 \oplus b_1A_1 \oplus b_2A_2 \oplus b_3A_2A_1$$

Like the a coefficients, the b coefficients can be 0 or 1. This can be extended to n variable, giving

$$
\begin{aligned}
f &= \oplus \sum_{i=0}^{2^n-1} b_iP_i \\
&= b_0 \oplus b_1A_1 \oplus b_2A_2 \oplus b_3A_2A_1 \oplus b_4A_3 \oplus \ldots \oplus b_rA_n \ldots A_1 \\
&\quad b_i \in \{0,1\} \text{ and } r = 2^n - 1
\end{aligned}
$$

This is known as the positive (true) RM expansion since all variables appear in true form.

The b and a coefficients are related by a modulo-2 two-variable transform matrix as follows:

$$\begin{bmatrix} b_0 \\ b_1 \\ b_2 \\ b_3 \end{bmatrix} = \begin{bmatrix} 1 & 0 & 0 & 0 \\ 1 & 1 & 0 & 0 \\ 1 & 0 & 1 & 0 \\ 1 & 1 & 1 & 1 \end{bmatrix} \begin{bmatrix} a_0 \\ a_1 \\ a_2 \\ a_3 \end{bmatrix}$$

$$\text{i.e., } b = T_2 a \text{ over } GF(2)$$

$$\text{where } T_n = \begin{bmatrix} T_{n-1} & 0 \\ T_{n-1} & T_{n-1} \end{bmatrix}$$

$$\text{and } T_1 = \begin{bmatrix} 1 & 0 \\ 1 & 1 \end{bmatrix}$$

Conversion between RM and Boolean can be achieved using algebraic manipulation, map methods (similar to K-maps), or tabular techniques.

If all the variables are complemented, a negative polarity results. If each variable can appear in either true or complemented form but not both, then we have a variety of fixed polarity generalized Reed-Muller (GRM) expansions. More expansions result if mixed polarities are allowed where variables can be in true or complemented form. One criterion for the minimization of these expressions is to find the polarity with the least number of terms, although minimizing the number of literals in product terms is also desirable. A number of techniques are available for minimization, including maps (e.g., K-maps) and tabular methods.

MULTILEVEL

The combinational logic circuits explained earlier are in sum of products form. This results in two-level circuits, which are normally AND/OR, although NAND or NOR gates may be used. Using algebraic tools such as decomposition, extraction, factorization, substitution, and collapsing, the logic can be transformed into multilevel form. Multilevel realizations are the preferred means of implementing large logic systems. They give more degrees of freedom in implementing Boolean functions and increase the potential for reusing subcircuits. To illustrate this, consider the following expression:

$$F = ABC + ABD + \overline{A}\,\overline{C}\,\overline{D} + \overline{B}\,\overline{C}\,\overline{D}$$

$$\text{Let } X = AB$$

$$Y = C + D$$

$$\text{Then } F = XY + \overline{XY}$$

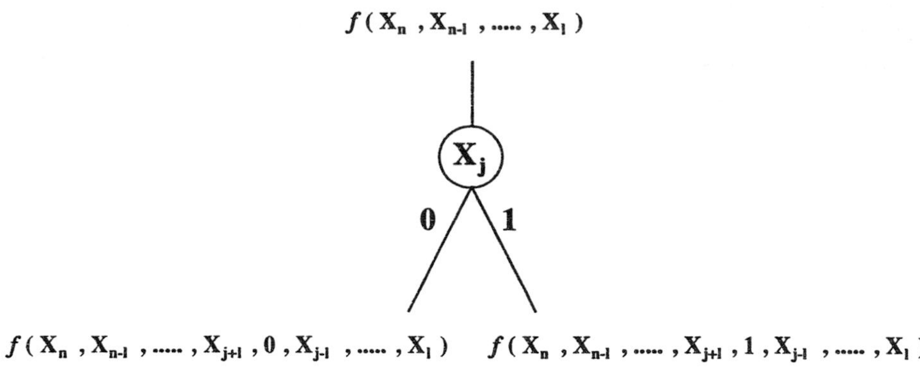

FIGURE 3. *Nonterminal node of Boolean function.*

This creates two new nodes *X* and *Y* which can connect to other nodes. This type of decomposition can be adapted to the exclusive_OR case.

Binary Decision Diagrams (BDDs)

The BDD is a popular tool for multilevel synthesis. It facilities sharing and its use can be extended to multi-outputs. The BDD is derived by repeated applications of Shannon's expansion theorem. Consider any n-variable function given in sum of minterms form. The function is expanded with respect to any variable x_j as follows:

$$f = \bar{x}_j f\,(x_n, \ldots, x_{j+1}, 0, x_{j-1}, \ldots, x_1) + \\ x_j f\,(x_n, \ldots, x_{j+1}, 1, x_{j-1}, \ldots, x_1) +$$

This can be represented as shown in Fig. 3. The subfunctions shown in parentheses are independent of x_j and may be expanded with respect to another variable. This is repeated until the subfunctions are reduced to logical constants having ones and zeros. These are known as terminal nodes.

Consider a three-variable logic function as follows:

$$f = \bar{x}_3\bar{x}_2\bar{x}_1 + x_3\bar{x}_2\bar{x}_1 + x_3\bar{x}_2x_1 + x_3x_2\bar{x}_1 + x_3x_2x_1$$

If the function is expanded with respect to x_1 first, then

$$f = \bar{x}_1(\bar{x}_3\bar{x}_2 + x_3\bar{x}_2 + x_3x_2) + x_1(x_3\bar{x}_2 + x_3x_2)$$

The subfunctions, shown in parentheses, are then expanded with respect to x_2 and x_3 and drawn as shown in Fig. 4a. It should be noted that each nonterminal node, shown as a circle, can be implemented using a 2 : 1 multiplexer with the variable in the circle acting as the control input. This device is also known as the 2-variable universal logic module (ULM), since it can implement any two-variable logic functions. In fact, it can be made using two-level AND/OR logic. Since each nonterminal node requires one ULM, effort is made to reduce their number using such standard rules as deletion and merger, as shown in Fig. 4b and Fig. 4c. This results in a reduced ordered binary

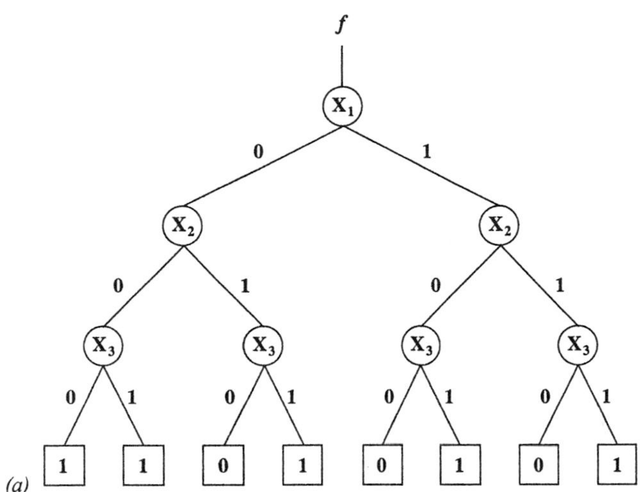

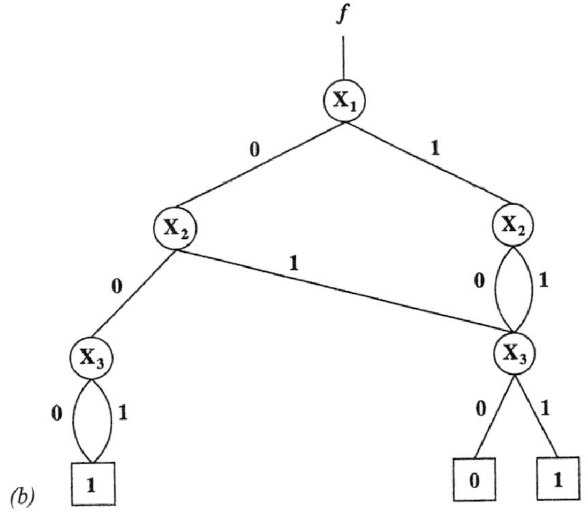

FIGURE 4. *A BDD for the design example. (a) binary decision tree; (b) reduction of redundant and insomorphic branches; (c) reduced ordered BDD.*

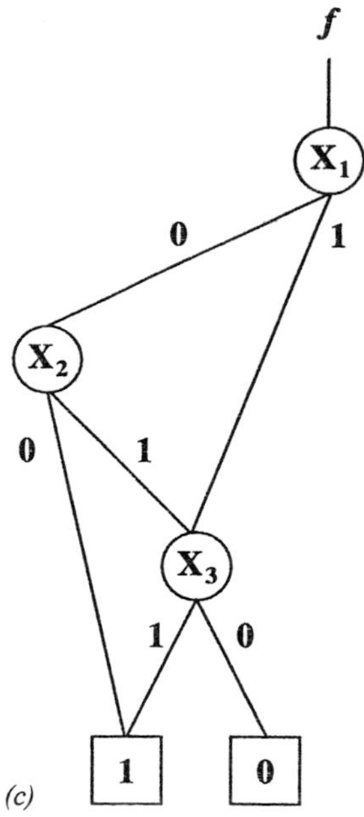

FIGURE 4. (continued).

decision diagram (ROBDD)—ordered since the same variable is used at any one level. It is known that different variable orders result in different ROBDDs, which may require more or fewer ULMs. Unfortunately, there is no easy way of finding the best variable order at present.

Finally, it should be noted that the same technique can be employed for the exclusive OR domain. The resulting structures are known as Reed_Muller BDDs (RMBDD) or functional BDDs (FBDD).

Sequential Circuits

In sequential circuits, also known as finite-state machines, the outputs at any time depend on the primary inputs applied at that time (present inputs) as well as previous inputs. Sequential circuits therefore consist of combinational logic and storage devices to remember previous inputs. This implies that the same input may produce different outputs, depending on the state of the circuit at the time the input is applied. The variables representing previous inputs or the state of the circuit are called state or secondary variables, to distinguish them from the primary (external) inputs. States that are defined by the state variables and primary inputs are called the total states, and there are up to 2^{S+P} of these. Variables S and P represent the numbers of state and primary inputs, respectively. The next state S_{t+1} is uniquely determined by the present state S_t and present input Y_t, hence

$$S_{t+1} = f(S_t,Y_t)$$

where f is the state transition function.

Present and next states can also be represented by S and S_+, respectively. If the output (primary output) Z_t is a function of the present state only, the circuit is known as a Moore machine, hence

$$Z_t = g(S_t)$$

where g is the output transition function.

If the output Z_t is a function of the primary inputs as well as the present state, the circuit is known as a Mealy machine, hence

$$Z_t = g(S_t,Y_t)$$

This implies that for every present state and input there may be a unique next state and output. In some cases, such as binary counters, the outputs may be the same as the next states. The next states are delayed and fed back to become the present states for the next cycle. If the memory devices (flip-flops) are controlled by a clock pulse such that changes only occur at specified times, the circuit is called synchronous; otherwise, it is asynchronous. Figure 5 shows a block diagram of a synchronous sequential circuit.

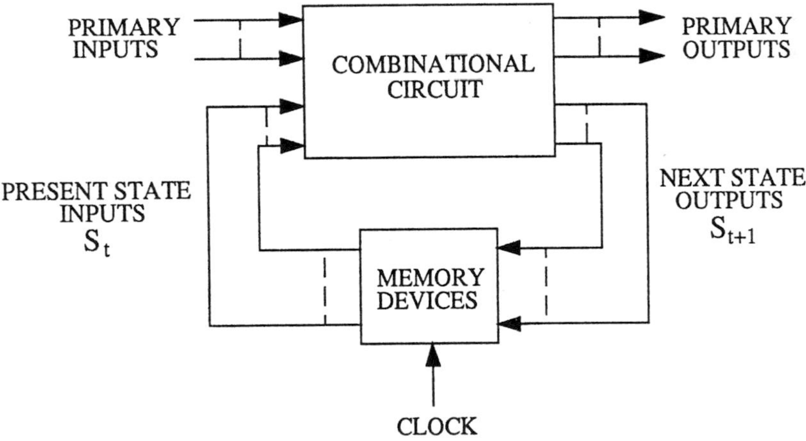

FIGURE 5. *Block diagram for a synchronous sequential system.*

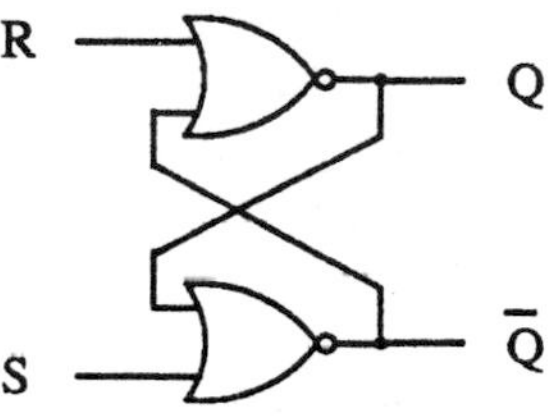

FIGURE 6. *Simple SR flip-flop.*

STORAGE DEVICES

The storage devices used to remember the state of the circuit are known as flip-flops (FF). Their outputs can change from one state to another, upon receiving the appropriate input signals. Each FF is capable of storing one bit (0 or 1). The four common types available are SR, JK, D, and T FFs.

A basic circuit of the SR/FF is given in Fig. 6, in which Q and $\overline{Q}$ are the output and its complement. A high signal on input S sets the output to 1, while a high signal on R resets it to 0. Both are stable states. Practical devices may have more complex circuits and other inputs, such as clock, preset, and clear. The preset and clear, if available, are known as asynchronous inputs because they are independent of the clock. S and R cannot be 1 simultaneously. The state equation relating the next state $Q+$ to the present state Q is given by

$$Q_+ = S + \overline{R}Q$$

The JK/FF is similar to the SR/FF with J and K replacing S and R, respectively, except that when $J = K = 1$, the output changes state. The state equation is given by

$$Q_+ = J\overline{Q} + \overline{K}Q$$

The D/FF is a delay FF with a single input D. The output assumes the value of the input when the device is clocked. The state equation is given by

$$Q_+ = D$$

The T/FF is a toggle device with a single input T. Each time an input pulse is received at T, the device changes state when clocked. The state equation is given by

$$Q_+ = \overline{Q}T + Q\overline{T}$$

Memory registers, shift registers, counters, and similar devices can be constructed by connecting FFs to each other, sometimes with additional logic gates. With n FFs it is possible to store n bits of data or count in binary from 0 to $2^n - 1$. Sequential circuits are generally synchronous (clocked). Asynchronous (unclocked) can be faster since they do not have to wait for clock pulses to change their states. This, however, increases the probability of malfunction. Variations in delays along different signal paths mean that the circuit may end up in a different state from what was intended. One must have a good reason to use unclocked circuits.

SYNTHESIS OF SEQUENTIAL CIRCUITS

Sequential circuits can in some cases be designed intuitively. For complex circuits, a systematic design procedure should be followed. Generally the starting point is a design specification in the form of statements. From this a state diagram and a state table are derived. Figure 7 and Table 4 show a two-state diagram and table for the JK/FF, which is a simple sequential circuit. The two circles labeled A and B correspond to states 0 and 1, respectively. In this case the next state is itself the output. The inputs on J and K that cause the transition are shown on the arcs. For example, $JK = 10$ or 11 will cause a transition from A to B.

The number of states may be minimized using standard procedures. The states are then given a state assignment (binary code). The assignment may be arbitrary, although techniques are available for finding economic assignments. At this stage a decision is made as to what FFs and other hardware are to be used. State and output equations are then derived. These may be minimized using K-maps or other methods before the circuit is implemented. Because different FFs behave differently, design

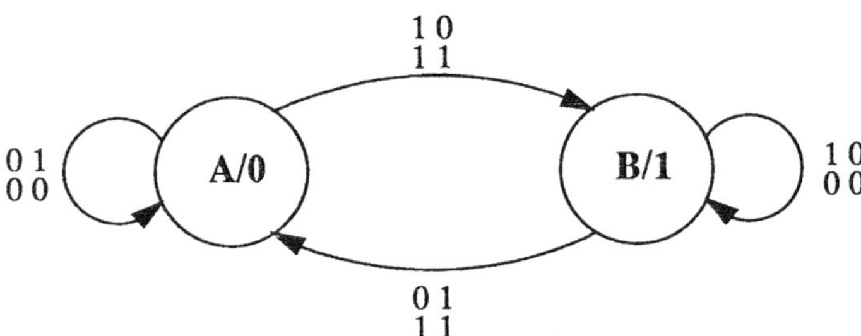

FIGURE 7. *State diagram for the JK flip-flop (Moore model).*

TABLE 4

Two-State diagram for the JK/FF.

PRESENT STATE	NEXT STATE/OUTPUT JK=00	01	10	11
A	A/0	A/0	B/1	B/1
B	B/1	A/0	B/1	A/0

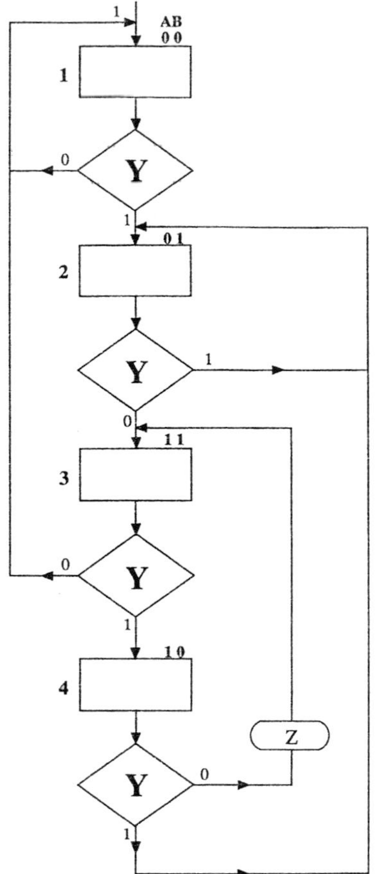

FIGURE 8. *ASM chart for the design example.*

procedures must be modified accordingly. Due to space limitations, the design method selected here is based on the algorithmic state machine (ASM) technique rather than on traditional methods. *D* FFs will be used to illustrate the procedure, although any of the others can be used.

Consider the following statement: A circuit is required to produce an output of 1 when the sequence 1010 is detected in a serial stream of data.

First an ASM chart is drawn, showing states and transitions. This is similar to the state diagram except that state boxes are used to represent the states and their codes. Outputs depending on the states only, if any, are shown inside these boxes; otherwise, they are shown in conditional output blocks, as shown in Fig. 8. Decision boxes show relevant inputs as opposed to all possible input combinations in the traditional state tables. This makes the technique more efficient for large practical designs.

The ASM chart shows four distinct states, numbered 1 to 4. Two FFs named *A* and

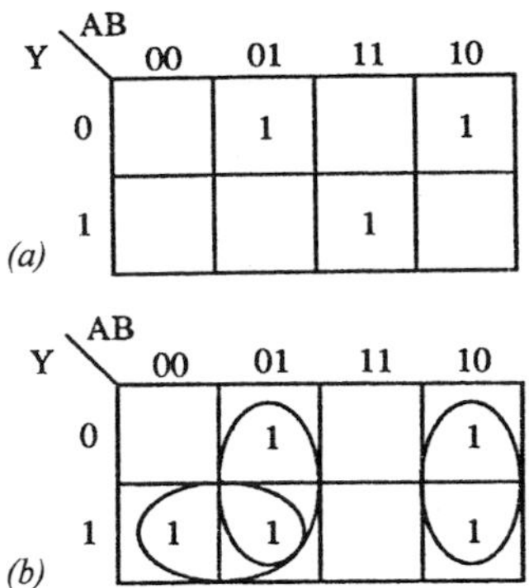

FIGURE 9. *Karnaugh map for the design example. (a) K-map for D_A; (b) K-map for D_B.*

B have a total $2^2 = 4$ possible state codes, namely 00, 01, 11, and 10. The input and output variables are labeled Y and Z, respectively. The reader may observe a typical design problem, which arises due to inadequate design specifications. In this case, it is assumed that patterns may overlap, hence 101010 produces two outputs. Should data not be overlapping blocks of four digits, the circuit would return to state 1 after state 4. (See ASM chart.) This was not clear from the original specifications.

Remember that the next state of a D/FF is the same as the present input. For FF A, therefore, the states where A is equal to 1 are identified, and terms representing the link paths leading to these states are ORed, hence

$$A_+ = D_A = \overline{A}B\overline{Y} + ABY + A\overline{B}\,\overline{Y}$$

similarly for flip-flop B

$$B_+ = D_B = \overline{A}\,\overline{B}Y + \overline{A}B\overline{Y} + \overline{A}BY + A\overline{B}\,\overline{Y} + A\overline{B}Y$$

$$\text{Output } Z = A\overline{B}\,\overline{Y}$$

The expressions for D_A and D_B are entered on K-maps, as shown in Fig. 9.

D_A does not simplify, but D_B reduces to the following:

$$D_B = A\overline{B} + \overline{A}B + \overline{A}Y$$

These expressions are implemented as shown in Fig. 10.

It should be emphasized that a design such as this is often implemented using PLDs. Registered PALs, for example, have AND/OR logic and D FFs on the chip and can be programmed by the user, provided she or he has access to a suitable programmer.

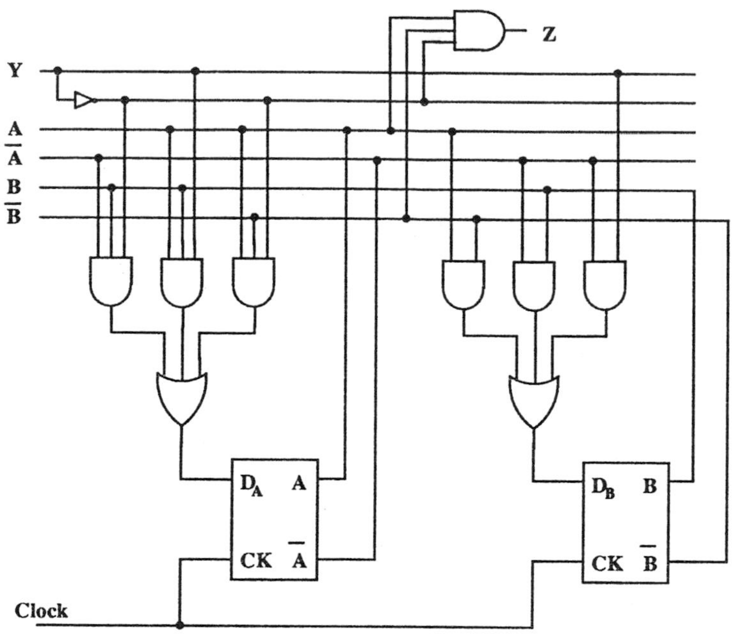

FIGURE 10. *Circuit diagram for the design example.*

LINEAR SEQUENTIAL CIRCUITS

Linear sequential circuits are finite-state machines with a finite number of inputs and outputs. The inputs, outputs, and state transitions occur at discrete intervals of time. Only linear components are used in these circuits. These are the modulo-2 adders (EXOR) and the unit delays (D FFs). The main feature of linear devices is that they preserve the principle of superposition. In other words, the output due to a number of input components is the sum of the outputs due to the input components acting separately. It should be noted that other logic devices such as AND, OR, NAND, and NOR are not linear.

The output of the unit delay assumes the value of its input when clocked. This can be represented by a D operator. The output Z of the unit delay is a delayed version of its input X, hence

$$Z = DX$$

For n-unit delays

$$Z = D^n X$$

Two types of linear sequential circuits will be described.

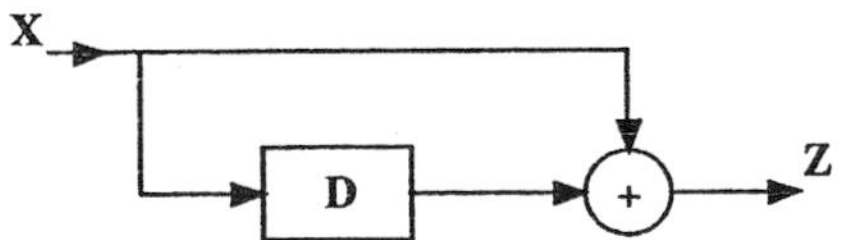

FIGURE 11. *A simple feedforward circuit.*

Feedforward Linear Binary Circuits

Figure 11 shows the simplest feedforward circuit with a single input and a single output. The output is the modulo-2 sum of the input and the delayed version of the same input.

$$\begin{aligned} Z &= X \oplus DX \\ &= X\,(1 \oplus D) \end{aligned}$$

The circuit has a transfer function $T(D)$ given by

$$T(D) = \frac{Z}{X} = 1 \oplus D$$

If the input consists of a binary sequence of 1's and 0's, it can be expressed by a polynomial in which the 1's and 0's are coefficients of the powers of a dummy variable. The sequence 1101 can be represented by the polynomial

$$1D^3 \oplus 1D^2 \oplus 0D^1 \oplus 1D^0$$

which simplifies to

$$D^3 \oplus D^2 \oplus 1$$

If this sequence is now applied to the circuit of Fig. 11, the output is the modulo-2 product of the input polynomial and the transfer function of the circuit.

Multiplication and division follow the normal rules, except that modulo-2 addition/ subtraction are employed. Addition and subtraction of modulo-2 polynomials are the same.

For example

$$D^2 \oplus D^2 = D^2 \theta D^2 = 0$$

$$D^3 \oplus D^3 \oplus D^3 = D^3$$

The circuit of Fig. 12 multiples the input polynomial by its transfer function, which is $1 \oplus D \oplus D^3$.

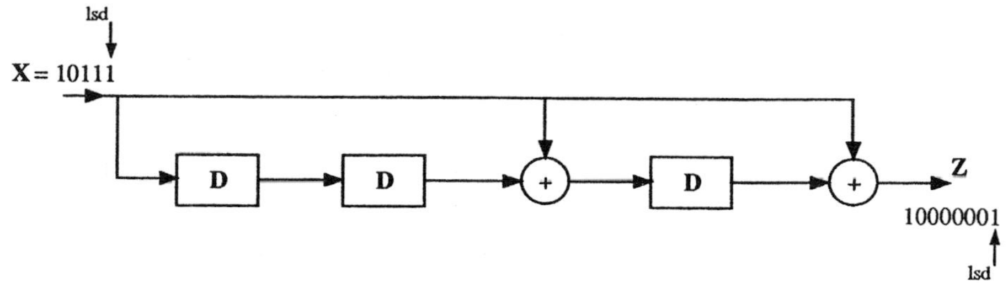

FIGURE 12. *Example of a feedforward circuit.*

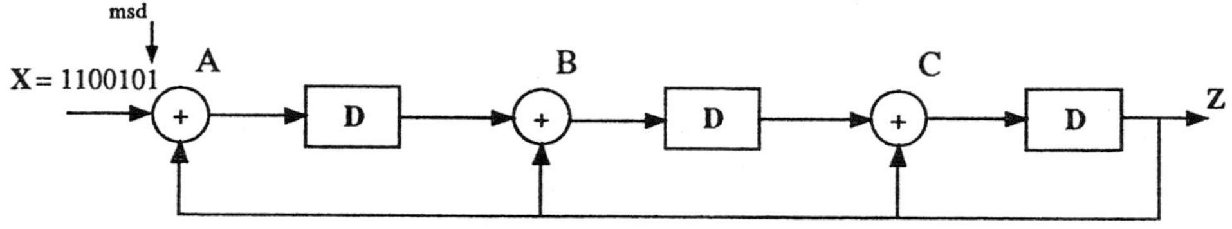

FIGURE 13. *Example of a feedback circuit.*

$$Z = (1 \oplus D \oplus D^3)(1 \oplus D \oplus D^2 \oplus D^4)$$
$$= 1 \oplus D^7$$

Other circuit configurations are also possible.

Feedback Linear Binary Circuits

Feedback circuits can be used for polynomial division. Different configurations are possible, but for the circuit given in Fig. 13, the most significant digit (msd) is fed in first, the msd of the quotient is delivered first, and the remainder is left in the register at the end of the division cycle with the msd to the right.

The circuit in Fig. 13 divides the input polynomial $1 \oplus D \oplus D^4 \oplus D^6$ in this case by the polynomial of the circuit, which is $1 \oplus D \oplus D^2 \oplus D^3$, giving output Z and remainder R.

$$Z = D^3 \oplus D^2 \oplus D \oplus 1$$
$$R = D^2 \oplus D$$

Note that the circuit can be modified as required by adding more stages and/or changing the tapings. For example, by removing EXOR C and its feedback connection, the polynomial describing the circuit changes to $1 \oplus D \oplus D^3$. The polynomial becomes $1 \oplus D^2 \oplus D^3$ if EXOR B is removed instead of C. These circuits are extensively used in coding and decoding circuits for error detection and correction in digital communication systems. It should be noted that the internal stages of the shift

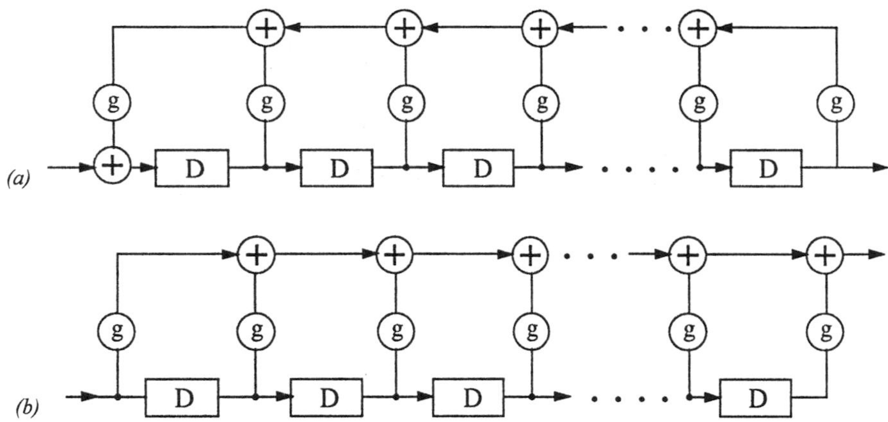

FIGURE 14. *(a) A general linear feedback circuit; (b) a general linear feedforward circuit.*

register (FFs) are actually modified. Alternative circuits are available in which the shift registers are read-only but not modified.

Figure 14a shows a general feedback circuit that is read-only and that is a member of the recursive digital filters family. Similarly, Fig. 14b shows a feedforward circuit, which is also known as a nonrecursive filter. The *g* coefficients indicate the presence or absence of tap connections.

Current Trends

LEVELS OF INTEGRATION

Digital circuits can be implemented using standard ICs on a circuit board. Many circuits can also be implemented in whole or in part, using such PLDs as PROMs, PALs, and PLAs. These can normally replace tens of SSI devices, such as gates and FFs. The PLDs are available in different sizes and configurations for either combinational or sequential circuits. Some of these devices can be erased and reprogrammed, which is convenient for prototype applications. PALs and PLAs are more suitable for random logic applications than the ROM/PROM families because they can implement a minimized sum of products expressions. Figure 15 shows part of a commercial PAL programmed to implement the circuit given in Fig. 10. This is achieved by entering the equation to the PAL programmer. The programmer produces a fuse pattern that is used to blow unwanted fuses. The connections marked (•) in Fig. 15 indicate intact fuses (connections). PAL devices are available in different sizes and configurations to suit different applications.

Once a design is tried and tested, it may be desirable to put it on a single chip. This has the advantages of small size, low power, reliability (fewer connections to go wrong) and security (difficult to copy). The cheapest route is the gate array. Gate arrays are

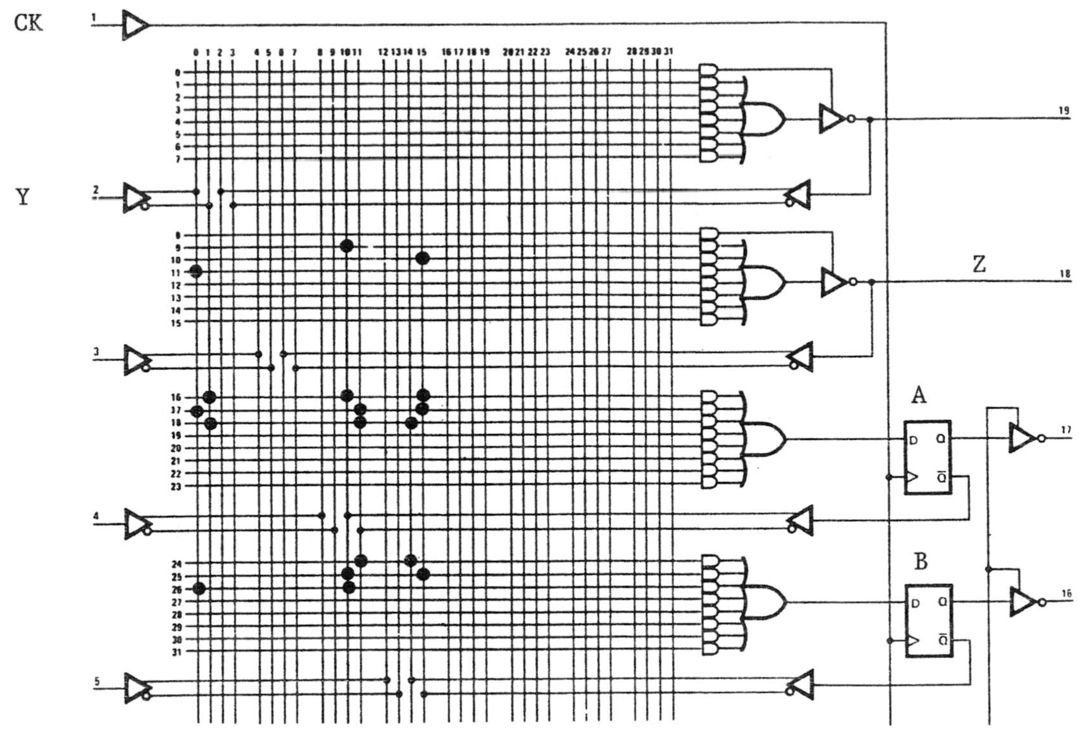

FIGURE 15. *PAL implementation of the sequential circuit in Fig. 10.*

standard ICs that are fully fabricated except for the last layer of interconnections. They have the equivalent of hundreds or thousands of gates on a single chip. They consist of identical cells, normally arranged in rows separated by channels for wiring and surrounded by input and output peripherals. The cells contain transistors and possibly resistors which can be connected as desired by the user. Electronic computer-aided design (ECAD) tools are used in these applications to enter the design (schematic capture) and simulate it to ensure that it would work correctly after fabrication. The computer will then place the components and route the design. Files will be generated that can be used for the final metallization stage. Typically 50 to 90 percent of the components on the chip are utilized, depending on the regularity of the design and the ECAD software used. The whole cycle can be completed in weeks. The gate array approach is known as semicustom. Field-programmable gate arrays (FPGA) are now available. These can be programmed by the user and reprogrammed if necessary, which is convenient for experimentation purposes. Assuming that a suitable programmer and ECAD tools are available, an average design can be implemented in one day.

The next level of integration is known as full custom. This is expensive and requires a full set of masks for fabrication, which may be anything from seven to fourteen, depending on the technology employed. A design may take a year or more to complete using the full-custom approach, and can only be justified for specialized applications or if the product is mass-produced. In some cases standard cells may be utilized. These are standard components already designed and tested, stored on a computer library. Custom-built chips are more efficient in terms of silicon utilization, as there are no wasted components, and result in a hand-tailed product. It must be appreciated that present-day VLSI devices with hundreds of thousands of components on a few square millimeters of silicon would not be possible without ECAD tools. A myriad of ECAD software packages are now available from a large number of suppliers.

One consequence of designing at the VLSI level is that the traditional minimization techniques described earlier may not be relevant. This is partly because the tools cannot cope with large multi-output logic systems and partly because the saving of a few gates at the VLSI level becomes insignificant, considering the cost of a gate.

Another approach that is gaining popularity is the synthesis from behavioral description. These formal methods of design require that the design description should be at a higher level of abstraction and the specifications of the design be formal and mathematically rigorous. Essentially the circuit is described in software rather than a schematic diagram. The most popular tool at present is known as VHDL. This stands for very large scale integration hardware descriptor language.

TESTABILITY

The rapid increase in circuit complexity, especially at the VLSI level, means that testability is becoming a major issue. It is no longer acceptable to design a circuit and leave the testing for someone else. The designer must take testability into account at an early stage and ensure that the circuit can be easily tested.

Electronic circuits are tested by applying signal waveforms to their inputs and observing the outputs. For digital circuits, the test patterns are binary vectors applied in succession. As the number of inputs increases, full functional testing becomes impractical. A circuit with n inputs will have a truth table with 2^n entries. At one test per μs, it would take thirty-six years to test a circuit with fifty inputs. The problem gets worse if the circuit is sequential. A popular fault effect model is the stuck-at model, where no single connection is stuck at zero (sa0) or one (sa1). This structured test normally reduces the number of tests to $2n$.

Because of feedback, testing of the sequential circuit is more complex. One approach for solving the problem is the design for testability. In this case the circuit is designed in such a way to simplify and minimize testing effort. The requirement is to increase the controllability and observability of the internal nodes with a minimal increase in the number of input and output pins.

Figure 16 shows the scan-in scan-out (SISO) approach. The diagram shows multiplexers inserted in front of the FFs

$M = 0$ gives normal operational mode

$M = 1$ puts the circuit in scan mode

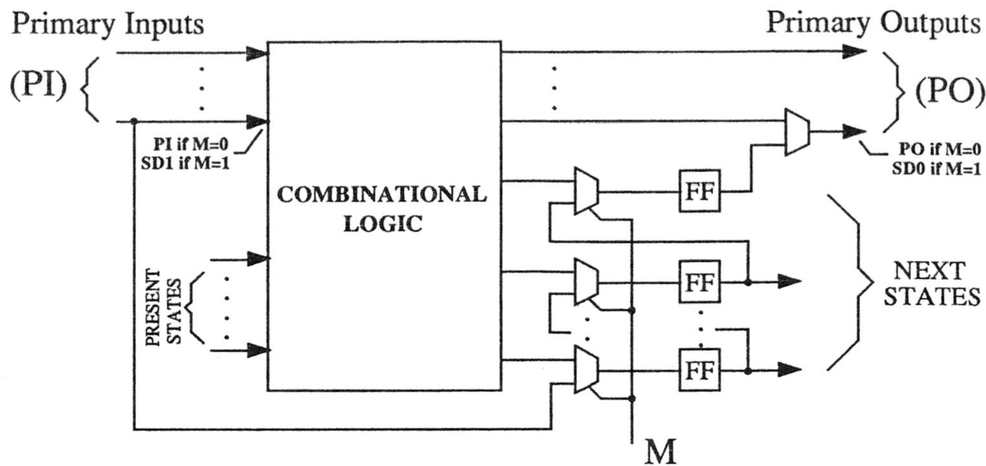

FIGURE 16. *Scan-in scan-out arrangement.*

In the scan mode the circuit is directly controllable by shifting in the required set values through the shift data in (SDI) and observable by shifting the content of the FFs through the shift data out (SDO). By carefully choosing test vectors, it is possible to make each FF go through the required transitions. Since the operational and test modes are never used simultaneously, SDI and SDO can share primary input and output pins with the circuit. Such test facilities add an overhead of about 5 to 20 percent.

Another approach is to design self-testing circuits. This is achieved by built-in testing facilities. This has the advantage of simplifying field services and maintenance. A common approach is the signature analysis based on the use of a source of test stimuli built on to the chip or PCB. This is simply a linear feedback shift register (FSR) that generates a pseudorandom sequence. If the output of the circuit shown in Fig. 17 is EXORed with the signal undertest, then the content of the register is modified in some way characteristic of the signal undertest. The modified bit pattern is the

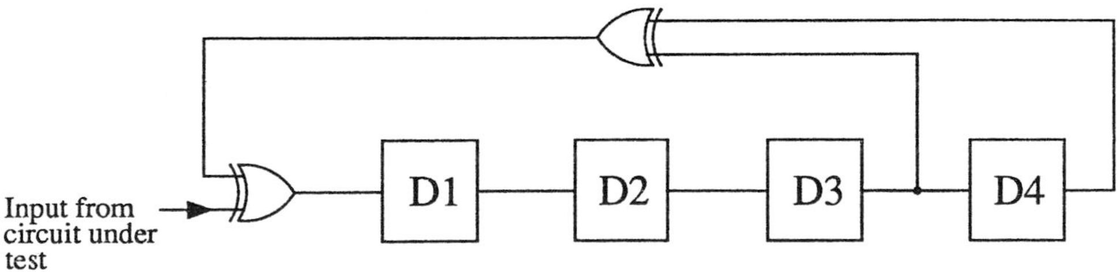

FIGURE 17. *A simple signature analysis arrangement.*

signature of the input source. If the procedure is repeated with a signal from a faulty circuit, then after the prescribed number of cycles the pattern generated is different from the fault-free signature, thus identifying a faulty circuit. Another commonly used facility is known as the built-in logic block observer (BILBO), which combines self-test and signature analysis. The built-in test strategy for VLSI chips is based on the idea that test patterns are generated and responses evaluated on the chip. This strategy must be balanced by the requirement to keep the silicon area and additional pins to a minimum.

BIBLIOGRAPHY

Almaini, A. E. A. *Electronic Logic Systems,* 3rd. ed., Prentice Hall, 1994.
Daniels, J. D. *Digital Design from Zero to One,* Wiley, 1996.
Dueck, R. K. *Fundamentals of Digital Electronics,* West, 1994.
Hill, F. J. and Peterson, G. R. *Computer Aided Logical Design with Emphasis on VLSI,* 4th ed., Wiley, 1993.
Pappas, N. L. *Digital Design,* West, 1994.
Roth, C. H. Jr. *Fundamentals of Logic Design,* 4th ed., West, 1992.

A. E. A. ALMAINI

METHODOLOGY FOR DOCUMENT ANALYSIS

Introduction

Information technology has provided powerful tools for document management; for example, word processors, computer-aided design (CAD) tools, and different E-mail, group support, archiving, and publishing systems. The acquisition of a new system in an organization usually solves problems of a subset of workers in some specific tasks. A new software system may enable an increase in the productivity of individuals in an organization but not necessarily an increase in the productivity of the organization as a whole. The acquisition of a new system has rarely been planned from the point of view of information management and business processes. Various incompatible systems have been supplied for different document management activities. As a result, much of the collective knowledge of organizations is stored in incompatible digital documents on different digital storage media. The current trends toward internationalization, networking, fusioning, and alliancing lead to the accumulation of incompatibility and information management problems.

The utilization of information in documents is currently much more technology-dependent than during the era of paper-based document management. Applications are platform-dependent, and documents are in most cases application-dependent. Information in digital documents is lost if the documents cannot be found or if they cannot be presented to human perception (*1*). Many such problems concern service-sector organizations (e.g., libraries) as well. Application dependency, inconsistencies, and problems in maintaining long-term access to digital documents are all well known in libraries and archives.

Many enterprises have begun major projects to turn their electronic document management (EDM) environments into environments with standardized information structures and effective utilization capabilities. The goal is to improve the quality of EDM and to improve the generation of business value by EDM (*2*). An EDM development project is usually also a *standardization* project, in which the intent is to agree upon rules that define the way information is represented in documents. Continuous Acquisition and Lifecycle Support (CALS) is an example of an international program to support enterprises in their EDM reengineering projects (*3*). The program has been initiated by the U.S. Department of Defense and is intended to support the standardization of EDM in both the armed forces and industry. In EDM reengineering and standardization projects, a profound *document analysis* is needed. In such an analysis, current documents and document management practices are studied and described and new document structures and document management practices are proposed.

In a standardization project of an organization or a group of organizations, the primary concern in document analysis is in the documents produced within the organizations. On the other hand, EDM development can also be important in cases in which there is little internal document production. For example, libraries interested in improving the quality of their digital library services need rather profound analysis concerning both the primary documents created outside the library and the secondary documents created within the library, which contain meta information about the primary documents. A library can also participate in an EDM development project as an expert on reader needs. For example, in a project standardizing documents created in the Finnish parliament and ministries, the Library of Parliament has provided valuable information about readers of documents and reader needs.

EDM Concepts

In EDM development and document standardization, organizations are interested in documents as a means of human information management: a means to cluster, organize, store, and transfer information. In particular they are interested in using computers and the digital form for information management. The content of a digital document may be authored by humans or by a computer, but the content is always intended for human perception. There is therefore a need for associated hardware, software, and at least one specified external representation for the content. When the notion of information is understood according to the sense-making theory of Dervin (*4*), as "the sense created in a situation, at a specific moment in time and space by a reader" (by which Dervin means a human reader), then the information in a document is always subjective. In this article, the following characteristics are regarded as essential to a *document*:

- It is intended for human perception, to be understood as information pertaining to a topic.
- It has content and one or more external representations.
- The content consists of parts, parts consist of symbols, and parts are structured to support human understanding.
- It is stored on media.
- It can be identified and handled as a unit.

Additional characteristics of a *digital document* are:

- The content is stored on digital media.
- The document is associated with hardware and software that can identify from the digital content the symbols and the structure of the parts and produce from them external representation to be perceived by humans.

Electronic document management in an enterprise does not only concern documents. Figure 1 shows the major EDM components (*5*). There are basically two types of entities in an EDM environment: activities and resources. The *resources* are of three different types: actors, documents, and systems. An *actor* is an organization or a person. *Systems* consist of devices, software, and data used to support the performance of activities. Out of all the recorded data in an environment, documents are those possessing the characteristics listed above. An *activity* is a set of actions performed by one or more actors. The broken lines in Fig. 1 show the information flow between activities and resources. Resources are regarded as information repositories in which the information produced in an activity can be stored or from which information can be taken and used in an activity. Information needed and produced during activities is stored in documents, in the heads and experience of people, in the organizational culture, and in systems. *Information* is thus anything that can be stored in a repository and used in an activity, or that can be produced by an activity and stored in a repository to be later used in an activity (probably in some other environment). In relationship to documents and systems, actors are called *users.*

An EDM environment may be a single organization. In the current networked world, however, business processes usually concern several organizations, and resources are more or less shared by those organizations. The EDM environments in which a specific organization or person is involved thus may be quite complex, and the information in an activity making sense to a human actor often comes from many different sources.

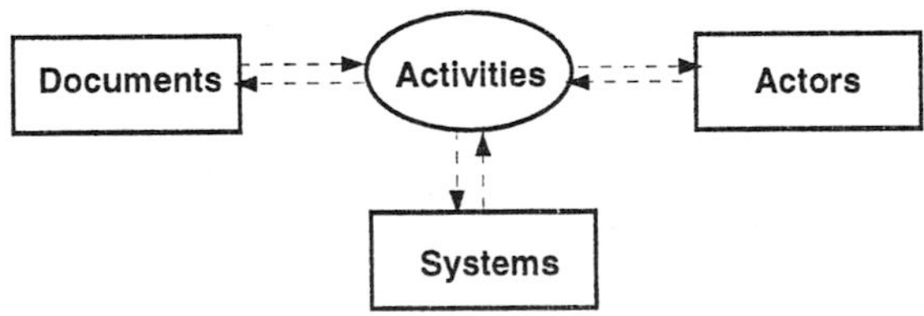

FIGURE 1. *Components of an electronic document management environment.*

Document Analysis as Part of Document Standardization

One of the approaches to solving the problems discussed in the introduction is document standardization using application-independent standard formats. In standardization the idea is to plan digital information structures and formats, taking into account future changes in systems instead of planning them for a specific software system. The rules associated with a document, document authoring, and the storage format are intended to help consistent understanding of the content by the authors and different readers, and also in situations in which the software and hardware changes. Sprague (*2*) suggests the development of an EDM strategy in an organization. Standardization can be taken as such a strategy.

STRUCTURED DOCUMENTS

The Standard Generalized Markup Language (SGML) is an international standard for defining and representing documents in an application-independent form (*6*). The standard is based on the idea of *structured documents*; before creating documents, their logical structure is first defined in a *Document Type Definition* (DTD). In the DTD, the hierarchic structure of the parts of a document is specified, and possible attributes are associated with those parts to add extra semantic information. In the case of documents, the structure and attribute values are indicated by markup. The Document Style Semantics and Specification Language (DSSSL) is a language used for defining a layout for documents with a specific DTD in a standard way (*7*). The Hypertext Markup Language (HTML) is an SGML application used in Internet publishing. Another more advanced standard intended for information distribution and transfer on the Internet is a new standard XML (Extensible Markup Language) developed by the WWW Consortium (*8*). The XML is a subset of SGML and allows documents in which the hierarchic structure is indicated by markup without associated DTD. The XML forms the nucleus of a planned standard family whose other important members are the languages for defining styles and hypertext links.

Factors supporting the use of SGML as a document format are discussed, for example, in the articles by Barron (*9*) and DeRose et al. (*10*). The following have been important objectives for Finnish companies and public sector organizations when embarking on SGML standardization projects (*11*):

- SGML supports long-term information deposit by internationally agreed-upon application-independent rules for defining and representing information structures.
- The production of different forms from the same content can be automated; for example, the HTML format needed for Internet distribution can be dynamically created from the same recorded content from which the paper document is printed.
- Advanced query facilities can be developed with different views for different groups of users.

RASKE AS A STANDARDIZATION PROJECT

One example of a standardization project is RASKE. The term RASKE comes from the Finnish words *Rakenteisten AsiakirjaStandardien KEhittäminen,* meaning the development of standards for structured documents. The project was commenced in spring 1994 by the Finnish Parliament and a software company in cooperation with researchers at the University of Jyväskylä (*12*). The Ministry of Foreign Affairs, the Ministry of Finance, the prime minister's office, and a publishing house also participated in the project.

The RASKE project was motivated by document management problems in the Finnish Parliament and government. Teams studying the legislative work carried out in Parliament identified, for example, the following problems concerning document management (*13*):

1. Incompatibilities of the systems used caused the need for repeated typing of the same piece of text, which in turn was a potential source of inconsistencies in documents.
2. Inconsistencies in document naming and document identifiers caused problems and extra work.
3. There was a lack of information management coordination between the ministries and between the government and Parliament.
4. In spite of the fact that almost all of the documents were digital, documents were mostly distributed on paper.
5. The retrieval techniques of different systems were heterogeneous.
6. The retrieval techniques of the electronic archiving system and the tracking system of Parliament were not satisfactory.
7. The future usability of the information in the archived digital documents was uncertain.

The document analysis in the RASKE project concerned four domains: the inquiry process, national legislative work, Finnish participation in the European Union legislative work, and the creation of the state budget. During the case analyses, various methods of analysis were tested and developed. Preliminary DTDs were designed for twenty-one document types, including, for example, government bill, government decision, government communication, private bill, special committee report, budget proposal, and communication of Parliament (*14*).

The work of the RASKE project during the period from 1994 to 1998 has been followed by several projects in which selected companies have developed and implemented SGML solutions for a specific subset of documents. The first implemented document repository in SGML form was the archive of laws and statutes, which was published by the Ministry of Justice in 1997. In Parliament, the application of SGML started in 1998, and the Ministry of Finance prepared the budget proposal for 1999 in SGML form. All of these documents are available to all citizens on the Internet free of charge. The analysis and methodology development work of the RASKE project is continuing in the EULEGIS project (European User Views to Legislative Information in Structured Form) funded by the Telematics Applications Programme of the European Commission and involving companies, universities, and public sector organizations in different European countries.

THE STANDARDIZATION PROCESS

Interorganizational document standardization covering many document types is an extremely complicated task, and it may take several years before the first standards are implemented. Of the potential SGML-based standards, HTML is the one that has been widely and flexibly adopted. It is, however, a format supporting Internet publishing but not the information management of other areas. Despite the availability of predefined standards for some other sectors as well [e.g., the CALS DTDs for the armed forces and industry (*3*), the TEI standard for humanities (*15*), and the DocBook DTD for books (*16*)], choosing standards to effectively support business goals and activities nonetheless requires considerable work and rethinking about document management in relation to business processes. A survey in Finland showed that many Finnish companies and public sector organizations are interested in and motivated to use SGML and are also participating in SGML activities, but few have operational solutions outside HTML (*11*).

Figure 2 shows a model for SGML-based standardization in an organization. The circles depict activities, also called *phases,* and the arrows show the control flow specifying the order for starting the activities. The small black circle indicates that all of the following three activities can be started either in parallel or in any order. The analysis phase produces preliminary standards for a specified domain. Design of new solutions usually requires evaluation of the preliminary DTDs parallel with the development of new work practices and selection of new systems. The new EDM solution will then be implemented. The solution may require many changes in work practices (*17*), hence careful evaluation of new solutions and training of the workers is important. After evaluation, the implementation may need corrections, further redesigning may be called for, or a new domain may be selected for analysis.

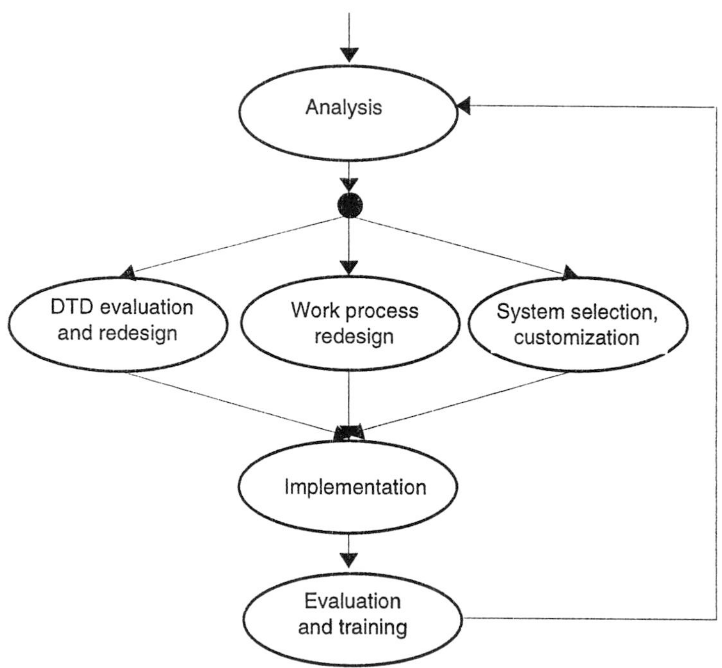

FIGURE 2. *A model for the document standardization process.*

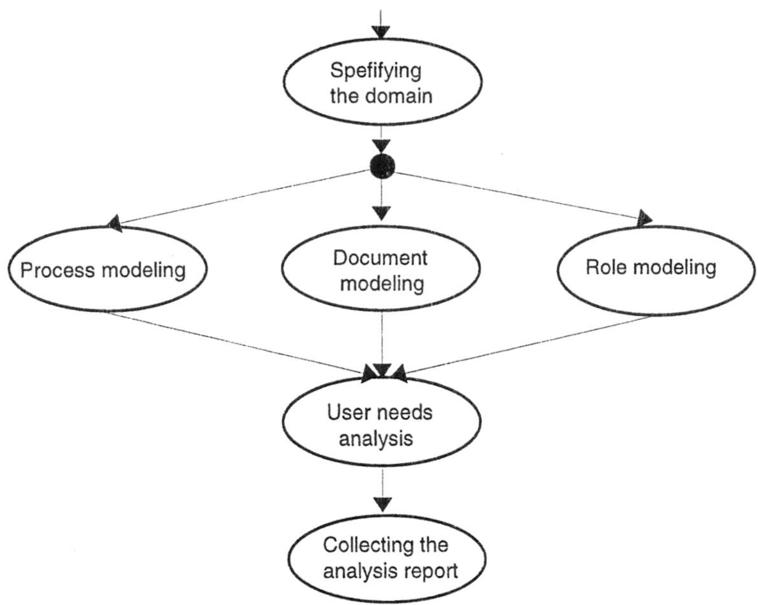

FIGURE 3. *A model for the document analysis process.*

THE ANALYSIS PROCESS

One of the goals of the analysis phase of Fig. 2 is to provide preliminary document standards to be further evaluated together with the redesign of work processes and systems. Other important goals are to support the following:

- Better understanding of the complex domain and the role of document management activities in business activities
- Better understanding of the needs of the actors
- Communication during the analysis and the subsequent standardization phases
- User training
- Continuous EDM development
- Specification of requirements for new systems

The analysts should be able to identify the problems inherent in current document management and to show the effects of those problems to the people dealing with the documents. The analysis should help people in the workplace to understand the differences between paper and digital documents and to know the opportunities offered by the digital media, hence the analysts should be EDM experts possessing the skills and means to communicate with the domain experts. The chosen method of analysis should help in dividing the complex analysis and communication task into manageable subtasks.

A model for the document analysis process is shown in Fig. 3. The process starts by defining and describing the domain to be analyzed. The domain is the activity whose document management the standardization and improvements will concern. An example of an analysis domain could be creation of the state budget or paper machine manufacturing. Figure 3 does not explicitly show iteration in the analysis. Once the domain has been defined, any of the subsequent phases may, however, reveal a need to correct or extend previously created models and descriptions. Basically all of the activities may thus proceed to some extent in parallel until the report of the analysis is finished. The domain definition is followed by process modeling, document modeling, and role modeling. Process modeling is used as a means of identifying smaller activities on the domain, the organizations responsible for them, and the documents created or used in those activities. Document modeling covers the description of document types, their life cycles, their contents, and their relationships to each other. In role modeling the most essential document users are identified and their document management activities are described. The user needs analysis studies the needs concerning future document management. At the end of the analysis process, the analysis report is collected and extended on the basis of the descriptions and models produced in earlier phases. The report includes suggestions for future improvements in document management.

Data-Gathering Methods

An extensive amount of data have to be collected during the document analysis phases. The ways in which the data were gathered in the RASKE project can be divided into three categories: project council meetings, literal sources, and interviews.

PROJECT COUNCIL MEETINGS

A council comprising the analysts and representatives from the document support departments of the organizations involved was set up. The council corresponds to the "document council" suggested by Sprague (*2*). At council meetings, the work products of the analysis were evaluated and discussed. These discussions were found to be an effective way of gathering information concerning current document management, requirements for the future, and additional data sources.

LITERAL SOURCES

The major literal sources can be divided into the following types:

1. Reports of earlier projects and working groups in the EDM area. Considerable activity had taken place during the previous year or two. The reports listed a number of problems and needs.
2. Printed documents in the analysis domain. Examples of documents were copied and carefully analyzed.
3. Existing written rules and standards concerning documents. Some of the rules were expressed in statutes, some were instructions given by ministries, and some were more

informal instructions. For example, there were written instructions for drafting government bills.

4. Systems manuals and instructions. Knowledge about current systems is important in identifying the benefits and problems in them.
5. General literature describing the domain. In the case of legislation, extensive literature is available.

INTERVIEWS

The interviews were divided into the following two types:

1. Informal interviews with experts in the domain. Interviews were conducted with people working with documents in the organizations. The interviews were supported by charts and other outcomes of the analysis. The domain experts were mostly chosen by the project council.
2. Structured user interviews. People using the documents in the domain either within or outside the subject organizations were interviewed to ascertain their requirements concerning document management. The interviews followed structured questionnaires. The goal of the interviews was to obtain more information about the work and tasks done in the user roles and about the needs associated with those roles. The basis for the design of questionnaires was the sense-making theory (*4*). The user needs were connected to situations in the work of the respondents.

Modeling Methods

Different modeling techniques are available for EDM components: methods for modeling document structures (*6, 18, 19*), work processes and user roles in them (*20*), and systems (*21*). None of the methodologies as such covers the modeling needs in an analysis project. In the RASKE project, the modeling methods were chosen from different methodologies and tailored for the purpose of document analysis. SGML was chosen as the method for describing detailed document structures. Elm graphs were used for graphical descriptions of document structures (*19*). The most important origins of the other modeling methods were in the object-oriented analysis (OOA) methodology (*22*), in information control nets (*23*), and in role modeling (*24*). One of the most important requirements for the modeling methods was the clarity of notions and models. Except for the DTDs, the models were not intended for computers but to support communication and understanding of the area by human readers.

DOMAIN DEFINITION AND PROCESS MODELING

The domain definition includes the identification of the activity whose document management the improvements will concern and the identification of the major organizational actors of the activity. Process modeling is used as a means to identify smaller activities, organizations responsible for them, and documents created or used in those activities. Variants of information control nets (ICNs) are suitable for describing relationships between activities, actors, and documents (*23*). Basically ICN models are process models showing a set of *activity* objects, a set of *resource* objects separated into input resources and output resources, mappings indicating the control flow among the activities, and mappings indicating the information flow. An activity may further be described as an ICN. Figures 1–3 already introduced special variants of ICNs. Figure 1 showed one activity circle, but no control flow. Figures 2 and 3 instead showed only the control flow and no resources or information flow. Also, the ICNs used in the domain definition and in the process modeling are special variants of more general ICNs.

Organizational Framework

As an ICN, an *organizational framework description* consists of an activity and a set of organizations as input resources. The organizational resources are used in the activity, and their participation can be regarded as an information flow to the activity. Figure 4 depicts the organizational framework of the domain "creation of the state

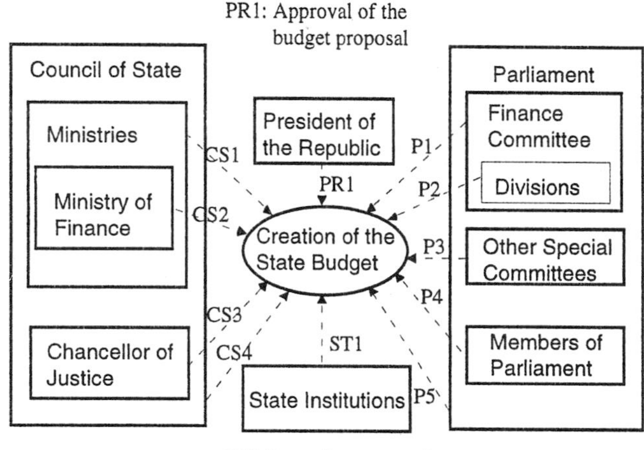

CS1: Preparing ministry proposals
CS2: Collecting the proposals of ministries and preparing the joint budget proposal
CS3: Checking legality
CS4: Presenting the budget proposal

P1: Discussing and reporting its comments concerning the budget proposal
P2: Discussing and working with special areas of the proposal
P3: Preparing statements concerning the area of the special committee
P4: Participating in committee work and voting in the plenary session, preparing budgetary petitions and motions to amend
P5: Presenting the budget after plenary session handling

FIGURE 4. *Organizational framework for the creation of the state budget.*

budget." In the graphical representation, the broken arrows from the organizations to the activity indicate the information flow. They are labeled by identifiers and associated with phrases briefly describing the tasks of the organizations in the activity. Hierarchic relationships of organizations are indicated by nested rectangles.

It is important in modeling EDM to know the relationships subsisting between the major activities, actors, and documents. The document output model and document input model show the business activities of the domain as a process and the organizational actors of those activities. The output model shows the documents produced in the course of the activities, and the input model shows the documents used in the activities.

Document Output Model

A *document output model* consists of a set of activities that are subactivities of the activity of the whole domain, a set of organizations as resources, and a set of document objects as output resources. In the organizational framework model the participating organizations were indicated as sources of information flowing to the domain activity. In the document output model, explicit information flow is shown only to documents. Organizations can be regarded as input and output resources at the same time. While performing their activities, organizations are not only sources of information; those working in the activities increase their experience and expertise and thus the organizations also increase their information resources. This information flow is not explicitly indicated in the document output model, however. In the graphical representation, organizations performing an activity are listed in the upper part of the activity circle.

An important difference between the process models described in this article and the original ICNs is in the use of control flow arrows. In ICNs a control flow arrow from activity A to activity B indicates that A must be completed before B can start (*23*). Information control nets were designed for office automation and there the specification of the relationship between the ending of one activity and beginning of another activity was important. In document analysis the intent is not to automate business processes. The major objectives of process modeling are to help in the identification of the activities, actors, and documents, and to facilitate human understanding and communication. The selection of the correct level of abstraction in the process models is therefore important. The purpose is not to describe all the special cases and details. In document analysis, modeling concerns real-life work processes in which many activities take place in parallel and the exact specification of the relationship of the ending of one activity and the beginning of another activity is rarely important, therefore a control flow arrow between activities A and B in the models of this article represents *weak control flow,* indicating that activity B begins after activity A has begun. Figures 2 and 3 were examples of the use of weak control flow to show rather complicated processes at a very general level of abstraction. Both processes include considerable iteration, but this is not indicated in the models by separate control flow arrows. The semantics of the model, however, also covers iteration.

Figure 5 shows a document output model for the creation of the state budget. In Fig. 5 the names of the document types produced in the relevant activities are

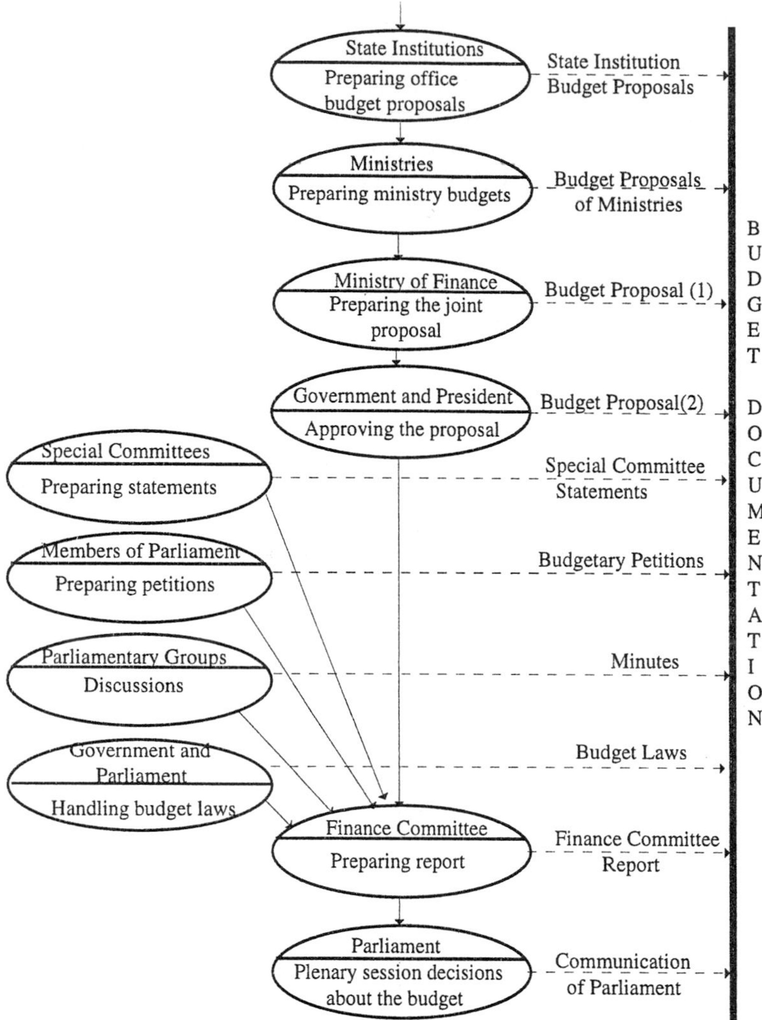

FIGURE 5. *Document output model for the creation of the state budget.*

indicated along the broken arrows. The number in parentheses following budget proposal refers to different versions of the same document object. The vertical balk line on the right represents the documentation created during an actual work process. Basically the organizations appearing in a document output model are the same as those in the organizational framework figure. For the sake of simplification, some of the organizations may, however, be left out if their tasks are clear. Others may emerge in the course of process description. For example, in the document outpout model of Fig. 5 the chancellor of justice and divisions occurring in the organizational framework model of Fig. 4 has been omitted, whereas the discussions of parliamentary groups has been added.

In the RASKE project, the document output models were found to be very useful in the user needs interviews in orienting the respondents to the domain. The models were sent to the interviewees before the interviews, and during the interview the respondents were able to comment on the models and indicate their own place in the model.

Document Input Model

A *document input model* is otherwise similar to the document output model except that instead of showing the documents produced by the activities, it shows the major documents used in the activities. In the processes analyzed in the RASKE project, the repository of the documents used was much larger than documentation created during the process. In general, the documentation used in an activity by an organization depends on the information needs of the people working in that activity. Document input models are therefore designed after the user needs interviews.

DOCUMENT MODELING

The document output model shows the document repository created in the domain. Document modeling is used to give more detailed information about a chosen subset of the document types in the repository. Document modeling may also concern new types not appearing in the current repository. Document modeling is divided into the following three phases:

1. Object modeling
2. State modeling
3. Content modeling

The origins of object modeling and state modeling are in the object-based modeling methodology of Shlaer and Mellor (*22*). In object modeling, document objects are identified and described, and their relationships to each other are described in a document-relationship diagram. The dynamic behavior of a document object over time is described in a state model. In content modeling, the structure of documents is analyzed. Content modeling includes the design of preliminary SGML DTDs. Much of the modeling of the three phases takes place in parallel and iteratively. Each of the phases is described below.

Object Modeling

In object modeling, a *document object* is an abstraction of a set of documents. An important question to be answered is: What are the real-world documents (or the sets of information) to be modeled as a document object? In the document analysis of standardization projects, the goal is to describe the information in units corresponding as closely as possible to those useful for the organization's performance in future

Private Bill is a legislative proposal made by a Member of Parliament. The proposal may be originally written either in Finnish or in Swedish. If the proposal is written in Swedish, the Translation Office translates it into Finnish. The document is printed by the Printing Office and published in the Series of Parliamentary Documents. Printed copies are stored in the Library of Parliament. The electronic form of the document is archived in the electronic text archive of Parliament, the original signed paper document in the archive of Parliament. A Private Bill may concern a Government Bill in which case it is sent to a Special Committee for preliminary work, and examined by the plenary session together with the Government Bill. A Private Bill may also be a proposal independent of any Government Bill. The Bill is approved or rejected in the plenary session.

FIGURE 6. *Description of the private bill object*

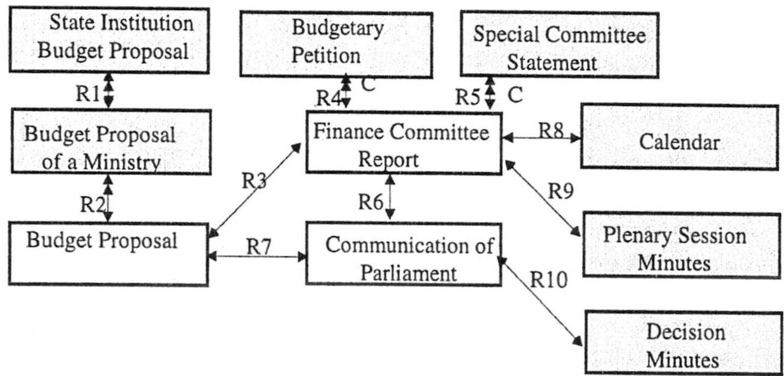

R1: Budget Proposal of a Ministry is based on State Institution Budget Proposals
R2: Budget Proposal is created on the basis of Budget Proposals of Ministries
R3: Finance Committee Report concerns the Budget Proposal
R4: Possible Budgetary Petitions of Parliament Members are taken into consideration during the preparation of the Budget Committee Report
R5: There may be one or more Special Committee Statements included in the Finance Committee Report
R6: Communication of Parliament is created on the basis of the Finance Committee Report
R7: Communication of Parliament is a reply to the Budget Proposal
R8: Finance Committee Report is mentioned in the Parliamentary Calendar
R9: Finance Committee Report is mentioned in the Plenary Session Minutes
R10: The decisions about the budget, included in the Communication of Parliament, are mentioned in the Decision Minutes

FIGURE 7. *A document-relationship diagram.*

document management systems. In current document management practices, however, the partition of information into documents does not necessarily best support information management. Currently a set of information items identifiable as a unit and pertaining to a topic may consist of several word processor files. For example, in Finland legislative documents are written in the two official languages, Finnish and Swedish. The Swedish translation of a government bill originally written in Finnish clearly belongs to the same information unit as the Finnish text. Currently, however, versions written in different languages are written as different files and also retrieved from distinct electronic archives in Parliament. In the RASKE project we decided to consider the translation of a piece of text as a part of the same document object as the original text. This decision is also taken into account in the process model in Fig. 5; it does not show different language versions separately.

A short description is provided in the object model for each document object class. Figure 6 shows the description of a private bill. The document objects and their relationships to each other are described graphically in a *document-relationship diagram* (D-R diagram), corresponding to the information structure diagram of OOA. Figure 7 shows the D-R diagram for documents created during the creation of the Finnish state budget. In the example, the standardization covers three documents: budget proposal, finance committee report, and communication of Parliament. In the diagram, the document objects of the standardization domain are depicted by white rectangles, the external documents by shadowed rectangles. A one-to-one relationship is depicted by a single arrowhead, a one-to-many relationship by a double arrowhead. A conditional relationship is indicated by the letter *C*.

State Modeling

In state modeling, the dynamic behavior of document objects over time is described by the *state transition diagrams* of OOA. A state transition diagram is a behavioral model showing the behavior of a specific document object over time. The activities shown in the diagram change the values of some attributes of the object. A state transition diagram for the private bill object is shown in Fig. 8. A state transition diagram consists of states, events, transition rules, and actions. A *state* represents a situation of a typical instance of the document object during its lifetime. Each document instance can only be in one state at any given time. In its *creation state,* a document instance comes into existence. An *action* is an activity that must be done with an instance upon arrival in a state. One action is associated with each state, but that action may consist of a sequence of activities. Since activities are associated with states and an object is in only one state at a time in a state transition diagram, the diagram cannot be used to graphically indicate parallel activities. Parallel activities can only be described in textual descriptions. An *event* represents an incident that causes an instance to move from one state to another. A *transition rule* specifies which new state is achieved if a particular event happens in a certain state. In its *final state,* the instance either becomes quiescent or it vanishes. A quiescent instance continues to exist but has no interesting dynamic behavior.

The life cycle of the object in Fig. 8 has seven states, each numbered, named, and represented by a box in the state transition diagram. The number and name of each state is written inside the box in bold. The actors and the action associated with a state are described inside the box. An arrow between the boxes illustrates a transition rule. The arrow is labeled with the event (label and meaning) that causes the instance to move from its present state to its successor state. State 1 is the creation state and state 7 is the final state. In some cases a document object may have a circular life cycle; it exists all the time and has an operational cycle of behavior. In the case of documents

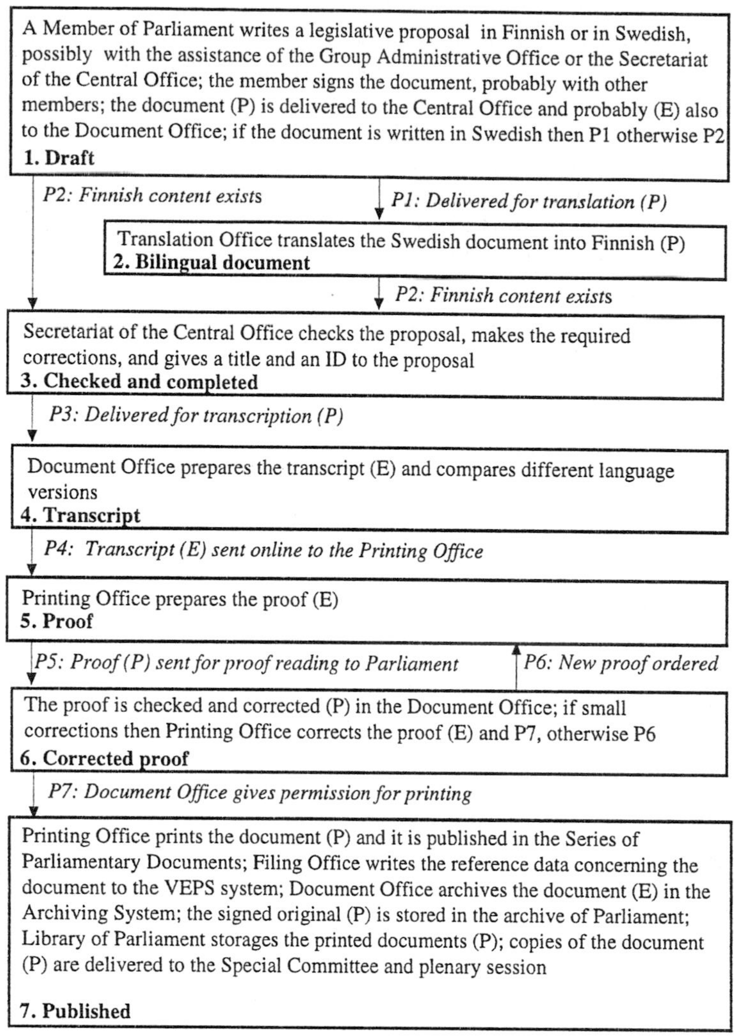

A Member of Parliament writes a legislative proposal in Finnish or in Swedish, possibly with the assistance of the Group Administrative Office or the Secretariat of the Central Office; the member signs the document, probably with other members; the document (P) is delivered to the Central Office and probably (E) also to the Document Office; if the document is written in Swedish then P1 otherwise P2
1. Draft
P2: Finnish content exists
P1: Delivered for translation (P)
Translation Office translates the Swedish document into Finnish (P)
2. Bilingual document
P2: Finnish content exists
Secretariat of the Central Office checks the proposal, makes the required corrections, and gives a title and an ID to the proposal
3. Checked and completed
P3: Delivered for transcription (P)
Document Office prepares the transcript (E) and compares different language versions
4. Transcript
P4: Transcript (E) sent online to the Printing Office
Printing Office prepares the proof (E)
5. Proof
P5: Proof (P) sent for proof reading to Parliament
P6: New proof ordered
The proof is checked and corrected (P) in the Document Office; if small corrections then Printing Office corrects the proof (E) and P7, otherwise P6
6. Corrected proof
P7: Document Office gives permission for printing
Printing Office prints the document (P) and it is published in the Series of Parliamentary Documents; Filing Office writes the reference data concerning the document to the VEPS system; Document Office archives the document (E) in the Archiving System; the signed original (P) is stored in the archive of Parliament; Library of Parliament storages the printed documents (P); copies of the document (P) are delivered to the Special Committee and plenary session
7. Published

FIGURE 8. *A state transition diagram for a private bill.*

handled in legislative organizations, a document object mostly has a born-and-die life cycle containing one or more creation states and one or more final states. The letter *P* in the text describing an action or event refers to a paper form and the letter *E* to an electronic form. The figure shows that a private bill is handled in the early stages of its lifetime mostly as a paper document. It may be written on a word processor but it is usually transmitted in paper form. It is not until its transfer from state 4 to state 5 that electronic means are employed, thus digital form is not effectively used. Depending on needs, state transition diagrams may be used to describe different kinds of activities concerning documents in a class. In the RASKE project, state transition diagrams were primarily used to describe document production. In some other cases, diagrams could be used to show the handling of a document in its final content and form.

Content Modeling

The main purpose of content modeling is to specify the hierarchic structure of the documents in the standardization domain. In the first stages of the modeling, the major components of documents in a class are described in a *document component description.* The relationships of the components to the components of documents in other classes are described in a *reuse table.* The reuse table is intended for analysis of the current reuse of structural components and for showing new possibilities for reuse. A reuse table is defined for each document object. The collection of reuse tables included in the content model is a way of showing the dependencies of different document types.

Most of the modeling in document analysis usually describes the current situation. In the identification of document objects, however, the analysis should be able to anticipate future needs. Grouping information into document objects may differ from current practices, and some of the document types may be totally new. Also, detailed content modeling should take into account the requirements for future EDM. The SGML offers a formal language with which to define the detailed structure of document content by a DTD. SGML authoring tools are available for creating and testing the DTD, and also for showing the DTD graphically. Elm graphs (*19*) were used for graphical descriptions in the RASKE project.

ROLE MODELING

In role modeling the use of documents by actors is modeled by role objects. A *role object* is an abstraction of the document management needs, tasks, and responsibilities of a group of people. Among existing object-oriented modeling methods, the method of Gottlob et al. (*24*) is flexible enough to describe role hierarchies in which a user can play different roles at the same time and in which roles can evolve. Figure 9 shows part of the role hierarchy for the document repository created during the creation of the state budget. Role types are depicted by circles. The role types are connected by arrows to the user class, or to the role types whose objects may take on that role. A person as a user of the repository is considered both as an instance of the root type and as an instance of each role type for which that person qualifies. A user in the *organization* role uses documents in the activities of an organization; for example, as a worker in the organization. The use of documents in a *person* role is not necessarily related to any organization. On the other hand, a user may also be in a person role and organization role at the same time. For example, a user may at the same time be a client of a public library and a citizen needing information preparatory to moving to another country. The double circle around the organization role indicates that a user may have roles in different organizations at the same time. For example, a person working in the Finnish Parliament as a member of Parliament can also be a minister in the Ministry of Finance. During ministerial vacations, a person may take on the role of several ministers at the same time.

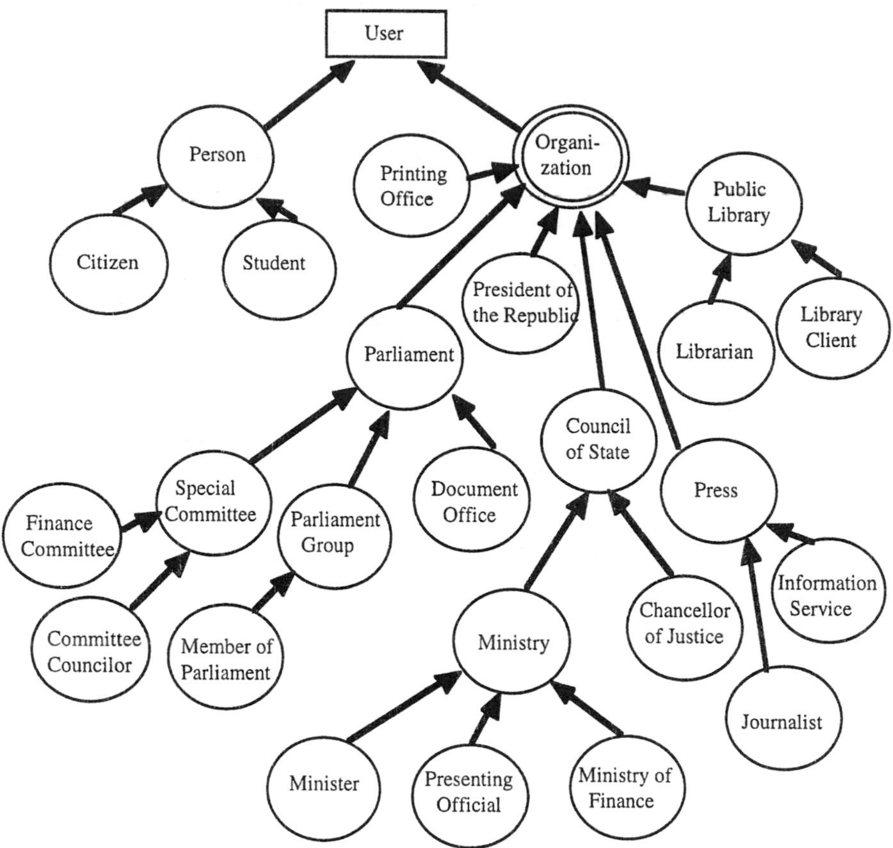

FIGURE 9. *A part of the role hierarchy for the creation of the state budget.*

With respect to a domain, roles can be divided into internal and external. The users in *internal roles* perform activities in the domain process, whereas the users in *external roles* use documents in some other activities, either in organization roles or as private persons. In the document analysis of companies, all the user roles may be organization roles. Documents created in the public sector are, however, intended for the public and their users may be in a person role not representing an organization in the use situation. Person roles can be classified in different ways; for example, citizen, student, immigrant, senior citizen. The clients of public libraries are typically in person roles while using documents.

Role modeling produces textual descriptions of roles—the way documents are used and the purpose of use. The relationship between document objects and role objects is described in a *document-role relationship table.* Figure 10 shows a relationship table for the document objects government bill, special committee report, and private bill, and for the role objects ministry, minister, presenting official, member of parliament,

	Governm ent Bill	Special Committ ee Report	Private Bill
Internal			
Ministry	C	U	U
Minister	C	U	U
Presenting Official	W	U	U
Member of Parliament	U	U	W
Document Office	T	T	T
Printing Office	T	T	T
External			
Press	U	U	U

FIGURE 10. *A document-role relationship table.*

document office, printing office, and press. In Fig. 10, the columns are labeled according to document objects and the rows according to role objects. The letters in the table indicate the type of activity performed by a role object with respect to a document object. If a user is responsible for preparing the content matter of a document and not writing and storing the document, then the relationship is indicated by a *C*. The letter *W* means that the user is creating the document content and writing the document. The user may also use a technical assistant for writing. The letter *T* indicates technical document processing (e.g., typing or archiving). The letter *U* refers to the use of completed documents.

Information concerning the most important user roles can be subsumed under role profiles, each of which includes the following data:

- Role name
- Related roles
- Business activities
- Document activities
- Systems used
- Situations in which documents are used
- Documents and parts of document used
- Problems and needs

Data for the profiles are collected at all phases of the analysis, especially at the interviews of the user needs analysis phase.

User Needs Analysis

User needs analysis should cover the document management needs of the individuals and organizations: documents, their use, the systems by which they are used, and the relationships of users. Some of the needs of participating organizations are a starting point for the analysis. More data about the needs of organizations are then collected from literal sources, in the project council meetings, and by the informal domain expert interviews. Needs concerning individuals and groups of persons are part of the needs of the organizations.

Data about the needs of persons are collected by user needs interviews. Structured questionnaires were used in the interviews in the RASKE project. In the questionnaires, data from the following areas were collected:

- Organization and tasks of the organization
- Personnel tasks in the domain
- Situations in which documents were used in the domain process and outside the process
- Documents and information produced and needed in the above situations
- Systems and databases used in the situations
- Problems and needs

The use of documents was associated with specific situations in the work of the respondents on the basis of the sense-making theory (*4*).

The user needs interview analysis produces corrections and extensions to the models created in phases started earlier, especially to the outcomes of role modeling. The analysis of the problems and needs is divided according to the document management components—systems, documents, work processes, and interrelationships between actors. The problems and needs of people in different roles are introduced in the final report, which also includes the above-described models and suggestions for improvements in the different document management activities of the organizations.

Conclusion

Nowadays documents are mostly authored using information technology. The use of digital data as information in some activities may, however, be impaired by unintegrated and inconsistent solutions. After storing information in nonstandardized ways, probably for three or four decades, the document management environment of a group of organizations working toward a common goal may be extremely complicated. To achieve effective utilization of digital media, careful analysis of the environment is needed. The analysis should cover all the components of document management: documents, their users and use, and the business processes in which the documents are used. The article introduced a methodology for document analysis: methods for data gathering, modeling, and user needs analysis.

In this article, document analysis was introduced as a phase in a document standardization project. As an example, the RASKE project, which developed standards for documents created in the Finnish Parliament and government, was introduced. In this project, SGML was selected as the document format and the document definition language. The use of other methods introduced in this article is not limited to SGML projects. Standardization may take place in different forms; for example, by the development of a quality system (*25*). Information specialists have an important role in the EDM improvement projects of organizations. Information services and libraries have extensive expertise in documents, their organization, and user needs. This expertise was also important in the RASKE project.

Acknowledgments

The results presented in this article evolved during the work of the RASKE project and the beginning of the EULEGIS project. Mika Hirvonen, Kirsi Heiskanen, Katri Kauppinen, Antti Lehtinen, Merja Lehtovaara, Virpi Lyytikäinen, Pia Norrila, Tero Päivärinta, and Pasi Tiitinen have contributed as RASKE researchers. The cooperation and extensive knowledge of experts in the Finnish Parliament and government as well as in many other organizations has been extremely valuable. Special thanks are owed to Olli Mustajärvi in the Finnish Parliament for his continuous support and cooperation. The financial support of the Finnish Parliament, Ministry of Foreign Affairs, Ministry of Finance, prime minister's office, Academy of Finland, Technology Development Center of Finland, and Telematics Application Programme of the European Commission is gratefully acknowledged.

REFERENCES AND NOTES

1. For more information about problems in electronic document management of organizations, see M. Bauer and J. Siegel, "Information Integration for Field Workers and Office-Based Professionals: 3 Case Studies," in *Information and Process Integration in Enterprises: Rethinking Documents,* T. Wakayama, S. Kannapan, C. M. Khoong, S. Navanthe, and J. Yates, eds. Kluwer Academic Publishers, Norwell, MA, 1998, pp. 95–108; D. G. Bell, D. G. Bobrow, O. Raiman, and M. H. Shirley, "Dynamic Documents and Situated Processes: Building on Local Knowledge in Field Service," in *Information and Process Integration in Enterprises: Rethinking Documents,* T. Wakayama, S. Kannapan, C. M. Khoong, S. Navanthe, and J. Yates, eds. Kluwer Academic Publishers, Norwell, MA, 1998, pp. 261–276; and T. Päivärinta and P. Tyrväinen, "Documents in Information Management: Diverging Connotations of 'A Document' in Digital Era," *Proceedings of the IRMA '98 Conference: Effective Utilization and Management of Emerging Information Technologies,* Idea Group, Hersley, PA, 1998, pp. 163–173.

2. R. H. Sprague, "Electronic Document Management: Challenges and Opportunities for Information Systems Managers," *MIS Q.,* **19**(1), 29–49 (1995).

3. J. M. Smith, *Introduction to CALS: The Strategy and the Standards,* Technology Appraisals Ltd, 1990. Links to CALS standards can be found, e.g., on the CALS page at http://cals.debbs.ndhq.dnd.ca/english/morecals.html (Sept. 2, 1998).

4. B. Dervin, "From the Mind's Eye of the User: The Sense-Making Qualitative-Quantitative Methodology," in *Quantitative Research in Information Management,* J. D. Glazier and R. R. Powell, eds. Libraries Unlimited, Englewood, CO, 1992, pp. 61–84.

5. A. Salminen, V. Lyytikäinen, and P. Tiitinen, "Putting Documents into their Work Contextin Document Analysis," to be published in *Inform. Proc. Mgt.*

6. C. F. Goldfarb, *The SGML Handbook,* Y. Rubinsky, ed. Oxford University Press, Oxford, UK, 1990.

7. Information Technology-Processing Languages—Document Style Semantics and Specification Language (DSSSL), ISO/IEC 10179:1996 (#), International Organization for Standardization, Geneva, Switzerland, 1996.

8. Extensible Markup Language (XML) 1.0, REC-xml-19980210, W3C Recommendation Feb. 10, 1998, http://www.w3.org/TR/REC-xml (Sept. 2, 1998).

9. D. Barron, "Why Use SGML?" *Electronic Pub.,* **2**(1), 3–24 (1989).

10. S. J. DeRose, D. G. Durand, E. Mylonas, and A. H. Renear, "What Is Text, Really?" *J. Computing Higher Ed.,* **1**(2), 3–26 (1990).
11. V. Lyytikäinen, "Rakenteisuuden hyödyntäminen elektronisissa dokumenteissa. SGML-pohjaisen dokumentaation tutkimus ja käyttö Suomessa 1997," Teknologiakatsaus 57/98, Tekes, 1998.
12. A. Salminen, M. Lehtovaara, and K. Kauppinen, "Standardization of Digital Legislative Documents: A Case Study," *Proceedings of the 29th International Conference on System Sciences,* IEEE Computer Society Press, Los Alamitos, CA, 1996, pp. 72–81.
13. A. Salminen, K. Kauppinen, and M. Lehtovaara, "Towards a Methodology for Document Analysis," *JASIS,* **48**(7), 644–655 (1997).
14. Results of the RASKE project have been reported in Finnish in: K. Kauppinen and M. Lehtovaara, "Organisaation dokumenttien rakenteen suunnittelu. Sovellusalueena valtiopäiväasiakirjat," pro gradu -tutkielma, Jyväskylän yliopisto, Tietojenkäsittelytieteiden laitos, 1995; V. Lyytikäinen, T. Päivärinta, A. Salminen, and P. Tiitinen, "Valtion talousarvioon liittyvien asiakirjojen rakenteistaminen, RASKE-projektin raportti," Eduskunta, 1997; P. Tiitinen, T. Päivärinta, A. Salminen, and V. Lyytikäinen, "Suomalaisten EU-lainsäädäntöasiakirjojen rakenteistaminen, RASKE-projektin raportti," Tietohallinnon selvityksiä, Ulkoasiainministeriö, Tietohallintolinja, 1997.
15. *TEI Guidelines for Electronic Text Encoding and Interchange (P3)* is made available by the electronic text center at the University of Virginia at http://etext.virginia.edu/TEI.html (Sept. 2, 1998). The text encoding initiative home page is at http://www.uic.edu:80/orgs/tei/ (Sept. 2, 1998).
16. The home page of the Davenport Group, the maintainers of the DocBook DTD, http://www.oreilly.com/davenport/ (Sept. 2, 1998).
17. K. Braa and T. I. Sandahl, "Approaches to Standardization of Documents," in *Information and Process Integration in Enterprises: Rethinking Documents,* T. Wakayama, S. Kannapan, C. M. Khoong, S. Navanthe, and J. Yates, eds. Kluwer Academic Publishers, Norwell, MA, 1998, pp. 125–142.
18. Information Processing-Text and Office Systems—Office Document Architecture (ODA) and Interchange Format, ISO-8613, International Organization for Standardization, Geneva, Switzerland, 1989.
19. E. Maler and J. El Andaloussi, *Developing SGML DTDs: From Text to Model to Markup,* Prentice Hall, Englewood Cliffs, NJ, 1996.
20. For process modeling methods, see B. Curtis, M. A. Kellner, and J. Over, "Process Modeling." *Commun. ACM,* **35**(9), 75–90 (Sept. 1992); J.-P. Tolvanen and K. Lyytinen, "Modeling Information Systems in Business Development: Alternative Perspectives on Business Process Re-engineering," *Proceedings of the IFIP TC8 Open Conference on Business Process Re-Engineering: Information Systems Opportunities and Challenges,* May 8–11, 1994, Upper Saddle River, Queensland Gold Coast, Australia, pp. 567–580.
21. For information systems modeling methods, see G. Booch, *Object-Oriented Design with Applications,* Benjamin/Gummings, Redwood City, CA, 1991; J. Martin and J. J. Odell, *Object-Oriented Analysis and Design,* Prentice Hall, Englewood Cliffs, NJ, 1992; J. Rumbaugh, M. Blaha, W. Premerlani, F. Eddy, and W. Lorensen, *Object-Oriented Modelling and Design,* Prentice Hall, Englewood Cliffs, NJ, 1991; E. Yourdon, *Modern Structured Analysis,* Prentice Hall, Englewood Cliffs, NJ, 1989; P. Coad and E. Yordon, *Object-Oriented Analysis, 2nd ed.,* Prentice Hall, Englewood Cliffs, NJ, 1991.
22. S. Shlaer and S. J. Mellor, *Object Lifecycles: Modeling the World in States,* Yourdon Press, Yourdon, New York, 1992.
23. Information control nets are introduced in C. A. Ellis, "Information Control Nets: A Mathematical Model of Office Information Flow," *Proceedings of the Conference on Simulation, Measurement and Modeling of Computer Systems, ACM SIGMETRICS Performance Evaluation Review,* **8**(3), 225–238 (1979); C. A. Ellis and G. J. Nutt, "Office Information Systems and Computer Science." *ACM Comp. Surv.,* **12**(1), 27–60 (1980).
24. G. Gottlob, M. Schrefl, and B. Röck, "Extending Object-Oriented Systems with Roles." *ACM Transac. Info. Syst.,* **14**(3), 268–296 (1996).
25. T. Päivärinta, A. Salminen, and T. Peltola, "Continuous Improvement of Electronic Document Management by a Quality System: A Case Study," *Proceedings of IRIS 21,* N. J. Buch, J. Damsgaard, L. B. Eriksen, J. H. Iversen, and P. A. Nielsen, eds. Dept. of Computer Science, Aalborg University, Aalborg, Denmark, 1998, pp. 701–715.

AIRI SALMINEN

SOFTWARE AGENTS IN LOGISTICS REPLANNING

Introduction

Most logistics operations are distributed both in terms of availability of resources and processing of information. Logistics operations in the context of military operations can be very complex, therefore various parts of military logistics are assessed and analyzed through simulation programs (simulations). These simulations are run distributedly and are efficient for analyzing logistics plans that are generated using uncertain or stochastic information. One of the concerns is how we integrate these simulations into a single system that meets the following objectives:

1. *Information sharing:* Simulations need to share information (input and output) among each other and with other dynamic databases.
2. *Real-time plan assessment:* Simulations should be able to use real-time data and thus use it to assess the plans in real time.
3. *Information presentation to users:* The integrated system should present the user (who could be a logistician, a member of the staff, or a military commander) with suitable information without overloading or losing vital information.
4. *User assistant:* The system should assist the user in taking corrective actions (i.e., replanning) at the appropriate time instead of only monitoring plan execution.
5. *Multiuser collaboration:* Finally, the integrated system should handle the collaboration among its users.

Various military contractors and universities have been trying to solve different aspects of this integrated system. Pennsylvania State University has been working in this area since 1994 and has demonstrated several key areas of research in the above context. In the first phase, we demonstrated a multiagent-based proof-of-concept distributed architecture (distributed intelligent agents for logistics—DIAL) that integrated the functionality of PORTSIM (port simulation, a simulation for port operations) and ICODES (integrated computerized deployment systems, a simulation for ship loading activity) prototypes (*1*). This led to the second phase of DIAL, an integrated system, in which we focus on building an agent structure by separating communication, message understanding, and reasoning as different layers (*25*). This agent structure is used to develop a logistician's assistant agent (along with a customized graphical user interface—GUI—for multiple user collaboration).

In this article, we shall describe the first phase of DIAL research work in detail, along with its relevance to other research work in distributed artificial intelligence (DAI). Neither effort in the first phase nor current research completely addresses all of the previously stated objectives. We shall give the list of basic readings that address the above issues at the appropriate places, however.

Background

Distributed artificial intelligence has emerged as a distinct subfield within artificial intelligence (*2*), which dates back to early work in Contract Net (*3*). The term DAI was "born" in the United States. The first official DAI meeting, called *The Workshop on Distributed AI,* was held in 1980 at the Massachusetts Institute of Technology in Boston (*4*). The main focus of DAI was on the ways of getting multiple automated entities ("agents") that interact appropriately toward a system-level goal. Early work on interacting agents was designed by a single designer who was mainly concerned with the general system's performance. The agents were not designed to have sufficient expertise to solve a problem single-handedly (e.g., information processing by distributed sensors; *5*). In parallel with the research in DAI, work was being conducted on the level of logical axiomatization of "single" agents (*4, 6*). In the early 1980s, researchers tried to bring the agent-centered view of modeling entities and DAI together, and asked questions regarding system behavior built with individually motivated agents that had been designed by independent designers. The research in this direction led to the emergence of the Multi-agent System (MAS), while the original stream became known as Distributed Problem Solving (DPS; *7*). While building MAS, coordination became an important issue. Coordination is defined as *managing dependencies between activities* (*8*). "Cooperation," "competition," and "collaboration" are considered different forms of coordination (*8*). In that aspect, DPS is sometimes called a cooperative DPS (CDPS) to stress cooperation in coordinating the agents (*9*). Cooperative DPS is viewed as a distributed search for the solution of a single problem where distributed agents share information and resources for the same goal (*10*). Research in MAS focused on the extreme end of the same spectrum (i.e., solve a single problem or task), while each of the agents has his or her own goal(s) and individual utilities (*4*).

Irrespective of the motivation of MAS and CDPS, negotiation exists in both streams, and is viewed as a communication process to further coordination. One example of the coordination process is problem decomposition and task assignment, which is a primary concern in planning and control problems (e.g., robot navigation and traffic management). This leads to the question of whether the problem must be decomposed and addressed centrally or by distributed agents that would coordinate without any central coordinator (*11*). In the case of distributed planning and control, the emphasis is either to develop social laws and protocol (at precompilation time) to ensure conflict resolution and convergence (*12*) or to promote the evolution of social laws through learning in negotiation (*13, 14*). Sometimes predefined social laws can be written as rules contained in a central entity that does problem decomposition, task assignment, conflict resolution, and so on. These central entities are called supervisor or controller, based on the degree of control exerted over the agents (*11*).*

Early work in DIAL can be categorized as research in distributed problem solving using a centralized task allocator or supervisor. DIAL can be more appropriately classified as a hybrid system since it also uses "data-dependency-based protocol" to formulate the flow of tasks to solve the replanning problem. With our recent focus on agent structure, we are moving toward a MAS stream of research in which various logisticians' assistants will be negotiating and facilitating multiuser collaboration.

---

*One central controller and several agents is a two-level hierarchical system.

Distributed Intelligent Agents in Logistics

The military logistics operation involves moving units (consisting of forces and equipment) from their bases (home stations) to theaters (destination). It is assumed that some event (e.g., a combat situation, a threat, or an economic crisis) has triggered the logistics operation. DIAL does not answer the question of when and how to develop a plan for a logistics operation due to the fact that it is an outcome of human (e.g., commanders) intervention, and subjective discussions. The logistics plan generated is called time-phased force deployment data (TPFDD). The representation of the TPFDD is very crucial to the architecture of DIAL;* however, it is not the focus of the DIAL research. The TPFDD captures the following suboperations:

1. Movement of certain forces to mobilization stations.
2. Movement of "advanced" forces to seaports and airports for departure to theaters.
3. Training of mobilized forces at various mobilization stations.
4. Movement of trained forces and their equipment to the points of embarkation (seaport and airports) by rail and road transportation.
5. Loading of equipment onto ships.
6. Arrangement of equipment on various levels and compartments of ships.
7. Airlifting of troops and equipment at airports.
8. Movement of ships to ports of debarkation.
9. Arrival operation at points of debarkation. This operation consists of all of the above operations in reverse order (i.e., moving troops from points of debarkation to theaters).

The TPFDD summarizes the duration of each operation that consists of starting time and finishing time of each operation. Table 1† explains various dates contained in the TPFDD (*15*). The TPFDD can be considered a schedule of movement for forces and equipment. The TPFDD might fail as an original schedule due to occurrences of some unexpected events, including a flood or storm, traffic, or a malfunction of equipment at port. One of the ways to validate the TPFDD schedule is to use these events as real-time sensor information in the simulation of each operation and compare the projected dates obtained from the simulation with dates in the TPFDD. If the projected dates differ from the TPFDD dates substantially, the commanders or logistician find alternate ways to meet the dates in the TPFDD. These alternate ways could range from minor enhancement of resources (to expedite movement and the training period) to changes in the unit itself. In current military practice, the simulation of the logistics suboperations are performed distributedly because the information required for simulation is distributed. Furthermore, under the current practice, human experts determine alternate ways to meet the schedule, therefore the objective of DIAL is *replanning,* which can be formally stated as: "Developing an architecture to

*Various research and development work is conducted by companies to represent TPFDD as dynamic and distributed data using object-oriented representation

†There are other dates mentioned in the TPFDD such as EDD (earliest delivery date) and FAD (feasible arrival date) that are hardly referred to and hence omitted from the table. Another crucial date is the G date, which is the date when forces must be mobilized or called by the president. This date does not appear in the TPFDD.

TABLE 1

Most Referred Dates in TPFDD

Unit ready to load date (RLD)	The date when forces (unit) must be rady to depart the mobilization station to port of embarkation (POE).
POE available to load date (ALD)	The date when forces must be available at POE to be airlifted or sealifted.
POD earliest arrival date (EAD)	The date when forces must arrive at the port of debarkation (POD)
POD latest arrival date (LAD)	The latest date when Forces must have arrived at POD. (LAD–EAD is the slack period.)
Destination required delivery date (RDD)	The date when forces must reach the destination (i.e., theater).

integrate various logistics simulations running distributedly and using the DPS concept to suggest or implement alternate ways to meet TPFDD dates."

Replanning is the means of fixing a plan to meet its original goal (if the plan is perceived to e infeasible to meet the goal). It should be noted that the original goal of DIAL is schedule maintenance; however, there could be various scenario-specific goals. One such goal is *unit integrity*. Unit integrity can be formally state as:

Definition 1: All the items of the same unit must be in the same location at all times.

This definition is a fallout of the principle of the aggregation in location theory (*16*), based on divisibility of physical objects. It states that all items of one unit must be transported in the same ship with their set of transportation assets or must be trained in the same mobilization station, for example. This is a scenario-specific goal*, which may not always be the system-level goal. The system-level goal of DIAL, however (since we use the DPS concept) was to maintain both TPFDD requirement and unit integrity.

Prior to explaining both the DIAL architecture and various key ideas in the architecture, we will mention certain assumptions on which the architecture was based. We will also explain the suitable readings at various implementation and theoretical level of details. The assumptions are as follows:

1. DIAL integrates two simulation drivers that simulate two logistics operations only—loading of a ship and arrangement of items in a ship. Under this assumption, the logistics for DIAL consist of movement of items of various units from the gate of entry of a seaport to different compartments of a ship. Multiple ships were not used, due to limitation of simulation drivers being developed simultaneously.
2. A deployable DIAL system is expected to monitor the plan execution and parameters (such as traffic and weather) affecting plan execution. Based on the monitoring information, DIAL is expected to assess a replanning situation and recommend corrective

*Unit integrity was a vital goal during Desert Storm logistics operation.

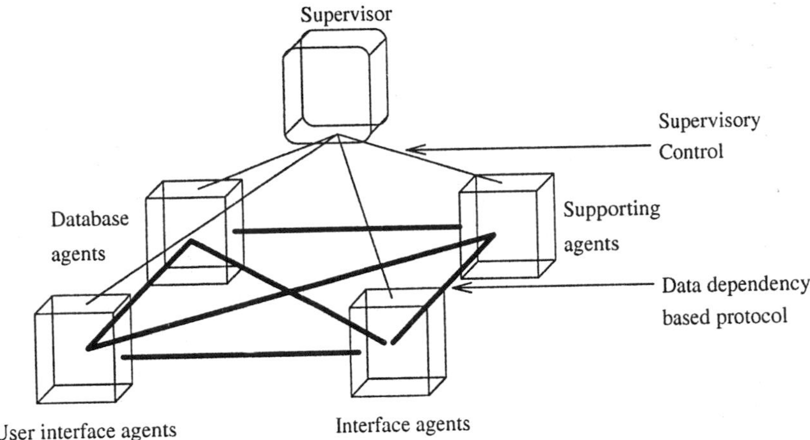

FIGURE 1. *Two-level hierarchies showing different components of DIAL.*

strategies. We assume the user of the DIAL proof of concept to detect the need for replanning, however, and request the DIAL system through a user interface to suggest corrective action. This assumption does not violate the replanning concept behind DIAL because the user can be treated as a sensor too.

DIAL Components

The DIAL system consists of the following components:

1. Supervisor for coordinating activities/task among agents
2. Interface agents, each interfacing a simulation program
3. Supporting agents, each checking for any violation of one of the criteria laid for solving the replanning problem
4. Database agent for storing and fetching legacy (and real-time) databases required for solving the replanning problem

Figure 1 shows the hierarchical system of DIAL. The following sections contain the details.

DATABASE AGENT

Unlike the role of a database server providing (consistent) data upon request, the database agent is intended to have additional roles. The following constitute the primary roles of the database agent:

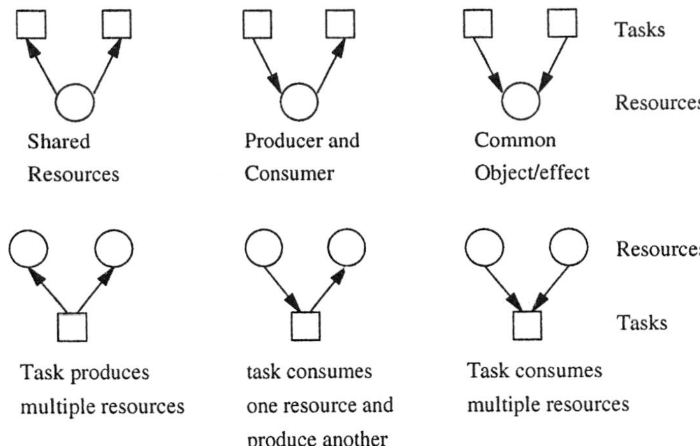

FIGURE 2. *Various activity/task and resource dependencies.*

server in such a way that intermediate solutions are pushed by the supervisor rather than the agent pulling or monitoring the information.

SUPERVISOR

Having described various roles of different agents in DIAL, we establish a coordination mechanism. We employ a central entity-based coordination as opposed to protocol-based distributed coordination or evolving coordination. We call the central entity a supervisor. Another reason for this entity being called a supervisor is that the supervisor does task assignment and checks the sequence of tasks to solve the replanning problem only; it does not dictate to the agent the means to solve each task. Before explaining the coordination mechanism followed by the supervisor, we will explain the representation of this mechanism at a generic level. The effort put in DIAL fits in well with the taxonomy developed by the Center for Coordination Science at MIT.

Coordination—that is, managing dependencies among activities (tasks)—can be represented by the relationships between resources used or produced by activities and the dependency of an activity over these resources (*20*). In Fig. 2, a circle represents a resource unit*, a rectangle denotes an activity, and an arrow denotes how the resource is used. Figure 2 shows six different types of activity-resource relationships and the associated coordination mechanisms.

1. Shared resource: One resource unit is used by two activities. The coordination mechanisms in this case are the following:

*In classical artificial intelligence, a unit "may be" denoted by the smallest indivisible piece of physical object or piece of information.

   a. If the resource unit is divisible and activities can use (consume) divided or partial resources, then assign the resources to activities (tasks).
   b. If the resource is reusable, then perform either of the two: (1) if the resource is reproducible (such as information) then make duplicates of the resource and let the first activity use the original resource and the second activity use duplicate resources, and (2) if the resource is reusable then schedule the activities that one activity uses the resource after the other activity is completed.
   c. If the resource unit is indivisible and nonreusable, then do task selection (e.g., through bidding or rule-based options).
2. Producer and consumer: An activity produces a resource that is required by another activity. The resource produced by the first activity can be either reusable or consumable.
3. Common object or effect: Two activities produce the same resources. The coordination mechanisms in this case are as follows:
   a. If the resource unit produced by two activities is divisible, then pick the "best" resource as elements of the original unit from either of the activities and merge the resource elements. An example of this are various activities producing a car, where resource elements are engine, chassis, suspension, and so on.
   b. If the resources unit is indivisible but can be duplicated, then embed a conflict-resolver activity to choose one resource from either of the activities.
   c. If the resource units are indivisible and cannot be duplicated (e.g., placing a cube at location X by crane or forklift), then pick only one activity. (In this case, we call activities conflicting activities.)
4. Dependencies between one task and multiple resources: The last three cases of task and resource dependencies can be broadly classified under this category, which poses less difficulty for coordination. In the first case, one task utilizing resources from two different sources requires synchronization of availability of resources to avoid (1) starvation or (2) deadlocks (*20*).

In DIAL, a resource is considered data, which may be legacy data or real-time data. An activity is considered a computation to be carried using the data as a resource. In coordination theory, activities are not associated with any activity (task) executor (or actor as they call it, and agent in DIAL). In DIAL, however, we call an activity a computation to be performed by an agent, therefore if two agents can perform the same activity then we denote them as two activities.

Consider a situation in which a logistician requests replanning. The supervisor requires determining a *process flow* that connects various activities and resources. This process flow (along with the coordination mechanism) essentially dictates the problem-solving procedure. In most architectures to date (*11*), the problem-solving procedure is embedded in the central coordinator. For example, we may embed the process flow as shown in Fig. 3 in the supervisor, based on which supervisor coordinates activity-data coordination among agents. For example, coordination point c_1, c_3, c_5 and c_7 requires the coordination of one activity and multiple data sources. From the process flow diagram, however, it may be observed that activities at coordination point c_1 and c_5 require some data, which could lead to starvation because data could not be produced unless the activity is executed and vice versa. The supervisor could therefore coordinate by either requesting that the activity executor execute the activity (i.e., perform the computation) with a partial data set or provide data from some other source (e.g., request data of the previous session from the database agent). Coordination points c_3 and c_7, however, require a schedule type of coordination mechanism related to coordination points c_2 and c_6, respectively. c_2 and c_6 requires coordination of

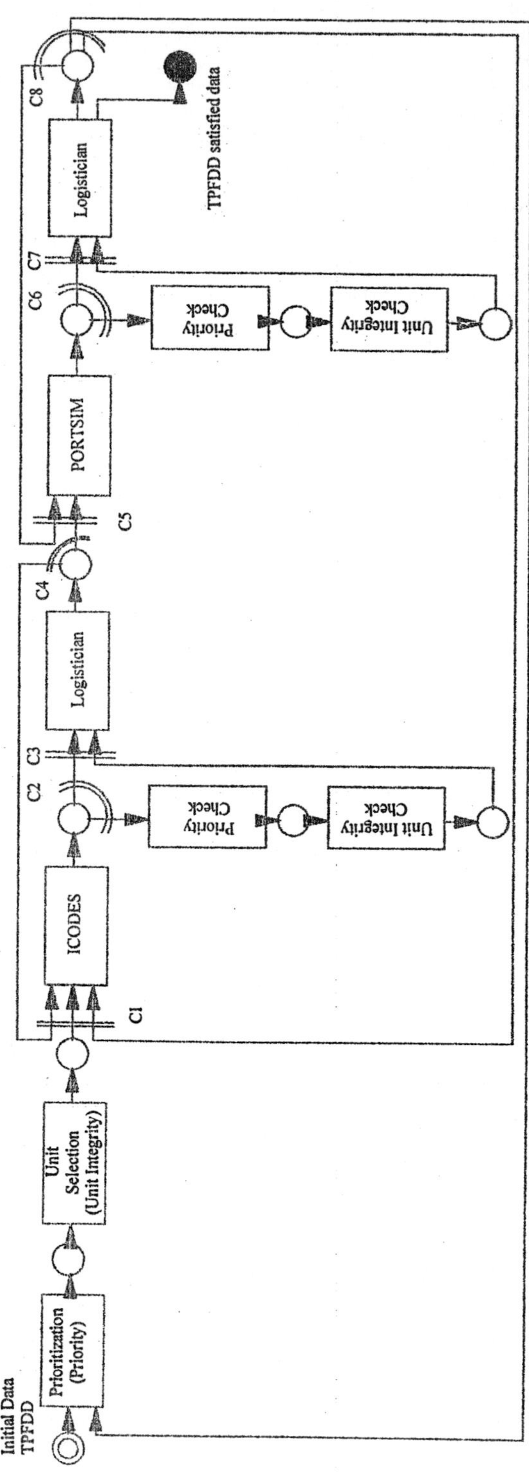

FIGURE 3. *A process flow to solve a particular replanning problem.*

multiple activities requiring the same resources. The supervisor schedules "priority check" and "unit-integrity check" activities prior to "logistician" activity because the latter activity requires data to be obtained from the former two activities. The coordination point c_8 also requires the coordination of multiple activities competing for the same resources. It must be noted that resources such as data can be duplicated and distributed among all activities; however, the supervisor elects selects one activity to restrict the proliferation of several replans in one session of replanning. The selection is entirely dependent on data provided by the logistician activity. In short, it may be noted that although various coordination points fall in the generic classification of activity and resource dependency structure, they do not have a generic coordination approach.

In DIAL, the supervisor does not follow an embedded process flow as the problem-solving procedure; rather, it lets the agents come up with a process flow based on data dependency. In this context, the approach in DIAL is similar to the partial global planning (PGP) approach (*21*), which is a bottom-up approach. In contrast to a top-down approach, in which a problem is decomposed and tasks are assigned to all agents, in a bottom-up approach each agent knows its task, but the solution of each task needs to be coalesced to form the solution of the global problem. It must be noted that both approaches are still cooperative DPS. It may be ascertained fairly and precisely that the top-down approach is a centralized approach and the bottom-up approach is a decentralized approach. In DIAL, the protocol based on which agents coordinate (i.e., the cooperation form of coordination) is based on data dependency. In this context, the role of the supervisor is as follows:

1. To form a coalition of agents to solve a replanning problem. Various activities required to solve the problem are determined by the supervisor*. Based on the required activities to solve the problem and the list of activities provided by the agents (called the registration process below), the supervisor forms a group of agents. The supervisor does not lay out the process flow, however. It is accomplished through data dependency, as described below.
2. To add an agent to a group of agents to remove data starvation.
3. To schedule or select activities in case multiple activities compete for the same data source and cannot resolve the competition based on data dependency.

From the perspective of the above roles, DIAL follows a hybrid approach—a decentralized approach for process flow determination and a centralized approach for problem decomposition and supervision.

Replanning Approach

The following steps constitute important stages in the replanning approach:

1. During the DIAL system initialization, each agent registers the activities (e.g., computation) that they can perform individually. The registration procedure will be described in

*The part of the problem-solving procedure of determining various activities is known as problem decomposition.

the next section. The registration procedure is similar to "different applications exporting CORBA methods in a Common Object Request Broker Architecture (CORBA) based environment" (*22*). This helps agents to even unregister certain activities dynamically. These activities are thus not used in problem solving. We do not use the dynamic feature in the replanning procedure, however.

2. The supervisor determines the activities that are required to solve the replanning problem. A replanning problem originating from the logistician specifies the activities to solve the problem, therefore task decomposition can be placed under a "medium" level of sophistication based on Ref. *23,* since it is done centrally through a table lookup of a list of registered activities. For example, a replanning problem requiring simulation of ship loading and maintenance of unit priority is specified by the logistician. Based on the table lookup the supervisor confirms the activities.
3. Problem decomposition follows the formation of a coalition of agents that are selected by the supervisor to perform those activities. A coalition is formed when each of the selected agents registers with a mediator by providing a list of data types (e.g., item number, priority, item description, weight, and volume) that it can output or produce. We call this mediator ttsession*. The mediator helps in determining the process flow through a matching procedure described below.
4. Construction of a successful process flow ensures data availability for execution of an activity (computation). In short, process flow contains starvation-free, deadlock-free, and supervised process sequences. Figure 3 is such a process flow, which is not embedded in the supervisor, but rather generated by the agents. This process flow contains all kinds of possible activities of the agents, such as the following:
   a. Use embedded rules to prioritize unit and item
   b. Use embedded rules to select units
   c. Use ICODES simulation
   d. Use PORTSIM simulation
   e. Check for priority maintenance
   f. Check for unit integrity maintenance
   g. Suggest the user for approval
5. As clearly stated in the DIAL objective, the system must suggest alternate ways to meet TPFDD requirements in case the simulation results are found unsatisfactory. The results of the simulation of ship loading are said to be unsatisfactory under the following circumstances:
   a. At least one item of a unit has not been loaded onto the ship (violation of unit integrity).
   b. The items (by weight) of a unit left on the dock are less than or equal to the sum of the items (by weight) of low prioritized units loaded onto the ship (violation of priority).

   The results of the simulation of cargo movement in a port are said to be unsatisfactory under the following circumstances:
   c. At least one item of a unit is moved to the dock after the ship departure time (violation of unit integrity and TPFDD).
   d. An item of a low-priority unit arrives at the gate later than an item of a high-priority unit, but is loaded before the item of the high-priority unit, therefore the item of high priority is loaded after the ship departure time (violation of priority and TPFDD).
   e. The average throughput time of all items of a high-priority unit is greater than the average throughput time of all items of a low-priority unit if the higher priority unit violates unit integrity (violation of priority and TPFDD).

   Under these circumstances, agents use precompiled rules to display appropriate simulation results and suggest alternatives. For example, the ICODES agent, unit integrity agent, and priority agent collectively suggest the following actions to the logistician:
   f. Shuffle (or substitute) unloaded items of a high-priority unit with the loaded items of a low-priority unit to maintain unit integrity of the high-priority unit, and thus

*ttsession is a ToolTalk message server.

eliminate the low-priority unit from being loaded onto the ship. The authorization of substituting items requires the discretion of the logistician and is only suggested by the agent.

g. Delete a unit from the TPFDD or abandon mobilization of a low-priority unit.
h. Delete a high-priority unit to facilitate the loading of several low-priority units.
i. Change the priority of the units.
j. Accept the partial list of loaded items of units as default constituents of the unit. (The unloaded items will not be considered for port simulation.)

The above list of suggestions does not involve innovative strategies such as searching for another ship to the same destination, offloading already loaded cargo in the ship to create more space, or even rearranging items in ships for space optimality. This is due to limitations of the ICODES simulation that was under simultaneous development and to keep information exchange between the simulation and the agent independent of the simulation program.*

Similarly, the PORTSIM agent, the unit integrity agent, and the priority agent collectively suggest the following actions to the logistician:

k. Change the arrival distribution of the items. (These essentially suggest to the logistician to increase the transportation resource, which in turn changes the arrival distribution.)
l. Delete items from the list.
m. Accept the units whose items cannot be loaded before the ship departure time. (These items will not be used in the ICODES simulation.)
n. Change the priority of units as well as items within a unit.

The PORTSIM agent, like the ICODES agent, does not suggest increasing resources in port or changing the dispatch rules because the PORTSIM simulation had not been designed to deal with changing resources and dispatch rule files.

6. It may be observed from the process flow diagram that each time a simulation is run and some violations are detected some corrective suggestions are offered to the logistician. The process is iterated until the logistician approves the modified TPFDD. At coordination point c_8, the supervisor selects the course of iteration (i.e., whether the simulation should be confined to repetition of PORTSIM or both PORTSIM and ICODES). This supervisory control is exerted based on the approval of the logistician.

As stated earlier, replanning is the means of correcting a plan if the execution of the plan does not accomplish the goal. DIAL uses a hybrid (decentralized and supervisory) CDPS procedure to simulate parts of the logistics plan/operation and determine suggestive actions as means of correcting the TPFDD. The next section describes the detail of the implementation process that has been elaborated in Refs. *24* and *1*.

Implementation Details

The primary implementation focus of DIAL is to enable the agents to communicate with legacy simulation programs and to use ttsession to develop a process flow. The following are main implementation steps in DIAL as a proof of concept for replanning:

1. DIAL integrates legacy systems. Interfacing legacy systems as a means of wrapping the simulation is an implementation achievement. There are several ways of interfacing an

*This limitation could be avoided when standards are developed for information exchange between agent and simulation such that the simulation program may change, but not the information exchange.

TABLE 2

The Agentclips 1.4 Functions for Communications

Agentclips function	Description
(new_server <string>)	Creates a server with named string.
(connect_bb <blackboard>)	Connects to the blackboard and sends its address and host name.
(bb_assert <facts>)	Connects to the blackboard and writes the facts or commands.
(receive_message)	Does blocked receive. If this is not called, other rules can be fired. If no rules need to be fired, it does blocked receive

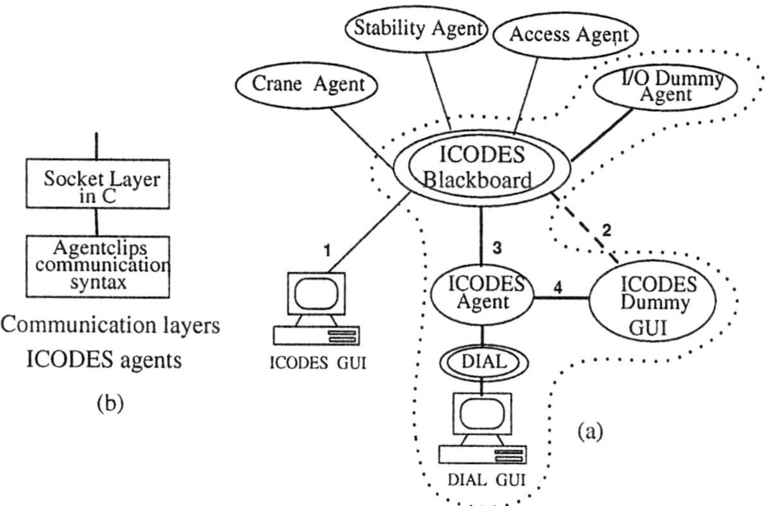

FIGURE 4. *The interface between ICODES and DIAL.*

application. We will describe how we interfaced PORTSIM and ICODES drivers and give suitable pointers to other interface methods.

a. Interfacing with ICODES

ICODES GUI allows a logistician to interact with the ICODES simulation. Loading, unloading, deletion, and substitution of items are different forms of interactions accomplished by the logistician through the GUI. The ICODES interfacing agent exerts the same forms of interaction as a "virtual" user of ICODES simulation. The ICODES GUI passes the logistician's interaction messages as procedural calls to the ICODES blackboard by invoking bb_assert (similar to assert in any clips program), as shown in Fig. 4a. The blackboard sends the message to appropriate ICODES agents based on the input templates sent by ICODES agents. All the communication (control and data) occurs through the blackboard.

In order to test the interface between the ICODES blackboard and the ICODES GUI, we created a dummy GUI (2 in Fig. 4a) that simulates the input-output behavior of the ICODES GUI. The ICODES dummy GUI, written in agentclips, could communicate with the ICODES blackboard by registering it as a new client-server. It could send and receive messages via the established sockets. Table 2 lists the four functions written in agentclips that could achieve this communication mechanism. Since the ICODES interface agent is written in C, we replaced these four functions written in agentclips to equivalent functions in C so that the agent forms a bridge between the ICODES blackboard and the ICODES dummy GUI, thus the ICODES interface agent being a daemon connects to the blackboard and gives its identity as an ICODES GUI (3 in Fig. 4a). At the same time, it also creates the ICODES GUI (which is a dummy GUI in our case) and gives the impression that the ICODES blackboard (4 in Fig. 4a) is creating the GUI. The ICODES interface agent need not translate the commands and inputs to clips facts because the underlying agentclips system takes care of it. As shown in Fig. 4b on the communication layers of agentclips, the real communication is achieved by a socket code written in C that has been replicated in the ICODES interface agent, therefore the ICODES interface agent sends and receives the contents of the facts directly. The dotted enclosure in Fig. 4 shows different components of the ICODES driver interface.

b. Interfacing with PORTSIM

Not all legacy sytems provide libraries to build dummy GUIs (e.g., ICODES). They do not provide source code to insert functions in the legacy system and transform into an agent program. It is therefore often required to invoke the complete legacy application as a separate process (similar to any Unix process). All the communication such as data transfer is accomplished through files (instead of sockets). PORTSIM is one such legacy simulation program, therefore the PORTSIM interface agent creates a file (accessible by PORTSIM application) that contains information regarding arrival times, description, dimensions, and priority of items.* Next, the PORTSIM interface through IPC (Unix interprocess communication) mechanism (fork and exec) invokes the PORTSIM driver. Upon completion of the PORTSIM dirver (by tracking the process number obtained via IPC), the PORTSIM interface agent reads the output file created by the PORTSIM driver.

c. Other interfacing mechanisms

In various legacy systems (after the advent of object-oriented programming and visual programming techniques), efforts are made to separate the graphical interface and the program, therefore standards are developed for how the graphical interface needs to communicate with legacy programs. A few such standards are Tcl/TK and Xlib tool kit libraries. Using these standards**, C and C++ programs (which can be used to write agent programs) can be written to be compiled with legacy programs.

After the advent of such user-level messaging systems as CORBA, several legacy systems have developed programs and standards to communicate with these programs through CORBA calls. These standards are used to develop different GUIs that can remotely communicate with the program. These standards, which were developed using the CORBA interface definition language (IDL), can be also used to write agent programs in any programming language. Developing CORBA IDL standards to communicate with a legacy program is the most advanced, efficient, and object-oriented way of enabling agents to access the programs.

After the advent of such user-level messaging systems as CORBA, several legacy

---

*The resource file and ship timing and arrival file were not allowed to be changed by the PORTSIM interface agent in the proof of concept

**These standards are popularly known as application interface (API).

systems have developed programs and standards to communicate with these programs through CORBA calls. These standards are used to develop different GUIs that can remotely communicate with the program. These standards, which were developed using the CORBA interface definition language (IDL), can be also used to write agent programs in any programming language. Developing CORBA IDL standards to communicate with a legacy program is the most advanced, efficient, and object-oriented way of enabling agents to access the programs.

Various databases (e.g., Microsoft Access, Oracle) provide their legacy query languages to communicate with those databases. Today we have commercially available libraries (even CORBA IDL) that can be compiled with C and C++ programs to enable these programs to access the legacy databases remotely.

In short, developing standards for communication between GUI interfaces and legacy programs facilitates the development of agents that can interface with those programs. The conventional way of invoking legacy programs as a process and thus communicating through files (e.g., PORTSIM) is much weaker than interfacing through messages and standard calls (e.g., ICODES), although process-level control and performance could be improved if the source code of the legacy programs could be compiled with agent programs.

2. In DIAL, the supervisor and agents are persistent objects (i.e., servers). In other words, DIAL itself is a persistent system. This means that the supervisor and agents must be running as servers in various hosts prior to the logistician accessing DIAL. Another reason for DIAL being a persistent system is that various agents need to be monitoring and looking for alternatives (i.e., replanning), even in the absence of any logisticians in the system. The following steps are followed to initialize DIAL as a persistent system:
   a. ttsession is a ToolTalk communication process that communicates with other ttsessions running on the network. It is assumed one ttsession is running on each host of the network. During its tart, each ttsession reads the ToolTalk types of databases. The ToolTalk-type database dictates ttsession (i.e., which application/agent to invoke upon receiving messages and what message patterns must be registered to deliver a message to those applications). This is accomplished by writing a script using ToolTalk language and invoking tt_type_comp, which updates the database.
   b. The supervisor is run on one of the hosts in the network, and it requests a set of ttsessions running on specified hosts to start agents. The instruction to start agents is already known to the ttsessions running on the specified hosts through a script-updated ToolTalk database.
   c. Upon starting, the agents join the ttsession running on the supervisor's host, which the supervisor has also joined.
   d. Each agent expresses its requirements and capability to produce (Table 3) to the supervisor through the ttsession.
   e. At this step, all agents have registered a few message patterns with the ttsession on the supervisor's host that enables the supervisor to form a group of agents depending on a logistician's problem (problem_assign operation in Table 4, Ref. *1*).

      The advantages of having a centralized messaging server is that each agent does not have to handle message pattern matching and message delivery. This is beneficial during process flow construction, which evolves through message exchanges among agents.
3. One of the main implementation details is how agents use ttsession to develop a process flow. The following steps illustrate this procedure:
   a. When a logistician starts a GUI, the GUI starts a process called user interface agent.
   b. The user interface agent joins the local ttsession and poses the problem and information regarding the local ttsession to the supervisor's ttsession.*
   c. The supervisor examines the problem and determines which agents are required to solve the problem. The supervisor uses Table 3 to determine the agents that are

*This means that supervisor's host is known to each user interface agent prior to the GUI run.

TABLE 3

Requirements and Capabilities of the Agents

Name of the agent	Requirement	Capability to produce
ICODES interface agent	cargo_unit_priority	stowplan
	cargo	stowplan
	cargo_seq	stowplan
PORTSIM interface agent	cargo_item_priority	time_cargo_seq
	cargo_seq	time_cargo_seq
Supporting agent	Cargo	cargo_priority
	Cargo	cargo_seq
	cargo, ship	select_cargo

TABLE 4

Control Messages

Operation	Usual sender	Usual receiver	Expected reply
confirm_data_types	Any Agent (say A)	Any Agent (say B)	ok_wait
problem_assign with agent identity	Supervisor	Any Agent	prob_done

capable of solving the problem. The selection method is simple and described in Ref. 1.

d. The supervisor assigns the problem to each agent (problem_assign operation in Table 4; *1*) and invites them to join the user interface agent's ttsession. This means that for each logistician it is possible that his or her agent might have joined several other user interface agents' ttsessions (Fig. 5).

e. Each agent of the group of selected agents registers message patterns. A message pattern consists of an operation name confirm_data_type (Table 4) and arguments indicating the types of data that the agent can provide. When an agent tries to solve an assigned problem, it looks for the input data. In the case in which the input data are not available, the agent sends a message with the operation name confirm_data_type and the data types as the arguments that the agent seeks. ttsession matches message and message pattern, and delivers the message to the agent who can provide the data. For example, the ICODES interface agent can initiate the ICODES simulation if prioritized cargo is available. This message fires up the priority agent to perform prioritization on units.

   This procedure might lead to deadlock or starvation, which means that an agent might be looking for data to solve a problem that itself results from the agent solving the same problem or the agent might be looking for data that no agent in the group can provide. In such cases, the DIAL system requires the supervisory role of adding new agents based on need. We have not implemented such a supervisory role in DIAL.

   In short, the underlying process flow is constructed through agent-to-agent interaction based on data dependency.

We have shown (*1*) that distributed ttsessions as message servers make the system

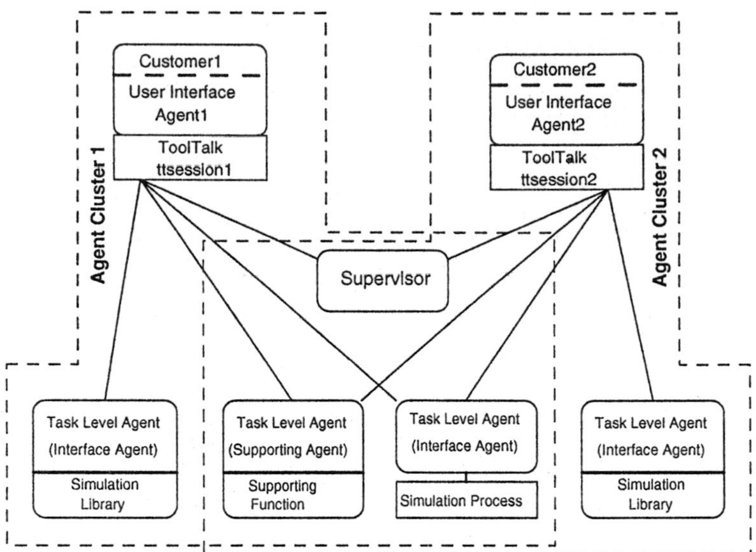

FIGURE 5. *DIAL architecture with distributed ttsessions.*

scalable in terms of the large number of agents or large number of logisticians accessing the system.

Results and Discussion

The DIAL proof of concept partially answers various objectives mentioned in the introduction. In this section, we shall evaluate those objectives qualitatively, as follows:

1. *Information sharing:* The input and output of the simulations are shared through the supervised process flow in which agents interfaced with the simulation programs communicate, resolve the data dependencies, and share input and output data. DIAL has achieved a reasonable step in accomplishing integration of simulation programs and information sharing.
2. *Real-time plan assessment:* DIAL has laid out the architecture for infusing real-time data in the simulation; however, it does not implement this part. The database agent with appropriate rules and interfaces with real-time data sources could trigger replanning, which is currently presented by the logistician through the GUI. We are currently undertaking research to include the uncertain information associated with real-time data to develop logistics plans with replanning eventualities. The second and current phase of DIAL allows the dynamic information architecture specification (DIAS) to collect weather information and use that information in the simulation of transportation in the continental United States.
3. *Information presentation:* There is not a well-defined procedure in which only suitable information regarding replanning could be presented to the user; however, guidance could be obtained from human-computer interaction and the logistics practitioners.

DIAL presents textual information of the plan from ICODES and PORTSIM with various alternatives, such as buttons, so it is possible that the user of DIAL may lose vital information. This objective requires further study and research.

4. *User assistant:* One of the main lessons learned from DIAL that has been pursued in the current phase of DIAL and will also be pursued in the future is to develop a logistician's assistant. ICODES and PORTSIM interface agents could be called logistician's assistants, as they suggest various replanning avenues to the logisticians. These alternatives are already programmed as rules in agents, however. It is possible that a logistician might be able to solve replanning using his own rules of thumb, which are not embedded in the agent. One of our proposed work is how to develop visual tools with which logisticians can solve replanning problems and agents can infuse the rule on the fly. Second, the agent might have a large number of alternative ways to correct the plan. The best alternative is dependent on the scenario-specific situation, however. Choosing the best alternative could be called metareasoning. The question of how to develop a metareasoning procedure is a research issue, and has been well highlighted in the current phase of DIAL.
5. *Multiuser collaboration:* DIAL (in both phases) accomplishes multiuser (multilogisticians) collaboration informally. DIAL reports the action of one logistician to the other. At a sophisticated level, however, there cold be several conflicts and confrontations among the action of logisticians. The actions in logistics replanning are various means of approving different suggestions. Such conflicts could be resolved by attaching utilities and solving a game-theoretic approach or using the hierarchy of logisticians in selecting or disregarding certain actions. We are not currently addressing multiuser collaboration in replanning.

Acknowledgments

The authors wish to thank the Army Research Office for its generous support (Grant DAAH04-96-1-0464) in pursuing this research.

REFERENCES

1. G. Satapathy, S. R. T Kumara, and L. M. Moore, "Distributed Intelligent Architecture for Logistics (DIAL)." *Internat. J. Exp. Syst. Applic.,* **14**, 409–424 (1998).
2. A. H. Bond and L. Gasser, "An Analysis of Problems and Research in DAI," in *Distributed Artificial Intelligence,* A. H. Bond and L. Gasser, eds. Morgan Kaufmann, San Mateo, CA, 1988, pp. 3–35.
3. R. G. Smith, "The Contract Net Protocol: High-level Communication and Control in a Distributed Problem Solver." *IEEE Trans. Computers,* **C29** (12), 1104–1113 (1980).
4. J. S. Rosenschein and G. Zlotkin, *Rules of Encounter: Designing Conventions for Automated Negotiation Among Computers,* MIT Press, 1994.
5. D. D. Corkill and V. R. Lesser, "The Distributed Vehicle Monitoring Testbed: A Tool for Investigating Distributed Problem Solving Networks," in *Blackboard Systems,* R. Engelmore and T. Morgan, eds. Addison-Wesley, 1988.
6. K. Konolige, *A Deduction Model of Belief,* Pitman, London, Morgan Kaufmann, San Mateo, CA, 1986.
7. E. H. Durfee and J. Rosenschein, "Distributed Problem Solving and Multiagent Systems: Comparisons and examples," *Proceedings of the 13th International Workshop on DAI,* M. Klein, ed. Lake Quinalt, WA, 1994, pp. 94–104.
8. T. W. Malone, K. Crowston, J. Lee, and B. Pentland, "Tools for Inventing Organizations: Towards a Handbook of Organizational Processes," *Proceedings of the 2nd IEEE Workshop on Enabling Technologies Infrastructure for Collaborative Enterprises,* Morgantown, WV, April 1993.
9. E. H. Durfee, V. R. Lesser, and D. D. Corkill, "Cooperative Distributed Problem Solving," in *The Handbook of AI,* vol. 4, Barr et al, eds. Addison Wesley, 1989, pp. 83–147.

10. E. H. Durfee, V. R. Lesser, and D. D. Corkill, "Trends in Cooperative Distributed Problem Solving." *IEEE Trans. Knowl. Data Eng.,* **1**(1), (March 1989).
11. F. V. Martial, "Coordinating Plans of Autonomous Agents," Ph.D. thesis, University of Saarbrucken, 1992.
12. Y. Shoham and M. Tennenholtz, "On the Synthesis of Useful Social Laws for Artificial Agent Societies," *Proceedings of the 10th National Conferences on Artificial Intelligence (AAAI-92),* San Diego, CA, 1992.
13. J. O. Kephart, T. Hogg, and B. A. Huberman, "Dynamics of Computational Ecosystems; Implications for DAI," in *Distributed Artificial Intelligence vol. II,* L. Gasser and M. Huhns, eds. Pitman, London, Morgan Kaufmann; San Mateo, CA, 1989, pp. 79–96.
14. M. Youssefmir and B. A. Hubberman, "Resource Contention in Multiagent Systems," in *Proceedings of the First International Conference on Multi-Agent Systems (ICMAS-95),* San Francisco, June 1995, pp. 398–405.
15. J. M. Shalikashvili, "User's Guide for JOPES (Joint Operation Planning and Execution System)," technical report, Defense Technical Information Center, http://www.dtic.mil/doctrine/jel/other_pubs/jopes.pdf, May 1995.
16. K. L. Myers and D. E. Wilkins, "Reasoning about Locations in Theory and Practice." *Computa. Intell.,* **14**(2); (1998).
17. A. Bestavorsa, K. J. Lin, and S. H. Son, *Real-time Database Systems: Issues and Applications,* Kluwer Academic, 1997.
18. B. Zhang and L. Zhang, *Theory and Applications of Problem Solving,* North Holland, New York, 1992.
19. M. R. Genesereth and S. P. Ketchpel, "Software Agents." *Commun. ACM,* **30**(7); 48–53 (1994).
20. K. Crowston, "A Taxonomy of Organized Dependencies and Coordination Mechanisms: Working Paper," technical report, School of Business Administration, University of Michigan, http://ccsmit.edu/CCSWP174.html, Aug. 1994.
21. E. H. Durfee and V. R. Lesser, "Using Partial Global Plans to Coordinate Distributed Problem Solvers," *Proceedings of the Tenth International Joint Conference on Artificial Intelligence (IJCAI-87),* Milan, 1987.
22. R. Ben-Natan, *CORBA: A Guide to Common Object Request Broker Architecture,* McGraw-Hill, New York, 1995.
23. K. Decker, E. H. Durfee, and V. R. Lesser, "Evaluating Research in Cooperative Distributed Problem Solving," in *Distributed Artificial Intelligence, vol. II,* L. Gasser and M. N. Huhns, eds. San Mateo, CA, Morgan Kaufmann, 1989.
24. G. Satapathy and S. R. T. Kumara, "A Multiagent Framework for Logistics Environment—DIAL," technical report, Pennsylvania State University, Industrial Engineering Dept., State College, PA, available at ftp://marie.iddr.ie.psu.edu/pub/dial.gz, Sept. 1995.
25. B. Reyns, S. R. T. Kumara, G. Satapathy, G. Smith, and J. R. Hummel, "Distributed Intelligent Agents for Logistics (DIAL): An Update," *Simulation Interoperability Workshop, spring 1998*, 98S-SIW-203, Simulation Interoperability Standards Organization, March 1998.

SOUNDAR R. T. KUMARA
GOUTAM SATAPATHY
MIRANDA L. MOORE

SOFTWARE RELIABILITY

Introduction

Software now controls banking systems, all forms of telecommunications, and process control in nuclear plants and factories, as well as defense systems. Even in households without a PC, many of the gadgets and the automobiles are software-controlled. Society has developed an extraordinary dependence on software. There are many well-known cases of tragic consequences of software failures. In popular software packages used every day, a very high degree of reliability is needed, because the enormous investment of the software developer is at stake. Studies have shown that reliability is regarded as the most important attribute by potential customers.

It is not possible to write software that is totally defect-free, except possibly for very small programs. All programs must be tested and debugged until sufficiently high reliability is achieved. Total elimination of all faults in large software systems is infeasible. Software must be released at some point; further delay will cause an unacceptable loss of revenue and market share. The developer must take a calculated risk and have a strategy for achieving the required reliability by the target release date.

In the recent past enough data have become available to develop and evaluate methods for achieving high reliability. Developing reliable software has become an engineering discipline rather than an art. For hardware systems, quantitative methods for achieving and measuring reliability have been in universal use for a long time. Similar techniques for software are coming into use due to the emergence of well-understood and validated approaches.

Here we will use the terms *failure* and a *defect* as defined below (*1*).

Failure: a departure of the system behavior from user requirements during execution
Defect (or fault): an error in system implementation that can cause a failure during execution

A defect will cause a failure only when the erroneous code is executed and the effect is propagated to the output. The *testability* of a defect is defined as the probability of detecting it with a randomly chosen input. Defects with very low testability can be very difficult to detect.

Some mathematical concepts are applicable to both software and hardware reliability. Hardware faults often occur because of aging. Combined with manufacturing variation in the quality of identical hardware components, the reliability variation can be characterized as exponential decay with time. On the other hand, software reliability improves during testing as bugs are found and removed. Once released, the software is reliable. Software will fail from time to time during operation when it cannot respond correctly to an input. The reliability of hardware components is often estimated by collecting failure data for a large number of identical units. For a software system, its own past behavior is often a good indicator of its reliability, even though data from other similar software systems can be used for making projections (*2*).

Development Phases

A competitive and mature software development organization targets high reliability from the very beginning of software development. Generally, the software life cycle is divided into the following phases:

1. Requirements and definition: In this phase the developing organization interacts with the customer organization to specify the software system to be built. Ideally the requirements should define the system completely and unambiguously. In actual practice, there is often a need to do corrective revisions during software development. A review or inspection during this phase is generally done by the design team to identify conflicting or missing requirements. A significant number of errors can be detected by this process. A change in the requirements in the later phases can cause increased defect density.
2. Design: In this phase the system is specified as an interconnection of units, such that each unit is well defined and can be developed and tested independently. The design is reviewed to recognize errors.
3. Coding: In this phase, the actual program for each unit is written, generally in a higher-level language such as C or C++. Occasionally assembly-level implementation may be required for high performance or for implementing input/output operations. The code is inspected by analyzing the code (or specification) in a team meeting to identify errors.
4. Testing: This phase is a critical part of the quest for high reliability and can take 30 to 60 percent of the entire development time. It is generally divided into the following separate phases:
    a. Unit test: In this phase, each unit is separately tested, and changes are performed to remove the defects found. Since each unit is relatively small and can be tested independently, they can be exercised much more thoroughly than a large program.
    b. Integration testing: During integration, the units are gradually assembled, and partially assembled subsystems are tested. Testing subsystems allows the interface among modules to be tested. By incrementally adding units to a subsystem, the unit responsible for a failure can be identified more easily.
    c. System testing: The system as a whole is exercised during system testing. Debugging is continued until some exit criterion is satisfied. The objective of this phase is to find defects as fast as possible. In general the input mix may not represent what would be encountered during actual operation.
    d. Acceptance testing: The purpose of this test phase is to assess system reliability and performance in the operational environment. This requires collecting (or estimating) information about how the actual users would use the system. This is also called alpha testing. This is often followed by beta testing, which involves actual use by the users.
    e. Operational use: Once the software developer has determined that an appropriate reliability criterion is satisfied, the software is released. Any bugs reported by the users are recorded but are not fixed until the next release.
    f. Regression testing: When significant additions or modifications are made to an existing version, regression testing is done on the new or "build" version to ensure that it still works and has not "regressed" to lower reliability.

It should be noted that the exact definition of a test phase and its exit criterion may vary from organization to organization.

Table 1 shows the typical fraction of total defects introduced and found during a phase (*3, 4*). Most defects occur during the design and coding phases. The fraction of defects found during the system test is small, but that may be misleading. The system test phase can take a long time because the defects remaining are much harder to find.

TABLE 1

Defects Introduced and Found During Different Phases

	Defects (%)		
Phase	Introduced	Found	Remaining
Requirements analysis	10	5	5
Design	35	15	25
Coding	45	30	40
Unit test	5	25	20
Integration test	2	12	10
System test	1	10	1

It has been observed that the testing phases can account for 30 to 60 percent of the entire development effort.

Software Reliability Measures

The classical reliability theory generally deals with hardware. In hardware systems the reliability decays because of the possibility of permanent failures. This is not applicable for software, however. During testing, software reliability grows because of debugging and becomes constant once defect removal is stopped. The following are the most common reliability measures used.

Durational reliability: Following classic reliability terminology, we can define *reliability* of a software system as:

$$R(t)=Pr\ \{\text{no system failures during } (o,t)\} \tag{1}$$

Transaction reliability: Sometimes a *single-transaction* reliability measure, as defined below, is more convenient to use.

$$R=Pr\ \{\text{a single transaction will not encounter a failure}\} \tag{2}$$

Both measures above assume *normal operation*; that is, the input mix encountered obeys the operational profile (defined below).

Mean time to failure (MTTF): The expected duration between two successive failures.

Failure intensity (λ): The expected number of failures per unit time.

Note that

$$MTTF = \frac{l}{\lambda} \tag{3}$$

Since testing attempts to achieve a high defect-finding rate, failure intensity during testing λ_t is significantly higher than failure intensity $t\lambda_{op}$ during operation. Test-acceleration factor A is given by

$$A = \frac{\lambda_t}{\lambda_{op}} \tag{4}$$

and is controlled by the test selection strategy and the type of application.

Example 1: For a certain telecommunication application, acceleration factor A has been found to be 10 in the past. For the current version, the target operational failure intensity has been decided to be 2.5×10^{-3} per second based on market studies. Then the target test failure intensity is

$$\begin{aligned}\lambda_t &= A \cdot \lambda_{op} = 10 \times 2.5 \times 10^{-3} \\ &= 2.5 \times 10^{-2}\, per\ second\end{aligned}$$

Defect density: Usually measured in terms of the number of defects per 1000 source lines of code (KSLOC). It cannot be measured directly, but can be estimated using the growth and static models presented below. The failure intensity is approximately proportional to the defect density. The acceptable defect density for critical or high-volume software can be less than 0.1 defects/KSLOC, whereas for other applications 5 defects/KLOC may be acceptable. Sometimes weights are assigned to defects depending on the severity of the failures they can cause. To keep the analysis simple, here we assume that each defect has the same weight.

Test coverage measures: Tools are now available that can automatically evaluate how thoroughly a software has been exercised. The following are some of the common coverage measures:

- Statement coverage: The fraction of all statements actually exercised during testing.
- Branch coverage: The fraction of all branches that were executed by the tests.
- P-use coverage: The fraction of all predicate use (p-use) pairs covered during testing. A p-use pair includes two points in the program, a point at which the value of a variable is defined or modified followed by a point at which it is used for a branching decision (i.e., a predicate).

The first two are structural coverage measures, while the last is a data-flow coverage measure. As discussed below, test coverage is correlated with the number of defects that will be triggered during testing (*5*). A statement coverage of 100 percent can often be quite easy to achieve. Sometimes a predetermined branch coverage, say 85 percent, may be used as an acceptance criterion for testing.

What Factors Control Defect Density?

There has been considerable research to identify the major factors that correlate with the number of defects. Enough data are now available to allow us to use a simple model for estimating the defect density. This model can be used in two different ways. First, it can be used by an organization to see how it can improve the reliability of its products. Second, by estimating the defect density, one can use a reliability growth model to estimate the testing effort needed. The model by Malaiya and Denton (*6*), based on the data reported in the literature, is given by

$$D = C \cdot F_{ph} \cdot F_{pt} \cdot F_m \cdot F_S \qquad (5)$$

where the five factors are the phase factor F_{ph}, the modeling dependence on the *software test phase,* the *programming team factor* F_{pt} taking into account the capabilities and experience of programmers in the team, the *maturity factor* F_m depending on the maturity of the software development process, and the *structure factor* F_s depending on the structure of the software under development. The constant of proportionality C represents the defect density per KSLOC. We propose the following preliminary submodels for each factor:

Phase factor F_{ph}: Table 2 presents a simple model using actual data reported by Musa et al. (*1*) and the error profile presented by Piwowarski et al. (*4*). It takes the default value of one to represent the beginning of the system test phase.

The programming team factor F_{pt}: The defect density varies significantly due to the coding and debugging capabilities of the individuals involved. A quantitative characterization in terms of programmers' average experience in years is given by Takahashi and Kamayachi (7). Their model can take into account programming experience of up to seven years, each year reducing the number of defects by about 14 percent.

Based on other available data, we suggest the model in Table 3. The skill level may depend on factors other than just experience. Programmers with the same experience can have significantly different defect densities, which can also be taken into account here.

The process maturity factor F_m: This factor takes into account the rigor of the software development process at a specific organization. The SEI capability maturity model level can be used to quantify it. Here we assume level II as the default level, since a level I organization is not likely to be using software reliability engineering. Table 4 gives a model based on the numbers suggested by Jones and Keene as well as reported in a Motorola study (*6*).

The software structure factor F_s: This factor takes into account the dependence of defect density on language type (the fractions of code in assembly and high-level languages) and program complexity. It can be reasonably assumed that assembly language code is harder

TABLE 2

Phase Factor F_{ph}

At beginning of phase	Multiplier
Unit testing	4
Subsystem testing	2.5
System testing	1 (default)
Operation	0.35

TABLE 3

The Programming Team Factor F_{pt}

Team's average skill level	Multiplier
High	0.4
Average	1 (default)
Low	2.5

TABLE 4

The Process Maturity Factor F_m

SEI CMM level	Multiplier
Level 1	1.5
Level 2	1 (default)
Level 3	0.4
Level 4	0.1
Level 5	0.05

to write and thus will have a higher defect density. The influence of program complexity has been extensively debated in the literature. Many complexity measures are strongly correlated to software size. Since we are constructing a model for defect density, software size has already been taken into account. A simple model for F_s depending on language use is given below:

$F_s = 1 + 0.4a$

where a is the fraction of the code in assembly language. Here we are assuming the assembly code has 40 percent more defects. We allow other factors to be taken into account by calibrating the overall model.

Calibrating and using the defect density model: The model given in Eq. 5 provides an initial estimate. It should be calibrated using past data from the same organization. Calibration requires application of the factors using available data in the organization and determining the appropriate values of the factor parameters. Since we are using the beginning of the subsystem test phase as the default, the data by Musa et al. (*1*) suggest that the constant of proportionality C can range from about 6 to 20 defects per KSLOC. For best accuracy, the past data used for calibration should come from projects as similar to the one for which the projection needs to be made. Some of the indeterminacy inherent in such models can be taken into account by using a high estimate and a low estimate and using both of them to make projections.

Example 2: For an organization, the value of C has been found to be between 12 to 16. A project is being developed by an average team and the SEI maturity level is II. About 20 percent of the code is in assembly language. Other factors are assumed to be *average*. The software size is estimated to be 20,000 lines of code. We want to estimate the total number of defects at the beginning of the integration test phase.

From the model given by Eq. 5, we estimate that the defect density at the beginning of the subsystem test phase can range between

$12 \times 2.5 \times 1 \times 1 \times (1 + 0.4 \times 0.2) \times 1 = 32.4$/KSLOC and

$16 \times 2.5 \times 1 \times 1 \times (1 + 0.4 \times 0.2) \times 1 = 43.2$/KSLOC, thus the total number of defects can range from 628 to 864.

Software Test Methodology

To test a program, a number of inputs are applied and the program response is observed. If the response is different from what was expected, the program has at least one defect. Testing can have one of two separate objectives. During debugging, the aim is to increase the reliability as fast as possible by finding faults as quickly as possible. On the other hand, during certification the object is to assess reliability, thus the fault-finding rate should be representative of actual operation. The test generation approaches can be divided into the following two classes:

1. Black-box (or functional) testing: When test generation is done by considering only the input/output description of the software, nothing about the implementation of the software is assumed to be known. This is the most common form of testing.
2. White-box (or structural) testing: When the actual implementation is used to generate the tests.

In actual practice, a combination of the two approaches will often yield the best results. Black-box testing only requires a functional description of the program; however, some information about actual implementation will allow testers to better select the points to probe in the input space. In a *random-testing* approach, the inputs are selected randomly. In a *partition testing* approach, the input space is divided into suitably defined partitions. The inputs are then chosen in such a way that each partition is reasonably and thoroughly exercised. It is possible to combine the two approaches; partitions can be probed both deterministically for boundary cases and randomly for cases that are not special.

Some faults are easily detected (i.e., have high *testability*). Some faults have very low testability; they are triggered only under rarely occurring input combinations. At the beginning of testing a large fraction of faults has high testability. The faults are easily detected and removed, however. In the later phases of testing, the faults remaining have low testability. Finding these faults can be challenging. The testers need to use careful and systematic approaches to achieve a very low defect density.

Thoroughness of testing can be measured using a test coverage measure, as discussed above. Branch coverage is a more strict measure than statement coverage. Some organizations use branch coverage (say, 85%) as a minimum criterion. For very high reliability programs, a more strict measure (e.g., p-use coverage) or a combination of measures (e.g., those provided by the GCT coverage tool) should be used.

To be able to estimate operational reliability, testing must be done in accordance with the *operational profile*. A *profile* is the set of disjoint actions, operations that a program may perform, and their probabilities of occurrence. The probabilities that occur in actual operation specify the operational profile. Sometimes when a program can be used in very different environments, the operational profile for each environment may be different. Obtaining an operational profile requires dividing the input space into sufficiently small leaf partitions and then estimating the probabilities associated with each leaf partition. A subspace with high probability may need to be further divided into smaller subspaces.

Example 2

This example is based on the Fone-Follower system example by Musa (*8*). A Fone-Follower system responds differently to a call, depending on the type of call. Based on past experience, the following types are identified and their probabilities have been estimated as given below:

A.	Voice call	0.74
B.	FAX call	0.15
C.	New number entry	0.10

D.	Database audit	0.009
E.	Add subscriber	0.005
F.	Delete subscriber	0.0005
G.	Hardware failure recovery	0.000001
Total for all events:		1.0

Here we note that a voice call is processed differently in different circumstances. We may subdivide event A above into the following:

A1.	Voice call, no pager, answer	0.18
A2.	Voice call, no pager, no answer	0.17
A3.	Voice call, pager, voice answer	0.17
A4.	Voice call, pager, answer on page	0.12
A5.	Voice call, pager, no answer on page	0.10
Total for voice call (event A)		0.74

The leaf partitions are thus {A1, A2, A3, A4, A5, B, C, D, E, F, G}. These and their probabilities form the operational profile. During acceptance testing, the tests would be chosen such that a FAX call occurs 15 percent of the time, a {voice call, no pager, answer} occurs 18 percent of the time, and so on.

Modeling Software Reliability Growth

The fraction of the cost needed for testing a software system to achieve a suitable reliability level can sometimes be as high as 60 percent of the overall cost. Testing must be carefully planned so that the software can be released by a target data. Even after a lengthy testing period, additional testing will always potentially detect more bugs. Software must be released even if it is likely to have a few bugs, provided an appropriate reliability level has been achieved. Careful planning and decision making requires the use of a *software reliability growth model* (SRGM).

An SRGM assumes that reliability will grow with testing time t, which can be measured in terms of the CPU execution time used or the number of man hours or days. The growth of reliability is generally specified in terms of either failure-intensity $\lambda(t)$, or *total expected faults* detected by time t, given by $\mu(t)$. The relationship between the two is given by

$$\lambda(t) = \frac{d}{dt}\,\mu(t) \tag{6}$$

Let the total number of defects at time t be $N(t)$. Let us assume that a defect is removed when it is found.

Here we will derive the most popular reliability growth model, the exponential model. It assumes that at any time the rate of finding (and removing) defects is proportional to the number of defects present. Using β_1 as a constant of proportionality, we can write

$$-\frac{dN(t)}{dt} = \beta_1 N(t) \tag{7}$$

It can be shown that the parameter β_1 is given by

$$\beta_1 = \frac{K}{\left(S \cdot Q \cdot \frac{1}{r}\right)} \tag{8}$$

where S is the total number of source instructions, Q is the number of object instructions per source instruction, and r is the object instruction execution rate of the computer being used. The term K is called the *fault-exposure ratio,* and its value has been found to be in the range of 1×10^{-7} to 10×10^{-7}, when t is measured in seconds of CPU execution time.

Equation 7 can be solved to give

$$N(t) = N(0)e^{-\beta_1 t} \tag{9}$$

When $N(0)$ is the initial total number of defects, the total expected faults detected by time t is then

$$\begin{aligned} \mu(t) &= N(0) - N(t) \\ &= N(0)(1 - e^{-\beta_1 t}) \end{aligned} \tag{10}$$

which is generally written in the form

$$\mu(t) = \beta_o(1 - e^{-\beta_1 t}) \tag{11}$$

where β_o, the total number of faults that would be eventually detected, is equal to $N(0)$. This assumes that no new defects are generated during debugging.

Using Eq. 6, we can obtain an expression for failure intensity using Eq. 11.

$$\lambda(t) = \beta_o \beta_1 e^{-\beta_1 t} \tag{12}$$

The exponential model is easy to understand and apply. One significant advantage of this model is that both parameters β_o and β_1 have a clear interpretation and can be estimated even before testing begins. The models proposed by Jelinski and Muranda (1971), Shooman (1971), God and Okumoto (1979), and Musa (1975–1980) can be considered to be reformulations of the exponential model. The hyperexponential model, considered by Ohba et al. (*2*) assumes that different sections of the software are separately governed by an exponential model with different parameter values for different sections.

Many other SRGMs have been proposed and used. Several models have been compared for their predictive capability using data obtained from different projects.

The exponential model fares well in comparison with other models; however, a couple of models can outperform the exponential model. We will here look at the logarithmic model proposed by Musa and Okumoto (*10*), which has been found to have a better predictive capability than the exponential model.

Unlike the exponential model, the logarithmic model assumes that the fault exposure ratio K varies during testing. The logarithmic model is also a finite-time model, assuming that after a finite time, there will be no more faults to be found. The model can be stated as

$$\mu(t) = \beta_o \ln(1 + \beta_1 t) \tag{13}$$

or alternatively

$$\lambda(t) = \frac{\beta_o \beta_1}{1 + \beta_1 t} \tag{14}$$

Equations 13 and 14 are applicable as long as $m(t) \leq N(0)$. In practice the condition will almost always be satisfied, since testing always terminates while a few bugs are still likely to be present.

The variation in K, as assumed by the logarithmic model, has been observed in actual practice. The value of K declines at higher defect densities, as defects get harder to find. At low defect densities, K starts rising, however. This may be explained by the fact that real testing tends to be directed rather than random, and this starts affecting the behavior at low defect densities.

The two parameters for the logarithmic model β_o and β_1 do not have a simple interpretation. A possible interpretation is provided by Malaiya and Denton (*6*). They have also provided an approach for estimating the logarithmic model parameters β_o^L, β_1^L, once the exponential model parameters have been estimated.

The exponential model has been shown to have a negative bias; it tends to underestimate the number of defects that will be detected in a future interval. The logarithmic model also has a negative bias. It is much smaller, however. Among the major models, only the Littlewood-Verral Bayesian model exhibits a positive bias. This model has also been found to have good predictive capabilities; however, because of computational complexity and a lack of interpretation of the parameter values, it is not popular.

An SRGM can be applied in two different types of situations: before testing begins and during testing.

BEFORE TESTING BEGINS

A manager often has to come up with a preliminary plan for testing very early. For the exponential and logarithmic models, it is possible to estimate the two parameter values based on the defect density model and Eq. 8. One can then estimate the testing time needed to achieve the target failure intensity, MTTF, or defect density.

Example 3

Let us assume that for a project the initial defect density has been estimated using the static model given in Eq. 5 and has been found to be twenty-five defects/KLOC. The software consists of 10,000 lines of C code. The code expansion ratio Q for C programs is about 2.5, hence the compiled program will be about $10{,}000 \times 2.5 = 25{,}000$ object instructions. The testing is done on a computer that executes 70 million object instructions per second. Let us also assume that the fault exposure ratio K has an expected average value of 4×10^{-7}. We wish to estimate the testing time needed to achieve a defect density of 2.5 defects/KLOC.

For the exponential model, we can estimate that

$$\beta_o = N(O) = 25 \times 10 = 250 \; defects$$

and from Eq. 8

$$\beta_1 = \frac{K}{\left(S \cdot Q \cdot \frac{1}{r}\right)} = \frac{4.0 \times 10^{-7}}{10{,}000 \times 2.5 \times \frac{1}{70 \times 10^6}}$$

$$= 11.2 \times 10^{-4} \, per \text{ sec}$$

If t_1 is the time needed to achieve a defect density of 2.5/KLOC, then using Eq. 9

$$\frac{N(t_1)}{N(O)} = \frac{2.5 \times 10}{25 \times 10} = \exp(-11.2 \times 10^{-4} \cdot t_1)$$

giving us

$$t_1 = \frac{-\ln(0.1)}{11.2 \times 10^{-4}} = 2056 \text{ sec } CPU \; time$$

We can compute the failure intensity at time t_1 to be

$$\lambda(t_1) = 250 \times 11.2 \times 10^{-4} \, e^{-11.2 \times 10^{-4} t_1}$$

$$= 0.028 \, failures/\text{sec}$$

For this example, it should be noted that the value of K (and hence t_1) may depend on the initial defect density and the testing strategy used. In many cases the time t is specified in terms of the number of man hours. We would then have to convert man hours to CPU execution time by multiplying by an appropriate factor. This factor would have to be determined using recently collected data. An alternative way to estimate β_1 is found by noticing that Eq. 8 suggests that for the same environment, $\beta_1 \times I$ is constant, thus for a prior project with a 5 KLOC source code, the final value for β_1 was 2×10^{-3} per sec. Then for a new 15 KLOC project, β_1 can be estimated as $2 \times 10^{-3}/3 = 0.66 \times 10^{-3}$ per sec.

DURING TESTING

The defect finding rate can be recorded during testing. By fitting an SRGM, the manager can estimate the additional testing time needed to achieve a desired reliability level. The major steps for using SRGMs are the following:

1. Collect and preprocess data: The failure-intensity data includes a lot of short-term noise. To extract the long-term trend, the data often need to be smoothed. A common form of smoothing is to use *grouped* data, which involves dividing the test duration into a number of intervals and then computing the average failure intensity in each interval.
2. Select a model and determine parameters: The best way to select a model is to rely on the past experience with other projects using same process. The exponential and logarithmic models are often good choices. Early test data have a lot of noise, thus a model that fits early data well may not have the best predictive capability. The parameter values can be estimated using either least square or maximum likelihood approaches. In the very early phases of testing, the parameter values can fluctuate enormously; they should not be used until they have stabilized.
3. Perform analysis to decide how much more testing is needed: Using the fitted model, we can project how much additional testing needs to be done to achieve a desired failure intensity or estimated defect density. It is possible to recalibrate a model that does not confirm with the data to improve the accuracy of the projection. A model that describes the process well to start with can be improved very little by recalibration.

Example 4

This example is based on the T1 data reported by Musa et al. (*1*). For the first twelve hours of testing, the number of failures each hour is given in Table 5.

TABLE 5

Hourly Failure Data

Hour	Number of failures
1	27
2	16
3	11
4	10
5	11
6	7
7	2
8	5
9	3
10	1
11	4
12	7

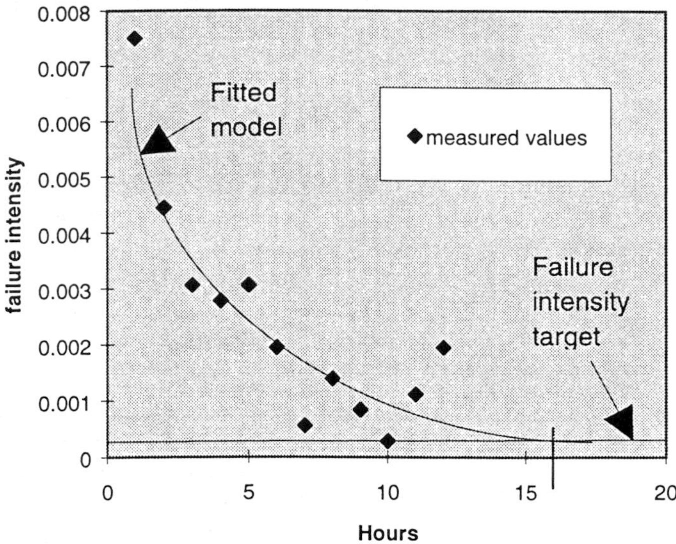

FIGURE 1. *Using an SRGM.*

We can thus assume that during the middle of the first hour (i.e., $t = 30 \times 60 = 1800$ sec) the failure intensity is 0.0075 per sec. Fitting all the twelve data points to the exponential model (Eq. 12), we obtain the following:

$$\beta_o = 101.47 \text{ and } \beta_1 = 5.22 \times 10^{-5}$$

Let us now assume that the target failure intensity is one failure per hour (i.e., 2.78×10^{-4} failures per second). An estimate of the stopping time t_f is then given by

$$2.78 \times 10^{-4} = 101.47 \times 5.22 \times 10^{-5} e^{-5.22 \times 10^{-5} \times t_f} \tag{15}$$

yielding $t_f = 56{,}473$ sec. (i.e., 15.69 hours), as shown in Fig. 1.

Investigations with the parameter values of the exponential model suggest that early during testing, the estimated value of β_o tends to be lower than the final value, and the estimated value of β_1 tends to be higher. The value of β_o thus tends to rise, and β_1 tends to fall, with the product $\beta_o\beta_1$ remaining relatively unchanged. In Eq. 15, we can guess that the true value of β_1 should be smaller, and thus the true value of t_f should be higher. The value 15.69 hours thus should be used as a lower estimate for the total test time needed.

The SRGMs assume that a uniform testing strategy is used throughout the testing period. In actual practice, the test strategy is changed from time to time. Each new strategy is initially very effective in detecting a different class of faults, causing a spike in failure intensity when a switch is made. A good smoothing approach will minimize the influence of these spikes during computation (*9*). A bigger problem arises when the software being tested is not stable because of continuing additions to it. If the changes are significant, early data points should be dropped from the computations. If the additions are component by component, reliability data for each component can be separately collected and the methods presented in the next section can be used.

It has been established that software test coverage is related to the residual defect density and hence reliability (*5*). The defect coverage C_D is linearly related to the test coverage measures at higher values of test coverage. For example, if we are using branch coverage C_B, we will find that low values of C_B, C_D remain close to zero. At some value of C_B, C_D starts rising linearly, however, as shown in Eq. 16.

$$C_D = -a + b \cdot C_B, \quad C_B > 0.5 \tag{16}$$

The values of the parameters a and b will depend on the software size and the initial defect density. The advantage of using coverage measures is that variations in test effectiveness will not influence the relationship, since test coverage directly measures how thoroughly a program has been exercised. For high-reliability systems, a strict measure such as p-use coverage should be used.

Reliability of Multicomponent Systems

A large software system consists of a number of modules. It is possible that the individual modules are developed and tested differently, resulting in different defect densities and failure rates. Here we will present methods for obtaining the system failure rate and the reliability, if we know the reliability of the individual modules.

SEQUENTIAL EXECUTION

Let us assume that for a system one module is under execution at a time. Modules will differ in how often and how long they are executed. If f_i is the fraction of the time module i is under execution, then the mean system failure rate is given by

$$\lambda_{sys} = \sum_{i=1}^{n} f_i \lambda_i \tag{17}$$

where λ_i is the failure rate of the module i.

Let the mean duration of a single transaction be T. Let us assume that module i is called e_i times during T, and each time it is executed for duration d_i, then

$$f_i = \frac{e_i \cdot d_i}{T} \tag{18}$$

Let us define system reliability R_{sys} as the probability that no failures will occur during a single transaction. From reliability theory, it is given by

$$R_{sys} = \exp(-\lambda_{sys}\, T)$$

Using Eq. 16 and 17, we can write the above as

$$R_{sys} = \exp\left(-\sum_{i=1}^{n} e_i\, d_i\, \lambda_i\right)$$

Since $\exp(-d_i\lambda_i)$ is R_i, single execution reliability of module *i,* we have

$$R_{sys} = \prod_{i=1}^{n} (R_i)^{e_i} \tag{19}$$

CONCURRENT EXECUTION

Some systems involve concurrently executing modules. They are required to run without failures for the system to operate correctly. In this case, the system failure rate is given by (*11*)

$$\lambda_{sys} = \sum_{j=1}^{m} \lambda_j \tag{20}$$

if there are *j* concurrently executing modules.

N-VERSION SYSTEMS

Multiple versions of the same program are sometimes used in some critical applications, such as defense or avionics. Each version is implemented and tested independently to minimize the probability of a multiple number of them failing at the same time. The most common implementation uses triplication and voting on the result. The system is assumed to operate correctly as long as the results of at least two of the versions agree. This assumes the voting mechanism to be perfect. If the failures in the three versions are truly independent, the improvement in reliability can be dramatic. It has been shown, however, that correlated failures must be taken into account.

In a three-version system, let q_3 be the probability of all three versions failing for the same input. Also, let q_2 be the probability that any two versions will fail together. Since three different pairs are possible among the three versions, the probability P_{sys} of the system failing is

$$P_{sys} = q_3 + 3q_2 \tag{21}$$

In the ideal case, the failures are statistically independent. If the probability of a single version failing is *p,* the above equation can be written for an idea case as

$$P_{sys} = p^3 + 3(1-p)p^2 \tag{22}$$

In practice, there is a significant correlation, requiring estimation of q_3 and q_2 for system reliability evaluation.

Example 5

This example is based on the data collected by Knight and Leveson (*12*), and the computations by Hatton (*12*). In a three-version system, let the probability of a version failing for a transaction be 0.0004. Then, in the absence of any correlated failures, we can achieve a system failure probability of

$$P_{sys} = (0.0004)^2 + 3(1-0.0004)(0.0004)^2$$
$$= 4.8 \times 10^{-7}$$

which would represent a remarkable improvement by a factor of $0.0004/4.8 \times 10^{-7} = 833.3$. Let us assume, however, that experiments have found $q_3 = 2.5 \times 10^{-7}$ and $q_2 = 2.5 \times 10^{-6}$. Then

$$P_{sys} = 2.5 \times 10^{-7} + 3 \times 2.5 \times 10^{-6} = 7.75 \times 10^{-6}$$

This yields a more realistic improvement factor of

$$0.0004/7.75 \times 10^{-6} = 51.6$$

Hatton points out that state-of-the-art techniques have been found to reduce defect density only by a factor of 10, hence an improvement factor of about 50 may be unattainable except by using N-version redundancy.

Tools for Software Reliability

Software reliability has now emerged as an engineering discipline. It can require a significant amount of data collection and analysis. Tools are now becoming available that can automate several of the tasks. Here names of some of the representative tools are mentioned. Many of the tools may run on specific platforms only, and some are intended for some specific applications only. Installing and learning a tool can require a significant amount of time, thus a tool should be selected after a careful comparison of the applicable tools available.

- Automatic test generations: TestMaster (Teradyne), AETG (Bellcore), ARTG (CSU), etc.
- GUI testing: QA Partner (Seague), WinRunner (Mercury Interactive), etc.
- Memory testing: BoundsChecker (NuMega Tech.), Purify (Relational), etc.
- Defect tracking: BugBase (Archimides), DVCS Tracker (Intersolv), DDTS (Qualtrack), etc.
- Test coverage evaluation: GCT (Testing Foundation), PureCoverage (Relational), ATAC (Bellcore), etc.
- Reliability growth modeling: SMERFS (NSWC), CASRE (NASA), ROBUST (CSU), etc.
- Defect density estimation: ROBUST (CSU).

- Coverage-based reliability modeling: ROBUST (CSU).
- Markov reliability evaluation: HARP (NASA), HiRel (NASA), PC Availability (Management Sciences), etc.

REFERENCES

1. J. D. Musa, A. Ianino, and K. Okumoto, *Software Reliability—Measurement, Prediction, Applications,* McGraw-Hill, New York, NY, 1987.
2. Y. K. Malaiya and P. Srimani, eds., *Software Reliability Models,* IEEE Computer Society Press, New York, NY, 1990.
3. A. D. Carleton, R. E. Park, and W. A. Florac, *Practical Software Measurement,* tech. report, SRI, CMU/SEI-97-HB-003, Carnegie Mellon University, Pittsburgh, PA.
4. P. Piwowarski, M. Ohba, and J. Caruso, "Coverage Measurement Experience During Function Test," *Proc. Int. Conference on Software Engineering,* Baltimore, MD, 1993, pp. 287–301.
5. Y. K. Malaiya, N. Li, J. Bieman, R. Karcich, and B. Skibbe, "The Relation Between Test Coverage and Reliability," *Proc. IEEE-CS Int. Symposium on Software Reliability Engineering,* Monterey, CA, Nov. 1994, pp. 186–195.
6. Y. K. Malaiya and J. Denton, "What Do the Software Reliability Growth Model Parameters Represent?" *Proc. IEEE-CS Int. Symposium on Software Reliability Engineering* (ISSRE), Albuquerque, NM, Nov. 1997, pp. 124–135.
7. M. Takahashi and Y. Kamayachi, "An Empirical Study of a Model for Program Error Prediction," *Proc. Int. Conference on Software Engineering,* London, England, Aug. 1985, pp. 330–336.
8. J. Musa, "More Reliable, Faster, Cheaper Testing Through Software Reliability Engineering," Tutorial Notes, *ISSRE '97,* Albuquerque, NM, Nov. 1997, pp. 1–88.
9. N. Li and Y. K. Malaiya, "Fault Exposure Ratio: Estimation and Applications," *Proc. IEEE-CS Int. Symposium on Software Reliability Engineering,* Denver, CO, Nov. 1993, pp. 372–381.
10. N. Li and Y. K. Malaiya, "Enhancing Accuracy of Software Reliability Prediction," *Proc. IEEE-CS Int. Symposium on Software Reliability Engineering,* Denver, CO, Nov. 1993, pp. 71–79.
11. P. B. Lakey and A. M. Neufelder, *System and Software Reliability Assurance Notebook,* Rome Lab, Rome, NY, FSC-RELI, 1997.
12. L. Hatton, "N-Version Design Versus One Good Design." *IEEE Software,* 71–76 (Nov./Dec. 1997).

YASHWANT K. MALAIYA